The Female Investigator in
Literature, Film, and Popular Culture

The Female Investigator in Literature, Film, and Popular Culture

LISA M. DRESNER

McFarland & Company, Inc., Publishers
Jefferson, North Carolina, and London

LIBRARY OF CONGRESS CATALOGUING-IN-PUBLICATION DATA

Dresner, Lisa M., 1967–
    The female investigator in literature, film, and popular culture /
Lisa M. Dresner.
      p.   cm.
    Includes bibliographical references and index.

    ISBN-13: 978-0-7864-2654-6
    ISBN-10: 0-7864-2654-3
    (softcover : 50# alkaline paper) ∞

    1. Detective and mystery stories, English — History and
criticism.   2. Horror tales, English — History and criticism.
3. English fiction — Women authors — History and criticism.
4. Detective and mystery stories, American — History and criticism.
5. American fiction — Women authors — History and criticism.
6. Women detectives in literature.   7. Women detectives in
mass media.   8. Popular culture — United States — History — 20th
century.   I. Title.
PR830.D4D74   2007
823'.0872099287 — dc22   2006026596

British Library cataloguing data are available

Cover images ©2006 photspin.

Manufactured in the United States of America

*McFarland & Company, Inc., Publishers
  Box 611, Jefferson, North Carolina 28640
   www.mcfarlandpub.com*

To the late Dr. Anthony J. Biancosino,
my high school jazz band teacher, mentor,
and dear friend, who taught his students the power
of hard work and perseverance, and who always
demanded "results — not excuses."

Acknowledgments

I am grateful to the many people who have helped me develop this project from a glimmer of an idea into its current form, particularly Bertrand Augst, Francine Masiello, Carol Clover, Betsy Wheeler, Denise Filios, and Dorothy Duff Brown. I am also grateful for the encouragement of my family and dear friends and for my excellent teachers at Riverside School, John Witherspoon Middle School, Princeton High School, the University of Michigan, and the University of California at Berkeley. I have also been fortunate to have the support of my generous colleagues at the University of Michigan Law Library, New England Institute of Technology, Providence College, Boston University, and Hofstra University. Finally, I owe special thanks to my former partner and able volunteer research assistant, Mike Greenfield.

Table of Contents

Introduction: The Mystery
of the Missing Theory

There have also been a few women detectives, but on the whole, they have not been very successful — Dorothy L. Sayers, "Introduction" to *The Omnibus of Crime*[1]

Although in the years since Ms. Sayers' dire report in 1928, there have been many popular female detectives, the scholarship on Anglo-American detective fiction to date still lacks a comprehensive theory that adequately theorizes the place of the female detective. Such theorizing as has occurred in the still-understudied field of detective fiction has tended to a masculinist perspective, defining the detective through qualities that are culturally coded as masculine: either the hyper-rationality of the intellectual detective or the casual violence of the hardboiled detective.[2] In these theoretical constructions, female detectives tend to be glossed over, omitted from consideration, or treated as if they were simply male detectives in drag.

Moreover, those scholars who *have* attempted to theorize the female detective have generally limited the scope of their conclusions to a single medium; their theories are applicable to print or film or television, but not to all three media. For example, Jacqueline Rose and Mary Ann Doane come the closest of the scholars who have written on this topic to articulating a theory of female detection on the silver screen. In her analysis of the gender politics of *Coma*, a film about a female doctor investigating a mysterious epidemic of comas at her own hospital, Rose points out that the film's narrative response to the female detective figure is the creation of a general atmosphere of paranoia, of madness "[a]s if there was an excess or danger in the very idea of the woman as detective (the idea that she might actually *look*) which produces its paranoid reversal."[3] Likewise, Mary Ann Doane notes the paranoia inherent in a cycle of films she terms

1

the "paranoid woman's films" and similarly links that paranoia to the investigating female gaze.[4] Rose's and Doane's formulations are apt not only for the discussion of these particular films, but for many others as well; indeed, I will argue below that in general, the act of female detection on film is entwined with intimations of madness.

The fact that Rose's theory is limited to a single medium is problematic, however — while it is accurate for female detectives in film, it does *not* hold true for female detectives in print or on television. Similarly, Kathleen Gregory Klein's study of professional female detectives in mystery fiction, *The Woman Detective: Gender and Genre*, makes a sound theoretical point: that these fictional female investigators tend to be portrayed as lacking either in femininity or in detecting ability, as if there were some sort of fundamental disjunction between the categories of "woman" and "detective."[5] Yet Klein's work — intentionally based upon a narrowly-defined group of texts in one medium — likewise does not consider all media. It is also, I believe, a theory that invites further study: While Klein makes a critically important observation, many nuances remain to explore.

In this study, I develop a more universally applicable theory explaining the place of the female investigator in fiction, film, and television — a theory that accounts for the seeming anomalies in, and contradictions among, earlier efforts to theorize the female investigator.

A Fatal Flaw? Theorizing the Female Investigator

The results of my study here may be, in one sense, profoundly discouraging to the feminist cultural critic. My research demonstrates that in all media, at all time periods, the Anglo-American female investigator is presented as in some measure fundamentally flawed, that she serves as a marker of the incompatibility of the cultural categories of "woman" and "investigator." These flaws can be seen in a myriad of works featuring female investigators, from the gothic thrillers of Ann Radcliffe in the 1790s to the mystery-romance television programs of the 1990s. The flaws in the female investigator differ, however, in severity and variety according to the medium in which she is portrayed: the female investigator is least limited as she is portrayed in fiction; somewhat more limited as she is portrayed on television; and most limited as she is portrayed in film, a medium in which she is routinely categorized as mad. I attribute these differences among media to the different looking relations between reader/spectator and character. Furthermore, the flaws in female investigators are directly linked to their placement in the nexus of desire. Even female investigators who are removed from the heterosexual nexus of desire — due to their age or sexual orientation — do not escape portrayal as flawed.

A Brief Overview of the Scholarship to Date on Detective Fiction

The general scholarship on detective fiction and film is extensive, although until quite recently, it was produced mostly by non-academics. A lively body of early and recent work in this area has been produced by fans, editors, mystery bookstore owners, librarians, popular book and film reviewers, and the authors and filmmakers themselves. Indeed, the most useful basic research tools in this field are still those produced by these "amateur" critics. Especially in the areas of film and television, comprehensive and finely-focused reference works written by non-academics abound, e.g., David Martindale's invaluable *Television Detective Shows of the 1970s*[6] or Dave Rogers' *The Complete Avengers,*[7] or Jack Condon and David Hofstede's *Charlie's Angels Casebook.*[8] Also notable is film historian William K. Everson's *The Detective in Film,*[9] marketed as a coffee-table book, but chock-full of useful reference information for scholars.

Moreover, much of the influential criticism of detective fiction has been written by non-academics (or by academics writing in non-academic guise). G.K. Chesterton, creator of the Father Brown mysteries, wrote the first critical essay in defense of detective fiction in 1902.[10] Dorothy L. Sayers, academic and creator of the popular series of detective novels featuring Lord Peter Wimsey, wrote some well-respected historical and generic commentaries on detective fiction that served as introductions to the several anthologies she edited.[11] Howard Haycraft, an editor at H.W. Wilson and Company, wrote *Murder for Pleasure: The Life and Times of the Detective Story*, a generic study of the detective story published in 1941.[12] Haycraft's 1946 anthology, *The Art of the Mystery Story*, includes critical essays by mystery authors G.K. Chesterton, Dorothy L. Sayers, S.S. Van Dine,[13] Erle Stanley Gardner, Raymond Chandler, John Dickson Carr, Rex Stout, and Dashiell Hammett; by reviewers Anthony Boucher[14] and Vincent Starrett; by law professor John Barker Waite; and even a literary-critical poem by humorist Ogden Nash.[15] It contains no contributions by professional academics writing as academics.

Writing in 1979, in the preface to one of the first avowedly academic studies of detective fiction, Leroy Lad Panek aptly notes:

> After forty years of criticism, the detective story is still an unexamined form; the handful of books and several hundred articles written about detective fiction have not gotten very far in coming to terms with it... Since the late twenties, most critics have been mesmerized by the idea of the puzzle and its relationship to the form [and not much else]... Another of the fundamental problems confronting the criticism of detective fiction is its field of focus. To date it has largely been very broad or very narrow: from general historical surveys and philosophic reactions to articles on single writers or books.[16]

Since the study of detective fiction has only recently gained legitimacy in the academy, it is not surprising that there has been too little avowedly academic criticism of this genre, even though academics are among the most avid readers of detective fiction.[17] Despite the popularity of the genre among academics, both as readers and as authors,[18] it is only relatively recently that academics have been willing to apply their critical talents to detective fiction openly.

One of the first academics to embrace the serious study of detective fiction was the chair of the department of popular culture at Bowling Green State University, Ray Browne. Under Browne's direction, the Bowling Green State University Popular Press published several early studies of detective fiction. While these studies provide competent overviews of the authors and sub-genres covered, their critical framework is largely that of the New Critics, Structuralists, and earlier literary critics: Browne's own *Heroes and Humanities: Detective Fiction and Culture* surveys several mystery authors from the perspective of the "writers' concern with the hero and his/her role in the humanities."[19] Gary Hoppenstand's *In Search of the Paper Tiger: A Sociological Perspective of Myth, Formula and the Mystery Genre in the Entertainment Print Mass Medium* applies consideration of myth and formula to several mystery sub-genres.[20] The longest chapter in George N. Dove's *The Police Procedural* likewise considers myth and formula in the police procedural subgenre.[21] Nadya Aisenberg's *A Common Spring: Crime Novel and Classic* similarly applies a structural analysis to crime fiction, then documents the influence of formulaic crime fiction on Dickens, Conrad, and Greene.[22] Panek's *Watteau's Shepherds* articulates its own theory of detective fiction. His "Backgrounds and Approaches" chapter sets out a theory of detective novels as "games, jokes, reactions to the adventure thriller and reactions to the established form itself."[23]

Some of these important early writings on the detective story define the genre in decidedly masculine terms. For example, in *An Introduction to the Detective Story*,[24] Leroy Lad Panek takes a male-centered and genre-studies approach to his subject. This approach leads him to exclude many novels — particularly novels featuring female detective characters — from his definition of "detective story."

Indeed, many critical studies of the detective story gloss over issues of gender. In a useful overview and discussion of works of criticism and attempts to theorize the mystery from a variety of perspectives, Larry Landrum himself gives short shrift to gendered readings and theorizations. Instead, he tucks any such readings away in a sub-section entitled "Multicultural Criticism" — implying a basic "otherness" to gendered readings.[25]

Three recent major studies of female detective fiction do seek to theorize the genre: Maureen T. Reddy's *Sisters in Crime: Feminism and the Crime Novel* (1988), Kathleen Gregory Klein's *The Woman Detective: Gender and Genre* (1988, 2nd edition 1995), and Sally R. Munt's *Murder by the Book?: Feminism and the Crime Novel* (1994). All have taken on a Herculean task, as the number of novels with female detective protagonists has skyrocketed. While these authors have inaugurated feminist theories of detective fiction, other areas remain somewhat neglected.[26]

As noted above, there has been little academic consideration of detective films and television series. What has been done has not fully theorized the place of the female investigator as portrayed in these media. Early writings on mystery-detective television series (e.g., Robert S. Alley's article on "Television Drama" and Lorna Sage's article on "Kojak and Co." in *Television: The Critical View*[27]) tended to give short shrift to — or simply ignore — female detectives. Although film studies, as a genre of academic criticism, has been in general commendably concerned with the role of gender, this has not led to much overlap between the work of those who theorize about gender in film and the work of those who theorize about detectives in film.

The lesbian detective novel has been addressed in part by a chapter of Sally Munt's study *Murder by the Book?: Feminism and the Crime Novel.*[28] Munt studies primarily the lesbian detective novels of the 1980s and early 1990s, observing that some early lesbian detective novels "are as much concerned with the process of becoming a lesbian as with the solution of a mystery."[29] Munt's interests in this chapter focus on the political underpinnings of the lesbian detective novel and a theorizing of these novels as attempting to construct lesbian identities.

There are still too few other theoretical studies of lesbian detectives,[30] however, although the number of lesbian detective novels is burgeoning.[31] The paucity of criticism of this genre may be partly due to its relative recency. Munt identifies 1977's *Angel Dance* by M.F. Beal as the first lesbian feminist mystery.[32] An essay by Joseph Hansen (author of a series of mysteries featuring gay male detective Dave Brandstetter) published in the 1984 revised edition of *Murder Ink* contains not a single reference to the lesbian as detective.[33] Another possible reason for the paucity of criticism in this area may be academic disdain for (and/or political misgivings about) lesbian "genre fiction."[34]

Moreover (perhaps partly due to the academic/political concerns noted above), the criticism of lesbian detective fiction that has been published has heretofore often focused on a relatively limited canon of early works[35] that tend to grapple with important lesbian/feminist topics, including, among others, Barbara Wilson's *Murder in the Collective* and *Gaudí Afternoon*,[36] Mary Wings' novels featuring detective Emma Victor,[37] and the early Kate Delafield novels by Katherine V. Forrest.[38] Both Wilson and Wings have also published articles explaining the genesis of some of their work and what they sought to accomplish by it.[39]

Thus, although there has clearly been some interest in female detectives in their various manifestations, there has yet to be a comprehensive study of the overlap between the categories of "woman" and "investigator" that spans a variety of genres and media. Hence, this project.

Terminology: Investigator vs. Detective

I have made the semantic decision to name the object of my study the "female investigator" rather than the "female detective" primarily for reasons of inclusivity. The word "detective" implies professionalism — not necessarily in the sense of ability but certainly in the sense of receiving a monetary reward and a certain amount of recognition for one's detective work. "Amateur detective," while allowing the inclusion of those who are unpaid but recognized for their detective work, leaves out those whom I assert below to comprise a very important category of investigators: those who investigate up to a point, but are ultimately unable to carry their investigations to a conclusion through their own efforts. This group of almost-detectives is most prevalent in the female gothic literature that is the subject of my first chapter. Since one of my main findings is that the cultural inconcinity caused by the placing of a woman in a role that has been culturally coded as masculine leads to the troubled role of the female investigator, it would be unthinkable to omit the grandmothers of the detective story from my study here. Thus, "female investigator" seems a more appropriate term to use than "female detective."[40]

Scope of Inquiry

This work does not include a chapter on the female investigator in the popular detective novel. To include one would be unwise. As I have noted above, entire treatises have been written on women in popular detective fiction. The overwhelming volume of detective novels with female protagonists makes it difficult both to survey the genre and to theorize it accurately. Since others have made this valiant attempt, I leave the field to them and seek to focus on other areas that are more understudied in the hope of developing a more universally applicable theory of the place of female detection in Anglo-American culture.

Most critical works have recognized the difficulty of making a comprehensive survey of female detective novels and have focused instead on a narrower subpart of the field.[41] These works have focused on a single author, like Agatha Christie,[42] or on a group of female authors,[43] or on a character, like Nancy Drew,[44] or on a group of characters,[45] or on a particular approach, like a sociological/bibliographical overview,[46] or on a sub-genre, like teenage-girl sleuths,[47] or on a group of texts from a particular perspective and time period, like the feminist female investigators of the 1980s and early 1990s.[48]

Having taken a few years off to complete a law degree, as I put the finishing touches on this work and re-checked the literature available on the female investigator, I was heartened to find that since I had begun my study, several dissertations had appeared that treated topics relevant to female investigators. Like the works that have gone before them, these studies tend to focus on an author or a group of authors or a group of films, and do not appear, from their abstracts, to attempt a unified theory of the female investigator in literature and popular culture.

In this work, I will similarly limit my scope by looking at several understudied genres that feature female investigative protagonists, while at the same time seeking to theorize the female investigator within and across generic boundaries. I make no claim to having produced a comprehensive survey of the female investigator in my chosen genres and media (although the film and television chapters do cover many representations of the female investigator in film and on television). Rather, I have sought to cover a sufficient number of works in each genre to convince the reader of the accuracy of my genre- and medium-based observations.

Areas of Inquiry: The Gothic Novel, Film, Television, and the Lesbian Detective Novel

I have selected four areas of inquiry that I believe are most understudied: 1. The female investigator in the Gothic novel. 2. The female investigator in the lesbian detective novel. 3. The female investigator on television. 4. The female investigator on film. The flaws of the female investigator play out in different ways in these different genres: In the gothic novel, the female investigator is an almost-investigator whose inquiries never reach fruition without the assistance of an outside party; in the lesbian detective novel, anxiety about the female investigator's dual roles as lesbian and investigator is displaced onto the female investigator's car and body; on television, the female investigator's flaws are closely connected to the socio-cultural norms when each series was produced; on film, the female investigator is always tinged with madness.

Tying It All Together: A Case Study of du Maurier's Rebecca

My final chapter examines how the same narrative of female investigation — Daphne du Maurier's classic gothic novel *Rebecca*— is transformed by its translation into lesbian detective novel, teleplay, and film. This examination of a single narrative as it is represented in various genres and media confirms the findings of the earlier chapters.

· 1 ·

The Female Gothic Novel
and the "Almost-Detective"

The female gothic novel[1] is a genre rife with "almost-detectives" —
investigating women whose attempts to discover a secret are only moder-
ately successful. Many of the tropes in this genre are relevant to our study
of female investigators. The secret in novels of this genre *is* eventually
revealed, but only partially due to the heroine's own efforts,[2] a narrative
structure that implies that even the best and brightest young women of
their generation share some fundamental lack. The arenas in which gothic
investigative heroines are most often tested are in the fields of (both oral
and written) language, vision, interpretation, identity, and the body. When
tested in these arenas, the heroine initially appears strong, yet has her
essential weakness exposed at the end. Furthermore, the gothic female
investigator's inability to detect fully seems inextricably linked to her position as a desiring subject. These "almost-detectives" show their greatest
inability to detect successfully when they investigate the male objects of
their desire.[3]

I will trace this trend through an examination of several best-selling
female gothic novels — Ann Radcliffe's *The Mysteries of Udolpho*, Jane
Austen's satire on the gothic novel, *Northanger Abbey*, Charlotte Brontë's
Jane Eyre, and Wilkie Collins's *The Woman in White* and *The Law and the
Lady*. I have chosen these particular texts because of their broad popular
appeal when they were published, for they are representative of the popular culture of the time. While often characterized as "women's literature"
today, these novels were popular reading for both genders when originally
published. *Udolpho* was a staple in the libraries of the educated through
the first half of the nineteenth century.[4] *Jane Eyre* was reviewed in such
popular journals as *The Athenaeum*, *The Spectator*, and *The Examiner*.[5]

9

R.F. Stewart notes that *The Woman in White* was so popular that "when published in book form, having already been serialized, the first impression of 1,000 copies ... sold in one day."[6] Moreover, *The Woman in White* inspired a wide variety of tie-in merchandising[7] and was so compelling that, according to Julian Symons, "Gladstone cancelled a theatre engagement to go on reading it, and Prince Albert sent a copy to Baron Stockmar."[8] Moreover, though his critical reputation later declined, Collins' writing remained extremely popular with the masses at the time of the publication of *The Law and the Lady* over fifteen years later.[9]

The Mysteries of Udolpho

In Ann Radcliffe's *The Mysteries of Udolpho*, heroine Emily St. Aubert initially demonstrates great investigative skill[10] in the areas of interpretation, language, and the body.[11] Early on in *Udolpho*, the narrative constructs Emily as a person who has been trained (admittedly against her nature) by her father to be skilled in interpretation, to respond in a thoughtful and sanguine manner to mysterious or unpleasant events.[12] Significantly, Emily gleans these abilities from her father *after* the deaths of her two brothers, implying that she has been granted a portion of the interpretive mastery inherent in patriarchal power as part of the paternal inheritance that might have gone to her brothers.[13]

Imprisoned in the castle of Udolpho by her evil step-uncle Montoni, Emily also demonstrates her mastery over language: She displays a great talent for eliciting pertinent information about castle denizens from her maid Annette and commands Annette on numerous errands aimed at gathering further information. The relationship between Emily and Annette as they express it through their use of language is in no wise an equal one. Emily constantly interrupts Annette's speech and criticizes her for its expanse and subject matter.[14] While Emily asks Annette questions that Annette answers honestly, she herself will not submit to Annette's probing:

> Emily interrupted her; "Have you heard no other music since you came to the castle — none last night?"
> "Why, did you hear any last night, ma'amselle?"
> Emily evaded this question by repeating her own [333].

Emily's assertion of linguistic power over Annette is clearly class-related.[15] Emily commands a similar power over some of the other servants, but she is not nearly as effective at dominating people of her own class (such as her aunt or Montoni) linguistically.

Emily also shows great physical daring[16] and strength of purpose in several ways: She jeopardizes her physical safety and her tenuous position in the household by exploring spooky dark towers (both alone and with a sinister servant) in an unsuccessful search for her imprisoned aunt. Later, she steadfastly defends her aunt from Montoni's wrath as the aunt lies dying. She also bravely carries out her aunt's last wishes in the face of severe threats from Montoni.

The narrative, however, constructs Emily as possessing several flaws that keep her from discovering what she wishes to know. The first flaw is a failure of language: while Emily shows great power over her social inferiors, like Annette, in her use of language, others who hold the same social status as she does, particularly men, use language to trick her. For example, Montoni's unscrupulous scheme to marry Emily off against her will to Count Morano in exchange for money depends on his deliberately misleading her into thinking that she is agreeing to sell off her childhood home when she writes a note to her uncle that can be interpreted as acquiescence to an arranged marriage.

The second flaw that disrupts Emily's investigative abilities is a failure of interpretation: Despite her father's careful attempts to train her in Stoic philosophy, Emily continually leaps to conclusions based upon insufficient evidence, and thus unfailingly misinterprets almost everything she sees and hears. A dead body behind an arras? It must be real. A mysterious stranger in the castle? It must be her long-lost love, Valancourt.

Some of Emily's interpretive problems are related to the third flaw — a failure of the body. Although she is physically daring in her pursuit of information, Emily has the unfortunate tendency to faint at the drop of a hat, which effectively denies her the possibility of fully investigating her hunches, particularly her hunches about dead bodies. For example, when Emily tries to investigate a supposedly deserted room that appears to be in use by some unknown person, she is overcome by terror at finding what seems to be a decaying body hidden behind a tapestry and never pursues her investigation far enough to discover that it's actually just a wax model. Similarly, when in search of her imprisoned aunt, whom she assumes may already be dead, Emily faints from discouragement and terror before being able to discover that her aunt is really still alive. Emily likewise leaps to a false conclusion about the identity of a real dead body she discovers in a another tower, then faints before she can ascertain its true identity.[17]

Emily's continual fainting spells signify her imprisonment in the world of the body — a body that the narrative constructs as intrinsically flawed because it is female. Whenever Emily reaches up to the arenas of vision and knowledge, the body pulls her back down, reasserting its superior claims on her by blocking her access to these arenas.

Emily's interpretive failures are underlined by the fact that in the peculiar shorthand universe of the female gothic novel, all of the questions Emily seeks the answers to *are* indeed answered, but never directly due to her own efforts. The narrative unfolds in such a way that her investigations can only achieve fruition through the efforts of others, as if the narrative would cede her too much power if it allowed her to discover anything directly herself. In the most striking example of this principle, near the end of the novel, Emily's many questions about the mysterious goings-on surrounding her own family and Chateau-le-blanc are finally answered by the disappointing expedient of having the abbess of a convent simply summon Emily to tell her the whole story.

Northanger Abbey

Many of the areas of challenge for the "almost detective" that appear in the other gothic novels I examine here can also be seen in Jane Austen's satire *Northanger Abbey* (originally bought for publication in 1803, but unpublished until after Austen's death in 1818). In some measure, of course, these similarities may be due to the fact that Austen's main object of satire *is Mysteries of Udolpho*,[18] which she skewers sharply. Yet the discourses of the gothic thriller that she emphasizes are still in play decades later in the other gothic works I examine: Like the gothic works it parodies, *Northanger Abbey* underlines the importance of language, interpretation, and investigative skill to its gothic heroine, Catherine Morland, while simultaneously undercutting her abilities in these areas.

Northanger Abbey clearly indicates the ambivalent relationship between the gothic heroine and written language.[19] First, the trope of the all-important heroine's journal is lampooned. When they are first introduced, Henry Tilney meets Catherine's suggestion that she may not keep a journal with mock disbelief:

> Not keep a journal! How are your absent cousins to understand the tenour of your life in Bath without one?... How are your various dresses to be remembered, and the particular state of your complexion, and curl of your hair to be described in all their diversities, without having constant recourse to a journal? [14].[20]

Here, Tilney acknowledges the association of femininity with writing only to undercut the potential power of that association by implying that "feminine" subject matter is unworthy of record or remembrance. Of course, such an implication is itself undercut by the ironic circumstance of its placement within a novel that is written by a woman and whose main subject matter is "feminine." Yet I would argue that Henry's "jokes" here (and as detailed below) resonate throughout the novel because of Henry's status as an authoritative speaker in the work. Henry is one of the only characters in the novel who is *not* broadly lampooned. As one of Austen's idealized male types, he is presented as the voice of reason, a master of interpretation with a wicked sense of humor and a voice very similar to that of Austen's sly narrators in this and other works. Especially because his voice is so close to the narrator's voice, Henry's pronouncements, even in jest, carry more weight than pronouncements by other characters.

Henry proceeds — in jest — to the subject of letter writing in a way that similarly disparages Catherine's authority over language:

> It is this delightful habit of journalizing which largely contributes to form the easy style of writing for which ladies are so generally celebrated. Everybody allows that the talent of writing agreeable letters is peculiarly female. Nature may have done something, but I am sure it must be essentially assisted by the practice of keeping a journal [15].

Henry's overvaluation of women's letter-writing potential clearly means the opposite here, as we see by his response to Catherine when she takes him seriously and hazards the opinion that men might sometimes be better letter writers than women:

> As far as I have had the opportunity of judging it appears to me that the usual style of letter-writing among women is faultless, except in three particulars ... [a] general deficiency of subject, a total inattention to stops, and a very frequent ignorance of grammar [15].

In this passage, the material and technical competence of women's letters is again typed as unworthy. Henry's later disclaimer that "[i]n every power of which taste is the foundation, excellence is pretty fairly divided between the sexes" (15) fails to erase the resonances of his earlier remarks.

We can also see the narrative itself casting doubt upon Catherine's control over written language: the chaise that is to carry her to a visit to Tilney's home at Northanger Abbey proves so crowded that "she [has] difficulty in saving her own new writing-desk from being thrown out into the street" (139) by Henry's father, General Tilney. The fact that a woman's writing desk is held by General Tilney as disposable (as opposed to the presumably more "feminine" parcels carried by his daughter's maid, in favor of which the writing desk is in jeopardy) underlines the tenuous affinity between women and writing in this novel. Moreover, when Catherine begins her suspenseful search of the mysterious ebony cabinet in her room, she is gratified in the extreme to find a "manuscript" hidden inside, but in the light of day finds it to be nothing more than a laundry list (154–157). The laundry list similarly implies the uselessness of women's writing: While certainly useful from the practical standpoint of getting laundry done, the laundry list — associated with female workers, washer-women — is useless from the upper-class Catherine's point of view; because of its subject matter relating to the material conditions of lower-class women's daily lives, it is of no importance to her.[21]

Northanger Abbey similarly emphasizes failures of interpretation among gothic heroines by having Catherine fail at almost every turn to interpret the meanings and motives of other people.[22] Indeed, the one time Catherine does interpret events correctly is used in the narrative to point out what a rare event this is in gothic novels:

> Mr. Tilney ... was talking with interest to a fashionable and pleasing-look-ing young woman who leant on his arm, and whom Catherine immedi-ately guessed to be his sister; thus unthinkingly throwing away a fair opportunity of considering him lost to her for ever, by being married already. But, guided only by what was simple and probable, it had never entered her head that Mr. Tilney could be married... [T]herefore, instead of turning of a deathlike paleness, and falling in a fit on Mrs. Allen's bosom, Catherine sat erect, in the perfect use of her senses, and with cheeks only a little redder than usual [41].

This passage is notable not only for its representation of the gothic hero-ine's tendency to misinterpret situations, but also for its emphasis on the bodily weakness that the gothic heroine tends to display when faced with disagreeable notions. Furthermore, by showing Catherine using her pow-ers of reason and observation to deduce Tilney's marital status, the pas-sage also implies that these powers are not possessed (or used, at any rate) by many gothic heroines.

The balance of the novel undercuts Catherine's interpretive abilities, implying that the common sense and mastery of the codes of her culture that she displays in the instance above are an exception to the way in which she normally interprets the world around her. After a series of mis-understandings about the true nature of relations between her brother and his fiancée, Catherine makes the biggest mistake of all, and incorrectly sus-pects General Tilney of having murdered his late wife.[23] Austen further underlines the stagnation of Catherine's interpretive skills near the end of the novel, when Catherine shows her surprise at how Henry interprets the

General's particularly desiring his son not to make a fuss over dinner as a mandate for a very fine dinner indeed: "[W]hy he should say one thing so positively, and mean another all the while, was most unaccountable! How were people, at that rate, to be understood?" (196). It is clear from this remark that Catherine has not mastered the social codes of her culture. Of course, the project of the novel is to demonstrate the inanity of these social codes through the innocent eyes of a young woman who doesn't understand them. Still, I would argue that the novel's insistence on Catherine's misinterpretations — of social codes and of more serious matters — points to this tendency to misinterpret as a major area of concern for the gothic heroine.

Similarly, the fact that Catherine cannot successfully use her detective skills to discover useful information, no matter how earnestly she wishes to do so, underlines the importance of this area for the gothic detective. Catherine's boldest attempts at investigation when at Northanger Abbey — opening an ancient trunk, exploring the mysterious ebony cabinet in her room, and making a secret expedition to the room where Mrs. Tilney died — all end ignominiously. Catherine finds only a counterpane in the trunk, the laundry list in the cabinet, and a disappointingly cheerful, modern aspect to Mrs. Tilney's last room. Furthermore, Catherine's investigations are not only unsuccessful, but they are also by no means secret. Catherine is surprised by Miss Tilney in her investigation of the trunk, and by Henry Tilney in her investigation of Mrs. Tilney's room. In both instances, she is very much ashamed, both of her groundless suspicions and of being caught in the act of pursuing them. The second notion is particularly important, for in these instances, the investigator finds herself investigated, caught in the visual and interpretive matrices of another instead of gaining the confirmation of her own visual and interpretive mastery that she had expected to gain through her investigation. The investigator who finds herself the subject of other investigations is just one of the many tropes from *Northanger Abbey* that resonates with tropes in *The Mysteries of Udolpho*.

Jane Eyre

We can see the patterns set up by *Udolpho* and parodied in *Northanger Abbey* followed in several other female gothic novels throughout the next century. In Charlotte Brontë's 1847 novel *Jane Eyre*,[24] for example, our plucky heroine Jane shows the same physical and moral courage as Emily

St. Aubert and Catherine Morland do — offering Rochester immediate assistance after his equestrian accident, rushing to save him when his bedroom mysteriously catches fire, and resolutely striking off on her own with no money to avoid a bigamous "marriage" with him.

Furthermore, the battle of wills between Jane and Rochester is fought largely on the field of vision: both characters initially construct themselves as viewing subjects who gain knowledge of others from seeing and interpreting their looking relations. In an early instance, Rochester tells Jane, "...[B]eware, by the by, what you express with [your eye]; I am quick at interpreting its language" (166–167) — a telling phrase, reflecting the link between language and vision. Jane does not suffer Rochester's construction of himself as reader and herself as text gladly, however, and soon after in their conversation she tells him, "I judged [the moral path you wish to take] by your countenance, sir; which was troubled when you said the suggestion had returned upon you" (168). Thereby, Jane effectively reads his glance as he has just read hers, and their battle is thus far a draw.

This battle of vision continues with many early instances of Rochester looking at Jane as if to establish power over her through the Gaze. One of the more intriguing battlefields of this visual contest is the collection of Jane's drawings. Rochester, having heard of Jane's drawings from his ward Adèle, abruptly demands to see them — "Fetch me your portfolio, if you can vouch for its contents being original" (156), he orders Jane. After initially doubting her skill, he queries her intensely about her state of mind when painting, and then styles himself an art critic, conceding only that "the drawings are, for a schoolgirl, peculiar" (158). These actions are quite coercive. The act of demanding — not requesting — to look at Jane's pictures, the expressions of her innermost thoughts, and setting himself up as a judge of their merit has the same valence as Rochester's other coercive visual acts, such as repeatedly making Jane sit well in the firelight so he can examine her (153, 161). Yet the contest is not entirely one-sided: when Rochester examines Jane, she examines him right back. Moreover, Jane's pictures also signify some of her privileged vision. For despite Rochester's rough treatment of Jane and her pictures, he is obviously touched and intrigued by their subject matter. The woman who can intrigue Rochester by her expression of her inner vision surely must be granted some visual mastery as well here.

Jane's visual relationship to the visiting house party at Thornfield is similarly ambiguous. As she surveys the party's arrival, Jane makes sure to keep the visual high ground: "Adèle flew to the window. I followed, taking care to stand on one side, so that, screened by the curtain, I could see without being seen"(195). Jane likewise initially uses back stairways to avoid being seen by the ladies of the party, while she hides in the darkness and enjoys watching them emerge in their evening finery.[25] Certainly, her visual relationship to the members of the house party here cannot be characterized as oppressive to them, yet it certainly expresses a form of knowledge-seeking: through it, Jane gains further knowledge of the members of the house party without allowing them any knowledge of herself.

The negative side of seeing without being seen resurfaces in the series of dreadful evenings Jane is forced to spend sitting ignored in a corner watching the gay party of visitors egg on the budding "romance" between Rochester and the socialite Blanche Ingram. In this case, even though Jane is the viewing subject, the power is held by Rochester. This seeming paradox can be explained by the power of self-specularization and performance, for the performative mode is one that coerces the spectator's powers of vision and interpretation, as happens here. As Rochester styles himself the lover of Blanche Ingram, he channels Jane's interpretation of events into the desired one and produces the desired effect, namely, that she becomes jealous.

Here, Jane's ability to see clearly is inversely proportional to her sexual desire. When she is jealous of Rochester and Blanche, she cannot see the true one-sided nature of their relationship. The link between Jane's impaired vision and her sexual desires is reinforced by the episode of the "gypsy woman." While Jane answers the traveling fortuneteller's queries and insinuations about her desire for Rochester chastely and circumspectly, she is at the same time unable to penetrate Rochester's disguise to discover that the gypsy woman is he.

At Rochester's marriage proposal, Jane initially appears to have regained the upper hand, as she again constructs herself as a privileged interpreter of Rochester's body, commanding him to place himself in her line of vision to be examined:

> "Mr Rochester, let me look at your face; turn to the moonlight."
> "Why?"
> "Because I want to read your countenance — turn!"
> "There! you will find it scarcely more legible than a crumpled, scratched page. Read on: only make haste, for I suffer" [283].

Rochester's comment about the illegibility of his countenance proves immediately prophetic. For while Jane describes herself as capable of superior vision, the narrative of their encounter actually emphasizes her *inability* to see. She can "scarcely see [her] master's face"(284), and, startled by an ominous lightning bolt, thinks "only of hiding [her] dazzled eyes against Mr.

Rochester"(284). This last quotation maps the relationship between vision, knowledge, and desire onto the body; Jane desires to resist the dazzling light (signifying knowledge) by burying her eyes in the shoulder of the man whose proposal of marriage she has just accepted (signifying sexual desire).[26]

Relations in the field of vision shift dramatically in the novel when Rochester is blinded and Jane returns home after a brief exile to nurse and marry her now-blinded and widowed employer. Here desire plays a somewhat different part than it has done previously: Jane is now able to fulfill her desire not because *she* cannot see, but because *Rochester* cannot see. Jane does not enjoy her uncontested visual superiority for long, however. As Rochester regains his sight bit by bit, the narrative notes that he is able to see the blue of Jane's dress and an ornament hung round her neck (476), thus repositioning her as an object of his vision. Indeed, the dress and ornament are peculiarly feminine details with which the narrative metonymizes Jane; the choice of these feminine-inflected details to represent Jane underscores the narrative's link between femaleness and visual objectification. Furthermore, the fact that the narrative ends [except for an update on the Rivers family] with Rochester looking at his infant son (476–477) reinforces Jane's role as the reproducer, not the producer, of meaning and culture.

While she is at least a formidable opponent (if not the eventual victor) on the field of vision, Jane is clearly vanquished on the field of interpretative mastery. Not only is Jane completely unable to solve the mystery of the strange laughter she hears from the top story of the mansion (until she is shown Bertha Mason on her wedding day due to the precipitous arrival of Bertha's brother), but she is also, in fact, unable to solve *any* of the mysteries that surround her. This incapacity is due not to the fact that she doesn't notice that things are strange or that she doesn't think about them at all, but rather to the fact that Jane's reasoning skills are in some ways parallel to Emily's physical skills in *Udolpho*—as soon as Jane might find out something interesting, she makes a conscious decision not to think or talk about the topic any more. For example, at the end of her second meeting with Rochester, Jane gets up to go because she is mystified by Rochester's discourse and his vague hints about his past:

> ... I rose, deeming it useless to continue a discourse which was all darkness to me; and, besides, sensible that the character of my interlocutor was beyond my penetration ... [169].

While Jane may display admirable self knowledge here, she learns no more of Rochester, and is reduced to the rather inefficient strategy of waiting until he wishes to tell her more of his past.

Part of Jane's inability to detect stems from her indefatigable politeness, which makes her reluctant to press others — especially servants — for information against their will.[27] When Mrs. Fairfax cannot enlighten her on the reason for Mr. Rochester's long absences, Jane swiftly desists from questioning her:

> The answer was evasive. I should have liked something clearer: but Mrs Fairfax either could not, or would not, give me more explicit information.... It was evident, indeed, that she wished me to drop the subject, which I did accordingly [159].

While this passage at least shows a healthy curiosity on Jane's part, sometimes her reticence is so great that she cannot even admit to the desire to know: When Jane overhears two servants discussing Grace Poole, who stop when they see her approach, she admits to no impulse to question them further: "...[T]he conversation was of course dropped. All I had gathered from it amounted to this — that there was a mystery at Thornfield; and that from participation in that mystery I was purposely excluded."(195) Jane's politeness here may be not only a marker of her class status, but also a marker of her gender, as politeness is gendered as a feminine Victorian virtue. Whatever the cause, Jane's complacent acceptance of her exclusion from a mystery bodes ill for her ability to investigate effectively.

Yet Rochester eventually *does* tell Jane more about his past *and* about the mystery surrounding "Grace Poole," since he and Jane inhabit the same gothic universe that Emily does in *Udolpho*; like Emily, Jane *will* have all of her questions answered, but these questions will be answered only at the whim of those whom she would investigate and not as the direct result of her own efforts — as if some mysterious agency has translated Jane's desires into action on the part of others instead of action on her own part.

This mysterious wish-fulfillment process requires that Jane earnestly desire to increase her knowledge while taking no physical or mental steps to do so. "I meditated wonderingly on this incident; but gradually quitting it, as I found it for the present inexplicable, I turned to the consideration of [other matters]" (177), she notes, puzzled about the strong emotions Rochester displays about his newfound contentment at home.

Sometimes, the agency for delaying Jane's investigations is displaced onto the general course of events. Certainly Jane at one point *intends* to question Rochester more closely, but the narrative never allows her to turn intention into action. "I wanted again to introduce the subject of Grace

Poole, and to hear what he would answer; I wanted to ask him plainly if he really believed it was she who had made last night's hideous attempt; and if so, why he kept her wickedness a secret" (187), she asserts, after she has saved Rochester from being mysteriously burned in his bed. Jane is thwarted in her quite reasonable search for an explanation of the previous night's events, however, by the fact that Rochester has already left his estate for several weeks, and that she will not get a chance to speak with him alone for several weeks after that. By the use of narrative stratagems like these, the entire structure of the novel limits the information that Jane can uncover under her own power.

The Woman in White

Even in the narration of novels more explicitly concerned with female detection, we can see this same limiting principle in operation. Wilkie Collins is noted for his depictions of strong, intelligent women, yet his most courageous heroines are not allowed to reap the fruits of their investigative labors directly. Marian Halcombe[28] in Collins's 1860 novel, *The Woman in White*,[29] is notable for her androgynous physical qualities, qualities that apparently give her the license to set herself up as an investigator. Though she may occasionally belittle her own detecting abilities, the narrative presents Marian as a decidedly strong investigator. This is evident in her investigative actions, the ways in which she presents herself and others present her as an investigator, her powers of observation and deductive reasoning skills, and her mastery over language.

Marian's actions establish her as an aggressive investigator when she is faced with any mystery, no matter how seemingly insignificant. When regaled with visiting tutor Walter Hartright's stories about the strange woman in white who accosted him on the outskirts of London and mentioned a nearby village, Marian is eager to investigate. "We really must clear up this mystery, in some way," she says. "...I am all aflame with curiosity, and I devote my whole energies to the business of discovery from this moment."[30] She promptly proceeds to pore over her mother's old correspondence and discovers a letter clearly identifying the mysterious woman as Anne Catherick, which conclusion she confirms by cross-examining Walter about his encounter with the woman in white. Moreover, fiercely protective of her half-sister Laura, Marian also mounts an investigative campaign to discover the plans of Laura's new husband, the slimy Sir Percival Glyde, and Glyde's sinister counselor Count Fosco.

Marian also clearly constructs herself as an investigator through the language she uses in describing her actions. When she realizes that Walter has a crush on her half-sister Laura, she phrases the discovery in investigative language: "I have discovered your secret — without help or hint, mind, from any one else" (95). She similarly describes a day spent exploring the new home she will share with Laura and Sir Percival as "a day of inves[t]igations and discoveries" (225). Likewise, when she and Laura have been followed by a mysterious figure on their walk, Marian sends Laura upstairs, then goes "at once to make [her] first investigations in the library" (286) to see if the Foscos could be responsible for the incident.

Walter similarly constructs Marian as a powerful investigator — especially in the field of vision — by the language he uses in describing her. In his descriptions of Marian, Walter focuses on her keen vision and perception: "[H]er penetrating eyes had contracted a new habit of always watching me" (91) he notes; she is the one "whose quick eye nothing escape[s]" (73).

Marian's ability to combine careful observation with deductive reasoning further constructs her as a skilled detective. Indeed, when she has sent Laura to an assignation with Anne Catherick from which both women have disappeared, she tracks Laura with the skill of any analytical detective:

> I detected the footsteps of two persons — large footsteps like a man's, and small footsteps, which, by putting my own feet into them and testing their size in that manner, I felt certain were Laura's.... I discovered a little hole in the sand — a hole artificially made, beyond a doubt. I just noticed it, and then turned away immediately to trace the footsteps as far as I could, and to follow the direction in which they might lead me.
>
> They led me ... a distance, I should think, of between two and three hundred yards, and then the sandy ground showed no further trace of them. Feeling that the persons whose course I was tracking must necessarily have entered the plantation at this point, I entered it too.... I discovered [a path], just faintly traced among the trees, and followed it.... I stopped at a point where another foot-track crossed it. The brambles grew thickly on either side of this second path. I stood looking down it, uncertain which way to take next, and while I looked I saw on one thorny branch some fragments of fringe from a woman's shawl. A closer examination of the fringe satisfied me that it had been torn from a shawl of Laura's, and I instantly followed the second path ... (312–313).

Marian also cross-examines Laura to deduce who has been hanging around outside Laura's door:

> "Was it a man or a woman?"
> "A woman. I heard the rustling of her gown."

"A rustling like silk?"

"Yes, like silk."

Madame Fosco had evidently been watching outside [329].

In these examples, Marian's use of deductive reasoning anticipates the analytic reasoning used by detectives such as Collins's Sergeant Cuff in *The Moonstone* or Sir Arthur Conan Doyle's Sherlock Holmes later in the century and pays homage to the reasoning used by Edgar Allan Poe's earlier sleuth Arsène Dupin.[31]

Marian also demonstrates a certain mastery over language in both its spoken and written forms. In terms of spoken language, Marian demonstrates the ability to overhear the conversations of others successfully without being detected herself. Her glee at overhearing a conversation between Glyde and his lawyer is evident: "I listened — and under similar circumstances I would listen again — yes! with my ear at the keyhole, if I could not possibly manage it in any other way" (248). Furthermore, in a tour de force, Marian creeps out on a window ledge and successfully overhears all of Fosco's and Glyde's plotting, gathering information that, had she been able to put it to good use, might have enabled her to save Laura without any outside aid.

In terms of written language, Marian demonstrates her narrative authority by narrating a good twenty percent of the story, more than any other narrator except Walter Hartright, and the parts that she describes are particularly gripping. Marian's narration is taken from her diary,[32] which is presented as an authoritative record of events: When she and Laura remember a legal detail differently, Marian hauls out her journal to prove she is right and then extrapolates: "In the perilous uncertainty of our present situation, it is hard to say what future interests may not depend upon the regularity of the entries in my journal, and upon the reliability of my recollection at the time when I make them" (307). Marian is also the one who suggests posting letters to Laura's lawyer to advise them in times of danger. She is also alert to possible threats to the security of her written language: Marian astutely doublechecks a letter she has posted and discovers that it has been tampered with. Though she modestly attributes this action to a womanly "impulse," it follows immediately on markedly suspicious behavior by both Count Fosco and Madame Fosco and should be taken as further proof of Marian's deductive reasoning skills (277–78).[33]

Yet despite Marian's apparent mastery of vision, language, and deductive reasoning, the text systematically strips her of each of these abilities before her narration is done. Marian, that keen observer of others, is introduced in the narrative as the *object* of Walter Hartright's gaze. Walter narrates:

I looked from the table to the window farthest from me, and saw a lady standing at it, with her back turned towards me.... I was struck by the rare beauty of her form, and by the unaffected grace of her attitude. Her figure was tall, yet not too tall; comely and well-developed, yet not fat; her head set on her shoulders with an easy, pliant firmness; her waist, perfection in the eyes of a man, for it occupied its natural place, it filled out its natural circle, it was visibly and delightfully undeformed by stays. She had not heard my entrance into the room; and I allowed myself the luxury of admiring her for a few moments, before I moved one of the chairs near me, as the least embarrassing means of attracting her attention. She turned towards me immediately. The easy elegance of every movement of her limbs and body as soon as she began to advance from the far end of the room, set me in a flutter of expectation to see her face clearly. She left the window — and I said to myself, The lady is dark. She moved forward a few steps — and I said to myself, The lady is young. She approached nearer — and I said to myself (with a sense of surprise which words fail me to express), The lady is ugly!

Never was the old conventional maxim, that Nature cannot err, more flatly contradicted — never was the fair promise of a lovely figure more strangely and startlingly belied by the face and head that crowned it. The lady's complexion was almost swarthy, and the dark down on her upper lip was almost a moustache. She had a large, firm, masculine mouth and jaw; prominent, piercing, resolute brown eyes; and thick, coal-black hair, growing unusually low down on her forehead. Her expression — bright, frank, and intelligent — appeared, while she was silent, to be altogether wanting in those feminine attractions of gentleness and pliability, without which the beauty of the handsomest woman alive is beauty incomplete....

"Mr. Hartright?" said the lady interrogatively, her dark face lighting up with a smile, and softening and growing womanly the moment she began to speak ... [58–59].

In this quotation, Marian is initially presented as the object of Walter Hartright's desire. Walter goes over Marian's body piece by piece, dividing it into sections, fetishizing it, measuring it against ideals of feminine beauty — a comparison in which Marian is the victor (because of her "natural" rather than artificially-enhanced approach to beauty — no stays for her!) until Walter reaches her face. It is significant that while Marian herself does similar visual breakdowns on the characters *she* describes, Walter is not among them. He himself is never implicated in the field of vision as she is, perhaps suggesting that Marian's powers of observation are valid only when she herself is not under scrutiny, only when she herself is not an object of desire.

Furthermore, note Marian's tenuous control over spoken language in this passage. While she is silent, she maintains her masculine attributes, but as soon as she begins to speak, betrayed by her voice, her strong demeanor becomes invaded by feminine attributes. Just as Marian cannot be an observer of the one who observes her, here she cannot overhear others while they hear her.

Note also the head/body: masculine/feminine split here. The spell of Walter's gaze is broken only when Marian's incongruous masculine head is revealed, implying, perhaps, that masculinity is not the proper object of comparison — and that a male face cannot be fetishized. Marian's strong point is this head, presumably the source of her "intelligent" expression. This intelligence is no empty promise, as Marian's demonstrated detective ability will show.

Marian puts this feminine body on the line for her investigation: as noted above, she climbs out on the verandah roof to spy on Fosco and Glyde and successfully manages to overhear their plotting. Yet she cannot do this until she transforms her body into more masculine lineaments through a change of clothing. She notes:

> A complete change in my dress was imperatively necessary for many reasons. I took off my silk gown ... because the slightest noise from it on that still night might have betrayed me. I next removed the white and cumbersome parts of my underclothing, and replaced them by a petticoat of dark flannel. Over this I put my black travelling cloak.... In my ordinary evening costume I took up the room of three men at least. In my present dress, when it was held close about me, no man could have passed through the narrowest spaces more easily than I [342].[34]

Here, the female body is presented as symbolic of excess, as a dangerous superfluity,[35] while the male body is presented as the norm, the ideal. Yet at her moment of seeming triumph, when Marian appears to have successfully overcome her female body in order to use it in her investigations, Marian is not allowed to put the information she learns to good use. Instead, the act of investigation she has committed attacks her body[36] — her exposure to the cold night air and a rainstorm while she's spying gives her a serious fever that keeps her from communicating what she has discovered. This implies some sort of inherent feminine bodily weakness — men wear similar thicknesses of clothing and don't get sick; women apparently need more protection. Worse yet, the fact that Marian is ill becomes part of the mechanism used to trap Laura and take her money, so that Marian's investigation — betrayed by her body — leads directly to the result it was meant to prevent. Moreover, Marian's bold investigation here marks the end of her power in the novel. From this point forward, all investigative activities are undertaken instead by the novel's male hero, Walter Hartright.

Marian's loss of power over language is also made complete here: Walter now takes over the main narration from Marian (whose diary has recorded much of the action so far), never to return it to her. It is also important to note that Marian's loss of investigative power is marked by the occasion of Count Fosco reading her diary and writing his own entry in it. Her writing has been discovered; his rises to power. Marian's investigative powers are promptly ended when she is herself investigated.

We can also see that Marian's problems as detective — like Jane Eyre's — are narratively linked to her location in the field of desire. In her diary, she reports a barely suppressed desire for Fosco:

> I am almost afraid to confess it, even to these secret pages. The man has interested me, has attracted me, has forced me to like him. In two short days he has made his way straight into my favourable estimation, and how he has worked the miracle is more than I can tell [240].

> He flatters my vanity by talking to me as seriously and sensibly as if I was a man. Yes! I can find him out when I am away from him — I know he flatters my vanity, when I think of him up here in my own room — and yet, when I go downstairs, and get into his company again, he will blind me again, and I shall be flattered again, just as if I had never found him out at all! He can manage me as he manages his wife and Laura, as he managed the bloodhound in the stable-yard ... [245].

> I do assuredly feel, even on this short acquaintance, a strange, half-willing, half-unwilling liking for the Count.... I certainly never saw a man, in all my experience, whom I should be so sorry to have for an enemy. Is this because I like him, or because I am afraid of him [246]?

Several important points of Marian's narration are worth noting here. First, the diminution in power that Marian undergoes in Fosco's presence: The line comparing Fosco's "management" of her to his management of Madame Fosco, Laura, and the dog associates Marian with weakness, subservient femininity, and animality. Second, the coerced aspect of Marian's desire: Phrases like "he has forced me to like him" and "a strange, half-willing, half-unwilling liking for the Count" underline the fact that Marian's desires are not under her own control here. Finally, the aspect of mystification: Phrases like "how he has worked the miracle is more than I can tell" and "when I go downstairs and get into his company again, he will blind me again" imply a mysterious, almost supernatural agency on Fosco's part that obscures Marian's vision and reason while she is in his presence.

Furthermore, Marian's loss of power when Fosco reads and writes in her diary emphasizes how desire is implicated in the loss of her investigative powers. By reading her diary, Fosco accordingly reads of Marian's attraction to him; investigated by the one whom she would investigate, she stands incriminated by her own hand. Fosco compounds the violation of her secret writing not only by reading it, but also by having the temerity to write an entry in her diary himself (significantly, the last entry in Marian's diary, as if the violation of her literary voice is so great that she can no longer speak with it). In one of the most spine-tingling passages in all of British literature, Fosco acknowledges that he has read Marian's entire diary and expresses his own attraction to her. Fosco's entry in Marian's diary, like a physical entry into her body, has the psychic effect of a rape,[37] and Marian is silenced by it.

Peter Brooks describes Fosco's reading of Marian's diary as a moment "in which our readerly intimacy with Marian is violated, our act of reading adulterated by profane eyes, made secondary to the villain's reading and indeed dependent on his permission."[38] I disagree with the implied universality of this statement. This interpretation suggests a rather proprietary attitude towards Marian's writings — it implies that the reader is in a voyeuristic relation with Marian's writing and is surprised/annoyed by the intrusion of Fosco as a competing voyeur. This seems to me a particularly "masculine" conception of reading: the reader and Fosco are seen as sharing a voyeuristic relation with Marian's writing, and the reader's discomfort is caused by the loss of power entailed in having Fosco usurp authority over the reader's reading of Marian's writing. I think there is a "feminine" response to Fosco's intrusion as well — a response based upon identification with Marian as writer and the violation of her writing, which implies the reader's violation as well.[39]

The Law and the Lady

The most competent of the gothic female investigators examined in this chapter is undoubtedly Valeria Woodville, the intrepid heroine of one of Collins's later novels that is now little known, *The Law and the Lady* (1875).[40] Like Emily St. Aubert, Catherine Morland, Jane Eyre, and Marian Halcombe before her, Valeria is both mentally acute and physically bold. Like earlier gothic heroines, she also investigates a man and what he may or may not have done to his first wife, in this case, a wife for whose murder the man has been tried and neither acquitted nor convicted. Instead, Valeria's new husband Eustace bears the burden of a Scottish "Not Proven" verdict. Valeria's discussion of its effect on her husband and the world at large is notable:

He knew, poor fellow, the slur that the Verdict left on him. "We don't say you are innocent of the crime charged against you; we only say, there is not evidence enough to convict you." In that lame and impotent conclusion the proceedings ended, at the time. And there they would have remained, for all time — but for Me [182].

This passage is noteworthy in two regards. First, Valeria calls the Not Proven verdict "lame" and "impotent"— interesting images of castration. Why would Valeria view the law as emasculated here? More importantly, what is her vision of a "masculine" law?[41] One that produces a guilty verdict? Surely, that cannot be what she desires, although culturally, a sense of rough justice is associated with masculinity. Declaring a man's innocence is traditionally much more associated with femininity than with masculinity. Perhaps it is rather the *in*decision of the "decision" reached that strikes Valeria as un-masculine. Valeria does deride the amount of time it takes the all-male jury to reach its "decision": "A jury of women would not have taken a minute!" (182) she snips. For Valeria, decisiveness and definition are masculine categories — uncertainty and lack of clarity are "lame" and "impotent" (i.e. feminine) categories. In this instance, Valeria crystalizes the Western cultural conception of order, decisiveness, and knowledge as masculine characteristics associated with the ideal masculine detective.

This dynamic is emphasized in the final sentence of the section quoted above: "And there they would have remained, for all time — but for Me" (182).Valeria here sets herself up in the masculine detective role, a point underlined by her bold capitalization of the word "Me"— a traditionally masculine assertion of self .[42]

Detection

Valeria's detection is notable both for the subject she investigates — male guilt — and for the various institutions of the patriarchy that are arrayed against her and over which she triumphs in order to investigate successfully. Valeria continues her investigation in the face of opposition from her husband Eustace (representing the institution of marriage), his friend Major Fitz-David (representing the institution of the military), her clergyman uncle Starkweather (representing the institution of the church), the Scots lawyer Mr. Playmore (representing the institution of the law), and Miserrimus Dexter's doctor (representing the institution of medicine).

Valeria is at her peak investigative prowess very early in her married life, when she has yet to become fully integrated into the Victorian patriarchal family structure: On her wedding day, Valeria catches Eustace crying. Although he attempts to allay her fears, she is still suspicious (22). She starts her investigations when, waking early after a few days of married life, she goes into her husband's dressing room, idly pokes through Eustace's dressing case, opens the false bottom to it, and finds a hidden picture of her new mother-in-law (23–24).

Valeria's investigative prowess is again highlighted when Eustace then tries to lie to her by telling her that an apparent chance meeting with her mother-in-law is really his mother's scheme for making Valeria's acquaintance. Valeria isn't fooled and gets Eustace to admit that he was lying — but not to tell her the truth (34–35). Upset by his reticence, Valeria resolves to solve the mystery and learn Eustace's secret (37). Using information from her landlady, Valeria learns that her mother-in-law's name is not Woodville but Macallan and seeks out the lady in question (41). Her mother-in-law confirms that Valeria is legally married, but refuses to tell her anything more (43). Valeria is undaunted, however.

In her next investigative tour de force, Valeria challenges the authority of two men — her husband Eustace and his friend, retired military man Major Fitz-David — who resist her investigations. When Valeria presses Eustace, he tells her not to question him about his past:

> If you could control your curiosity ... we might live happily enough. I thought I had married a woman who was superior to the vulgar failings of her sex. A good wife should know better than to pry into affairs of her husband's with which she has no concern [54].

Note that here, investigation and inquiry are denigrated by being classified as "curiosity" (54), a "vulgar failing" (54) associated with femininity. When Valeria reiterates her desire to know the truth, Eustace sternly tells her his secrecy is "[f]or [her] own good" (54) and gives her a dire warning (54–55). Far from being cowed by these obstacles, Valeria is spurred on by them and resolves to investigate further (55). Valeria instantly takes action and proceeds to Major Fitz-David's house, out of which she has seen Eustace emerge (55). What Valeria does next is an intriguing mixture of spying and investigation. Although Valeria charms her way into the Major's good graces by her feminine disguise, she also uses proof of her previous successful investigations in order to persuade him to aid her. Valeria tells him that she has discovered that her real last name is now Macallan (62). Proof of her successful investigation alone, however, is not enough to persuade the Major to aid her: Combining brains with a feminine gesture of submission, she impulsively kisses his hand (63). This feminine deferral prompts the Major to begin his explanation. When the Major becomes evasive, Valeria again credits her gender for her ability to overcome his will:

> A man in my place would have lost all patience, and would have given up the struggle in disgust. Being a woman, and having my end in view, my resolution was invincible. I fairly wore out the Major's resistance, and compelled him to surrender at discretion [65].

Here, Valeria turns a stereotypically negative feminine trait — nagging — to her advantage and presents her victory over the Major in masculine, military language.

The Major tells Valeria that he is bound by an oath of honor — a masculine ideal — not to reveal Eustace's terrible secret. Valeria nevertheless manages to sidestep the masculine oath of honor and extracts the critical admission from the Major that information about her husband's secret is hidden in the very room in which they are sitting, gaining, moreover, his permission to search it (72–74). By her astute reading of the Major's unintentional glances at a bookcase and a broken vase that matches the vase on that bookcase (79–80), she realizes that the key to Eustace's past must lie in the bookcase — a series of deductions highlighting Valeria's visual and interpretive mastery. By opening the Major's keepsake book of his former love affairs — i.e., investigating male desire — Valeria discovers a secreted photograph of Eustace with an unknown woman (86–90). Then, by being courteous to the Major's lower-class protegée, she discovers the book that reveals her husband's secret — "An Account of the Trial of Eustace Macallan for the poisoning of his wife" (91–94). After reading the ominous title page, Valeria promptly faints, suggesting that she, like other Gothic heroines, is not immune to bodily weakness (94). Note that unlike Emily in *Udolpho*, however, Valeria's bodily crisis is precipitated by real — not imagined — bad news.

Valeria's next barrier to investigation is the disapproval of her clergyman uncle Starkweather — her erstwhile guardian, who represents not only the church, but also the patriarchal family unit. The vicar strongly disapproves of Valeria's plan to clear Eustace. Valeria answers that she will first read the trial (121) and will then proceed as follows:

> I shall first try to form some conclusion (after reading the Trial) as to the guilty person who really committed the crime. Then, I shall make out a list of the witnesses who spoke in my husband's defence. I shall go to those witnesses, and tell them who I am, and what I want. I shall ask all sorts of questions which grave lawyers might think it beneath their dignity to put. I shall be guided, in what I do next, by the answers I receive. And I shall not be discouraged, no matter what difficulties are thrown in my way [121].

Although Valeria's impassioned, yet sensible, speech here fails to convince her uncle of the soundness of her plan, he at any rate does not impede it, and Valeria continues her investigations.

Just because she has overcome opposition, however, that does not mean that Valeria's investigations always go smoothly. Valeria's first (and manifestly incorrect) theory about how Sara Macallan has died is that Eustace's beautiful cousin, Mrs. Helena Beauly, is the poisoner. Indeed, Valeria sets forth a credible amount of circumstantial evidence to support her theory (184–187). Accordingly, she determines to ask advice from Eustace's old friend Miserrimus Dexter and, if he agrees with her, to go undercover to spy on Mrs. Beauly (188).

Valeria highlights her physical courage and commitment to investigate when she boldly goes to see the mad Miserrimus Dexter accompanied by her mother-in-law. Yet here too, her bravery does not necessarily imply investigative mastery. When Valeria mentions to Dexter that he had ideas of his own about the death of the first Mrs. Macallan, Dexter reacts oddly. "At that, he suddenly raised his eyes, and fixed them with a frowning and furtive suspicion on my face," Valeria relates. "'How do you know I have ideas of my own?' he asked, sternly" (216–217). This odd behavior might suggest to Valeria that Dexter knows more about the death than he is telling, but it doesn't.

Valeria's investigative mastery is also undercut when she again misreads Dexter's character and involvement in the death by misreading his reaction when she tells him of her investigative mission. Dexter becomes agitated and only calms down when Valeria makes it clear that she does not know the whereabouts of the person she suspects (242). Here too, Valeria evinces no suspicion that Dexter is upset because he has guilty knowledge.

Valeria seems at one point during her visit to be successfully investigating by using her femininity as a tool (just as she has used it successfully with Major Fitz-David before), yet she cannot follow through on the implications of what she discovers. On the one hand, she uses Dexter's low opinion of women's minds to elicit information, prefacing one of her most probing statements with: "I am only an ignorant woman ... and I daresay I am quite wrong" (249). On the other hand, when her intimation that she suspects the first Mrs. Macallan of being deliberately poisoned throws Dexter into a frenzy of excitement and anxiety (249–250), she does not attribute his frenzy to its right cause — guilty knowledge. Instead, Valeria blithely allows Dexter to confirm her wrongheaded suspicion that Mrs. Beauly poisoned the first Mrs. Macallan (251). Dexter and Valeria accordingly decide that she will go undercover using the name of Woodville — the name under which Eustace married her — in order to gain the confidence of Mrs. Beauly, or of Mrs. Beauly's maid. What happens next seems like it supports Valeria's investigative prowess, but in fact undermines it. On the one hand, while undercover — as herself — Valeria successfully finds evidence that undercuts Dexter's stated reasons for suspecting Mrs. Beauly. On the other hand, this successful investigation on her own leads directly to Valeria's eventual dependence on men as partners in her investigation. She decides to go to Edinburgh to question her husband's lawyers. As traveling alone is not an option for Valeria, her faithful old friend Benjamin insists upon accompanying her on the train. She does, however, persuade him to let her tackle the lawyer alone. She notes:

> My experience of the world is not a very large one.... But I have observed that, in nine cases out of ten, a man will make concessions to a woman, if she approaches him by herself, which he would hesitate even to consider, if another man was within hearing [271].

Valeria's naiveté as an investigator is underscored by the contrastingly sharp perception of Mr. Playmore, the Scots lawyer. Mr. Playmore instantly divines, upon hearing Valeria's story, that Dexter has something to hide (275–277). To be fair, however, when Mr. Playmore has persuaded Valeria of Dexter's duplicity, it is Valeria who correctly deduces that Dexter is only hiding information about the death and is not himself the murderer, as Mr. Playmore suspects him to be (277–278).

The last male barrier to her investigations that Valeria overcomes is Miserrimus Dexter's doctor. Valeria boldly decides that she will risk another visit to Dexter to find out his secret, even in the face of a doctor's opinion stating that Dexter may suddenly snap and go entirely insane if his nerves are bothered — an act that demonstrates both her physical courage and her resolve to complete her investigations (281–282).

Yet Valeria's commitment to investigate in the face of opposition does not remain entirely immune to adverse influence by men. For instance, Valeria mulls over the information that she has obtained from the Trial and from Dexter's statements and correctly deduces that Dexter must have stolen a missing room key to the poisoned woman's room. Yet this sign of her deductive mastery is juxtaposed against Valeria's explicit submission to a man's will. She notes: "...I promised beforehand to do nothing, without first consulting [Mr. Playmore's] opinion..." (305). This statement is the more striking given that repeatedly throughout the narrative up to this point, Valeria has consulted men about her plans, but has previously proceeded to do exactly as she pleases.

Valeria's investigatory powers sink to a low point when her mother-in-law persuades her to give up her search (312). But no sooner does Valeria give up than the apprehension that she is pregnant (313) makes her change her mind. For her child's sake, Valeria decides to press on (313–314). The pregnancy makes Valeria a clear servant of the patriarchy again, for, although the reader does not know the gender of the child at this point, Valeria is carrying Eustace's son and heir. The pregnancy reinforces the fact that Valeria's detection is being done not on her own account, but on behalf of her men.[43]

While the pregnancy empowers Valeria in one way (by inspiring her to keep investigating), it also marks an important shift in the narrative to a diminution of Valeria's investigatory powers and a devolution of these powers onto the male figures in the narrative. As Valeria is symbolically disabled by her pregnancy, the physical acts of detection now begin to be performed by men. For example, a letter arrives detailing how Mr. Playmore has confirmed Valeria's deduction about Dexter's sneaking into the poisoned woman's room by tracking down a servant (315–316).

In keeping with Valeria's reduced investigative powers, the key to finding the missing papers is *not* generated by Valeria, but by Mr. Playmore, who has the idea of sending a man to New York to find the person who would have thrown away the household litter. The message from America says to "open the dust-heap" at the house where the poisoned lady died (364). This dust-heap is something Valeria has already seen, including the scraps of paper strewn in it, yet she has not made the logical assumption that scraps torn up and thrown away usually wind up in the dust heap. Valeria fails completely in her interpretation here.

The more Valeria becomes reintegrated into the patriarchal family unit, the more her investigatory powers — and her desire to investigate — fail her. For instance, Mr. Playmore asks Valeria to come to Edinburgh to consult about the dust heap, but Valeria refuses to take part in this aspect of the investigation, choosing instead to meet the recovering Eustace in London.[44] Moreover, when it turns out that she must meet the ailing Eustace in Paris instead, she writes Mr. Playmore that she will take no further part in the investigation at all — a decision that makes Mr. Playmore and Benjamin take over the investigation. As Valeria's investigative power wanes here, the investigative power of the men rises: Mr. Playmore consults Benjamin about how to put together torn-up documents, and Benjamin eagerly sets about making experiments. Indeed, Benjamin, who before was unenthusiastic about the project, now eagerly sets about trying experiments of his own (370–371).

Although Valeria is reunited with a weakened Eustace in Paris and sets about nursing him back to health — an ironic echo of the nursing position in which Eustace found himself in relation to his sickly late wife — Valeria finds their reunion insufficient to effect her entire happiness. She notes:

> I still felt secret longings, *in those dangerous moments when I was left to myself,* to know whether the search for the torn letter had, or had not, taken place. What wayward creatures we are! With everything that a woman could want to make her happy, I was ready to put that happiness in peril, rather than remain ignorant of what was going on at Gleninch [373–374, emphasis mine]!

Note first here that the urge to investigate strikes Valeria only when she is *alone,* i.e., not in her "proper" place in the family unit by her husband's and mother-in-law's sides. Note further the gendered nature of the longing expressed here: Valeria chides herself for being dissatisfied while she has all that a *woman* could want — not all that a *person* could want. In contrast, the investigating Scots lawyer Mr. Playmore has a wife (273), yet *he* appears perfectly able to combine marriage with the investigation of a mystery. This suggests that for men, investigation and desire are perfectly compatible, whereas for women, they are somehow mutually exclusive.

Identity and Naming

Throughout the novel, Valeria's identity is inflected by the names people call her, an issue to which she is exquisitely sensitive. For instance, when Major Fitz-David addresses her as "dear Mrs Woodville," Valeria retorts: "Call me by my right name, sir.... I have made a discovery. I know, as well as you do, that my name is Macallan" (62). The Major later ignores Valeria's request that he call her Mrs. Macallan, however, and addresses her as Mrs. Woodville instead (66). When Valeria calls him on it, he explains, simply: "Your husband wishes me to persist" (66). This blunt denial of Valeria's wishes emphasizes the way in which Valeria's identity is subsumed by that of her husband.

Another character who bridles at the thought of addressing Valeria as "Mrs. Eustace Macallan" (210–211) is Miserrimus Dexter, albeit for a different reason: doing so reminds him of the unfortunate death of Sara, the first Mrs. Macallan (211). Valeria tells Dexter her first name in order to satisfy his curiosity:

> "My name is Valeria," I said.
> "A Roman name," remarked Miserrimus Dexter. "I like it.... I shall call you Mrs[.] Valeria. Unless you disapprove of it?"
> I hastened to say that I was far from disapproving of it [211].

The fact that Dexter chooses to refer to Valeria as Mrs. *Valeria* underlines her detachment from the patriarchy, as she uses neither her husband's nor her father's name. Yet the "Mrs." underlines the fact that even she cannot escape the patriarchal stamp and still echoes the Major's earlier insistence on refusing to call her Mrs. Macallan without her husband's permission.

Writing and Narrative

Valeria's relationship with writing and narrative throughout the novel is ambiguous at best, with even her moments of mastery in these areas often undercut by hints that she is not really in control of them. This relationship with writing and narrative follows a trajectory like a Bell curve: the beginning and end of the novel throw doubt on Valeria's ability to control them, and only the middle of the novel seems to allow her any mastery over them at all.

The novel opens with Valeria's relationship to writing severely in jeopardy, and the particular piece of writing in question is directly connected to Valeria's sexual desire. The very first narrated plot point of the novel has Valeria signing the marriage register incorrectly at her own wedding and then re-signing it with trembling fingers (8).[45] This uncertainty in writing occurs at what should be the peak of Valeria's desire for her husband Eustace Woodville — the consummation of their love in matrimony. The implication here is that feminine desire and masculine control over language may be mutually exclusive. (As we shall see later, Valeria's stumble here also prefigures the complex issues of naming and identity that pervade the narrative.)

The narrative (as told by Valeria — like Jane and Marian, she is a strong first-person narrator) then flashes back to their courtship, and Valeria promptly recalls an earlier instance when she lacked control over writing — again, an instance where the writing in question is directly related to Valeria's sexual desire. This time, the problem is one of interpretation rather than physical prowess. Before approving their marriage, Valeria's uncle has requested a character reference for Eustace from a mutual acquaintance. His terse, neutral reply is interpreted quite differently by uncle and niece: Valeria's uncle, adept at reading between the lines, rightly suspects that "[t]here is something under the surface in connexion with Mr Woodville, or with his family, to which Major Fitz-David is not at liberty to allude" (20). Valeria, at the peak of her desire, suspects nothing in the writing, however; on the contrary, when Eustace gallantly tries to release her from their engagement, she throws herself upon him and begs him to marry her as he has promised.

Valeria's relationship with legal writing is more ambiguous than the uniformly negative relationship with writing inflected by desire detailed above. On the one hand, others believe that Valeria's intention to prove Eustace's innocence is useless because they doubt her command of an important piece of writing, the account of Eustace's trial. For instance, before Eustace leaves Valeria, he responds to her entreaties only with the command, "Read the Trial" (107) — a command suggesting that the written legal record can never be contradicted. Likewise, Major Fitz-David and Valeria's father's old clerk Benjamin also refuse to believe that Valeria can help Eustace, reiterating the supremacy of the written legal record: "You have not read the Trial," Valeria is told (109).

Despite others' expectations that she will be mastered by the written legal record, however, Valeria boldly carves out her opposition to the unchallenged dominance of the written word and indeed, to the legal system itself:

> The facts are enough for *me*.... We know he is innocent. Why is his innocence not proved? It ought to be, it must be, it shall be! If the Trial tells me it can't be done, I refuse to believe the Trial. Where is the book, Major? Let me see for myself, if his lawyers have left nothing for his wife to do [109; emphasis in original].

Here, Valeria challenges the masculine-identified sphere of written official legal findings with the feminine-identified sphere of reality and lived experience — "the facts."

Similarly, as the narrative progresses, Valeria responds to a negative piece of desire-inflected writing with a positive defense of her mastery of legal writing. Eustace, too cowardly to take his leave of Valeria in person, makes clear his intention to desert her permanently in writing, by leaving her a letter urging her to annul their six-day marriage (131–133). Instead of accepting the decision set forth in this writing, however, Valeria boldly writes her own letter back to Eustace, affirming her intentions:

> What the Law has failed to do for you, your Wife must do for you.... The only chance that I can see of winning you back to me, in the character of a penitent and loving husband, is to change that underhand Scotch Verdict of Not Proven, into an honest English verdict of Not Guilty.
>
> Are you surprised at the knowledge of the law which this way of writing betrays in an ignorant woman? I have been learning, my dear: the Law and the Lady have begun by understanding one another. In plain English, I have looked into Ogilvie's Imperial Dictionary; and Ogilvie tells me [the definitions of Not Proven and Not Guilty] [116].

Note here Valeria's strategic alignment of herself with authoritative writing through her consultation with Ogilvie's dictionary. Her control and use of the dictionary symbolize her control over language, writing, and the law.

Moreover, in her characterization of the above letter to Eustace to her reading audience, Valeria simultaneously embraces and distances herself from authoritative written speech. She makes the self-deprecating comment that her letter is "[p]oor enough as a composition" (117), yet she bolsters her mastery of writing by noting that she "could write a much better letter now" (117) and that her letter had the merit of being "the honest expression of what [she] really meant and felt" (117)—again a submission of masculine-identified writing to feminine-identified lived experience.

Valeria's account of the trial itself continues her ambiguous relationship with legal writing. On the one hand, her trial account initially shows a strained relationship with language. In describing the title page and indictment alone, she twice refuses to write words that upset her:

> I cannot prevail upon myself to copy, for the second time, the horrible title-page which holds up to public ignominy my husband's name.... I shall not copy the uncouth language [of the indictment], full of needless repetitions (and, if I know anything of the subject, not guiltless of bad grammar as well) ... [124–125].

Although Valeria shows here that legal language has power over her, she simultaneously reasserts her own power over legal language by her criticism of the indictment's "needless repetitions" and "bad grammar."

Valeria's actual presentation of the Trial to her readers and her analysis of it underscore her increasing mastery over language, however. She sets out the import of the prosecution's questioning of its first witness and notes what the defense will have to establish in its cross-examination of this witness (139–140). Valeria's cogent analysis here is borne out by the actual substance of the defense's cross-examination, in which the defense lawyer does *exactly* what she predicts he will try to do. Valeria's mastery over the trial narrative is reinforced as she continues her über-narration of the meaning and import of various testimony throughout the trial as a frame around the testimony she presents to the reader: she aptly tells the reader what the testimony will establish or has established and how the case is shaping itself. Indeed, at one point, Valeria even provides a formal summary of what the prosecution and defense have proven so far (152).

Yet Valeria's mastery over the Trial transcript is incomplete. She makes one serious misreading of character that will prove important later, although its import is not obvious to the reader at this time: Valeria interprets a passage in the Trial transcript where Eustace's friend Miserrimus

Dexter is described as trying to keep the police from searching Eustace's room as necessarily meaning that Dexter is Eustace's "thorough good ally" (152). This serious misreading later keeps Valeria from solving the mystery as quickly as she otherwise might have done.

Overall, however, Valeria's mastery over writing and narrative proves at its peak when she challenges the legal system's version of events in the trial transcript, justifying Collins's choice of *The Law and the Lady* as the title of his novel. Later events in the novel seem designed to undercut whatever mastery over writing and narrative Valeria has previously shown.

For instance, Valeria's mastery over writing begins to slip when she arranges to visit Dexter for the last time, with her faithful friend Benjamin as her companion and note-taker (324–325). Interestingly, the task of writing falls to the man here, although Valeria is theoretically supposed to be in charge of when the writing will start and stop (325). The interview underlines Valeria's increasingly shaky hold on discursive mastery: Valeria's first attempt to lead Dexter to speak of the mystery almost causes him a complete mental breakdown (331–336). Then, Valeria almost loses her chance to learn the truth from the rapidly deteriorating Dexter when she tries to discourage him from telling what seems like an unrelated story. Only belatedly does Valeria realize that the story may hold the key to the mystery (337).

Moreover, Valeria's lack of control over language continues in this scene as Dexter becomes delirious and starts babbling disjointed clues about what happened with the poisoned woman, namely that a letter that would clear Eustace exists and has been disposed of as waste paper (344–345). Valeria does not understand the meaning of Dexter's words here, but sends a transcript of Benjamin's notes to Mr. Playmore and keeps a copy to puzzle over herself. Another sign of Valeria's lack of mastery over meaning and interpretation at this point in the narrative is that Mr. Playmore correctly interprets the reference to the letter, while Valeria remains mystified (351–354). Mr. Playmore searches Eustace's former house for the torn letter. Not finding it, Mr. Playmore correctly surmises which servant must have disposed of the letter. To find the servant, now in New York, he makes arrangements with Valeria (354–355). Mr. Playmore also correctly interprets an address in Dexter's ramblings and sends one of his clerks to find that Dexter had keys made to Eustace's diary and to the drawer in which it was kept (356).

The last incident in which Valeria demonstrates any control over writing occurs when she tries to negotiate the inherent conflict between her life as an investigator and her role as Eustace's wife. Besieged again by a letter from her mother-in-law saying that Eustace will have her, if only she will give up her investigation, Valeria writes a deceitful letter in return: she writes only the truth, but omits all reference to her ongoing investigation (362–363). Interestingly, this successful deceit is practiced on a woman, not a man, perhaps suggesting that Valeria's mastery of language here is more effective because it does not face masculine interpretation.

Valeria's role then shifts from being one who informs others about the results of her investigations to one who simply learns of the investigations of others. She then receives at Paris a letter from Benjamin detailing the progress of the investigation (374–375). At this point, Valeria is so far removed from the act of investigating that she is discovering information at a third or fourth remove from its original discovery: The agent sent to America finds out information about the letter and passes it to Mr. Playmore, who passes it to Benjamin, who passes it to Valeria. This is certainly a far cry from Valeria's initial solo investigative tour de force in the Major's study. Then, Benjamin's letter tells her, he himself has gone up to Gleninch to arrange to have men search the dust heap with Mr. Playmore for the missing letter (378). This turn of events implies that finding the letter is clearly a man's job.

Indeed, the torn letter is found and painstakingly pieced together by a group of *men*. It turns out to be a letter written by Eustace's first wife explaining her suicide. Valeria's response to this solution of the mystery is to disavow her own efforts and abilities at investigation:

> It was all my doing ... [a]nd yet, what I had done, I had, so to speak, done blindfold. The merest accident might have altered the course of later events. I had over and over again interfered to check Ariel, when she entreated the Master to "tell her a story." If she had not succeeded, in spite of my opposition, Miserrimus Dexter's last effort of memory might never have been directed to the tragedy at Gleninch. And again, if I had only remembered to move my chair, and so to give Benjamin the signal to leave off, he would never have written down the apparently senseless words which have led us to the discovery of the truth [396].

Note how Valeria highlights the uselessness of her attempts to control discourse here.[46] Indeed, her efforts to shape a dialogue with a man are pronounced almost ruinous.

The Law and the Lady ends with a scene reminiscent of *The Woman in White* or *Jane Eyre*: a tableau of Valeria, Eustace, and their newborn son. But part of that tableau is a reference to the letter — the suicide note of the first Mrs. Macallan, which Valeria wisely urges Eustace not to read, as it indicts Eustace as an unloving, cold husband. Although it may seem

as if Valeria has control over language and writing here, in that she tells Eustace not to read the letter and he follows her advice, the suicide note carries another valence as well. Valeria can also be seen as endangered by the suicide note: The note speaks of another woman's real-life experience of the disappointments of marriage and the dangers of a female desire that is not fully reciprocated. Valeria may well wish to suppress the letter not only to protect Eustace, but also to protect herself— not only because of what it tells of another woman's past with Eustace, but also because of what it portends for her own future with him.

* * *

The Law and the Lady is simply the most extensive example of the limitations placed upon the female investigator by the gothic form. Throughout this chapter, we have seen how the heroine of the female gothic is typed as an "almost-investigator." No matter how strong her desire to investigate, and no matter how strong her linguistic and interpretive mastery, she is never allowed to bring her investigation to a successful conclusion through her own efforts.

◆ 2 ◆

Lesbian Detectives
Have Car Trouble

The number of lesbian detective novels is burgeoning. In their study *Sleuths in Skirts: Analysis and Bibliography of Serialized Female Sleuths*, Frances A. DellaCava and Madeline H. Engel list 41 lesbian detective series characters.[1] Yet while there are some excellent essays on lesbian detective fiction, there still is more work to be done in this field. The relative paucity of criticism of this genre may be partly due to its relative recency. Sally R. Munt identifies 1977's *Angel Dance* by M.F. Beal as the first lesbian feminist mystery,[2] and a 1984 essay by Joseph Hansen (author of the mystery series featuring gay male detective Dave Brandstetter) contains no references to lesbian detectives.[3] Another possible reason for the paucity of criticism in this area may be academic disdain for (and/or political misgivings about) lesbian "genre fiction."[4]

When I began working out my theory of the flawed female detective, I naively assumed that lesbian detective fiction would serve as the exception that proves the rule. It seemed obvious to me that fiction written by and for lesbians and starring lesbian protagonists should be exempt from the patriarchal influences that pervaded other narratives of female detection. Who more than lesbian detectives would be exempt from being objectified by the male gaze? Surely, I thought, this immunity from the gaze would produce a set of profoundly competent female detectives with nary a flaw. As it turns out, I was dead wrong.

Lesbian detectives have by far the most car trouble of any subset of fictional detectives. Their cars catch on fire, get keyed, get car bombed, get crushed by movie stunt cars, run out of gas, get flat tires, hit rocks, stall in the middle of chases, almost run off the road, get stolen, have their door latches stick, cough up smoke, have their radiators boil over, get parking tickets, get towed, spend a lot of time at the shop, break down, get followed without them realizing it, and keep getting left behind when the detective needs them.[5] I will argue that in the lesbian detective novel, the lesbian detective's car metonymizes the detective herself, and that what happens to her car symbolizes her psychic reality.

As noted below in the television chapter, competence in transportation is a key index of a female investigator's freedom.[6] On a scale from *Charlie's Angels* (detectives are highly competent at managing all forms of transportation) to *Murder, She Wrote* (detective can't even drive), however, lesbian investigators fall far closer to *Murder, She Wrote* than to *Charlie's Angels*. Several lesbian detective series appear to have made a running gag out of their protagonists' troubles with their automobiles. Lesbian investigators' cars get ticketed, towed, and totaled at a rate far exceeding that suffered by the average male investigator — or even the average straight female investigator.[7] Somehow, male investigators don't seem to have much car trouble.[8] This may be related to the car as phallic symbol.

Several other unexpected tropes appear in the world of lesbian detective fiction. There is an undercurrent of self-blame and/or a lack of self-reliance that runs through many lesbian detective novels. While all kinds of detectives make tactical errors, the lesbian detective is far more likely to blame herself explicitly for an error. Lesbian detectives also tend to get rescued a lot, like latter-day gothic heroines.[9] True, their rescuers may now be female, but the detectives themselves are still placed in a disempowered position by being unable to rescue themselves from danger. This rescue-from-danger theme adds a certain romance-novel quality to the lesbian detective novel.

There is also a surprising tendency for competence in the lesbian detective world to split along a butch/femme axis. Generally, the more butch the lesbian investigator, the more savvy she seems to be about the workings of the world in general and the case she's working on in particular. Even among relatively butch lesbian investigators, however, there are sometimes surprising lapses of perception and common sense. The emphasis on the butch model of lesbian self-presentation may be related to the fact that most lesbian sleuths are modeled more after the American hard-boiled type of detective than the Continental great thinker type of detective.[10]

Finally, the lesbian investigator's competence appears to be directly related to her place in the field of vision and the field of desire.[11] When the lesbian investigator finds herself investigated and pursued as a sexual object or overcome by desire, her investigative skills are usually in abeyance. On the other hand, when the lesbian investigator is apart from desire, her competence increases. Moreover, lesbian detectives seem to be beset with relationship troubles. The course of true love seldom seems to run smooth for them.

Nell Fury

My introduction into the world of lesbian detective fiction came from reading *The Two-Bit Tango*, Elizabeth Pincus's first novel starring San Francisco private detective Nell Fury. This novel initially seemed to confirm my preconceptions. Nell Fury is a tough-talking, wise-cracking professional private eye who specializes in cases with some connection to the queer community. She winds up solving the mystery handily in *The Two-Bit Tango*[12] and its two sequels, *The Solitary Twist*[13] and *The Hang-dog Hustle*.[14] Overall, Nell exudes an aura of competence as she goes about the details of her detective work. (The convincing detail may stem from the fact that Pincus herself worked as a private detective[15] — following in the footsteps of Dashiell Hammett, who worked as a Pinkerton operative before starting his literary career.)

Despite her overall aura of competence, however, Nell has several subtle flaws that replicate those we have seen in female detectives in other media and genres.

Competence

One would think that a butch investigator like Nell, who seems to operate mostly outside the field of vision, might accordingly achieve a higher level of investigative competence than heterosexual female investigators who are subject to the male gaze. Instead, the novels portray Nell as less-than-competent, especially when she tries to deal with technology or when she investigates men: In *The Two-Bit Tango*, Nell has difficulty getting a phone number for a female client in LA, even though she has the client's name and address and has talked to the information operator (33). Somehow, a heterosexual male investigator friend of hers is able to use his contacts to get this information — information that anyone could get from an operator or a reverse telephone directory.

Nell does show some competence in *Tango* when she surprises a young wanna-be investigator who is breaking into Nell's apartment and is able to deal with this milquetoast intruder effectively (70–72). When Nell herself tries to break into a house to investigate a few pages later, however, she is shown to be incompetent: She gives away her presence by gasping at a scene of violence she witnesses and winds up getting shot in the shoulder by her panicked client (74–75).

This juxtaposition of competence with incompetence is a pattern repeated throughout the series. When Nell and her friend Phoebe are kidnapped, Nell attacks one of the kidnappers with an elbow to the groin and whacks him in the face (119). Yet her physical abilities are insufficient to get her and Phoebe to safety. The other kidnapper still has his gun trained on them — they are still damsels in distress in dire need of rescue. Rescue comes from another woman, Nell's gun-happy client Olive (119–120). Nell wryly refers to the scene as something like in 'Charlie's Angels' [*sic*] (126). This is a particularly appropriate reference, since a major trope of *Charlie's Angels* is women rescuing other women.

Nell has great difficulty interpreting others' actions. Far into *The Two-Bit Tango*, she finds out that she has been fooled by her client's impersonation of the client's missing twin sister (123). Nell also suffers periods of unnecessary — and damaging — self-doubt about her perceptions. In *The Solitary Twist*, Nell twice spots a man who seems to be tailing her or her client but doubts the evidence of her own senses:

> [H]ad I conjured him up all along — a fabrication, a human mirage, a figment of my fervent imagination? Something solid to fixate on in my otherwise flailing investigation [52]?

Nell also sometimes makes naive assumptions. In *Twist*, when she sees the city worker she's tailing surreptitiously hand a mysterious manila envelope to a worker on a construction job the city is overseeing (61), Nell blames herself for being too suspicious: "I sighed. Here I was, traipsing around in disguise like a bumbling spy out of *Get Smart*, and Gold was just conducting a little city business" (62). Not until over seventy pages later does Nell accidentally discover that the envelope is part of a bribery scheme (133–135). Even then, Nell is so surprised at that information that, she says, "I almost fell off my stool" (133). Nell also momentarily loses track of the supervisor as she's tailing him (59–60).

The Solitary Twist makes clear that Nell has lousy perception when it comes to noticing that she herself is being followed — that is, when she is the object of the male gaze: "I was so preoccupied, in fact, that I failed to see the man in the steel gray Mercury who fell into traffic behind me and parked at the far end of Ramona, watching with cold, yellow eyes as I unlocked my apartment door and stepped inside" (151). Nell gets even more careless when she follows a lead to Minneapolis and is kidnapped by the yellow-eyed man. The narrative here highlights her failures in perception:

> I took a quick glance around, but didn't see anyone looking my way. My eyes must really be losing their keenness. Because as I dug my picklocks out of my pocket, a figure popped out of the darkness and clasped a cool hand across my mouth [177].

Although Nell struggles, she is overcome by her attacker's strength. It is interesting here that the attack on Nell occurs just as she is attempting to perform a phallically-cathected act — putting a picklock into the hole of a lock. Even more interestingly, Nell blames her failure on her failing vision — as if her act of investigating, of attempting to assume the male gaze, provokes a failure of her own vision.

Insult is added to injury when Nell's kidnapper tells her that he has not only followed her from San Francisco but that he has also tailed her for the last several days without her noticing (180). When the kidnapper takes her to her client, Nell guesses incorrectly about her client's true identity (187). When freed, Nell realizes that she's been looking to solve the mystery in all the wrong places, that she's "been traipsing around one step behind all the action" (195).

Nell's imperfect sense of her own personal danger is again underlined in the third Nell Fury novel, *The Hangdog Hustle*. Nell is ambushed again, a situation she again blames on faulty perception:

> Unfortunately for me, I ignored one of the princip[al] lessons of private-eye boot camp: always be aware of your surroundings. As I blithely inserted the key into the lock, I felt a presence hovering to my left. I turned, vaguely cognizant of someone tall with a mass of dark hair. Ah, it must be Merle.
> Whop!! A blow caught me at the side of the neck. I staggered backwards. S/he was tall ... but the dark crown was actually a woolly black ski mask.... I groped frantically for my briefcase, hoping to use it as a weapon. But a second wallop came quickly, another fist to the head that sent me reeling to the carpet like a woozy drunk, counting stars... [55–56].

As in the previous example, Nell is stopped here when in a phallically-cathected act — inserting a key into a lock.

When Nell follows a lead to Memphis, the bad guys get the drop on her yet again — again when she is attempting to enter a room to investigate:

> ...[T]he office door opened a crack. Then it swung fully inward. A white man with a hooked nose and a shock of carroty hair smiled and said, "Come on in."
> I stepped into the dimly lit space and opened my mouth to pose a ques-

tion. That's when I felt something hard and cylindrical nudge the front of my coat. I gasped and stumbled back but Carrot Head pressed tight against me and whispered, "*Come in*, Ms. Fury." Then he poked me again with the solid rod.

I caught a glimpse of polished black metal kissing fabric [166].

This is an exceedingly odd passage — chock-full of the imagery of heterosexual male aggression. The imagery signals that Nell is about to be shown at her weakest and least effectual. Nell is promptly tied up with other victims in a room doused with gasoline and about to be set afire (169) She wets her pants (169) and launches a completely ineffectual, doomed attack on their captors while she is still tied to a chair (169). For her trouble, she only topples over and gets a cut on the cheek (169) When the room is set ablaze, Nell and her fellow-victims are again in the damsel-in-distress position. Improbably, they are rescued in the nick of time by a fantasy-female figure: "[a]n angel ... in the form of a towheaded woman in 501s and a motorcycle jacket" (170).

Besides being ambushed frequently, Nell also keeps being betrayed by her body. In *The Hangdog Hustle*, for example, Nell is following suspects around Alcatraz and overhearing incriminating information when her foot slips on a piece of broken glass and startles her prey (125).

Nell combines the themes of unexplained incompetence, being betrayed by her body, finding that her physical attempts at conflict are insufficient, and needing to be rescued by a woman in the denouement of *The Hangdog Hustle*. First of all, Nell spots the murderer she aims to bring down just as her car is being ticketed. Rather than enlisting the aid of the officer giving her the ticket, Nell makes the illogical choice of taking time to call a client and having the client call the police for her (198). Then, after following the murderer into a music store, she is again betrayed by her body: "I made my mistake when I skirted a massive amplifier and tripped over a wire.... [T]he commotion drew Mason's attention (198–199)." Nell's clumsiness precipitates a hostage crisis. Again, she makes an unsuccessful attempt at physical combat: When she whacks the hostage-taker with a guitar, he hangs onto his gun and points it straight at her. Nell is again in the "damsel-in-distress" role as she finds herself "staring down an infinite tunnel of gun barrel" (199). Again, Nell is rescued by a woman — this time by a tough female San Francisco Homicide Inspector (199).

Driving

Nell's relationship with motor vehicles is highly problematic. Nell ends the first chapter of *The Two-Bit Tango* by telling her client that her car is "out of commission" (7). Indeed, the car is more seriously out of commission than Nell admits — it needs "a new clutch and engine overhaul" (7). She and her client decide to walk (7).

Nell is reduced to riding around hilly San Francisco on a Schwinn bicycle (16). This may reflect her own ambivalence about her car. She describes her car problems thus:

> My ailing VW Rabbit was stalled in front of the warehouse loading dock, collecting gull droppings. I didn't know whether to fix it, junk it, or give it to [an artist friend] for one of her mixed-media installation pieces [16].

In fact, Nell actively resists fixing her car when she's handed a wad of cash she doesn't think she's earned, despite a friend's urgings:

> "Nellie ... Get your car fixed. Or trade it for a better one."
> "I don't need a car!"
> "Who ever heard of a private eye without a car?"
> I thought really hard. "Jessica Fletcher" [29]!

It is telling that Nell invokes Jessica Fletcher here, since, like Jessica, she winds up doing a significant amount of investigating from her bicycle.

Because she never gets around to fixing her car, Nell is also forced to borrow cars. Even borrowed cars make her uneasy: The "tinny AM radio" in a borrowed car annoys her (37). This borrowed car (and every car Nell touches) serves as a focal point for her problematic relationship with law and authority. Nell promptly gets a parking ticket on the borrowed car (56), which she ignores. She then defiantly parks in the same place *again* and gets *another* ticket (59).

Nell's problems with transportation are not shared by Phoebe, Nell's cab-driver ex-lover. When Phoebe picks up Nell's rental car and drops it off in front of Nell's home, the car stays "ticket free" (84) until Nell gets it. Yet soon after Nell gets possession of the rental car, it starts attracting traffic tickets (101).

The denouement of *The Two-Bit Tango* is also highly transportation-related. After Nell rescues two kidnapped women from their captors (161–166), she then tries to flee their captors in her car, which skids (168) and gets hit by the captors' car (168). However, she successfully concludes the chase by slowing down when she hears the police (finally, Nell pays attention to the law!), while her pursuers wreck their car in a fatal crash trying to escape (169). Still, Nell's bad car-luck dogs her. Nell leaves the rental car near the scene of the fatal crash and returns the next day to find that it has been towed (175).

It is interesting, then, that Nell receives a transportation-related reward at the end of the first novel. Nell's client and her client's sister — the woman whom Nell rescued — give Nell "a baby blue vintage Mustang convertible with a black interior" (193) as a long-term loaner car. The last image in *The Two-Bit Tango* is an empowering image of a woman about to hit the open road:

> I sat in the driver's seat of the Mustang for a while, running my fingers over the steering wheel and the buttery leather upholstery. Even the cracks felt nice. I adjusted the mirrors, messed around with the stick, and imagined zooming around everybody's favorite city.... I hustled inside to grab my sunglasses. It was time to take this pony for a ride [193].

At least, this *seems* like an empowering image. But notice how we don't actually see Nell driving — just anticipating the joy of driving. This foreshadows Nell's continued problematic relationship with driving in the second Nell Fury novel, *The Solitary Twist*.

Initially, Nell seems to be enjoying her loaner Mustang, noting that it makes her feel "almost as cool as Thelma and Louise" (26) — an interesting reference, since Thelma and Louise are lawbreakers who get away with it, at least for a while. Nell, too, seems to have better luck with her own careless parking habits: she parks in a forbidden yellow zone without getting a ticket (26) and later comments that the car is "mercifully free of tickets" (52).

Things are not as rosy with the car as they seem, however. Nell notes that the Mustang, initially so "cool," soon becomes too hot: "My black convertible top made the Mustang heat up like an oven" (60). Moreover, the Mustang does not escape a parking ticket when Nell forgets about street cleaning (200) — perhaps a reference to the female-coded expectation that women are supposed to remember about things like cleaning. Most importantly, however, Nell's moment of greatest competence in the narrative is juxtaposed with the complete destruction of the Mustang. *Immediately* after Nell improbably outruns an entire SWAT team to tackle a hostage-taker and rescue her client's daughter (204), the car — which represented the female bonding and freedom of *Thelma and Louise* — is destroyed in a freak accident:

> As if that wasn't enough destruction for one day, I heard a resounding squeal of tires and raised my battered head in time to see a pickup truck race down Market Street, zoom off a movie set stunt ramp, apparently lose control in mid-air, and land upside down with a sickening splat on top of my beloved pale blue vintage Mustang convertible [205].

The Mustang is turned into "a flat, metal pancake bleeding powder-blue hunks of wreckage" (217). Like The *Two-Bit Tango*, however, *The Solitary*

Twist ends with an image of Nell hitting the road, as she embarks on a surprise road trip with her lover (225–226).

The third Nell Fury novel, *The Hangdog Hustle*, opens with Nell again driving a problematic vehicle — a friend's Datsun B210, described variously as a "dented-up hatchback," a "bucket of bolts," and a "mud-colored monster" (17). The Datsun doesn't sound good, either: Nell notes that it "cough[s] a bit of smoke" (39) and "hiccup[s] raucously" (49). When the Datsun breaks down (70), Nell is reduced to traveling by foot, cab, Muni train, bicycle, and a borrowed Acura. Nell leaves the dead Datsun in a the grocery store parking lot, and when she calls to check on it, it has mysteriously disappeared (103).

Nell also has trouble with another form of transportation — a ferry. According to the narrative, Nell should be extremely competent using ferries and should be familiar with the San Francisco ferry schedules — she notes that she had spent several *years* working as a deckhand for the very ferry company she uses (120). Yet Nell stays on Alcatraz Island following a pair of suspects for so long that she literally misses the boat — the ferry back to the mainland — and is forced to stay on the island overnight (126).

Later in the novel, Nell's broken-down missing Datsun is stolen (apparently by someone better at making it start than she is), crashed, and then abandoned (190). Like the flattened Mustang in *The Solitary Twist*, the Datsun is totaled: "The car was a twisted blob of mud-colored metal and spiderwebbed glass. The passenger side was so mangled I couldn't even rescue any trinkets from the glove compartment" (190). The glove compartment here might be read as female genitalia, a hidden, private box containing cherished trinkets. Its destruction bodes ill.

To replace the totaled Datsun, Nell buys a "navy-blue Mitsubishi pickup truck with a dent in the rear fender and a fake cowskin seat cover in the cab" (196). As in the other novels, the truck attracts the ire of the law: just two pages after Nell tells us she's bought the truck, she notes that it has gotten a ticket (which she ignores) (198).

As do the first two novels, *The Hangdog Hustle* ends with an image of driving. It is a more subdued image of driving in this novel, however: rather than hitting the open road, Nell tools around San Francisco with her dying client, off to buy clothes for her daughter (204).

Cherry Aimless, Nancy Clue, and the Rest of the Girls

As we saw through the examination of *Northanger Abbey* above, we can learn much about a genre from works that parody it. Mabel Maney has written a delightful trio of novels that parody both lesbian romantic fiction and juvenile girls' fiction.[16] In them, we can also trace a parody of the lesbian detective novel. The trilogy highlights the key elements common to the lesbian detective novel: car trouble, self-blame, rescues, and an index of competence that appears related to butch/femme roles and to the investigator's place in the field of vision. *The Case of the Not-So-Nice Nurse, The Case of the Good-for-Nothing Girlfriend*,[17] and *A Ghost in the Closet*[18] chart the adventures of Cherry Aimless (based on girls' series heroine Nurse Cherry Ames), Nancy Clue (based on Nancy Drew), and a sundry crew of their gay and lesbian fellow sleuths who join them in their various adventures. Their close friends span the spectrum of traditional lesbian and gay roles, from the very butch Midge and the very femme Velma (and the very butch George and very femme Bess in Nancy's hometown), to the "baby dyke" Lauren and the African American butch Jackie, to their gay chums, the Hardly Boys. Their world is populated with an endless supply of lesbian gym teachers, librarians, mechanics, newspaper reporters, gas-station attendants, nuns, English teachers, and home economics teachers, as well as several gay male drama coaches, antique dealers, and interior decorators. Heterosexual men appear only as villains, unless they are children. Positive heterosexual female characters usually turn out to be closeted lesbians, or at least to be lesbian-friendly. Female characters who blindly support patriarchal privilege tend to be evil.

All three novels in the trilogy make their chief villains symbols of the patriarchy. In *The Case of the Not-So-Nice-Nurse*, corrupt priests, symbolic of the male bias of organized religion, are the main villains. In *The Case of the Good-for-Nothing Girlfriend*, Nancy's abusive father Carson Clue, a prominent attorney, and Police Chief Chumley, symbolic of the male bias of the law, are the main villains. In *A Ghost in the Closet*, the evil Dr. Fraud, symbolic of the male bias of the medical establishment in general and of the psychiatric community in particular, is the chief villain.

The Case of the Not-So-Nice Nurse

The first sentence of the first Cherry Aimless novel, *The Case of the Not-So-Nice Nurse*, plants its heroine, Cherry, firmly in the field of vision:

> Cherry Aimless cut an attractive figure as she dashed through the crowded lobby of Seattle General Hospital, her striking royal blue nurse's cape sailing behind her and her crisp white cap perched precariously on rumpled curls. Her rosy cheeks were even more flushed than usual... [7].

As in this passage, Cherry is constantly flushing and blushing throughout the trilogy, suggesting a lack of control over her body. The first incidents in the novel also establish Cherry as a person betrayed by her body: While taking a short cut, Cherry trips and falls into a pile of newspapers, then literally runs right into her boss (7–9). In one sense, these incidents establish Cherry as someone who cannot control her body and the forces that surround her. Cherry's trip onto the newspaper pile foreshadows the trouble she will have understanding words and meanings later in the trilogy. Her collision with her boss similarly prefigures problems she will encounter due to her blind trust in authority figures. On the other hand, it is the newspapers and Cherry's boss who probably get the worst of their encounters with Cherry. Like a young Gracie Allen, although Cherry takes a literal, innocent approach to the world around her, she always eventually comes up on top, even though she may not understand how she got there.

Cherry is generally a sturdy girl, but like Marian Halcombe in *The Woman in White* and Emily St. Aubert in *Mysteries of Udolpho*, her body betrays her at moments of high excitement. Cherry faints from surprise and exhaustion at one point and faints again a few hours later after she has killed a murderous priest (148, 166). In *The Case of the Good-for-Nothing Girlfriend*, after Police Chief Chumley's death, Cherry faints again (235). This is a bit odd, since Cherry is supposed to be a nurse, but fainting seems to be her standard response to the killing of evil males who deserved it. Cherry is not the only detective in the trilogy who faints: Nancy similarly faints when she hears that housekeeper Hannah Gruel has not been released from jail on her say so (138).

In a parody of the juvenile series convention of advertising recently published and forthcoming novels in the same series, the narrative tells us that Cherry, who worships her hero Nancy Clue, has already "earned a reputation as a detective" (10–11). Yet Cherry is actually what Seymour Chatman would call a fallible filter: She constantly misinterprets the meanings of events around her, so that her perception is far inferior to that of the implied reader.[19] Not only does Cherry have a blind trust in authority figures, but she also has a blind trust in almost every person she meets. No matter what suspicious behavior she sees, Cherry struggles to find the most innocent, positive explanation for it. The result is a constant irony, as Cherry, locked into her own limited perceptions, misinterprets the world around her and her place in it.

Like Nell Fury, Cherry doubts the evidence of her own senses. When Cherry hears a cry for help and runs out of the hospital ward to investigate, she's bamboozled by a mendacious priest who claims he hasn't heard anything. Instead of standing her ground, Cherry retreats, not only outwardly, but also inwardly: "Cherry looked around the quiet room. Obviously, nothing had happened. Feeling foolish, she blushed some more. 'I've got to get more sleep; now I'm hearing things!' she said to no one in particular..." (16). Similarly, when fierce Head Nurse Marstad tells Cherry a fairly obvious lie, Cherry blames her own faculties rather than blame an authority figure:

> Cherry was so confused. She was sure Lana had arrived with the book. "But Nurse Marstad would never lie about a thing like that. Oh, I must have imagined the book belonged to Lana the same way I imagined hearing a call for help" [17]!

The narrative thus continually re-emphasizes Cherry's inability to interpret the world around her correctly. Even Cherry's dog Lady is portrayed as more astute than Cherry herself is when it comes to sensing prowlers: "[Lady] knew there was something out there in the night, even if her mistress didn't!" (35).

Also like Nell Fury, Cherry and the lesbian chums she will later meet love driving, but have an inordinate amount of trouble with their cars. Nancy Clue drives a "sporty yellow convertible," and she "handle[s] the swift car with skill" (114). Nancy's beloved car will see a lot of mechanical failures in the next installment of the series, however.

Cherry identifies highly with her car — a "1953 dark blue Buick" (note the similarity to the color of Cherry's nurse's cape) — as her alter ego: "'It's not a very glamorous car,' she thought, comparing it to the flashy red convertible with white leather seats parked in the next space. 'But it's sturdy and dependable, just like me'" (25). That alter ego is violated early in the novel, just moments after Cherry begins a long road trip. As Cherry is pulled over in a gas station, studying a map (a male-identified activity), "a strange man wearing a fedora pulled low over his face reache[s] into her car and snatche[s] her purse" (25)! The fact that the car/Cherry is violated by this male intrusion is underlined by the traditional identification of the purse with women's genitalia and by the use of the word "snatch," a slang word for female genitalia. Cherry, whose name connotes the hymen of a virginal, pre-sexual girl, screams, as if her first act of intercourse/loss of innocence has occurred (25). The purse-snatcher, startled by her cry, drops her purse, and Cherry vows to be more careful in the future with her purse, which contains a mysterious parcel she is charged with delivering (25–26).

The car, and Cherry, are violated again at Cherry's next rest stop.

Significantly, this violation occurs when she has been reading the lesbian novel that was part of her "secret package"—another transgressive female activity, like driving and map-reading. This time, two men block Cherry's car, and one of them accosts her as she sits in it, even opening her car door to menace her further (30). The opening of the car door, like the purse snatching, symbolizes a violation of the car-as-Cherry. Cherry's car is attacked again when her enemies steal the title and registration from it and report it stolen (75). Cherry's lesbian Aunt Gertrude also has *her* car stolen (89–90).

Like the Nell Fury novels, *The Case of the Not-So-Nice Nurse* ends with an image of driving: Cherry runs to Nancy's yellow convertible on her way to accompany her newfound chums on a road trip to solve another mystery (184).

The Case of the Good-for-Nothing Girlfriend

The next novel in the series, *The Case of the Good-for-Nothing Girlfriend*, starts on a note of automotive frustration, as Nancy's road trip with her chums hits a car-related snag. Nancy's car has "hit a rather large rock and made the most awful clanking noise before rolling to a dead stop at the side of the road"[20] (11). Nancy and Midge finally have to push the car to town, where it's fixed by a flirtatious lesbian mechanic, one of a series of lesbian mechanics and tow-truck drivers who populate the series (28, 32–34). The fact that Nancy's car metonymizes Nancy herself is underlined when the police put "an All Points Bulletin out on [Nancy's] car" instead of on Nancy herself (39).

Shortly after the last accident, lesbian sex winds up causing yet another car accident for the group:

> Velma had taken her mind off the road ahead for only a split second, but it had been long enough for the car to veer off course and crash into a boulder. Midge ... vowed that next time she would keep her hands to herself when Velma was driving [64].

The implication here is that lesbian sexuality and car trouble are linked.

Nancy's flair for taking useful courses and being well versed in obscure fields of knowledge is brought up, then immediately undercut:

> "That course I took in auto mechanics sure has come in handy on this trip," Nancy joked bravely as she hopped down off the bumper. Then her face grew cloudy. "I fear this car isn't going anywhere without a tow truck," she sighed.
> Midge frowned. "The radiator's busted and all the vital fluids have leaked out," she added [65].

Nancy has theoretical automotive knowledge,[21] but is unable to actually fix her car. Interestingly, Nancy's 1959 Chrysler doesn't have a spare tire (73). This seems odd in a large car of this era. The missing spare serves as an image of the girls' symbolic castration as they lose all of their transportation power. Likewise, the lost "vital fluids" recall the "precious bodily fluids" in the classic film *Dr. Strangelove, or: How I Learned to Stop Worrying and Love the Bomb* (Stanley Kubrick, 1964). The lost fluids similarly represent a loss of potency here.

Throughout *The Case of the Good-for-Nothing Girlfriend*, Cherry remains completely incapable of interpreting signs that to the reader are eminently suspicious — partly because she distrusts herself and partly because she is incapable of impugning the motives of others. Cherry's naiveté makes her trust a couple who are clearly jewel thieves, even though many clues suggest their true nature. When Cherry discovers a strange woman in her car with ample evidence to suggest that the woman is one of the jewel thieves following the group, her first thought is that she herself has made a mistake; her second thought is that the intruder has done so: "'What happened?' Cherry cried. 'Did you trip and fall into our car? These convertibles are a real hazard sometimes'" (122).

Like Cherry, Nancy has difficulty suspecting the patriarchy of wrongdoing — especially her "chum" Police Chief Chumley. It takes a long time for her to realize that he is evil.

A car is the instrument of revenge the girls take on evil Chief Chumley, who has conspired to hide Carson Clue's long-term abuse of Nancy and to railroad housekeeper Hannah Gruel into jail. Although the girls are actually attempting to shoot Chief Chumley after he has shot at them, they do not succeed in doing so. But as they chase him with their car in reverse, they accidentally run him over instead (234). Interestingly, this accidental killing is precipitated when the decidedly femme Velma tries to use a gun — a weapon of phallic privilege.

A Ghost in the Closet

The third novel in the series, *A Ghost in the Closet*, teams Nancy Clue and her lesbian chums with the Hardly Boys — a gay parody of the Hardy Boys series of juvenile fiction. Just as in the 1970s television series discussed below, Nancy is not allowed to continue detecting with an all-female retinue. Instead, Maney makes the Hardly Boys co-detectives with Nancy and her friends, and the Hardly Boys take over a good part of the narrative, with many segments of the novel devoted to their adventures alone.

The Hardly Boys are aligned with the traditionally masculine domain of high-tech consumer consumption through their gadgets: The Hardly Boys Official Detective Kit (98); The Hardly Boys Mold Making Kit (98); The Hardly Boys Fingerprint Collecting Kit (102); The Hardly Boys Special Evidence Camera (103); The Hardly Boys *Spy Book* (106); The Hardly Boys Decoding Machine (111); and The Hardly Boys Cave Exploring Kit [!] (123). This contrasts sharply with Nancy and her chums' relationship with tools and technology. The girls don't own these tools themselves — when Nancy dusts for fingerprints, she is forced to use the Hardly Boys Fingerprint Collecting Kit, not a kit named after herself (102).[22]

Virginia Kelly: African-American Amateur Lesbian Sleuth

The Virginia Kelly series, by Nikki Baker, features an African-American lesbian amateur detective.[23] The second and third novels in this series, *The Lavender House Murder*[24] and *Long Goodbyes*[25], showcase recurring themes in lesbian detective novels: car trouble, uncertainty, and rescue.

Car Trouble

Early in *The Lavender House Murder*, Virginia and her friend Naomi find themselves with a broken-down car whose radiator has overheated (7). In a scene reminiscent of Maney's Nancy Clue/Cherry Aimless series, Virginia and Naomi are "rescued" by several other women (10). Virginia carries on a romance with one of her rescuers, attracted by her automotive expertise. "The car girl, it turned out, was called Jo.... I thought of her, names aside, as the car girl, as if she had been born the minute she refilled our radiator" (102).

In *Long Goodbyes*, since her car is out of commission, Virginia carpools with friends in order to get back to her hometown for her high school reunion (19). She explains: "My car was in the shop again. My Italian car[,] which was a work of art not made to be driven.... [T]he car was at its best standing still in the garage" (19). Virginia's carlessness makes her dependent on others: She accepts a ride from her old high school English teacher in his ancient car and hitches a ride home from her reunion with a girl whose companionship she doesn't really want (53, 82–84).

Virginia borrows her father's old car in order to follow her old flame Rosey around town, but her automotive tailing is ill-starred, and Rosey catches her at it (112). After they talk, Virginia waits all afternoon in a mall parking lot with the car's motor running, then continues to follow Rosey until she runs the car out of gas (120). After Virginia gets the car refilled, she promptly gets pulled over by a police officer for speeding (122–124). Moreover, we find out that the heater in the car is working poorly, as if Virginia's sheer presence makes good cars go bad (147).

Madness

Stephen Soitos rightly notes that "[I]n the Kelly series..., one finds a perspective far less perspicacious and omnipotent than normal."[26] This is actually an understatement. Indeed, Virginia appears particularly vulnerable to charges of insanity, ineffectiveness, and physical insecurity. In *Long Goodbyes*, Virginia constantly uses words that impugn her own sanity: "[T]he words made me feel a little crazy; they even sounded a little crazy when I got them out of my mouth," she says (155). Or, "I chalked that theory up to paranoia" (155). Or, "...I wasn't so sure about not being crazy" (183). "Call me crazy" she says (215), and mentions "the craziness of [her] actions regarding Rosey" (217).

Other characters similarly impugn Virginia's sanity. Her friend Sandra tells her: "Virginia[,] you're really out of control.... You followed some woman you hadn't seen or heard from for ten years like a psycho stalker all afternoon and then you're surprised when she's weird about it" (158–159). Sandra also calls Virginia "paranoid" (161).

Uncertainty and Ineffectiveness

In the *Lavender House Murder*, when she's framed for the murder of a promiscuous fellow guest at the guesthouse where she's staying, Virginia sets about investigating. Virginia is a fairly ineffective detective, however. She sees crucial clues to the murderer and to the writer of a note left on the murdered woman's body. Virginia sees a mysterious woman leaving a note for the murder victim, yet does not tie this to the note left on the murder victim's body, until she stumbles across a notebook in the note-leaver's room with threats written in it (71, 131, 173). Even then, it is Virginia's friend Naomi who makes the explicit connections between the notations in the notebook and the note found on the body (174). Virginia and Naomi are then held at gunpoint by the note-leaver, who conveniently shoots herself after alleging that although she planned to kill the murder victim, she actually stumbled onto the body after the deed was done (188–190). Although Virginia correctly assesses that the note-leaver is telling the truth, and although Virginia does correctly accuse the real murderer, she does neither of these things confidently. In fact, she's quite wishy-washy about her solution of the case: "It was just an educated guess, but it made sense to me," she explains (193). Although Virginia's story explaining the identity of the murderer makes perfect sense, she is easily shaken from it when the murderer herself offers her own explanation. Virginia even offers an apology to the murderer, before *another* character notices blood on the murderer's tennis shoes (197)!

In *Long Goodbyes*, Virginia similarly doubts her senses. For example, Virginia thinks that she sees her old flame Rosey push a little old lady (48–49). Yet when she confronts Rosey about this incident, Rosey lies, and Virginia doesn't realize the truth until later (74, 109).

Virginia sometimes seems downright incompetent as an investigator, making stupid deductions. Despite having seen a high school girl run crying from her male high school teacher's house on a Saturday night and knowing that the girl and the teacher have been interrupted by a former tutee of the teacher's, Virginia has absolutely no suspicion that any form of sexual abuse could have been going on between the teacher and the high school girl (179). Plenty of clues that Virginia and the reader have already been given point to such an interpretation, but Virginia has no suspicions at all (55, 118, 119).

In fact, Virginia is so clueless that she accidentally confronts the murderer in *Long Goodbyes* without realizing that she's doing so. "I had the uneasy feeling I might be missing something — maybe something really important.... I was beginning to realize, numbly, that there was something important here I was still missing" (208, 212).

Rescue

Like Nell Fury and the girls in the Nancy Clue mysteries, Virginia is often physically rescued by other women. In *The Lavender House Murder*, Virginia is only able to leave the presence of a gun-wielding psychopath because her friend Naomi talks them out of the room (189–190). At the end of *Long Goodbyes*, like a heroine in a horror movie,[27] Virginia believes she has killed a psychopathic murderer — only to have him rise up and try to kill her again (227–229).

Like Nell, Virginia is rescued by a butch — her new lover Spike (229–231), who hits the murderer over the head with a bottle of Chianti (230–231). Interestingly, Spike is accompanied in her rescue of Virginia by Andre, a straight African-American man who has a history of treating women badly and who has previously physically assaulted Virginia himself (when she threatened to tell his pregnant wife that he had been having an affair with and fathered a child of one of the murder victims) (200–201). Virginia at first thinks that Andre is her rescuer, since he's holding the relevant Chianti bottle (230). Because she thinks he's rescued her, Virginia decides not to tell his wife after all (230). When Andre tells her that Spike is her real rescuer, Virginia blithely continues to sell out the sisterhood: "After everything I'd been through, I didn't imagine that Andre's character flaws much mattered anymore and whatever he said about it I wasn't sure Spike could have overpowered [the murderer] all by herself" (231).

Harriet (Harry) Hubbley

Jackie Manthorne's Canadian lesbian gym teacher amateur detective, Harriet "Harry" Hubbley, has a similar experience to Virginia Kelly when she goes back to her 30th high school reunion in *Deadly Reunion*.[28] This novel highlights several of the themes seen in previous novels and also plays up a theme we have not fully explored yet: relationship troubles.

Relationship Problems

Unlike more stereotypical male detectives who seem completely in control of their love lives, the love life of the lesbian detective is complicated and uncertain. Many love triangles evolve, not necessarily of the detective's choosing. In *Deadly Reunion*, Harry is in a very long-term relationship with her lover Judy, yet feels compelled to let Judy follow her wish of having an "open" relationship and taking another lover (10). Harry herself winds up sleeping with her old friend Vivi out of loneliness, even though she really just wants an exclusive relationship with Judy and even though she feels, at best, ambivalent about her own freedom to sleep with other women (54, 69). Like Virginia Kelly, Harry meets up with a teen crush for whom she had felt unrequited lust, gets to fulfill her teenage fantasy, but ultimately finds that it does not meet her expectations (54–56, 70). Similar problems arise in many of the other lesbian detective novels examined here: Nell Fury has an on-again off-again relationship with her love Tammy Rae Tinkers, with problems arising when Tammy moves away, and a few liaisons on the side when she can't have Tammy; Cherry Aimless is caught in a love triangle between the irresponsible Nancy Clue and the stalwart Detective Jackie Jones; and Virginia Kelly is in the middle of an extended painful breakup with her lover Emily and pursues inappropriate women whenever the opportunity presents itself.

Car Trouble

Early in *Deadly Reunion*, we learn that Harry's real car is a clunker with a "stiff steering wheel, squishy brakes, balding tires and cranky transmission," though she's driving a better rental car now (14). While driving, Harry misses the exit she intends to take off the highway, and she drinks so much at a reunion event that she is forced to get a ride home with an old classmate (14–15, 96, 102). This last driving-related mistake puts her at the mercy of others (including the murderer) for transportation (102).

Mike, the pastor, brings Harry's car back to her, and they go for a ride, during which Harry realizes that she could be driving with a killer: "Maybe she should drive back to town. It could be dangerous to be in the car alone with someone, especially now that they were driving through the woods. But, then again, she was driving. She was in control" (114–115). Or so she thinks — when Mike makes an unexpected comment, Harry nearly drives off the road (116).

Competence and Self-Doubt

Although Harry has successfully solved a mystery before, she still doubts her abilities. Harry also displays certain incompetent tendencies. She loses her purse (125), then gets conked on the head when she goes by herself into an old, gloomy church to retrieve it (128). Harry gets conked on the head even though she has heard a suspicious thud behind her before she is attacked — when she sees no one, she mistrusts her own senses and proceeds (127).

Harry misses the key to the entire mystery, that the promiscuous murder victim had AIDS. She has to be told this by a doctor classmate (173), even though she herself had observed the victim's unnatural, unhealthy thinness (13). Harry doesn't even really solve the mystery. One suspect just confesses to Harry that she whacked the murder victim over the head but didn't drown him (177–178), and Harry isn't even sure of the identity of the real murderer until he attacks her (179).

Kate Delafield

Kate Delafield is a professional lesbian detective, strongly allied with the law in that she works for the Los Angeles Police Department. She appears in several novels by Katherine V. Forrest, a noted author and editor of lesbian fiction. Here I examine two early Kate Delafield novels, *Murder at the Nightwood Bar*,[29] the second novel in the series, and *The Beverly Malibu*,[30] the third novel in the series.

Driving

At first glance, it seems that Kate doesn't have the car problems that plague some other lesbian detectives. *Murder at the Nightwood Bar* opens with an image of Kate driving her partner Ed Taylor around and continues with a series of vignettes where Kate is at the wheel (1, 40, 59, 71, 97). Taylor only drives Kate around once, however (143). *The Beverly Malibu*, like *Murder at the Nightwood Bar*, similarly opens with Kate driving her Plymouth police car up to a crime scene. Kate even finds a parking place on Rodeo Drive during the Christmas shopping rush, and *The Beverly Malibu* ends with an image of Kate driving (215, 274). It turns out, however, that despite her seeming mastery of the automobile, Kate has the biggest car problem of all the lesbian detectives discussed here. She has lost her lover in a fatal car crash and is still grieving over her loss.[31]

Competence and Physicality

In *Malibu*, Kate shows confidence and keen attention to detail. She also is impervious to criticism by her colleagues for her thoroughness: "She would acknowledge neither humor nor fault in the thoroughness of her methods, however aggravating they might be" (13). She is smugly aware that she has a wiser, more cautious view of the case than her partner, Ed Taylor, does; she deftly manipulates him to keep him working:

> Let Taylor nurse his improbable theory[;] she would not argue with him — not for some time yet. She knew too well how he would withdraw his attention from a case for which he had lost his eagerness, to go through only the bureaucratic motions required of him. Allowing him to follow his own scents would keep his nose on the trail [33].

Here, Kate is basically calling Taylor a dog, a subhuman creature. This is an interesting twist on the traditional cultural construction of women as subhuman, intuitive beings. Kate is also physically imposing: "You're a good size for a woman in the police, you look very capable," gushes a witness. "I'd rather have a fine big policewoman like you in my corner than some little bitty thing" (38–39). "You look very capable," another witness echoes (84). Yet Kate's physical competence is not complete. She almost gets swallowed whole by a treacherous sofa with very soft cushions (94, 96, 97, 102). She also shows physical weakness:

Kate sagged against the wall. "I've had it for now, Ed."

> Her confession was one he would never make: in their unequal relation-
> ship he jealously guarded his masculine pride [160].

This physical weakness is represented as a double-edged sword. Although her weakness itself can be seen as a failing, Kate's ability to be honest about her capabilities is presented as more honest — perhaps more secure — than Ed's inability ever to admit weakness.

Kate's competence is undermined by her superior officers' treatment of her in *Malibu*: When she's interviewing a little old lady witness alone, surely not a dangerous assignment, Kate's commanding officer checks up on her (261). It is difficult to imagine the commanding officer checking up on a male officer interviewing a little old lady in this way.

Outness

Many lesbian detective novels deal with issues of being closeted, especially at work. Early in the series, Kate Delafield doesn't dare come out because of the extreme homophobia of the LAPD (60–61). *Long Good-byes,* Virginia Kelly is similarly semi-closeted for professional reasons (17).

Sexuality

Kate is a butch with a fear of "turning femme," though *The Beverly Malibu* places her in the uncomfortably new femme position when she gets a crush on an older woman: "Why was this woman, so many years her senior, so very attractive to her? She was drawn by Paula Grant's strength qualities — and there was no precedent for it. She had always been attracted to a very different sort of woman, a woman with softer, more responsive attributes..." (62).

Kate then finds herself even more in the "femme" position when a young witness, Aimee Grant, takes the lead in seducing Kate:

> Aimee took Kate's face between her hands.... Aimee's mouth became pos-
> sessive; her tongue brought surges of desire, keenly specific heat to Kate's
> legs, the tongue-strokes creating astonishing weakness ... [Aimee] took her
> mouth away from Kate's. "Shouldn't we go to bed," she said, not a ques-
> tion.... In Kate's darkened bedroom she stripped off Kate's clothing. Her
> hands on Kate's shoulders, she backed Kate onto the bed, lowered her naked
> body onto hers.
> Kate knew she should assert herself with this woman who had assumed
> control of her. But some entity had taken possession of her body, had ren-
> dered it helpless....

> A woman had never done this to her first, she thought dimly some time later.... Never, she never came first with a woman [188–189].

Later, Kate is again very submissive in a sex scene with Aimee, including letting Aimee pull her to her bedroom by her belt[32] (195–196). Kate's discomfort with this "role reversal" echoes the concerns of earlier real-life lesbians living under a rigid "butch-femme" distinction, a distinction that in ways privileged butch positioning and made any slippage to a femme positioning "shameful."[33]

Kate also becomes involved with Aimee even though ethics and police procedure would forbid the relationship. "I have no business being involved with a witness in a capital murder case," she admits (200). Kate, who is about forty years old (202), is upset that Aimee is only twenty-five (199). She feels her very sanity is affected by the relationship: "I feel like I'm not a sane woman around her" (203). Kate defines "femme" here as being "not in control" (204).[34]

Detection

Kate is not a particularly effective detective. In *Murder at the Nightwood Bar*, she misses the identity of the murderer (188–189). In *The Beverly Malibu*, plenty of clues alert the reader to the likely identity of the murderer on pages 208–209, but Kate skips right over them, and she instead trusts her male partner's wrongheaded theory (210).

In *Malibu*, Kate does finally figure out who the murderer is, based not on deduction but on a chance sighting — a glance at the murderer's face after she's committed a second murder (227–232). Even then, Kate doesn't deduce the motive for the murder (230), although ample clues have been provided to the reader as to the murderer's motive. Kate also has trouble convincing anyone of her theory. Her partner Ed is skeptical at first: "Kate, is this one of those women's intuition things?" he asks (232). Even when he believes her, he slams her in a way that deals with femininity:

> "Partner," he said softly, nodding, "your say-so is good enough for me. But this isn't *Murder, She Wrote*. We can't do a thing without proof, we can't take her in without [probable cause]" [239].

After Kate finally deduces the motive, she then berates herself for missing an obvious clue (245).

* * *

The ambivalence about law, detection, and female competence seen in the Kate Delafield series is emblematic of the other series discussed above. This profound tension between the individual feminist and the patriarchal institutions within which she works, between the marginalized and the included, and between butch and femme finds its expression in a number of ways, most tellingly the symbolic disablement of the carphallus symbol that haunts so many of the works discussed above.

◆ 3 ◆

The Socio-Cultural Determinants of the Role of the Female Investigator on Television[1]

"Tell me, Miss Holt, how did you become a dick?" asks the enigmatic jewel thief in the premiere episode of *Remington Steele*, his double entendre reminding the audience of the expected link between detection and phallic mastery. His remark makes it clear that, although the female detective has been present on television since the 1950s, her legitimacy was still in question in the early 1980s. In this chapter, after a theoretical consideration of the genre-based differences between the female detective in film and on television, I consider other topics relevant to the female detective on television: violence, transportation, disposability, bracketing, identity, and multiple audiences. The chapter concludes with a historical overview of how the place of the female detective on television has been influenced by the socio-cultural forces operating in different eras.

Why Film and Television Differ in Their Portrayal of the Female Investigator: A Theory

The overall picture painted by the programs I examine in this chapter is rather a gloomy one for the female detective on television. No matter how intelligent and athletic she is, her investigative powers are always in some way suspect and subject to external patriarchal control. Yet there *is* some good news: the different visual style of commercial television seems to produce a less inherently "masculine" form of spectatorship than does film, for the competing discourses of program and advertisement produce a polyphony absent on film. The very fact that there is more than one "voice" present on commercial television works against the monolithic (masculine) perspective often seen in Classical Hollywood cinema. This is particularly true in that a large percentage of advertising on television has always been directed at the female consumer, even advertising during programs that don't seem particularly aimed at women. Thus, there often exists on television a "female" voice, or at least a voice aimed at the female spectator, which presents alternative realities to those represented within traditional television program narratives.

The result of this polyphony and of the fact that television is, in general, watched much more casually (with interruptions, talking back to the screen, simultaneous activities, natural lighting, etc.) than film is, is that the television camera's power to absorb the attention of the spectator, especially the male spectator, is weakened. From this weakening of the camera's power comes a weakening of the spectator's identification with the apparatus and concomitantly with the Gaze. Accordingly, the phallic identification with the Gaze/camera/protagonist/investigator experienced by the male spectator in the case of cinema is less present in the case of television. This means that on television, there is less of an identificatory problem for the spectator caused by the placement of a woman in the role of protagonist/investigator than there is in cinema. Little wonder, then, that on television, there is seldom that driving insistence on the madness of female detectives that one sees so frequently in film, as I will discuss below. Rather, as we will see here, television opens itself more easily than film to a variety of identifications and critical interpretations on the part of both male and female spectators.

Violence and the Female Detective

The question of women as perpetrators of violence against men has not yet been studied sufficiently. The possibility of women using physical violence against men breaks a strong American cultural taboo, as can be seen by the way the news media, in its reporting on the women's movement of the early seventies, heavily foregrounded women's karate training as newsworthy over other, more substantial issues.[2] Accordingly, very few female detectives on television have been portrayed as capable of effective violence. Emma Peel and her immediate predecessor on *The Avengers* Cathy Gale are quite unusual in that they are portrayed as using advanced martial arts skills on men. Honey West is similarly physically competent.[3]

Although other female detectives on television may use physical force, their violence is usually muted in some way. On the television series *Batman*, for example, while Batman and Robin punch their male attackers, Batgirl is relegated to throwing ineffective-looking acrobatic high kicks.[4]

On *Charlie's Angels*, the Angels usually wind up holding a gun on criminals, not hitting them. On *Remington Steele*, Laura Holt does occasionally tackle a criminal from behind or hit one on the head with a frying pan, but she never throws a straight punch face to face. (To be fair, physical violence is not portrayed as naturally the domain of males on the more progressive *Remington Steele* either. When "Steele" lands his first punch, he yelps and nurses his injured hand.) On *Moonlighting*, although the first episode shows us Maddie demonstrating how to throw a punch on David, this skill apparently disappears as she becomes a detective. In the same episode, she is portrayed as so incompetent with a gun that she fires blindly six times and misses a killer at close range; in another episode, she is reduced to biting a killer's ankle to stop him.

Other female detectives on television appear completely incapable of violence. The otherwise feisty Jessica Fletcher of *Murder, She Wrote* doesn't throw punches (though her aging male counterpart *Cannon* does). Genteel Sally McMillan of *McMillan and Wife* and Jennifer Hart of *Hart to Hart* would never *dream* of punching anyone, although their equally genteel husbands appear quite capable of defending themselves when the need arises.

The body of the female detective is a fascinating site, not only as a potential source of violence, but also as a potential recipient of violence. In *film noir*, the body of the male detective often suffers brutal beatings as part of a ritualized demonstration of power relations between men. Although the male detective may receive beatings during the course of his investigation when his knowledge is still incomplete, he often survives to turn the tables on his former attackers and to beat them when he is closer to solving the mystery.

This paradigm does not work for the body of the female detective. When female detectives are threatened, it is usually with the prospect of rape or of outright murder. Somehow the old adage "Never hit a girl" has been ingrained in our culture to such a degree that we are absolutely horrified to see a man hit a woman's face, although we have been desensitized to the same action between two men (and to other actions more genuinely harmful to women.) It is ironic how, on *The Avengers*, where women *were* allowed to participate in physical violence against men, there was still an unwritten rule that "no woman should be killed" on the show.[5]

Transportation and the Female Detective

The connection between women and their (lack of) control over transportation is another rich field of study. As they are presented in popular media, women are overwhelmingly portrayed as passengers rather than as drivers; if women do drive, often either their driving is shown to be inferior in some way to men's driving or their driving is used to signify some deeper transgressive element in their nature.

As an example of the first tendency, on the television series *Batman*, Batgirl must make do with her Batgirlcycle (a motorcycle with a sidecar) while Batman and Robin own the Batmobile, the Batcopter, the Batboat, and numerous other transportation devices. It is also interesting to note that the motorcycle owned by Batgirl cannot simply be identified as a Batcycle; rather, it is marked with the qualifier "girl" to show its otherness — and, by implication, its inferiority — to the genuine Batarticles.

The second tendency — the portrayal of women's driving as transgressive — can be illustrated by an example from Hitchcock's suspense film *Notorious*: Early in the film, rebellious Alicia Huberman deliberately tries to frighten her passenger, staid government agent T.R. Devlin, by driving wildly while she is drunk. By the end of the film, a reformed Alicia is curled up contentedly in the passenger seat of Devlin's car as he drives her to safety after rescuing her from a group of Nazis.

It is also important to note that the problem with women and transportation is by no means limited to cars. One need only try to count how many women commanded the bridge of starships on *Star Trek* and its several latterday spinoffs until the premiere of *Star Trek: Voyager* to realize that this problem is pervasive.

To some extent in the nineteen-sixties, and particularly in the nineteen-seventies, the relationship between women and transportation improved, however, reaching an all-time high in the mid-seventies. This increased competence with cars may reflect the women's liberation movement of the seventies. Many early-to-mid-seventies television series about "liberated" women showed those women moving on to new independent lives by driving off to a new city, e.g., the opening titles to *The Mary Tyler Moore Show*, *One Day at a Time*, and *Alice*.

Many female detectives on television are affected by this discourse, both positively and negatively. Some have their power enhanced by their clever use of transportation; others are undercut by their disenfranchisement from transportation. Charlie's Angels are especially noteworthy for their enhanced transportation skills: they pilot almost every conceivable type of vehicle during the show's run. Cagney and Lacey are similarly capable: almost every episode shows them driving around New York. Moreover, during the first of several *Cagney and Lacey* reunion tv-movies in the mid-nineties,[6] one says to the other that she really misses *driving around together* and solving crimes.

Some programs give out mixed messages or negative messages about women and transportation: the opening credits of *Hart to Hart*, for example, begin with a powerful image of Jennifer Hart in her sportscar attempting to pass her husband Jonathan in his sportscar on a winding mountain road. Yet one of the closing shots of the credits shows Jennifer losing control of a dune buggy and plunging off a dock. At the other end of the spectrum, Jessica Fletcher of *Murder, She Wrote* never drives at all.

The most curious case may well be that of *Remington Steele*, a program that grapples with issues of gender inequality quite extensively. On this show, the male and female detectives both drive on occasion, but usually skirt the driving issue altogether — they are *both* driven by their long-suffering chauffeur Fred.

Disposability/Replacability of the Female Detective on Television

The female detective on television is ultimately disposable or replaceable, particularly if she works with a male partner. Emma Peel of *The Avengers*, Sally McMillan of *McMillan and Wife*, Nancy Drew of *The Hardy Boys/Nancy Drew Mysteries*, Dee Dee McCall of *Hunter*, and Jill Munroe, Sabrina Duncan, and Tiffany Welles of *Charlie's Angels* all were disposed of and/or replaced before the series' end. This pattern suggests that women detectives are unnecessary in and of themselves, or that they are exactly equivalent to one another and therefore infinitely substitutable.

The explanations advanced by these narratives for the departure of a female character are themselves suggestive. The common explanations for a female detective's disappearance are death or marriage, which is the equivalent of death for women in most narratives, in that it marks the end of their story: nothing further about them is deemed worth narrating. Sally McMillan is killed off (presumably because she's *already* married to the series' hero). Emma Peel's husband, believed dead, is resurrected so that she must leave her espionage work to go to him. Dee Dee McCall leaves her police job to get married. Nancy Drew's disappearance is never explained (perhaps because she's too young to die or get married.) Sabrina Duncan's disappearance from *Charlie's Angels* is explained by a double trope of femininity: she is both married and pregnant.[7]

The removal by marriage is a common explanation for the disappearance not only of female detectives but also of many female characters on television (e.g., Shirley on *Laverne and Shirley*). I recall not a single instance in which a *male* character's absence is explained by his marriage. It just doesn't happen, even when real events might seem to suggest it. When Fox Mulder leaves *The X-Files*, his absence is not explained by a marriage, even though actor David Duchovny was actually leaving the series in order to spend more time with wife Téa Leoni.

In this area, as in so many others, *Charlie's Angels* is a partial exception to the general rule. When Angel Jill Munroe leaves, she doesn't die or get married. Instead, she heads to Europe to race on the international circuit.[8] The departure of Angel Tiffany Welles (Shelley Hack) is explained simply by her deciding "to stay East for awhile."[9]

The reasons that female stars leave television detective shows are similarly interesting. An inordinate number of contract, creative, and working-conditions disputes spark their departure. Often, these disputes turn on women's issues: Diana Rigg left *The Avengers* because the producers, according to her co-star Patrick Macnee, were "male chauvinist pigs." Pamela Sue Martin apparently left *The Hardy Boys/Nancy Drew Mysteries* for similar reasons. Susan Saint James left *McMillan and Wife* in a contract dispute.[10] Kate Jackson, Emmy-nominated for her work on *Charlie's Angels*, left the series after she became unhappy with the way the series was evolving and after producers denied her time off to take what became Meryl Streep's Academy Award-winning role in *Kramer vs. Kramer*.[11] Almost all of these actresses were labeled "difficult" by the contemporary media and were generally portrayed very differently from actors who stood up to producers.[12]

The Female Detective and Bracketing/Emphasis Shifts

The female detective on television is often bracketed by male detectives and not allowed to investigate independently. This can be seen by the overwhelmingly large number of shows in which the female detective has a male partner or partners. Almost every series discussed below has the female detective bracketed thus, sometimes at the expense of the original source of the material. Thus *Honey West* pairs Honey with a male partner who does not exist in the series of books upon which the show is based, and *The Nancy Drew/Hardy Boys Mysteries* eventually teams Nancy up to work *with* the Hardy boys, though the two juvenile series (at least through the seventies version on which the show is based) do not feature this kind of crossover. The exceptions to this rule prove to be partial exceptions, at best. Even the highly independent Charlie's Angels have Charlie and Bosley lurking in the background. Cagney and Lacey are subject to the demands of a male boss and have male colleagues. As noted above, Jessica Fletcher is often dependent on men to give her rides to the scene of the crime. In fact, I have not been able to think of a single successful female detective on television who truly operates unbracketed by men. There really is no popular female detective equivalent to Lieutenant Columbo on *Columbo*, who is the central figure of his own show and is surrounded by faceless uniformed cops whose own characters are never delineated and who appear to exist merely to assist him.

Moreover, in many of these shows that are at least nominally about female detectives bracketed by men, there is a tendency for the female detective to become de-emphasized on her own show. The series attempts to shift the focus onto the male characters as the series progresses. Thus, for example, "Sweet Kathleen," a very late episode of *Police Woman*, focuses on Lt. Crowley to the almost complete exclusion of the series' heroine, Pepper. Likewise, the last episode of *The Girl from U.N.C.L.E.* focuses more on Mark Slate than on April Dancer.

Gender, Commodity, Identity, and the Female Detective on Television

The identity of the female detective on television is less stable, less fixed than the identity of her male counterpart. The female detective goes undercover (a task that *Charlie's Angels* raised to a high art) much more frequently than her male counterparts do, so much so that television critic Diana Meehan devotes an entire chapter of her book about female characters on prime-time television to "the decoy." She is often seen in disguise, in drag.

But even when she is not officially "undercover," her identity appears constructed. This can be seen through the use of fashion and style in the construction of the female detective's identity. More than most male detectives, the female detective often sets the style for a whole era with her wardrobe. One need only consider Emma Peel in her leather catsuits, Honey West in her leopard-skin wardrobe, Charlie's Angels trying on uniform after uniform, and fashionista Vallery Irons to see that for the female detective on television, the fashion medium is the message.

The relationship between the female detective on television and fashion/style is complicated by the commodification of the body of the female detective for the female consumers who watch detective programs. Much of the female detective's style is directly aimed at female consumers: Emma

Peel's entire wardrobe was available for purchase and was designed expressly for that purpose. The feathered Farrah-Fawcett look seen on *Charlie's Angels* dominated teenage-girl hairstyles for over a decade.

Multiple Audiences

The fact that the female detective's identity is fluid, ever-changing, allows programs about female detectives to blend fantasy and reality. This mixture of the two states allows for one of the most distinctive features of the female detective television program: the mixed messages about — and mixed responses of viewers to — the role of women on the program. Larger societal anxieties about gender roles are often played out through the body of the female detective in an uneasy binary — the portrayal of the female detective both represents and disavows gender problems.

This binary explains the multifarious viewer reactions to the same text. Some viewers see *Charlie's Angels* as nothing more than a "jiggle-fest," while others see it as a truly progressive program. *Charlie's Angels* is neither one nor the other of these things — it is both. Almost all of the other programs discussed in this chapter are also "both" — both progressive and regressive, both empowering and disempowering to women, portraying the female detective as both capable and incapable. Yet they are seldom equally "both." The various social and political movements of the last five decades have left their mark on the texts of female detective programs, and our historical analysis below will demonstrate how the delicate balance of power on these programs is intimately affected by their socio-cultural context.

A Historical View

The tendencies detailed above play out very differently for the female detective on television according to the era in which she is represented. More so than any other medium, television is bound to a reflection of the time during which it was created. Accordingly, while the female detective on television is always represented as flawed, the nature of that flaw varies considerably from era to era. The close readings below will demonstrate some of these shifts: Television programs of the 1950s, like the tepid television version of *The Thin Man*, reflect the domestic focus of their era by domesticating their female (and male) detectives to the point where Dashiell Hammett's charming creations are almost unrecognizable. Television programs of the 1960s, like *Honey West* and *The Avengers*, allow their female detectives an increased measure of autonomy. This autonomy is carefully circumscribed, however, by a pairing with male partners who can cut them down to size, and by an extreme specularization of their bodies that is consistent with the aesthetics of the pop era. Nineteen-seventies television detective programs reflect the contemporaneous women's movement by portraying female detectives, like the protagonists of *Charlie's Angels*, who are allowed to detect without much male interference and who show an increased facility with firearms, physical combat, and transportation. Yet shows like *Charlie's Angels* and *Police Woman*, which were popular with both male and female audiences, undercut their protagonists by specularizing them to a previously unseen degree, highlighting the public's ambivalent response to the women's liberation movement. The 1980s programs, like *Moonlighting*, *Remington Steele*, and *Cagney and Lacey*, reflect some of the tensions detailed in the best-selling 1984 advice book *The Superwoman Syndrome*, as their protagonists struggle to balance their careers with the demands of romance and family. The post-feminist television detective programs of the 1990s, like *The X-Files* and *VIP*, use elements of fantasy and pastiche that fit the post-modern sensibility of their era. They are post-feminist in the sense that they take for granted women's competence in a wide variety of traditionally masculine skill areas, but simultaneously work to disempower their strongest female characters through a variety of regressive strategies: "woman in jeopardy" plots, the feminizing of tomboy characters, etc. The one unchanging variable in these diverse programs is that the female detective is always flawed — she is never an all-powerful figure.

The Femmes Not-So-Fatales of the Fifties

One of television's first forays into female detection came with a television version of the *Thin Man*. Unlike her namesake in the Dashiell Hammett novel and the tremendously popular series of films, who exemplified the relative sexual freedom and autonomy of women in the 1930s, the Nora Charles of the late–50s television series (Phyllis Kirk) lacks the verbal, sexual, and gnomic authority of her earlier counterparts: she is not particularly witty, charming, or perceptive.[13] While the Nora of the big screen (Myrna Loy) often faces overt resistance to her attempts to detect alongside her husband Nick, she nevertheless persists in her investigations and often talks herself out of trouble with her quick wit. The Nora of the small screen, however, seems uninterested in (and untalented at) investigation. For example, in a 1958 episode entitled "The Art of Murder," Nora witnesses the flight of a man who has accidentally killed his landlord. Far from being able to recognize the killer (who happens to be a quick-change artist) when he visits her in disguise *twice* in order to determine what she has seen, Nora is entirely unsuspicious of his motives. When he attacks her, instead of screaming or fighting back, Nora acts completely helpless and faints. (She is only saved from death by the fact that the murderer is too tenderhearted to kill her in cold blood and makes do with kidnapping her instead.) Nick, who has done little independent detecting, eventually frees her with a great deal of help from the police. The television series' rendering of Nick Charles (Peter Lawford) is almost as tepid as its rendering of Nora. He seems to have little initiative or flair compared to the Nick of the silver screen (William Powell). This bland series fits perfectly with the domesticated ethos of the fifties: "Detectives" let their own investigative work be subsumed by larger entities representing the Law; men rescue women; and women are perfect hostesses — Nora politely offers the disguised murderer something to drink — but not good for much else.

The socio-cultural forces affecting the *Thin Man* can be seen through a comparison of the novel, film, and television versions. Although the Nick of novel and films retained his ties to the police (he was a former New York City police officer himself), he did the bulk of his investigating on his own, using police assistance sparingly. Furthermore, the Nick of the silver screen retained his ties to the criminal element he had befriended in his police work. The films made much of the class difference between Nick (who had started out poor and married into money) and Nora (heiress to the money into which he married) by contrasting their diverse groups of friends: his, policemen and petty criminals; hers, upper-crust socialites. The class differences so honestly portrayed in the film are completely obscured by the television series. It is very difficult to imagine the television Nick Charles taking a case for a petty thief or asking members of the criminal element for help in his investigations. Rather, in the television series, Nick seems born to money, not married to it.

This change may have been necessitated by the changing socio-economic climate of the United States between the thirties and the fifties. In the depression-weary thirties, a hardworking man with little money was a familiar sight, and men's masculinity could not be tied exclusively to the size of their paychecks, since such a standard would be impossible for most to reach. If a blue-collar worker should marry rich, he might be perceived as fortunate, not as a freeloader. During the economically healthy fifties, however, when relatively few men were out of work, men's economic power — typically symbolized by the ability to provide for a family consisting of an unemployed wife and several children — became an important marker of masculinity. In such a cultural context, having Nick unemployed and living off his wife's money might make him a less pleasurable locus of identification for a male viewer. Thus, the fifties series downplays that aspect of his life. Nora's loss of a strong economic identity in the television series is symbolically disempowering, and might in some measure explain the portrayal of her as the helpless house-wife.

We can see a more recent example of this phenomenon in the opening voiceover to the seventies *Thin Man* knockoff *Hart to Hart.* Due, I would suggest, to men's anxieties about the nascent Women's Liberation movement, in this version, the male member of the seventies couple is "a self-made millionaire" who has continued working, and the audience is given the distinct impression that his homemaker wife is the member of the couple who has married money.

Nick and Nora clones Pam and Jerry North (Barbara Britton and Richard Denning) had enjoyed earlier success on television in the early 1950s in *Mr. and Mrs. North* (1952–1954). The television series version of *Mr. and Mrs. North* also had a strong female lead who challenged her husband. As Pamela North, Barbara Britton was sometimes competent. In an early episode, "The Doll House," Pamela browbeats a seemingly sympathetic character who turns out to be in cahoots with criminals. Yet other episodes undercut her authority in a variety of ways.

An earlier short-lived series that I have been unable to view[14] sounds like one of the more intriguing female detective series of the 1950s. *The Gallery of Mme. Liu-Tsong* (Sept. 1951-Nov. 1951) starred Anna May Wong as an art gallery owner/detective.[15] Interestingly, a description of the ½-hour-long show notes no regular male characters, suggesting that Mme. Liu-Tsong detected alone, rather than being domesticated as a member of a heterosexual couple.[16] Significantly, she is portrayed as a businesswoman, a characterization reminiscent of the strong businesswomen of 1940s film, rather than the happy housewives of the fifties. I also find it interesting that such an early television female detective was a woman of color,[17] a characterization to my knowledge not repeated on television until the advent of *Get Christie Love!* in the 1970s. One might speculate that a single businesswoman of color with investigative powers was a bit too groundbreaking a characterization for the 1950s, and that these factors may have accounted for the series' short run. Perhaps Mme. Liu-Tsong was a *femme-trop-fatale* for the fifties.

The Sirens of the Sixties

The popular mystery fiction of the 1960s ushered in new era of opportunities for female detectives to be more physically active in their investigations. These books allowed for the creation of strong female investigators who were a far cry from the prim housewife-investigators of the fifties, even if the books seemed primarily aimed at a male audience looking for titillation and thrills. I am not convinced that this is necessarily the case, but it seems to be a popular critical stance on this fiction. Kathi Maio, for example, says:

> ... [T]he kind of thriller heroine who'd carry a gun was usually much less appealing to women than those old-fashioned spinster masterminds. Created with male audiences in mind, heroines with names like Modesty Blaise ... all had the killer instinct and a body to die for. These were boys' fantasies, these bombshells who enjoyed lobbing bombs and spraying rooms with Uzi fire. This purposely titillating melding of sex with violence held little appeal for most women.[18]

Even though these female investigators tended to be fantasy figures (Modesty Blaise was a self-made millionaire due to the proceeds of the world-wide crime network she had headed in an earlier stage of life), they reflected the real-life cultural construction of young women in the sixties as having more autonomy and sexual freedom than their older sisters. For example, in the early sixties,[19] Peter O'Donnell created the aforementioned Modesty Blaise as the heroine of a comic strip for British newspapers, a strip that was so popular that he went on to write many books about the character. Besides being independently wealthy, Modesty (often described by commentators as a "female James Bond") is a master of martial arts and firearms, takes full advantage of her desire to sleep with men she finds appealing, and is handily provided with a male companion who adores her in a sexually undemanding way — a remarkably powerful position. Although she uses the help of her partner Willie to foil complex international conspiracies and often takes his advice, she is clearly the senior partner and final authority of their team. While the character of Modesty Blaise never successfully made the transfer from print to film or television (an unpopular and *bad* movie came out in the late sixties; a failed television pilot aired in the early eighties), other characters like her *did* make it to the small screen in the sixties.

The 1965–66 series *Honey West* was based on the paperback series by G.G. Fickling (a pseudonym for Gloria and Forrest K. Fickling.)[20] Although the books seem aimed primarily at men and do not exactly present a strong feminist slant (professional private eye Honey is constantly losing her clothes in stormy seas or strip poker games) they *do* show her working on her own to solve mysteries while staunchly ignoring the efforts of handsome Lieutenant Mark Strong to make her quit work and marry him.

The television series, on the other hand, although at least partially aimed at women — the commercials aired during the first episode include one for deodorant, one for cosmetics, and one that shows girls improving their social lives by using mouthwash — makes Honey *less* independent. Instead of having Honey investigate crimes independently, the series teams Honey up with a male partner — Sam Bolt (John Ericson), her dead father's junior partner in the detective agency — and although Honey and Sam's relationship starts out as egalitarian, it quickly deteriorates into a war of the sexes. The first episode of the series, "The Swingin' Miss Jones," shows Honey (Anne Francis) planning the team's investigative strategies (which Sam obediently implements) and successfully using judo and gas pellets to subdue criminals not only when she faces danger alone, but when Sam is present as well. Honey and Sam have a friendly, mildly flirtatious relationship, and Sam seems untroubled by the fact that his boss is female. Yet by the time the last episode, "The Abominable Snowman," airs, Honey and Sam fight constantly. Sam is much more aggressive and angry towards Honey than he was earlier: he scolds Honey for lifting some evidence, grumbles about the investigative strategy she maps out for them, and finally hurls at her what the audience is meant to understand as the ultimate insult: "Career women!" Interestingly, the short-lived *Honey West* was produced by Aaron Spelling, who would later become a driving force behind the groundbreaking *Charlie's Angels* and the less feminist *Mod Squad* and *Hart to Hart*.

Although the British-made sixties television series *The Avengers* originally featured two male secret agent leads, various cast changes eventually led to a popular male-female pairing that exploited sexual tension in a way that made it marketable in America.[21] On the surface, the witty pair of John Steed (Patrick Macnee) and Emma Peel (Diana Rigg) appear to be a remarkably egalitarian detective team. They usually detect separately, then compare notes, and Emma is remarkable among female detectives for her ability to use physical force to subdue male assailants. A look behind the scenes of the series, however, reveals the producers' deliberate agenda to position Emma to be simultaneously the object of masculine desire and the locus of narcissistic feminine identification. The name "Emma Peel" — coined by the press officer for the *Avengers*, Marie Donaldson — points to the male spectatorship expected for the *Avengers*. As *Avengers* expert Dave Rogers describes the genesis of the name,

[Donaldson] realised that the new character had to have man appeal, and as she played around with the phrase in her head she couldn't help thinking Man Appeal, M appeal — Emma Peel. She liked the sound of the name and the producers jumped at it.[22]

The word "peel" suggests that Emma is just a step away from peeling off her clothes, clearly making her (slightly) hidden body a fetish object for male viewers. On the other hand, Emma Peel's entire wardrobe was from the beginning made to be marketed to female spectators — "The first collection of clothes designed specifically for a television programme to be adapted in its entirety for retail distribution."[23] Of course, the marketing of consumer goods (and the consumer ethos) to spectators of film and television is nothing new,[24] but in the era when the *Avengers* aired, it was seldom done in quite so calculated a manner.

Even without this behind-the-scenes information, however, it is clear that the *Avengers* undercuts Emma Peel's investigative authority in subtle ways. For example, in an episode about mind manipulation entitled "Too Many Christmas Trees," it initially appears that Steed has been brainwashed by his hosts at a sinister house party to which Emma has invited him. But after Emma mistakenly knocks out one of Steed's secret allies, the audience discovers that Steed's mind has never been subject to outside control. On the contrary, it turns out that *Emma's* mind was implanted with the suggestion to invite him to the party in the first place. Another episode, "Mission Highly Improbable," has the subtitle "in which Steed falls into enemy hands and Emma gets cut down to size." This subtitle suggests that it is only Emma who *deserves* to be "cut down to size" for being a woman who transgresses cultural norms, even though at various points in the action *both* Steed and Emma get shrunk by a miniaturizing machine. Steed's phallic authority, emphasized throughout the series by his ever-present umbrella, is particularly underlined in this episode. When a full-sized Emma teases the shrunken Steed by asking him "Is *everything* proportional?" he promptly reinscribes himself as a phallic figure by grabbing a big pen(is)[25] and stabbing a villain in the ankle with it in order to help Emma in her fight to escape. Emma actually has a long history with the pen-as-phallus-substitute. In the first *Avengers* episode telecast in the United States ("The Cybernauts"), Emma places her life in grave jeopardy by borrowing a pen from Steed, a pen which turns out to be transmitting homing signals to a murderous android. "Mrs. Peel, throw the pen away!" Steed shouts as the android bears down on her. "Throw me the pen. The pen ... throw it to me!" The underlying message is clear: bad things happen to women who usurp phallic authority, and they cannot be saved unless they are willing to return phallic privilege to men, its rightful owners.

It is also telling that Emma's exit from the show (due to the fact that Shakespearean actress Diana Rigg was mistreated by the show's sexist producers)[26] is sparked by the reappearance of her long-lost husband, who had been presumed dead in an aviation accident. All of a sudden, Emma's investigative career is over, and she leaves the show to be replaced by another young female sidekick for Steed. Apparently, no matter how compelling they may be as characters, female sidekicks are ultimately expendable.[27]

Not all of the female investigators on television in the sixties were as strong as Honey West and Emma Peel. *The Girl from U.N.C.L.E.*, a campy spinoff of the popular series *The Man from U.N.C.L.E.*, featured the male-female pairing of secret agents April Dancer (Stefanie Powers) and Mark Slate (Noel Harrison) battling outrageously over-the-top villains reminiscent of those seen on the contemporaneous series *Batman*. The premiere episode, "The Mother Muffin Affair," begins by constructing April as spectacle. As the episode opens, she and guest secret agent Napoleon Solo (in a crossover appearance from *The Man from U.N.C.L.E.*) are trapped in a room and need string to escape. Solo unravels April's wool turtleneck sweater, leers at her, then belatedly offers her his jacket. The episode also constructs April as less perceptive than Solo: He recognizes that a fortune teller is really the villainous Mother Muffin (Boris Karloff in drag!), while April doesn't. Moreover, April is presented as a poor fighter. When they are confronted with a cadre of villains, April runs into the ladies' room to escape. April also has mixed success with trying to charm her way out of danger. Her attempt to flirt with a cop to get rescued fails, as does her attempt to flirt with one of Mother Muffin's henchmen. Only at the end of the episode is she allowed some competence when she kisses one villain and dispenses a Vulcan neck pinch, thereby distracting them long enough for Solo to disable the other villains.

Other episodes in the series similarly construct April as a poor fighter. In "The Dog-Gone Affair" (airing 9/13/66), although April accidentally throws Mark in a judo move, the rest of the episode does not allow her to demonstrate her fighting ability. When they are both fighting villains, Mark tackles the big bad guy and is shown in an extended fight scene. April, on the other hand, goes after an old man, and although we are given to understand that she hits him over the head with a bottle, the incident isn't shown. April herself gets karate chopped into unconsciousness, tied to a chair, menaced with a fly-fishing rod, and hung upside down over a pool of piranhas. Although the episode does present April as smart (she finds the lost dog they are after), persuasive (Mark accedes to her suggestions about what they should do next), and athletic (she escapes the piranhas under her own power), she does not come across with the same power that Emma Peel and Honey West do.

The final episode of the series, "The Kooky Spook Affair" (airing 4/11/67), in which Mark and April prowl around a spooky ancestral estate that Mark has inherited, shows how the trends that started earlier continue. Despite the title of the series, this episode focuses more on Mark than on April. Mark continues to have long, physically demanding fight scenes, while April appears only after the fights are over and gets told to stay in her room a lot by Mark.

The episode is notable in that a man, Mark, gets accused of hysteria by a woman, April. (As we will see in the chapter on film below, it is usually the female detective on film who gets accused of madness.) After Mark is attacked by a man who looks like a fifteenth-century pirate, no one believes him, and April says to him: "With all your hallucinations and hysteria, I'm going to miss you." She continues to think Mark is nuts when he says someone has taken his gun and communicator. The tables soon turn, however, when April loses her own gun, a symbolic loss of phallic authority. Moreover, when April sees the same mysterious pirate that Mark saw, he accuses *her* of having visions or of being suggestible. This effectively transfers the accusation of madness from the male detective to the female detective and (like the episode of the *Avengers* where it appears that Steed has been brainwashed but it turns out that Emma really has) re-asserts the male dominance in the partnership.

The *Mod Squad* featured a relatively helpless and ineffectual female detective as part of a trio of troubled young criminal offenders who are recruited by the police to investigate crimes as undercover operatives. In the premiere episode, waiflike Julie Barnes (Peggy Lipton), the daughter of a prostitute, is required to date a suspect for information; when her cover is blown and he returns to her apartment to slap her around, she collapses and is completely unable to defend herself. Only the fortuitous arrival of her male partners Linc Hayes and Pete Cochran (Clarence Williams III and Michael Cole) prevents her from undergoing a severe beating.[28] Although Julie *is* smart enough to figure out where a set of blackmail pictures must be, she is not allowed the daring physical task of breaking into an office and retrieving them — that job falls to rich white male Pete rather than to Julie or to African-American male Linc. Julie is consistently left out of the physical work of detection: When Julie, Linc,

and Pete are closing in on the villains' hideout, Linc and Pete send her to phone for help while they use physical force to subdue the villains; then, they insult her competence by joking that with their luck, she'll get lost. Julie's authority is further undermined by the fact that she is also shown as unable to control transportation — she doesn't drive in this episode. Pete, the car *owner*, is the driver; when he's working elsewhere, Linc takes over the driving duties.

The Early Seventies

Ironically, the most competent female detective shown on television in the early seventies (in fact, one of the most competent female detectives *ever* shown on television) was a cartoon character. The inimitable Velma Dinkley of Saturday morning's teen detective show, *Scooby-Doo, Where Are You?*,[29] solved puzzling mysteries with ease. Velma and her friends Freddy Jones, Daphne Blake (voiced by Heather North), and Norville "Shaggy" Rogers [30] (and their great dane Scooby-Doo) traveled rural America in their van, solving the mysteries that cropped up wherever they went. While others in her gang of friends might stumble upon a clue or make an occasional deduction, the final solution of the mystery and the explanation of how the evidence pointed to the culprit and the culprit's probable motive were Velma's domain. Velma's competence was of a peculiarly Sherlockian type: she specialized in deducing the man-made causes of "impossible" or seemingly supernatural events, and she was usually correct in her suspicions.[31]

Yet Velma's investigative competence did not go unchallenged. Other than solving mysteries, her main function on the show was to provide suspense by losing her thick glasses and groping for them helplessly — invariably around the feet of whichever creepy monster was terrorizing the teens that week. This assault on Velma's vision, a thinly-veiled metaphor for her investigative ability, counteracted her image as an all-seeing, all-knowing detective.[32] Also, as the show progressed, Velma's mystery-solving competence declined from being almost entirely her own doing to becoming shared somewhat with her companions — particularly Freddy — although Velma retained the privilege of providing the final solution.[33]

The early episode "That's Snow Ghost" (1969) illustrates how Velma's competence is established, then systematically undercut. Velma correctly identifies objects as Tibetan (as opposed to Chinese) and notices the clue that there is sawdust in the Snow Ghost's footprints. She also shows physical competence in helping Fred chisel Shaggy and Scooby out of an ice block. On the other hand, Velma's physical competence is undermined in a number of ways. First, she is kidnapped by the Snow Ghost and chained to a log headed for a chainsaw — a classic damsel-in-distress position. To add insult to injury, she is rescued not by one of her human friends, but by Scooby, the dog. Second, in this episode, as in countless other episodes, Velma's glasses get taken. Third, this episode highlights the fact that driving is a male, not a female activity: Fred, goofy Shaggy, and even the dog Scooby drive the snowmobile. Velma and Daphne do not.[34]

Velma's character was written out of the mid-to-late '80s versions of the show.[35] Eventually, the characters of Fred and Daphne were also dropped. Instead, the puppy character of Scrappy-Doo (Scooby-Doo's nephew) took over the investigative role from Velma. Scrappy becomes the same intrepid interpreter of clues that Velma has been. So the investigative role is shifted from an adult woman to a puppy. This puppy acts as the embodiment of a young, know-it-all boy, much like the annoying protagonist of *Star Wars Episode I: The Phantom Menace*.

Quite a different series was *McMillan and Wife*,[36] which featured another "detective couple" with a mostly non-detecting wife. Stewart ("Mac") and Sally McMillan (Rock Hudson and Susan Saint James) are an amiable couple: he's San Francisco's dapper police commissioner; she's his adoring socialite wife. In *Television Detective Shows of the 1970s*, David Martindale describes the sexual politics of the series thus:

> [Mac] was ... a hands-on type who preferred investigating murders to flying a desk. Sally, on the other hand, was an amateur when it came to crime, but she tagged along anyway — occasionally helping, more often hindering.... [An] oft-used plot device was placing Sally in jeopardy. She was constantly being abducted or shot at by men harboring feelings of unrequited love.[37]

In a typical episode, "Cross and Double Cross," Sally misses Mac so much when he goes undercover as a gangster that she is impelled to make sure he's all right by dressing up as a hooker[38] and going to a seedy nightclub to get a glimpse of him. Instead of ensuring Mac's safety, however, Sally's action winds up jeopardizing his cover. Episodes like this one reinforce the audience's perception that while Sally may be a great wife, she's a lousy detective.[39]

Due to a contract dispute, Susan Saint James left the series at the end of the 1975-76 season. Sally died in a plane crash, and the show continued without her, its title shortened simply to *McMillan*. Apparently, the role of "wife" was unnecessary.[40]

The 1974-75 season saw the debut of *Police Woman,* which featured European American female police sergeant Suzanne "Pepper" Anderson[41]

(Angie Dickinson). While *Police Woman*'s title suggested that it focused on the investigative work of its lead, the narrative treatment of her undercut her investigative potency by subjecting her to sexual threats. In *Where the Girls Are: Growing Up Female With the Mass Media*, Susan J. Douglas notes:

> ... Pepper's main job as a cop was to go undercover as a prostitute, stripper, gangster's moll, or aspiring porno queen to set the black widow's trap. But she wasn't the predator, she was the prey.... [I]n her low-cut, fringed sheath or jumpsuit, Pepper was invariably found out by the bad guys and always had to be rescued by the white, male cavalry, the *real* cops.... Often she was rescued just as she was about to be raped or sexually violated in some other way. So the audience got to fantasize briefly about a woman who dared to do a "man's job" getting her just deserts.[42]

This tactic of allowing a woman some autonomy while punishing her for using it is emblematic of the media's schizophrenic view of women in the seventies. On the one hand, showing a woman employed in a powerful position relative to the Law undercuts the women's movement's claims of employment discrimination and oppression by the social order. On the other hand, showing a woman too much in control of the Law might pose a threat to the current patriarchal order.

The opening titles to *Police Woman* reflect the series' ambivalence about its female star. The titles start with a shot of Pepper looking competent while aiming and firing a gun. Then comes a shot of Pepper laughing, then a shot of her screaming, then a shot of a woman's bare legs (presumably Pepper's) walking downstairs (in a shot that could be entitled "half a nude descending a staircase"), then a shot of someone grabbing Pepper and shaking her head, then a shot of Pepper dolled up as a hooker (with the camera panning down from her face to her breasts), then a shot of her in disguise as an air hostess, then a (male) fist in brass knuckles heading toward the camera, then shots of Pepper's male co-workers, then a shot of a police car whose window shatters. These titles portray Pepper as simultaneously strong and vulnerable.

The series premiere, entitled "The End Game," which aired September 13, 1974, presents Pepper as strong and competent,[43] though emotional, and she is not particularly sexualized. The opening vignette shows Pepper and her co-workers in the criminal conspiracy unit — boss Sgt. Bill Crowley (Earl Holliman), scruffy vegetarian Pete Royster (Charles Dierkop), and capable African American Joe Styles (Ed Bernard) — all responding to a robbery in progress. Pepper draws and fires her gun with her co-workers, but she is not part of the final takedown; instead, she comforts a dying police officer. After he dies, Pepper is much more emotional than the other police officers — she cries, takes a drink from a bottle of liquor she keeps hidden in a file cabinet, and then asks to take the next day off work. None of her male co-workers is shown crying.

Pepper is also portrayed as the nurturing member of the team who has empathy with victims and is able to bond with them. When Crowley questions a former hostage, he doesn't get the whole story. Pepper, however, eventually gets the witness to admit that she was raped in addition to being held hostage.

Despite being feminized in other ways, Pepper isn't particularly sexualized by her dress in this episode. She generally wears pants and pantsuits. The appearance of female victims in this episode, however, seems to determine their fate. The raped hostage is a career gal with a butch haircut. A stay-at-home mom with a very *femme* hairdo is subjected to an almost identical hostage-taking scenario, but is *not* raped.

Pepper is portrayed as smart: she figures out that the hostage-taking bank robbers are from Las Vegas. Yet Pepper's relationship to violence is ambivalent. In the episode's second shootout, Crowley, but not Pepper, shoots one of the robbers. In the episode's final shootout, Pepper wields an enormous shotgun and kills a robber, but she kills the robber with whom the white male audience that *Police Woman* was presumably hoping to attract[44] is least likely to identify: Pepper shoots and kills a black female robber — who also wields an enormous phallically-cathected shotgun — rather than one of the white male or white female robbers who also make up the robbery gang. The diegesis also uses this moment to emphasize Pepper's femininity by showing her in shock after killing the robber. In contrast, when her male colleagues kill someone, they look somber, not devastated.

In another early episode, "Flowers of Evil" (airing 11/8/74), Pepper is still portrayed as a woman who's trying hard to be tough, but who is still prey to her emotions. At a grisly murder scene involving a little old lady, a fellow cop tells her: "I wouldn't go in there if I were you, Pep. It's been over a week." Pepper boldly responds, "I can hack it" and goes to investigate the scene. While she doesn't cry, she does look ill.

In this episode, Pepper is still fairly de-sexualized in the clothing she wears. She wears a shirt and pants in one scene, a t-shirt and pants in another, a polo shirt and pants in another, a scoop-neck shirt and pants in another, pants and a denim jacket in another, and a reasonably modest shirt and wraparound skirt in another. She is shown to be not unaware of fashion, however, as she identifies expensive clothes on the elderly murder victim. The sexiest outfit Pepper wears in this episode is a low-cut nurse's uniform, but it's still a top and pants, not a dress.

In contrast to the way that Pepper, the moral center of the show, is allowed to dress androgynously, this episode, like the premiere, punishes other women who have masculine characteristics. The villains of the episode are a trio of lesbians who steal from and then murder the elderly residents of the retirement home they run. Crowley describes them thus: "One of them looks like she ought to be driving a diesel truck. The other two read pretty much the same, maybe a little more discreet." The three lesbians are all stereotyped: one, a former military nurse, is very, very butch; one is very, very *femme*; and one, who turns out to be a switch-hitter who dates and controls both the others, is both feminine and commanding. The one who is shown to feel the most guilt and to be the least involved in the murders is the *femme* lesbian, who has a wavy hairdo and dresses very femininely. The one who initially appears to have physically committed the murders is the butch. Later, however, it turns out that the switch-hitter did the actual killing.

The episode also tacitly endorses the tactics police used before the Stonewall riots to entrap gays and lesbians. Pepper flirts shamelessly with the switch-hitter boss to get hired at the retirement home so she can investigate undercover. More disturbingly, during an interrogation, Pepper claims that she was the object of her lesbian college roommate's desire in order to persuade the *femme* to give the police information that will convict the switch-hitter, with whom she is hopelessly in love, rather than to take the fall for her.

The episode further implies that lesbians are always on the make. The switch-hitter, who must have her hands full with two girlfriends on the premises, leers at Pepper and tries to get Pepper to change into her low-cut nurse's uniform in front of her. Pepper deflects her, but the groundwork was laid for a similar "les-ploitation" scene two years later on another series. The "Angels in Chains" episode of *Charlie's Angels* aired on October 20, 1976,[45] and features a butch prison matron leering at the Angels as she orders them to open their towels to get sprayed with disinfectant.

An episode from the series' second season, "Pattern for Evil" (airing 10/03/75), shows a more clearly sexualized, feminized Pepper. Early in the episode, she wears a skirted suit rather than the pants favored in prior episodes. She then goes undercover as a model to expose an extortion ring preying on garment manufacturers, and accordingly appears in two cheesecake scenes where she models a revealing swimsuit with cut-out sides and a low-cut pink pajama set. Moreover, cops in New York with whom Pepper's co-workers are coordinating ogle surveillance film that includes shots of Pepper in a skimpy top and tight pants.

Although Pepper does some good investigating by eavesdropping and photocopying secret information, Crowley is the one who demonstrates investigative mastery by interpreting what she has found. This episode, like the first two discussed, shows Pepper's forte to be gaining the trust of women in order to extract information from them: Pepper chats up the wife of a criminal couple to learn more about the extortion racket.

One of the last episodes of the series, "Sweet Kathleen" (airing 3/15/78), nearly does away with Pepper entirely. Pepper must go to court to testify in a case, leaving the episode's focus on Crowley and her other co-workers. Pepper appears only very briefly in this episode, leaving the deductive work and gunplay to the men. The producers still squeeze in a scene where Pepper wears a low-cut nightgown while bringing coffee to Crowley and a guest and a scene where Pepper acts maternally towards Crowley, telling him not to stay up too late working on the case. Perhaps Pepper's virtual disappearance allows the episode to focus on a pretty ex-con's attempt to seduce and then kill Crowley. Having Pepper around would hamper that scenario. (For good measure, an over-eager police recruit also throws herself at Crowley in this episode). Even so, Pepper is extremely de-fanged in this episode. She brandishes her gun briefly in the final scene, but to no effect. In comparison, Crowley is presented as a supremely capable, phallic figure. He chases robbery suspects, shoots at them, and kills one of the robbers. Moreover, Crowley is shown to have known all along that the ex-con's affection for him was feigned. He has just been stringing her along in order to incriminate her.

Throughout the series, there is sexual tension between Pepper and Crowley, both divorced. Crowley is particularly bitter about his divorce in "Pattern for Evil," grousing, "She took me for everything but my shorts," and "You know what I miss about marriage? Nothing." In the premiere episode, Pepper appears jealous when Crowley flirts with a bank teller. In "Flowers of Evil," Crowley kisses Pepper on the forehead. Pepper and Crowley also cook dinner together, while an enlightened Crowley cooks up his mother's sauce recipe.[46] In "Pattern for Evil," Crowley takes Pepper as his date to a formal affair. In "Sweet Kathleen," Pepper massages Crowley's shoulders and purrs, "This case really has you tense," and Crowley leans his arm on Pepper's thigh as she sits on his desk. At the end of the episode, Pepper and Crowley leave the office together, presumably to spend at least part of the evening together.

Diana Meehan takes a positive view of *Police Woman*, viewing Pepper's constant need to be rescued simply as a generic topos. Meehan categorizes most of the female detectives of the fifties, sixties, and seventies as "decoys," tracing the model for later female decoys back to the character of Casey Jones (Beverly Garland), "a New York policewoman in a 1957 '*Dragnet*-style'" show called *Decoy*.[47] Meehan's positive reading of *Police Woman* emphasizes that Pepper Anderson gets "emotional warmth and acceptance" from her co-workers and asserts that they provide her with "a sense of community and family that divorcée Anderson did not have in her home life."[48] It seems to me, however, that assuming that Anderson needs a "substitute family" because she is a divorced woman is also problematic.

Get Christie Love!, which featured African American female police detective Christie Love (Teresa Graves), premiered during the same season as *Police Woman*, and it is often described as the black version of *Police Woman*. It seems more likely, though, that it was inspired by the popular subgenre of the early seventies blaxploitation film that featured African American women hunting down criminals who had hurt their loved ones: the Pam Grier films *Coffy* (Jack Hill, 1973), *Foxy Brown* (Jack Hill, 1974), *Friday Foster* (Arthur Marks, 1975), and *Sheba, Baby* (William Girdler, 1975) and the Tamara Dobson films *Cleopatra Jones* (Jack Starrett, 1973) and *Cleopatra Jones and the Casino of Gold* (Chuck Bail, 1975).[49]

The made-for-television movie that was later turned into the series is called simply *Get Christie Love!* (dir. William A. Graham, aired 1/22/74). It sets Christie up as a force to be reckoned with. The first time we see Christie, she's dressed as a hooker, rejecting the advances of a racist potential client. Shortly thereafter, she is menaced by, but competently apprehends, a serial killer who preys on prostitutes. Immediately thereafter, she is set on the track of Helena Varga (Louise Sorel), a drug lord's girlfriend, in order to glean information.

Christie boldly faces most physical challenges. When a hit man attacks her in her hotel room, she struggles with him and eventually tosses him to his death from her 15th-floor balcony. When another hit man shoots a witness and shoots at her, she shoots him dead. When Helena hits her, she hits Helena back and twists Helena's arm behind her back. When she is menaced by a thug with a knife, she whacks him with her purse and uses some (admittedly not wholly convincing) martial arts moves to subdue him.

Christie isn't infallible, however. When she's snooping in a suspect's apartment and she hears someone come in, she hides timidly in the closet, only to be discovered, to her chagrin, by her amorous boss Casey Reardon (Harry Guardino).[50]

Christie generally displays mental toughness. When Helena accuses Christie of being a cop and calls her on it, instead of backing down, Christie threatens her and demands information. Yanked off the case, Christie shows her persistence by continuing to investigate. Christie also shows an immunity to overempathizing with suspects: she coolly threatens the safety of Helena's son in order to obtain information about the drug lord's scheme.

Christie's driving competence is mixed. On the one hand, she is shown driving a lot, both by herself and with a male or female passenger, and she's generally presented as a capable driver. On the other hand, some of her driving ends badly. When she's chasing a murderous hit man, she gets in a crash and totals her own car. When she's driving in a borrowed car, she gets tailed and then almost run off the road. Although she manages to hop out of the car and shoot fiercely enough to run the other car off the road, she is unable to protect her passenger from getting fatally shot.

While mixing professional competence with a sexually suggestive demeanor was a tactic that worked to keep later female detective shows (like *Charlie's Angels* and *VIP*) on the air, it did not save *Get Christie Love!* Douglas postulates that the series may have faltered because "viewers didn't buy a female cop who smirked suggestively to criminals 'You're under arrest, sugah.'"[51] J. Fred MacDonald, author of *Blacks and White TV*, suggests that the show's demise stemmed from "an unbelievable character acting out poorly written scripts in a tired genre" and suggests that actress Teresa Graves' own insistence on less violence in the show might have lost the show viewers.[52] Interestingly, despite these accusations of a lack of verisimilitude, "the series was ... based on the adventures of a real-life ... [female] detective ... who served as a technical advisor and even contributed a few stories" to the series.[53] Indeed, author Dorothy Uhnak, whose detective novel *The Ledger* was made into the series pilot, had a realistic view of women in police work from her own first-hand experience:

> Uhnak ... joined the police force at age twenty, battling her way to Detective First Class in the jealously male ranks of the New York Police Department during the pre-feminist 1950s.... Although awarded two medals for heroism, one after single-handedly disarming a serial rapist twice her size who was holding a gun to her head, she was demoted back to patrol rank for taking pregnancy leave.... The protagonist [of her novel *The Bait*], Christie Opara, became the prototype for the short-lived *Get Christy* [sic] *Love*[!] television series.[54]

So, perhaps "lack of verisimilitude" arguments about the demise of *Get Christie Love!* (of which there are many) reflect society's low expectations of women's abilities rather than any concrete difference between women's abilities and how they are portrayed in a feminist television series.

Moreover, television programs marketing a female African American protagonist to a mixed-race/mixed-gender audience were extremely rare at the time,[55] and the fact that the show lasted a season indicates that it must have had some genuine merit. Particularly during this era, the success of an African American star at the box-office was no guarantee of similar success on television. The disparity might be due to the fact that movie success is judged by box-office receipts, allowing regional audiences to have a strong effect on the overall success of a movie, while television success is judged by Nielsen ratings, requiring that a television show appeal to a previously selected group of viewers. An interesting parallel is the case of *Shaft* (1971),[56] a film whose immense box-office success led to two sequels, *Shaft's Big Score* (1972) and *Shaft in Africa* (1973). Yet the *Shaft* television series, starring Richard Roundtree, the same charismatic actor who had been a success in the films, lasted only seven episodes in the 1973–1974 television season.[57]

THE NANCY DREW MYSTERIES: NOT HARDY ENOUGH?

It should come as no surprise to the reader that the seventies, which spawned the greatest number of television programs centered around women in any decade before or since, also produced a slew of television programs aimed at young female viewers, although these were not always produced as independent shows but were often paired up with similar programs aimed at young male viewers.[58] Thus it makes sense that this decade should bring to television two famous children's detective book series (both products of the Stratemeyer syndicate, though the first 23 Nancy Drew mysteries were penned by Mildred Wirt Benson)[59] to produce *The Hardy Boys/Nancy Drew Mysteries* There is nothing inherently sexist about the fact that the episodes about the Hardy Boys and Nancy Drew alternated each week. It is interesting to note, however, that Nancy's close female friends George and Bess (butch and femme, respectively) are downplayed in the television series, although they are featured quite prominently in the books. Furthermore, after one season, the network decided to cut many episodes of the Nancy Drew series and to make Nancy an occasional co-investigator with Frank and Joe Hardy (played by '70s teen idols Parker Stevenson and Shaun Cassidy) on their series instead. This move eventually led star Pamela Sue Martin to quit in protest. Although

Martin was replaced by a new Nancy Drew (Janet Louise Johnson) who worked with the Hardy Boys, the network cut all further solo Nancy Drew episodes, and eventually cut out Nancy's character entirely.[60]

CHARLIE'S ANGELS: FEMINISTS IN BIKINIS

It may seem odd that all the programs I have listed above featured women working as part of heterosexual couples or with a group of men,[61] especially considering the dawning of the women's liberation movement in the sixties and early seventies. Certainly, programs featuring solely female detectives were conceived of and aired during the seventies, but only one, a show that had a documented appeal to male spectators as well as female spectators — Charlie's Angels — was successful at that time.[62]

Charlie's Angels, which made its debut in 1976, is an interesting case in which a primarily female cast is allowed to work together as a detecting team. As the opening credits reminded viewers each week, the original "Angels" Sabrina, Jill, and Kelly (Kate Jackson, Farrah Fawcett-Majors, and Jaclyn Smith) were former rookie police officers who had been frustrated at being assigned to "women's jobs" at the LAPD (that is, they were fleeing sexual discrimination in the workplace) and had consequently quit to work for the reclusive private detective Charlie Townsend (played in voiceover by John Forsythe). Although the fact that Charlie is never seen puts him in a powerful position in relation to specularity, since he is not himself subject to the gaze,[63] it also limits his ability to be a locus of identification for the spectator. By definition, the audience never sees Charlie engaged in the act of detection, even though he is supposed to be a master detective. The only other male detective in sight is middle-aged bachelor John Bosley (David Doyle), who is portrayed as a glorified administrator for the detective agency with little sexual or investigative power of his own. This leaves the field free for the women detectives to take center stage, and unlike Pepper Anderson, when these women need to be rescued, the rescue comes from another woman, not a man.

Charlie's Angels in no way deserves its role as whipping boy for the television industry. Yet it is often derided by critics as television's worst of the worst.[64] Even television apologist David Bianculli uses it as a metaphor for bad television:

> Rejecting the entire medium of television on the basis of Charlie's Angels is no more logical or defensible — or sporting — than rejecting the entire motion picture industry on the basis of Porky's.[65]

Bianculli's use of the word "sporting" is telling. It is a word traditionally used by elite men, and its use evokes an image of television critics as elite men, who shouldn't sully themselves examining the worst of the worst — the vulgar, the female.

Many critics, both in the seventies and more recently, have credited the program's success to its appeal to a male audience enraptured by three attractive braless female protagonists and have bewailed the ascendancy of "jiggle" television.[66] Certainly, "jiggle" *was* an element of the show, which also carried the "woman in jeopardy" theme to new extremes.

Yet critics who dismiss this show as mere "jiggle" discount the series' tremendous appeal to female spectators. It is proof of the program's diverse spectatorship that the series plummeted in the Nielsen ratings *not* after the queen of jiggle Farrah Fawcett left the show, but rather after Kate Jackson, who played Sabrina ("the smart one"), left the show. While sex objects may be interchangeable, complex, developed characters are not. John Fiske notes:

> ... [W]omen have told me how much they enjoyed *Charlie's Angels* when it appeared on their screens in the 1970s, and that their pleasure in seeing women taking active, controlling roles was so great that it overrode the incorporating devices that worked to recuperate the feminist elements in its context back into patriarchy.[67]

Fiske here uses the example of male and female spectators' different responses to *Charlie's Angels* to discuss how spectators bring in outside experiences to aid in the interpretation of what they see on television. I would say that Fiske's interpretation makes it sound a bit like the *real* agenda of *Charlie's Angels* is this re-incorporation of women into patriarchy and that female spectators who liked the program were selectively blinding themselves to its anti-feminist elements.[68] I view the program from the opposite perspective: I would say that the converse is true — that *male* viewers selectively blinded themselves to the show's feminist elements by concentrating on the Angels as objects of desire. Frankly, the fact that women are presented as objects of desire is no surprise for the average female viewer — it's certainly something women see all the time. But the fact that women are working together and don't really appear to need men at all as professional partners or as romantic partners poses a pretty heavy threat to the average male viewer, since he is *not* usually surrounded by that kind of imagery.

Susan J. Douglas notes the appeal to female spectators of a program that showed women working together to help other women, that acknowledged the existence of sexism and was not afraid to use the words "male chauvinist pig," and that portrayed women triumphing over individual evil men, if not over the patriarchal system as a whole.[69]

I strongly agree with Douglas that part of *Charlie's Angels'* appeal to female spectators is also based on the portrayal of the Angels as active consumers on the burgeoning market of jobs for women. Every episode, the Angels go undercover working at different glamorous and exciting jobs. On an undercover job at a small circus, for example, Kelly is a stunt motorcycle rider, and Sabrina apprentices as a clown. At a racetrack, Sabrina races stock cars in a competition for women drivers. Jill plays tennis on the pro circuit. Kelly is a magazine photographer. While some of the undercover jobs clearly play to the jiggle audience — the Angels undercover as inmates at a women's prison-cum-bordello, as cheerleaders, as beauty pageant contestants — usually only one Angel (or two, at most) was placed in the jiggle role per week.[70] The others were shown working at interesting, challenging jobs. In a sense, they were instant role models to young women (and older women as well) who were considering their career options in the seventies, that era of what seemed like limitless opportunities for women.[71]

On the other hand, it would be misleading to say that there is "one" female response to *Charlie's Angels*. In *Women Watching Television: Gender, Class, and Generation in the American Television Experience*, Andrea L. Press examines variations in women's responses to *Charlie's Angels* based on their generation. She notes that older women viewers, who presumably viewed the series when it originally aired, focused on the Angels' camaraderie and work lives and enjoyed the show. Press found that younger women who had grown up in a post-feminist environment, however, resisted identifying with the Angels, focusing less on the Angels' work lives and more on the Angels-as-sex-objects aspect of the show.[72]

Moreover, even female critics are far from unanimous on the worth of *Charlie's Angels*. Ella Taylor calls *Charlie's Angels* "ostensibly a show about three young policewomen [sic] but actually an excuse for sexual titillation and ersatz violence."[73] Yet for good or ill, the show continues to be a central reference for American culture. In the late 20th and early 21st century, there have been two films updating the series, and other TV series — like *The Ricki Lake Show* and *That '70s Show* — have paid homage to *Charlie's Angels*.

One of the more compelling reasons to think of *Charlie's Angels* as having a more feminist subtext than is generally recognized is the positive links between women and transportation that it routinely displays. Each Angel has her own distinctive sports car, complete with car phone (not the ubiquitous luxury in the 1970s that it is today). Many scenes (and the series' opening titles) show the Angels driving somewhere to investigate or chasing criminals in their cars. As noted above, the program also positions women as experts in transportation. Not only is Kelly an accomplished stunt motorcycle rider, and Sabrina a tough stock car racer, but Jill returns to the series in later episodes as a formula one race car driver on the international racing circuit.

Furthermore, the fact that the Angels were portrayed as highly competent at traditionally masculine activities may be inferred to have had a huge influence on the show's female audience when we consider how seldom women were portrayed engaging in these activities in other shows of the time. According to a content analysis of all prime-time and Saturday-morning television shows aired during 2-week sample periods in the Fall of the 1975-76 and 1976-77 television seasons, women performed only 17.3% of the driving and 10% of the firearms use that occurred.[74] An enormous percentage of that driving and firearms use by women *must* have taken place on *Charlie's Angels*. (Although the opening titles to many series in the seventies showed women driving, as noted above, these series tended to be sitcoms in which the action took place indoors, and thus did not permit their female characters to drive on a weekly basis.)

Like *The Avengers*, *Charlie's Angels* also drew female viewers with fashion. According to *Entertainment Tonight: Charlie's Angels Uncovered*, the clothing budget for *Charlie's Angels* was $20,000 per episode.[75] Farrah Fawcett's Hugh-York designed[76] hairstyle influenced female hairstyles around the nation for years.

Male critical emphasis on the "jiggle" aspects of *Charlie's Angels* and the snide dismissal of the rest of the show's content may actually be compensatory strategies by which men can disavow elements of the show that may be unsettling to them — elements that portray women as self-sufficient and portray some men in a less-than-flattering light. We can see the difference between female and male critical responses to *Charlie's Angels* by the intertextual references that are made to it on a television program of the mid-nineties, stand-up comic Margaret Cho's short-lived sitcom, *All-American Girl*. On the September 28, 1994 episode of *All-American Girl*, twentysomething Margaret and her friend Ruthie play *Charlie's Angels* during slow times at their sales jobs and eagerly look forward to watching a *Charlie's Angels* marathon together. After they have a fight about work, Margaret goes home and watches the marathon alone with her brother. When he criticizes *Charlie's Angels*, she starts explaining to him that the show is about women rescuing women, about their relationships and friendships with each other. In so doing, Margaret realizes that the Angels "are friends first and Angels second"[77] and decides that her friendship with Ruthie is more important than their professional differences. As Margaret heads off to apologize to Ruthie, her brother sneers, "I'd hate to think you learned an important life lesson from a mid-seventies jigglefest," but then eagerly settles down to watch a titillating part of the show.[78] So, what we see is a young man surrounded by images of women who are strong and supportive of each other completely disavowing the seriousness of that aspect of the show and instead preferring to consider the female characters solely as objects of desire. *Et tu, Angels*-bashers?

Three Mystery-Romances of the Eighties

The 1980s gave rise to a spate of self-consciously cinematic mystery-romance television series. The successful *Hart to Hart* (1979–1984), which featured a happily married pair of investigators, was closely followed by two other popular series that featured heterosexual couples running private detective agencies — *Remington Steele* (1982–1987) and *Moonlighting* (1985–1989). Their blend of investigation with sexual tension recalls one of the underlying themes of *film noir*, and indeed, all three series exploited the *noir* aesthetic to varying degrees. I would argue that this similarity is no accident and, in fact, makes perfect sense given some of the similar social circumstances present in the late 1940s/early 1950s and the 1980s. Both periods of time followed closely on an era of unprecedented freedom and economic power for women, and both eras accordingly produced complex cultural negotiations that first acknowledge and then diegetically neutralize the threat that sexually and economically independent women pose to a capitalist patriarchal system.[79] Of the three series, *Remington Steele* is by far the most interesting to film historians, feminists, and psychoanalytic critics.

FILM SPECTATORSHIP AND IDENTITY IN *REMINGTON STEELE*

In terms of film, although all three series in early episodes pay homage to the *Thin Man* films of the 1930s and early 1940s (and *Hart to Hart* models its detective couple after Nick and Nora Charles to the extent that they are happily married, exchange witty banter, and have a cute dog), only *Remington Steele* maintains a constant self-conscious stream of references to classic cinema. Indeed, the male protagonist, Remington Steele, is himself a film buff who interprets the reality around him in terms of classic films: in every episode of the series, he finds some aspect of his situation that triggers a full reference — complete with title, studio, release date, main actors, and plot summary — to a classic film, then applies his knowledge of the plot in order to plan his next move (with varying degrees of success.) It is interesting to note that it is the male member of the detective couple who has privileged access to the cinematic here, though his implied visual and interpretive prowess is somewhat undercut by the fact that his cinematically inspired solutions to mysteries are usually incorrect.[80] (Perhaps this phenomenon occurs because Steele goes too far in his spectatorship by identifying heavily with screen stars — for example, he chooses the names of characters played by Humphrey Bogart for his aliases — and by blurring the distinctions between life and art.[81])

Feminisms of the Eighties: Few and Far Between: Furthermore, *Remington Steele* manipulates cinematic tropes to make a feminist point. The series inverts the usual *film noir* plot that requires a professional male detective to investigate a mysterious female potential romantic partner who has walked into his office, and to determine whether she is good or evil. E. Ann Kaplan notes:

> The *film noir world* is one in which women are central to the intrigue of the films [but not safely contained in traditional female roles].... Defined by their sexuality, which is presented as desirable but dangerous to men, the women function as the obstacle to the male quest. The hero's success or not depends on the degree to which he can extricate himself from the woman's manipulations. Although the man is sometimes simply destroyed because he cannot resist the woman's lures ..., often the work of the film is the attempted restoration of order through the exposure and then destruction of the sexual, manipulating woman.[82]

In contrast, in the *Remington Steele* series, Laura Holt is the *female* professional detective forced to investigate a jewel thief who has assumed an identity she knows is false — that of her fictitious boss, Remington Steele. In this case, the woman's integrity is a known quantity, while the character of the male interloper is murky.

Remington Steele (at least in its surface text) is unapologetically feminist in its approach, a refreshing difference from both *Hart to Hart* and *Moonlighting*, both of which pander to the 1980s backlash against the images of strong women that were prevalent in the 1970s. *Hart to Hart's* antifeminist bias can be summed up by a brief analysis of the program's opening credits. The opening voiceover, spoken by Jonathan and Jennifer Hart's chauffeur Max (Lionel Stander), makes the program's distinction between "male" and "female" values quite clear:

> This is my boss, Jonathan Hart: a self-made millionaire. He's quite a guy. And this is Mrs. H. She's gorgeous. She's one lady who really knows how to take care of herself.

While the surface meaning of "she's one lady who really knows how to take care of herself" might be read in a neutral context as "she's good in a fight," the context here implies that Jennifer Hart (Stefanie Powers) takes care of herself by marrying well, not by having a lucrative career of her own as her husband does. Jonathan Hart (Robert Wagner), in fact, continues working as the head of Hart Industries although the program makes it clear that he is wealthy enough to retire for life. Less charitably, one might read "she really knows how to take care of herself" as a gloss on "she's gorgeous." That is, she's gorgeous for someone in her late thirties and is doing a good job of preserving her beauty — the symbolic capital that landed her her advantageous marriage in the first place. That Jennifer Hart's quintessence is her status as married woman is suggested by the fact that she is introduced merely as *Mrs.* H., whereas Jonathan Hart is introduced by both his given and his family name. The use of an initial for Jennifer Hart's last name in the opening sequence is also worthy of note. Narratively, this choice can be explained by the fact that Max, the chauffeur, calls Jonathan and Jennifer Hart "Mr. and Mrs. H." Yet this overly casual form of address — the generic "Mrs." supplemented merely by an initial to suggest the man to which the "Mrs." belongs — seems to imply that Jennifer Hart is merely a place marker, that the exact identity of Jonathan Hart's wife is not intrinsically relevant.[83]

Moonlighting, while not as obviously regressive as *Hart to Hart*, projects a more subtle antifeminist viewpoint.[84] Although the female protagonist, Maddie Hayes (Cybill Shepherd), is a business owner — the owner of the detective agency that she now runs and thus nominally the boss of her male partner in detection — she is constructed as incapable of handling her own economic affairs. Maddie, a former model, now runs the agency herself because it is the only one of her numerous investments not sold or stolen by her crooked accountant. Why Maddie does not simply return to modeling in order to earn a living is never made clear. Although she is technically in a position of power, the program emphasizes Maddie's weaknesses: she can't handle money well; she is an amateur and must thus rely heavily on help from her professional partner, David Addison (Bruce Willis)[85]; and she is sexually frustrated, and consequently vulnerable to sexual teasing and approaches by David.

Remington Steele, on the other hand, plunges boldly into the topic of gender-based job discrimination in its first-season opening voiceover, in which series protagonist Laura Holt describes her genesis as a detective and her decision to invent a male boss when she realizes that no one wants to hire an independent female private investigator:

... So I studied and apprenticed ... but absolutely nobody broke down my door.... So I invented a superior — a decidedly *masculine* superior. Suddenly, there were cases around the block.[86]

This matter-of-fact depiction (and implicit criticism) of gender bias is a recurring theme throughout the program. The jewel thief who comes to impersonate the fictitious Remington Steele is consistently treated with far more respect by the public than is his "associate" Laura Holt, even though she is the one who solves the vast majority of their cases. The program consistently emphasizes Laura's frustration with this bias and its inherent unfairness. Even during the third-to-last episode of the program, Laura complains about being called "the little woman" by her partner in a marriage of convenience. More remarkably, when one of her two suitors in the episode refers to her behind her back as "the little woman," the other *corrects* him, making the point that references belittling women, so to speak, are unacceptable whether or not the women are actually present.

Julie D'Acci, however, points out that *Remington Steele* was not entirely immune to the effects of the '80s backlash. She quotes a *Los Angeles Herald Examiner* article by Elaine Warren that berates the program for quickly feminizing Laura's character.[87] Although I would not deny that this is true to a certain extent, I think the effects of a patriarchal system of language and meaning on the series are generally expressed in more subtle and complex ways than simply having Laura act "feminine."

Gender, Author-ity, Identity: All of the material *Remington Steele* might provide for film and feminist critics is nothing compared to its rich supply of material for the psychoanalytic critic. Laura Holt inhabits a subject position remarkable for a female subject: Right from the beginning of the series, she is presented as a powerful, knowing subject with many of the same qualities as the Name-of-the-Father.

First of all, Laura's investigative powers are essentially self-generated, rather than gleaned from the representatives of patriarchy. Her abilities are *not* inherited from a father or a father-figure as are those of Honey West and V.I. Warshawski.[88] Neither are Laura's abilities inherited from the traditional machinery of patriarchal law — Laura Holt has not been trained by a police academy as have Kinsey Millhone, Charlie's Angels, and Cagney and Lacey. Nor are they absorbed from a male partner, as are the abilities of Nora Charles, Julie Barnes, Jennifer Hart, Maddie Hayes, and Emma Peel.

Instead, Laura Holt is a rare creature — a self-taught female investigator. When she joins forces with "Remington Steele," her investigative powers are already fully formed. While she may learn about criminal behavior from him, in general, the early seasons of the program emphasize Steele's amazement at Laura's perception in solving mysteries. Furthermore, the fact that Laura's knowledge is self-generated seems deliberately emphasized by the opening season voiceover in which she tells the audience that she "studied and apprenticed," but never tells us *with whom*. That the gender and exact identity of Laura's teachers are left vague refutes the paradigm of knowledge being controlled and passed on by father-figures. The voiceover implies that it doesn't matter with whom Laura studied; what matters is that she was an active seeker of knowledge rather than a passive recipient of it — that she has authored her own identity as a professional woman.

This is quite rare among female detectives. It is interesting to note that even the fiercely independent feminist investigator Modesty Blaise has gained much of her knowledge of the world through the help of an old father-figure scholar (and much of her fighting ability from her male friend Willie Garvin.) Peter O'Donnell has written of how he felt it necessary to explain the genesis of Modesty Blaise's abilities in a far more detailed way than would have been necessary if she had been a male character doing the same things:

> ... I faced a major problem. With a James Bond, or a Saint, or a Bulldog Drummond, you don't have to explain how he got to be so smart, so skilled in karate or kung fu or whatever is the fashionable form of unarmed combat, so accurate with a gun, so knowledgeable about weapons, explosives, knockout drops, cars, planes, helicopters, and everything else a hero needs to know in order to beat the bad guys. He's a *hero*, so naturally he knows all that stuff, doesn't he? But girls don't come quite so ready-made.... I need[ed] a background for her which would make it feasible, within the license of fiction, that she should have all the attributes needed for her task....[89]

The fact that Laura herself narrates the voice-over (which disappears in later seasons of the show) may also seem, at first glance, to contribute to her author-ity. We should be wary, however, of automatically connecting the act of narration with complete control over events. As Kaja Silverman notes, although the voice-over *can* become such a locus of extreme authority that "it becomes a 'voice on high,' ... a voice which speaks from a position of superior knowledge, and which superimposes itself 'on top' of the diegesis," this generalization is only true to the degree that the narrating voice "preserves its integrity" by remaining disembodied and removed from the fiction.[90] Furthermore, Silverman suggests that "to the degree that the voice-over preserves its integrity, it also becomes an exclusively male voice."[91] Laura's voice-over, however, does not preserve its integrity by remaining disembodied, but is, in fact, narrated over shots of herself that accurately reflect the events she details.

Compare the unseen Charlie Townsend who narrates the opening voice-over on *Charlie's Angels* over ironic shots of the "Angels" that belie his narration. When Charlie's voice-over says that his employees "were assigned many hazardous duties," when they graduated from the police academy, the corresponding shots show how they were assigned to "female" police positions like switchboard operator and crossing guard. His assertion that he "took them away from all that" is similarly followed by shots of the Angels armed and dangerous. Unseen, Charlie is allowed the luxury of irony.

It is fascinating that the central premise of the *Charlie's Angels* opening titles — that women in the work force need a man's protection to get fair treatment — is actually the same as that of the *Remington Steele* opening titles, though one communicates its message ironically and one in a straightforward manner. The two programs are also similar in the sense that both rely on an exposed female labor source to gain glory for a male boss whose identity is in some way obscured. The Angels are just as eager to find out what Charlie looks like as Laura is to find out what Remington Steele's real name is.

Laura also is in a powerful position with respect to her ability to "author" another human being: her fictitious boss Remington Steele (named after a typewriter and a football team), whom she uses to increase her own success as a private investigator. The individual parts of the name Laura chooses, "Remington Steele," resonate in many cultural and psychic registers denoting masculinity. First, the typewriter is itself a symbol of authority, of the traditionally patriarchal privilege of controlling language. Second, "Remington" recalls both a firearm — a symbol of phallic authority — and the Western painter Frederic Remington, noted for his powerful scenes of men penetrating, investigating, and subduing nature, traditionally coded as feminine. Moreover, the football team in question, the Pittsburgh Steelers, has been particularly successful in another male arena, that of professional sports. Furthermore, the name Steele suggests both the unbending metal that provides the frame for that phallic mainstay of modern architecture, the skyscraper, and the unlawful profession of the male jewel thief who eventually comes to impersonate Remington Steele. Finally, the combination of Remington and Steele also suggests the popular brand of electric shaver, another symbol of masculinity. We see, then, Laura's parody of the markers of masculinity through her choice of a name that is vastly overdetermined as masculine.

Furthermore, Laura authors a real human being: the jewel thief who assumes Remington Steele's identity as part of an unsuccessful plot to steal some jewels that Laura is assigned to guard. Now, it may at first seem that the power relations in this case favor the jewel thief, since he takes over Remington Steele's identity against Laura's will, banking on the fact that she cannot produce a real Remington Steele to refute his claim of identity. Laura's power over naming is also initially undercut by the fact that although she desires to find out the jewel thief's true identity — her first-season opening voiceover ends with "I don't even know his real name" — he refuses to enlighten her. Yet Laura soon recognizes and exploits the advantages of having a real person who can act as a figurehead for her agency, and she thus begins to look less like the sorcerer's apprentice and more like an executive who has negotiated a symbiotic relationship with the representative of a hostile takeover.

Although the jewel thief initially seems to be a master at authoring himself, since he possesses a multitude of alternate alibis and legitimizing passports[92] to help in his work, a shocking development in the first episode of the 4th season reveals that his self-authorship is, in fact, a compensatory measure for his *lack* of identity: his birth illegitimate, he has no idea who his father is or what his real name is.[93] His trip to Great Britain to investigate a potential lead about his father's identity proves a failure, a failure only mitigated by Laura's gift to him of a fake U.S. passport bearing the name Remington Steele. Thus, Laura has progressed from having the "Remington Steele" name and identity usurped from her control to bestowing these attributes freely upon the recipient of her choice.

Several later incidents further reinforce Laura's structural position as the giver of name and identity: At the end of the regular series,[94] the jewel thief, hounded by the Immigration and Naturalization Service as an illegal alien, is forced to marry Laura in order to retain the right to live and work in the United States. His citizenship is contingent upon hers — a neat reversal of the pattern in which women are expected to gain their national, personal, and professional identities from their husbands. In this case, however, the jewel thief is forced to adopt Laura's *fatherland* as his own.

Furthermore, it is Laura who, in the final episode of the series, discovers the true nature of the jewel thief's paternity (he is actually the son of a fellow jewel thief, Daniel Chalmers, who had acted as his criminal mentor for years) and persuades his father to tell him the truth, thus providing him with an identity for the fourth time. Significantly, however, the jewel thief's father dies immediately before revealing the jewel thief's real name. (The jewel thief's question "Not that it matters after all this time, but what's my real name?" is answered by a shot of his father suddenly slumped over in death.) The jewel thief is correct: his real name does *not* matter, precisely because he has grown into the original identity provided for him by Laura; she is more the author of his identity than Daniel is, which is not least indicated by the fact that Laura has given him a legitimate profession squarely within the framework of patriarchal law, a profession he has ultimately chosen over the illegitimate profession taught him earlier by Daniel.

My Father, Myself?: Yet Laura's control over paternity and identity is by no means absolute. Her own father has been largely absent from her life, having abandoned her, her sister, and her mother when Laura was 16. Although the fact that Laura grew up in a female-dominated household does not seem to have hurt her at all professionally, she *is* typed as someone whose knowledge of families is flawed and artificial, as opposed to the jewel thief, who is coded as a repository of authentic knowledge about family structures: When Laura confides to the jewel thief that she always envied the "perfect" family next door, who never raised their voices or argued, he says that although he spent his childhood bouncing around from aunts to cousins and back, he learned that *real* families argue. Thus, even though *both* grew up fatherless, somehow, the male figure is given a privileged narrative voice in the definition of the family.[95]

The series also implies that Laura's problems with men are due to distrust stemming from her father's abandonment. The program constructs Laura as undersexed: She has had one failed live-in relationship sometime before the start of the program's narrative, but she has no serious steady relationship during the many years she and the jewel thief work together. Furthermore, the series precludes the possibility of household female solidarity in the absence of the father. Although we might expect Laura to bond with her mother and sister, she confides to the thief that she and her mother do not have a great relationship.

Laura's heavy *authority* over the jewel thief may stem from an inner conflict over her absent father. Laura's attempts to author "Remington Steele" represent a strategy for replacing her absent father by becoming a father figure herself. From this theoretical perspective, Laura's revelation of the jewel thief's true paternity becomes her deliberate renunciation of the paternal/authorial role. After all, Laura need not tell the jewel thief the truth, since Chalmers is reluctant to reveal himself. Yet by forcing

Chalmers to reveal himself, Laura makes a conscious choice to give up her place as the author of the only stable identity the jewel thief has ever known so that he can reclaim his "true" identity. What motive impels Laura to renounce her authority so completely? Perhaps her renunciation of a parental role is a necessary condition to the eventual consummation of their long-standing flirtation. It might indeed prove difficult for the jewel thief to love Laura on equal terms while she is positioned as the author of his identity. Once the jewel thief's own identity has been established externally, Laura becomes a less problematically cathected object choice.

Gender and Commodity: Despite her considerable power over names and identities in her professional life, Laura's personal life still reflects the unenviable position of a woman in a patriarchal system that builds social bonds among men through the exchange of women. Drawing on the work of Claude Levi-Strauss, Luce Irigaray has argued that heterosexual marital and sexual transactions often use women as objects whose exchange (from father to son-in-law or rival to rival) is a pretext for forming homosocial bonds between men.[96] This paradigm can be seen operating full force during the first and last seasons of the series. While the middle seasons of the series leave Laura pretty much a free agent — i.e., celibate — sexually, the opening and closing seasons of the series position her as a potential object of exchange between pairs of men.

During the first season, the jewel thief "Steele" and Laura's male assistant Murphy Michaels (James Read) challenge each other by both expressing a romantic interest in Laura. It is clear that Laura's worth as an object of exchange is increased by the fact that two men want her at the same time.[97] In fact, it seems that Laura's romance with "Steele" is only viable under circumstances that position her as such a commodity: Shortly after Murphy leaves the show at the beginning of its second season, "Steele" and Laura agree to maintain a platonic friendship, an arrangement which is honored for several seasons.

Although, during the last season, the couple begins to date again, something about their rekindled romance — a romance with no rival for Laura's affections in sight — rings false. For example, while on an undercover assignment at a counseling retreat for couples, the pair end up fighting over their differences instead of expressing affection for each other.

Furthermore, the wedding-for-immigration-purposes between Laura and "Steele" that caps the last of the regular-series shows (a string of post-series episodes followed) is coded by several textual markers as a false wedding — not as the proper resolution to a romantic comedy. First, Laura is not

the originally intended bride. Instead, "Steele" had planned to pay a prosti-́
tute to marry him. This casual substitution of Laura in the prostitute's role
reinscribes the idea that women are interchangeable commodities.[98] Second,
when Laura marries "Steele," she is covered with mud. Though Laura's
disheveled appearance represents her professional life (she has become bedrag-
gled while subduing a suspected criminal), it also symbolizes that her marriage to "Steele" is not truly legitimate, that it is marred by the circumstances
that have led to it. Finally, the wedding is the culmination of a madcap chase
in which the couple only escape a dogged INS agent by leaping aboard a
fishing-boat and persuading a fish cleaner masquerading as the captain to
"marry" them at sea, which he does in Spanish — a language foreign to both
Laura and the jewel thief. The fact that the language of the wedding is not
the language of the bride and groom symbolically undercuts the already tenuous legality of the proceedings.[99]

Laura's wedding to the jewel thief can apparently only be legitimized
when it is reconstructed as an exchange between men. In the first of a series
of three television movies that promise to resolve the series, the narrative
drags in an entirely new character — Tony Roselli (Jack Scalia) — who interrupts Laura's and the jewel thief's honeymoon-for-immigration-purposes
and promptly establishes himself as a serious rival to Steele in Laura's
affections.

It is no accident that Laura and the jewel thief's honeymoon (and
Laura's flirtation with her new love interest) takes place in Mexico. *Remington Steele* frames Mexico as a place that is radically Other — a place that
encourages sexual abandon in normally staid women, specifically in Laura.
In an early episode, we learn that Laura has had a wild time at a convention in Acapulco several years earlier, so wild a time that when the same
conventioneers run into her later while she is working on a case, they chase
her around screaming "Acapulco."[100]

It is particularly interesting that Laura's new love interest, Roselli, who
first appears as a jungle guide in the wilds of Mexico, where Laura and the
jewel thief are spending their false honeymoon, is explicitly modeled after
the Michael Douglas character (Jack Colton) in the film *Romancing the
Stone* (Robert Zemeckis, 1984).[101] The jewel thief takes one look at the
interloper and makes *Romancing the Stone* his movie reference for the
episode, a rather uncharacteristic choice, considering that the jewel thief
usually refers only to classic films; it is an appropriate *thematic* choice,
however, in that the narrative of *Romancing the Stone* concerns a female
romance writer who encounters a real-life embodiment of her literary creation who (like the jewel thief) proves difficult for his creator to control.[102]

The struggle for Laura's affections continues through all of the television movies that resolve the series. Like the jewel thief, the stranger proves not to be what he first appears to be either—he is a government agent in trouble with his own agency, and he collaborates with Laura and the jewel thief for his own ends. Interestingly, his friendship with "Steele" grows as he romances Laura—their bonding does indeed seem predicated on affection for (and the prospect of exchanging) the same woman.

Laura's final consummation of her relationship with the jewel thief is marked as dependent on her rejection of the government agent as a romantic prospect. This is made explicit in two scenes in the final television movie: First, Roselli makes an overt romantic proposition to Laura, to which she replies that although she might have taken him up on it several years earlier, her heart now belongs to the jewel thief, with whom she has worked hard to build a trusting relationship. This is the first time that Laura has made a direct statement that she has officially chosen the jewel thief as her sole romantic partner. This implies that Laura (and, by implication, women in general) cannot "choose" a romantic partner—or be chosen by one—in a social vacuum, but that the choice of one partner must be a conscious selection of one partner *over another*. (We see exactly the same dynamic at work in the episodes of *Moonlighting* in which Maddie chooses to sleep with David only *after* she has slept with and rejected her old boyfriend Sam Crawford (Mark Harmon), who—like Roselli—is not a regular series character and appears to have been brought in for the sole purpose of providing David with romantic competition.)[103]

Second, after Laura and the jewel thief have decided to finally consummate their relationship and he is blithely carrying her upstairs to bed, the phone rings and she answers it. It is Roselli. After briefly reiterating her rejection of him, Laura hangs up and she and the jewel thief proceed upstairs, ignoring the phone as it starts to ring again. As they reach the top of the stairs, the camera cuts to a shot of their bedroom window with the lights on, then off. Then the camera slowly draws back from the darkened window to include a shot of the whole castle. This is the last shot of the entire series. So far, this could be the ending to any one of a number of romantic comedies that use metonymic references to signify sexual consummation, from the falling blanket ("the walls of Jericho") in *It Happened One Night* to the drawn bed curtains of *Adam's Rib* to Asta's paws covering his eyes at the end of *The Thin Man*.[104] Over this traditional image track, however, the grating sound of the perpetually ringing phone continues (the castle apparently lacks an answering machine), robbing the scene of its romantic aura and giving it instead a jarring, discordant tone.

That tone reflects the sexual politics of the scene: it seems that the union between the jewel thief and Laura can only be maintained through a continual reminder that she is a potential object of exchange between men.

Mixed Messages for Troubled Times: In sum, *Remington Steele* sends mixed messages to its female spectators about the role that feminism should play in their professional and personal lives. On the one hand, the program acknowledges the existence of sexism and suggests that, in an ideal world, women should not face job discrimination. On the other hand, the program's "solution" to the problem of gender discrimination is that women perform men's jobs without taking credit for their work, thus essentially upholding the *status quo*. In terms of women's sexual desires, the program implies that while "nice girls do," they *don't* (have sex with men they desire) until they have undergone an exhaustive process of examining themselves and their prospective partners, and until they have been properly "won" in response to a challenge from another man.

I would argue that these mixed messages are a direct result of the conflicting attitudes about women's work and women's sexuality prevalent in the eighties. The mass culture of the eighties in general punished working women with the myth of the superwoman who obsessively got all of her professional work, housecleaning, and childrearing done with no outside assistance.[105] While Laura is unburdened with children, the culture of *Remington Steele* uses a similar tactic of portraying Laura as misguided in her extreme devotion to her work. While the sex-positive rhetoric born of the Sexual Revolution still circulated, the rise of the AIDS threat meant that the freewheeling sexuality of the seventies was now in disrepute, and women *were* encouraged to check out the background of prospective partners (though perhaps not quite so thoroughly as Laura checks out the jewel thief's background). Thus, *Remington Steele* reflects the ambivalent attitudes of its era.

AN APPARENT EXCEPTION TO THE RULE: *MURDER, SHE WROTE*

Ironically, the innocuous-looking little-old-lady mystery-writing sleuth Jessica Fletcher (Angela Lansbury) of *Murder, She Wrote* (1984–1996) has had much greater success than younger, flashier investigators. The program was a huge ratings success for over a decade, often placing in the top 10. Interestingly enough, according to *TV Guide*, *Murder, She Wrote* even drove the seemingly indomitable *Moonlighting* off the air in 1989, when the two programs were scheduled opposite each other.[106]

Plots on *Murder, She Wrote* follow a relatively simple formula: A murder occurs and the police accuse an innocent person (usually an acquaintance of Jessica's) of the crime. Jessica Fletcher hobnobs with the suspects, remembers a telltale piece of evidence, and rushes off to confront her suspect in a deserted place. The suspect confesses, but then attempts to flee or to harm Jessica. Fortunately, Jessica always has an ally in hiding for just such contingencies. The true murderer is captured and the innocent suspect is freed; justice prevails.

In many ways, the program grants Jessica impressive investigative authority: She is always correct in her final accusation (even if she is temporarily misled during the course of an investigation), and she always succeeds in bringing the murderer to justice. We might expect this in a program whose title explicitly constructs Jessica as an author in control of "murder." We might also expect this in a program in which the female lead actress has a great deal of authority herself. [As a result of Angela Lansbury's threat to leave the show (she was getting bored with the role), she was made executive producer of the show and therefore presumably obtained extensive script-control.] Furthermore, *Murder, She Wrote*'s consistently high ratings protected the program from the kind of network tampering to which less successful programs are subjected.

Because of its ratings success, then, the show was not subject to the same kinds of outside social and economic pressures that molded the development of concurrent shows (particularly *Cagney and Lacey*, discussed below). It is worth speculating, however, on the causes of *Murder, She Wrote*'s success, in order to determine why the image of Jessica Fletcher was appealing to a large, diverse audience of viewers. Some might suggest that *Murder, She Wrote*'s scheduled airtime after the high-rated *60 Minutes* practically guaranteed the program a large audience. If this were true, though, what made Jessica easy for the older, largely *male* audience of *60 Minutes* to identify with?

First of all, Jessica is coded as not-female through the fact that she herself neither fits the description of the typical object of masculine desire nor expresses any sexual desire herself. She is a post-menopausal celibate woman, although she has several close male friends and the occasional mildly-flirtatious admirer.[107] The widowed Jessica, however, does not flirt much herself, and thus becomes a comfortable locus of identification for men in that identification with her does not entangle the spectator in uncomfortable trajectories of desire.[108] Furthermore, she upholds the banner of patriarchy by her unquestionable devotion to the memory of her late husband, Frank. Finally, Jessica is kept from being typed as a monstrous virago, as many powerful older women on television are,[109] both by the desexualization noted above and by her construction as helpless in that still pre-eminently masculine arena: transportation. When asked during a 1994 television interview about similarities between herself and the character she played, Angela Lansbury conceded that while she and Jessica Fletcher were similar in many respects, she really wished that Jessica would learn to drive.[110]

That's right, Jessica, the consummate author who controls the destinies of many men, never operates a motor vehicle.[111] Although she rides a bicycle and jogs, these low-tech means of transportation are quite unsuited to the pursuit of criminals, so Jessica is reduced to catching rides with others (usually men) when she wants to confront a suspect. This lack of independence concerning transportation means that Jessica is never really *alone* when she elicits a confession from a murderer, and thus she is never solely responsible for the murderer's capture. While the show gives Jessica full credit for her intellectual prowess, it defines the *enforcement* of Law as men's province, and thus circumscribes her work firmly within an already-existing patriarchal bureaucracy. Although *Murder, She Wrote* does not portray the forces of law enforcement as monolithically well-meaning and all-powerful (quite the opposite, in fact, as Jessica bests many a self-satisfied, misguided police officer), the show never questions the machinery of law enforcement itself, only the judgment of individuals operating within the system. An episode about Jessica operating as a private detective completely outside the reach of patriarchal Law would be an unthinkable concept.

A 2003 TV-movie[112] shows that Jessica has still made no progress in her quest for transportational independence. She still cannot drive and is forced to get rides with others, which presents some hazards. At one point, the car in which she rides gets run off the road. In another crisis, Jessica is forced to flag down and hitch a ride with a total stranger in order to get to the scene of a buried treasure.

CAGNEY AND LACEY: WOMAN-TO-WOMAN DETECTIVE WORK

Other than *Charlie's Angels*, the only commercially successful program to focus on an all-female investigating team has been *Cagney and Lacey* (1982–1988). The show follows Chris Cagney (Sharon Gless) and Mary Beth Lacey (Tyne Daly), a pair of New York City female police detectives. The gender of the series' detectives was no accident: sparked by Molly Haskell's contention in her classic '70s feminist film critique, *From Reverence to Rape: The Treatment of Women in the Movies*, that the wave of '70s "buddy movies" did not include women, writing partners Barbara Avedon and Barbara Corday and producer Barney Rosenzweig set out to make a female "buddy movie" of their own.[113] The script of that movie, written in 1974, endured years of indifference from Hollywood studios; but the story eventually made it onto the small screen in a smash-hit 1981 TV-movie, which was then transformed into a regular television series.[114] Despite good ratings and high popularity among women, the television show was soon canceled by network executives, and only made it back on the air due to a massive letter-writing campaign (ten times the size of the most recent recall letter-writing campaign) by women viewers, due to the fact that *Cagney and Lacey reruns* over the summer placed number 1 in the ratings, and due to the fact that Tyne Daly won an Emmy that fall for her portrayal of Mary Beth Lacey.[115]

Since Julie D'Acci's comprehensive work *Defining Women: Television and the Case of Cagney and Lacey* (a work inspired by the politics of the rocky broadcast history of the program) provides readers with a complete history and feminist critique of the program, I will make only selected remarks about it here. First, D'Acci notes that the program's content, while at first overtly feminist, was deliberately softened over the years in order to broaden the show's appeal.[116] This phenomenon was emblematic of a larger trend in which the trajectories of many other programs of the '80s and early '90s that initially featured strong women characters "softened" or "feminized" these characters in some way, usually by subjecting them to pregnancy and/or marriage. Consider the following: Murphy Brown on the eponymous show (who gets pregnant accidentally and bears a son when she wants a daughter),[117] Rebecca Howe on *Cheers* (who goes from being portrayed as a fiercely competitive businesswoman to being portrayed as a man-crazy incompetent), policewoman Jackie on *Roseanne* (who gets pregnant accidentally and finally agrees to marry the baby's father, whom she does not love),[118] Molly Dodd on *The Days and Nights of Molly Dodd* (who gets pregnant accidentally and gets engaged to the baby's father), and teenage intellectual Andrea on *Beverly Hills, 90210* (who gets pregnant accidentally and — going against her initial instinct to have an abortion — marries the baby's father).

Second, the prospect of female partnership sent CBS executives into a tizzy of homophobia. Ironically, the very "buddy" relationship on which Avedon and Corday had based their entire concept of the tv-movie and television series was the aspect of the program that worried the network, as the network became frightened that viewers might think Cagney and Lacey were partners inside the bedroom as well as on the street. Network brass replaced the first-season Cagney (Meg Foster) with blond actress Sharon Gless because they thought Foster "came across ... as being masculine." A CBS executive told *TV Guide* that Cagney and Lacey "were too harshly women's lib.... We perceived them as dykes."[119] I find it fascinating that the whole idea of Cagney and Lacey being lesbians[120] was so upsetting to network executives regardless of how well the show was doing in the ratings. The fact that *women* loved the show apparently had little sway with them; it seems like they were instead genuinely worried that *men* might be upset by the portrayal of two independent women who didn't fit neatly into traditional media patterns of desire.[121] Although *Charlie's Angels* might have seemed to pose a similar threat to male viewers (in a reverse of the *Bonanza* rule, no Angel's boyfriend lasted more than an episode unless the Angel in question was going to retire), as I have argued above, these male viewers could easily disavow the picture of self-sufficient female friendship by concentrating on the Angels as objects of desire. But *Cagney and Lacey* offered male viewers no such out. The two detectives dressed for the most part in comfortable working women's clothes — I can't say I personally recall any episodes with wet t-shirts or bikinis[122] — and were women in their early forties — not traditional television objects of desire as Charlie's Angels were.[123]

Moreover, in a series of mid–1990s reunion movies Cagney and Lacey are allowed a rare privilege for female characters on television: aging. Stars Gless and Daly "jokingly refer to the [first of these movies] as *Cagney and Lacey: The Menopause Years.*"[124]

The Late '80s and Early '90s

After *Cagney and Lacey's* progressive vision, opportunities for the presentation of strong female detectives on television sadly declined. Detective Dee Dee McCall (Stepfanie Kramer) partnered with her big hunk of testosterone of a partner Hunter (Fred Dryer) on the action police drama *Hunter*, is hardly a feminist icon. A typical plot might include McCall getting raped, then clinging to Hunter for reassurance. He tracks down the rapist and cheers her up.

In another episode, entitled "Requiem for Sgt. McCall," we learn that McCall's late husband was a police sergeant who was shot by a hit man claiming self-defense when he got too close to the truth on a murder investigation. In classic female detective tradition, McCall sets out to clear her true love's name. In light of my earlier remarks about women and violence, it *is* remarkable that McCall actually punches the paroled hit man full in the face when he taunts her in public. The reaction of the narrative to her aggressive behavior is, however, no surprise: her superiors order McCall to back off and blame her for the result of her actions.

When she complains to her boss that he has tied her hands, he replies, "You tied your *own* hands, McCall, when you hit that guy in the chops." When McCall is later framed for the hit man's murder, she is suspended from active duty. Now, *Hunter* often relies on the right-wing late '80s premise that a bad legal system keeps good cops from catching criminals because it insists too much on trivia like suspects' rights. So actually, there are many episodes of the show in which Hunter, McCall, or both find that they are asked to stop their investigations because they're accused (falsely, of course) of trampling on a bad guy's rights like Dirty Harry. What's interesting is that when it's McCall, as in this case, she really *does* stop investigating. Instead, Hunter discovers who the murderer is and where there's going to be a showdown, then picks up McCall so she can see the dénouement. Although McCall tries to stop the murderer from killing again by drawing her gun, the murderer (a rich young woman) is unimpressed and refuses to drop her weapon until the Real Cop (and Legitimate possessor of the Phallus), Hunter, pulls out *his* gun. In the epilogue, even though she didn't actually solve the case, a proud McCall beams as her husband receives a posthumous citation of valor and says that the most important thing is that *his* reputation is finally cleared (never mind the fact that they've finally solved a woman's murder).

Significantly, McCall's character leaves the force to get married — shades of Emma Peel. Her replacement, Joanne Molenski (Darlene Fluegel), is killed off three months later, leaving Hunter to hunt alone, untrammeled by female assistance.

Two made-for-television movies in the 2000s updated the series, but not the dynamics between Hunter and McCall. In *Hunter: Return to Justice* (NBC, airing 11/16/02), McCall is engaged to someone else (who conveniently dies so that she can team up with Hunter again). McCall has been assigned to the pink-collar ghetto of the Juvenile Division in her local police department. McCall gets kidnapped and used as a hostage. When McCall is attacked, Hunter pushes her down and saves her. In contrast, when Hunter himself is attacked, he kills both the gunman and his accomplice.

In *Hunter: Back in Force* (NBC, airing 4/12/03), McCall and Hunter work together as a team again. While Hunter captures four armed bank robbers using only his service revolver, it takes two female cops (including McCall) to arrest one male prison guard. Hunter punches, shoots, and kills people in this narrative, while McCall spends her time getting leered at by the guard she later needs help arresting.

Also notable is the treatment of another female police officer in this made-for-television movie. When an anonymous female cop spots a suspect and attempts to disarm him by brandishing a gun, she is stabbed in the back for her trouble. For picking up the phallus, she is punished by the penetration of the knife, a symbolic rape that serves as retribution for her challenge to the patriarchal order.

The late 1980s also offered viewers a young African American female investigator, Officer Judy Hoffs (Holly Robinson), on *21 Jump Street*, a show about a multiracial group of police detectives in their early twenties who routinely went undercover as high school and college students to solve campus crimes. The sexual politics of the show were reminiscent of the early seventies. As the lone female detective in the group, Holly is shown performing a disproportionate amount of caregiving to troubled teens. She is required to do a disproportionate amount of decoy work as well. One particular episode could be straight out of *Police Woman* except that it doesn't require Holly to dress like a slut: In a classic "woman-in-jeopardy" role, Holly goes undercover in a wheelchair to catch a rapist who preys on disabled co-eds. Unable to get him to attack her on land, she lures him to a deserted gym by taking a moonlight swim. Both *Hunter* and *21 Jump Street* use their female detectives disproportionately in decoy roles, perhaps reflecting the late-eighties/early-nineties anti-feminist backlash.

PROGRESSIVE VISIONS? *PRIME SUSPECT* AND *UNDER SUSPICION*

In the 1990s, it became permissible to mention sexism again, at least on PBS, which didn't have many sponsors to worry about offending. The BBC television mini-series *Prime Suspect* and its sequels show Detective Chief Inspector Jane Tennison (Helen Mirren) openly battling the entrenched sexism of the old boy network in the London police department, even to the point of resigning at one point when she is unfairly passed over for promotion. *Prime Suspect* (airing in America on PBS in the early-to-mid–1990s), which was based on the experiences of a real-life female Detective Chief Inspector,[125] opens with DCI Jane Tennison begging her boss to be assigned to a murder case in her new precinct, since she finds herself shut out of the case-assignment loop. Like *Cagney and Lacey* and *The X-Files*, the *Prime Suspect* series have been exhaustively analyzed from a feminist perspective. The general consensus is that, while acknowledging the realities of sexism, the series suggests that the only solution for feminists is to incorporate themselves within the mechanisms of patriarchy.[126]

The wild success of the *Prime Suspect* series in America inspired a short-lived copycat commercial network program set in the states. *Under Suspicion* (1994–1995) featured a young female police detective who faced distrust, resentment, and even open insubordination from her male colleagues on account of her gender. Yet the show's acknowledgment of the existence of sexism, its portrayal of her and of women in general, was not particularly feminist, or even ideologically neutral. In the premiere episode, when she is assigned to handle the "woman problem" of a uniformed female officer who accuses her partner of sexual harassment, our heroine follows the duo to a coffee shop, where a nosy waitress tells her without any urging that they had been having an affair. Armed with the knowledge that the female officer has been using the harassment complaint to get a transfer away from her male partner, our heroine confronts the pair, informs them that their punishment for having concealed the truth is that they must continue to work together, and threatens them both with a worse fate if the female officer doesn't immediately drop the harassment charges. She parlays her success in "resolving" this problem into a plum assignment investigating the disappearance of her former partner/mentor. The messages to viewers: A. Women lie about sexual harassment. B. There is no solidarity among women; they just use each other and men to get ahead. Significantly, our heroine has no female friends; rather, her only focus is her missing partner, a married man whom she nevertheless idolizes in much the same way that Dee Dee McCall idolizes her dead husband. Like McCall, her first priority is also to clear a man's name. We see, then, that the fact that a program acknowledges sexism is no guarantee that it eschews patriarchal generic conventions.

THE X-FILES: PLAYING WITH GENDER ROLES?

The popular series *The X-Files* (1993–2002) is more science fiction than mystery series,[127] and has garnered quite a bit of academic attention already. Because it has been so thoroughly studied by others[128] (it is apparently popular among academics), I will touch only upon a few salient points and will examine fan responses to the series as a barometer of the expectations of the 1990s audience.

The *X-Files* represents male and female ways of knowing in an interesting way. FBI agents Dana Scully (Gillian Anderson) and Fox Mulder (David Duchovny) investigate weird phenomena. One's a scientifically-inclined skeptic and one believes firmly in the supernatural. The "catch" is that the *female* partner Scully is the skeptic, while the *male* partner Mulder is the "true believer." At first glance, *The X-Files* might seem to be progressive in assigning "the rational approach" to the female detective and "the intuitive approach" to the male detective, since Western culture usually assigns these roles in the opposite way, and since Western culture usually privileges the (masculine) rational, scientific approach. Since Mulder is eventually right in his intuitive suspicions on a regular basis, however, the seemingly progressive *X-Files* is similarly privileging masculine knowledge over feminine knowledge.[129]

Viewers' responses to the show are quite interesting on this point.[130] An examination of conversations in mid–October 1994 on the Internet newsgroup alt.tv.x-files, a forum for fans of the show, demonstrates that viewers are quite savvy about the politics of knowledge. One conversation thread complains that Scully's character has been gradually backing away from her scientific skepticism by not challenging Mulder more after his supernatural explanations of strange events and by not asking more challenging questions herself after witnessing "all sorts of weird shit." Although it is distressing that the show's writers seem to make Scully lose her intellectual edge, it is heartening to see aware viewers lamenting that fact.[131] Furthermore, it is obvious that many male fans of the show admire Scully for her mind: GA is IDDG! (Gillian Anderson is Intellectually Drop Dead Gorgeous!) was a common closing remark on articles in the newsgroup.[132]

In later seasons of the series, some disturbing anti-feminist trends appear. In addition to playing damsel in distress in more commonplace situations, Scully also gets kidnapped by aliens, is implanted with a device related to alien procreation, and battles cancer.[133] Her eggs are also stolen by the government, which produces a genetically-engineered girl who is Scully's biological daughter.[134] She is also impregnated with a part-alien baby by a conspiracy and is forced to put the baby up for adoption.[135]

While the spectators of the *X-Files* writing on the internet may not represent the entire television viewing audience,[136] their aware spectatorship indicates that there is a complex relationship between narrative and audience response. Their perceptive comments may indicate that some theories of spectatorship give spectators — both male and female — too little credit for being able to examine what they see critically.

VIP: A PASTICHE OF THE NEW MILLENNIUM

Like *Charlie's Angels*, *VIP* (1998–2002) appeals to multiple audiences on many levels. Women can identify with several strong female protagonists,[137] while men can fetishize the scantily-clad bodies of these same protagonists. *VIP* plays as a pastiche of earlier detective shows: The sisterhood and the flirty fashions recall *Charlie's Angels*. The fashion focus also recalls *The Avengers*. The imposter pretending to be a world-famous detective recalls *Remington Steele*. The campy humor of the show often recalls the classic 1960s series *Batman*. The ensemble cast of four white women and two men of color recalls racially-mixed ensemble shows, like *The Mod Squad* and *21 Jump Street*.

Despite the fact that all the female leads are strong characters, they are each undercut in their own ways. Like the women of *Charlie's Angels*, the women (and men) of *VIP* remain single. Like the women of *Charlie's Angels* and the men of *Bonanza*, they have a habit of falling for people who are unavailable/unsuitable.

The women of *VIP* are all types: There is the cute computer nerd Kay Simmons (Leah Lail), the tough ex–KGB agent Tasha Dexter (Molly Culver), the Mafia princess Nikki Franco (Natalie Raitano), the flaky fashionista California girl Vallery Irons (Pamela Anderson), and her fashionista sidekick Maxine Delacruz (Angelle Brooks).

All are capable and competent in their respective fields — computer technology, combat, pyrotechnics and cars, and fashion. Yet the series undercuts their abilities on a regular basis. Tasha, the most physically competent of the women, takes the brunt of the undercutting — the series seems to delight in humiliating her. Tough girl Tasha gets "feminized" on a fairly regular basis: she gets trapped with Val and is forced to wear Val's ultra-femme clothing; she gets brainwashed and develops an interest in women-centered television; she gets injected with truth serum and winds up telling Val with a giggle that Val has really nice hair. Nikki, the second-toughest female character, also gets undercut, in her case mainly by her juvenile flirting with fellow VIP employee Johnny Loh (Dustin Nguyen). In contrast, Val, the most femme of the *VIP* women, has a success rate against villains that is completely unmerited by her skills or brains, and is presented as the "real" heroine of *VIP*. One episode even goes so far as to show how the entire detective agency breaks up when she is away.

The success of *VIP* with both men and women, I would postulate, is due to its *Charlie's Angels*-like ability to combine jiggle with a community of strong female characters.

* * *

The universality of the flaws of the female detective over the decades is striking. It's not that there are no male detectives in an anti-hero role — Jim Rockford of the *Rockford Files* comes to mind — but rather that there are no female detectives in a super-competent role. We have yet to see a female detective on television as competent as Peter Falk's *Columbo*, who despite his feigned incompetence is always one step ahead of the bad guys, never fooled, and never beaten.[138]

• 4 •

Why Female Investigators in Hollywood Film Are Intrinsically Mad

Female investigators in film are insane. They are called "nuts," "cranks," "wacky," "obsessed," "paranoid," "highly neurotic," "hysterical," "demented," "unbalanced," "screwy," "dizzy," "dotty," "peculiar," "strange," "eccentric," "crazy," and "mad" by other characters within the diegesis of the films in which they appear, by the narrative structure of these films, and by critics analyzing these films. This paradigm differs from those I have discussed in my consideration of how the female investigator is portrayed in the gothic novel, in the lesbian detective novel, and on television. What is it specifically about the medium of film — as opposed to print or television — that encourages this association of female investigation with madness?

I demonstrate below that the spectator's relationship to the cinematic apparatus and the way in which Hollywood's cinematic codes have become inflected with sexual difference combine to make the position of a female investigator in Hollywood film structurally untenable. This disjunction between the female investigator's role and the structure within which she is placed produces a collision of codes in the cinematic text, eliciting the symptom of madness.

Detection and Spectatorship

In *The Imaginary Signifier*, Christian Metz asserts that the film spectator's "primary cinematic identification" is with the cinematic apparatus — the camera as it represents the spectator's own look — and only secondarily (by association) with characters within the film.[1] My claim is that because the position of a detective or investigative protagonist in film is very similar to the position of the cinematic apparatus, the spectator forms a deep (almost primary) identification with an investigative protagonist — a stronger identification than the normal secondary identification the spectator would form with another type of protagonist.

There are several similarities between the functions of the cinematic apparatus and the investigative protagonist: 1. The function of both camera and investigator is specular — both look. 2. The function of both camera and investigator is informative — both uncover information. 3. The function of both camera and investigator is evaluative and interpretive — both interpret images and events through framing — the camera literally; the investigator, metaphorically. 4. Both camera and investigator function as representatives of larger psychic structures — the camera stands in for the Gaze; the investigator stands in for the Gaze and (often) for the Law. 5. The function of both camera and investigator has been inflected by sexual difference — both typically privilege a formulation in which there is a male viewing/investigating subject and a female viewed/investigated object.

How might these similarities between the cinematic apparatus and the figure of the investigator affect the cinematic spectator's identificatory relationship with an investigative protagonist? I postulate that all investigators in film — by the very nature of their position — act as relays between spectator and apparatus. Metz has pointed out that certain characters (even characters paradoxically off screen) within a film's diegesis may act as "relays" between the apparatus and the spectator, promoting identification between the spectator's look and the specular functions of the apparatus.[2] It is logical to extrapolate from Metz's argument that the effectiveness of different characters as relays of this sort should be directly dependent on their relationship to the Gaze. Those characters accorded the most privilege in looking relations serve as the most effective relays between spectator and apparatus, while those characters accorded the least privilege in looking relations serve as the least effective relays.[3]

We can see that the investigator ought to hold a special, privileged position as a particularly effective relay between spectator and apparatus as opposed to the protagonists of other film genres. The protagonist of the average musical, western, romantic comedy, or melodrama is likely to be at least partially aligned with spectacle and visual meaning instead of with authoritative vision.[4] In contrast, investigative protagonists, almost by definition, have a privileged position in looking relations. The investigator's function is not only to see facts that are hidden, but also to change the way other characters (and the spectators) see those facts — to make them look like what they really are. This "creative" visual power — this ability to guide others' vision into a particular channel — endows the investigator with a control exactly analogous to the control that the apparatus exerts upon the spectators.

I have framed the theory above in gender-neutral language, yet it is generally acknowledged that gender has a strong influence on looking relations in film. Does gender affect this paradigm? Yes, very much so: Indeed, the influence of gender on cinematic codes and on individual spectators' relationship to the apparatus is directly responsible for the insistent cinematic trope of the mad female investigator.

In her influential article, "Visual Pleasure and Narrative Cinema," Laura Mulvey notes, "In a world ordered by sexual imbalance, pleasure in looking has been split between active/male and passive/female."[5] This sexual difference in spectatorship inflects the camera/investigator equation thus: If cinematic codes promote male spectatorial pleasure[6] by identification with the camera through a relay with a visually-privileged character, and if the investigator is a particularly important locus of such relays, then it is vital for the male spectator to identify with the investigator to ensure that he gains the greatest possible pleasure in looking.

The success of this identificatory relay will be helped or hindered by the gender of the investigator on screen: If the investigator is male, this identification between spectator and relaying character should proceed smoothly, especially since investigation — like spectatorship — has been coded as a masculine activity. If the investigator is female, however, this identification might require a more complex negotiation between spectator, character, and camera, since both spectatorship and investigation are emphatically coded as not-feminine activities.[7]

Spectatorship and investigation have been coded as "not-feminine" activities because the object to be looked at/investigated in these activities is traditionally female, while the spectator/investigator is traditionally male. Such firmly entrenched cultural coding may be difficult for spectators to overcome: If the male spectator has been conditioned to be looking *at* a female character on-screen, it may be difficult for him to make the transition to looking *with* a female character when the narrative requires it.[8] Similarly, it may be difficult for the male spectator to make the transition from looking *with* a male protagonist at a transgressive female object[9] to looking *at* the male object of a female character's gaze/investigation.

Being forced into such new ways of looking may cause the male spectator unpleasure — a problem for a Hollywood film. Only limited amounts of spectatorial unpleasure are allowable in Hollywood film, as opposed to avant-garde film, which often seeks to permanently unsettle spectators. Whereas avant-garde film often seeks permanently to disrupt familiar ways of looking, Hollywood film — conservative in the extreme — seeks ultimately to reestablish familiar visual codes. Although some amount of spectatorial unpleasure can be a desirable goal of a Hollywood film (e.g., to produce a sense of tension or anticipation in the spectator), this spectatorial unpleasure is only desirable as far as it can eventually be resolved; the tension produced by an element of unpleasure must in some way be released. As long as spectators are given some outlet by which they may disavow the elements of the enunciation that cause them unpleasure, though, the dictates of Hollywood film will be satisfied.

To allay spectatorial unpleasure, the enunciation of Hollywood film has evolved a number of strategies. Chief among these is the cinematic trope of madness — a state which allows otherwise contradictory elements to coexist. Madness allows the simultaneous acknowledgement of and disavowal of elements in the enunciation that might cause the spectator unpleasure.

Since female investigators in film pose an intrinsic structural problem for a male-focused enunciation, we should not be surprised to find that the trope of madness follows close on the heels of any appearance of a female investigator. Madness is the logical enunciatory response to a subgenre requiring female characters to fill a structural position that has been over-determined as masculine.

The enunciation *must* respond to the challenge of the gazing, thinking, ordering, acting female protagonist — Mary Ann Doane notes: "The intellectual woman looks and analyzes, and in usurping the gaze she poses a threat to an entire system of representation. It is as if the woman had forcefully moved to the other side of the specular."[10] It is this "threat to an entire system of representation" that evokes the omnipresent intimations of madness that dog the female investigator on film. Indeed, Doane has noted that problems of male identification with an investigating female gaze are responsible for the "paranoia" seen in the sub-genre of "the woman's film" she terms "paranoid woman's films."[11] She is quite correct in her observation.[12] My project here will demonstrate that Doane's observation about the cycle of "paranoid woman's films" must be radically extended. My research below demonstrates that almost *every* film featuring a female investigator contains some kind of intimation of madness —

not necessarily paranoia, but some word, identification, gesture, or symbol that evokes the intrinsic madness of the female investigator on film.

The ways and situations in which the trope of madness asserts itself are myriad. This study explores a broad range of them through an examination of several films featuring female detectives: *Coma* demonstrates how the entire structure of a film can be explicitly inflected by the idea of madness, while *The Silence of the Lambs, Hannibal, Copycat, Murder By Numbers*, and *The Avengers* demonstrate how the suspicion of madness can remain unstated (or jokingly stated) and yet be unmistakably implied by other elements of the enunciation. *Blue Steel* demonstrates that the trope of madness appears independently of the gender of the film's director. *Black Widow* and *Goodbye Lover* demonstrate that the trope of madness appears independently of the gender of the investigated villain. *Charlie's Angels* and *Charlie's Angels: Full Throttle* demonstrate that the trope of madness appears independently of the gender of the producer. *Cleopatra Jones, Foxy Brown*, and *Friday Foster* demonstrate that the trope of madness appears independently of the race of the female investigator. *Nancy Drew, Reporter, Smart Blonde, Compromising Positions*, and *Manhattan Murder Mystery* demonstrate that the trope of madness appears independently of the female investigator's marital status. *Murder on a Honeymoon, Murder, She Said*, and *Murder Most Foul* demonstrate that the trope of madness appears independently of whether or not the female investigator is actually constructed as a specularized object of male desire. *A Question of Silence, Dear Detective*, and *A Taxing Woman* demonstrate that the trope of madness appears in foreign films as well as in Hollywood film. *Thriller* demonstrates that the trope of madness appears even in feminist avant-garde films. *Stranger on the Third Floor, Phantom Lady, Insomnia*, and *The Mad Miss Manton* demonstrate how the trope of madness can be metaphorized or displaced. *Fargo* demonstrates that the trope of madness intrudes into films purportedly based upon real-life events. Finally, critics' responses to two gothic films — *Suspicion* and *Secret Beyond the Door* — demonstrate the male spectator's investment in believing that the female investigator is mad.

Coma: *Paranoia as Genre*

The enunciation of *Coma* (Michael Crichton, 1978) casts doubts on its female investigator's sanity at two levels: Within the diegesis, the female investigator, Dr. Susan Wheeler (Genevieve Bujold) is forced to undergo a psychiatric evaluation due to her investigative efforts, and the psychiatrist concludes that she is "rather paranoid and upset." Moreover, the film's entire narrative structure supports the suggestion that Wheeler is neurotic: Dr. Wheeler *incorrectly* suspects a massive conspiracy of illicit transplant-organ harvesters in a case where there proves to be only a single culprit. If her conspiracy theory had been proven correct, the narrative would have reinscribed her authority. Since she is mistaken in her suspicions, however, the film's narrative structure defines her as paranoid.[13]

Jacqueline Rose correctly correlates the suggestion of madness in *Coma*'s enunciation responds with the fact that the traditionally male role of the detective is filled by a woman:

> ... [I]n *Coma* there is a kind of perfecting of the hermeneutic code, the basic code of detection and suspense, but also its inversion because it is a woman who occupies the place normally given to the male protagonist.... [W]hat this releases is a kind of paranoia across the whole space of her investigation as she starts to believe [mistakenly] that everyone is against her. As if there was an excess or danger in the very idea of the woman as detective (the idea that she might actually *look*) which produces its paranoid reversal....[14]

Thus *Coma*'s enunciation undermines the female investigator's authority, so that rather than focusing on what she sees, the film's spectator instead focuses on who sees her.[15] This strategy positions the male spectator willy-nilly to look at her instead of with her, allowing him to disavow her competence. It is logical, given what we have postulated above, that Rose chooses a type of madness — paranoia[16] — to describe this film's enunciatory response to the "problem" of female investigation.

Blue Steel: *The Trope of Madness Is Independent of Gender of the Writer/Director*

What is the source of this enunciatory manipulation that undercuts the mastery of the female investigator? Is it purely a result of sexism on the part of male writers and directors who consciously make films that male audiences will find palatable? Probably not. Indeed, the enunciatory strategies of a great many films that are either scripted or directed by women mirror the enunciatory strategies in films scripted or directed by men. For example, several 1940s Gothics that cast doubt on the sanity of their female investigative protagonists are either scripted by or based on novels by women: *Rebecca* (Alfred Hitchcock, 1940) is co-scripted by Joan Harrison and based on the novel by Daphne du Maurier; *Suspicion* (Alfred

Hitchcock, 1941) is co-scripted by Joan Harrison and Alma Reville (with a third male writer); *Shadow of a Doubt* (Alfred Hitchcock, 1943) is co-scripted by Sally Benson and Alma Reville (with Thornton Wilder); *Phantom Lady* (Robert Siodmak, 1944) has Joan Harrison as associate producer.[17]

A more recent example of this phenomenon, Kathryn Bigelow's 1990 film *Blue Steel*,[18] undercuts the investigative authority of its female protagonist even as it gives a feminist twist to a classic film noir plot. Megan Turner (Jamie Lee Curtis) is a rookie police officer who deftly foils a robbery attempt by shooting an armed man, only to find herself under investigation for murder when a mysterious man steals the robber's gun. The man, aptly named Eugene Hunt (Ron Silver), then starts shooting people with bullets that have Megan's name carved on them, makes her acquaintance, and begins a romance with her. She eventually discovers his deception and finally kills him (after several attempts) when he attacks her.

At first glance, this scenario might seem to put Megan in no worse a position than any male film noir detective who is framed for murder and eventually discovers that his new love interest is responsible for the charges. Yet there is a crucial difference in enunciation between *Blue Steel* and the typical film noir that undercuts Megan Turner's narrative authority: In *Blue Steel*, the spectator knows more than Megan does. In contrast, most films noir of this type limit the spectator's vision and knowledge to roughly the same as that of the male investigator. Of course, camera angles and the like are seldom precisely coincidental with the look of the male investigator,[19] but they are usually close enough so that the spectator is in possession of roughly the same amount of information as he is. But in *Blue Steel*, the spectator knows the murderer's identity from the beginning, while Megan is completely unaware of his identity until he essentially reveals it to her himself. Moreover, Megan has no investigative impulses about Eugene. This implies that — despite her job as enforcer of Law — Megan's role is less that of an investigator than of a horror film victim: the suspense in the film is created by audience uncertainty over what the murderer will do to Megan, rather than any uncertainty over who the murderer is. Thus, the narrative irony of the enunciation aligns spectators at least partly with the murderer, if in no other way than that they are in possession of more information than Megan is, and thus cannot avoid experiencing a certain distance from her character because of their superior knowledge.

The effect would be entirely different if Megan had knowledge superior to that of the spectators, as many male investigators do. Frank Krutnik notes the example of Sam Spade (Humphrey Bogart) in *The Maltese Falcon*, the paradigmatic detective of the tough investigative thriller, whose authoritative masculinity most later film noir protagonists do not so much replicate as suggest and complicate. Krutnik describes a scene in which Spade appears to lose control of his temper during a meeting with criminal Max Gutman. When Spade leaves the building, however, the spectators see that he is smiling to himself, and that their previous interpretation of events was incorrect. Krutnik interprets the effect of Spade's superior knowledge thus:

> The reversal of knowledge here works along the lines of a "gag," for it is a stratagem which reconfirms the mastery of Spade/Bogart by raising and then disavowing the possibility of his defeat, transforming him in a moment from apparent failure to definitive master. The film repeatedly replays such scenes of triumph, serving to validate Spade as a figure of superior knowledge in comparison with the spectator.[20]

Where the enunciation of *The Maltese Falcon* overdetermines Sam Spade's narrative authority by allowing him knowledge superior to the spectator's knowledge, the enunciation of *Blue Steel* undermines Megan Turner's scopic and narrative authority by allowing her knowledge inferior to the spectator's knowledge.

The epistemological dynamics of *Blue Steel* demonstrate that a woman in the director's chair does not guarantee the ability and sanity of the female investigator onscreen. Which factor is decisive, then, in determining that a female investigator will be portrayed as mad? Could the problem be related to the fact that the female investigator in film is usually investigating within the confines of heterosexual desire, that she is investigating men? If male protagonists in Hollywood films — even non-detective films — are often granted a privileged role in relation to vision due to their alignment with the camera as desiring subjects, then we might read them as being in some way constructed by Hollywood codes as "natural" investigators, particularly "natural" investigators of women. If women — the "unnatural" investigators — investigate men — the "natural" investigators, then it might not surprise us to see the female investigator's role complicated by the fact that her intended prey has looked back at her, has turned her own weapon of vision against her, and that under this unexpected scrutiny she appears mad. Obviously, this dynamic seems to operate in *Blue Steel*. An examination of the slightly earlier film *Black Widow* demonstrates, however, that female investigators on film can be just as vulnerable to intimations of madness when they are imbricated in a web of homosexual desire as when they are in the more-often-seen context of heterosexual desire.

Black Widow *and* Goodbye Lover: *The Trope of Madness Is Independent of the Gender of the Culprit*

Like *Blue Steel*, *Black Widow* (Bob Rafelson, 1987) might be read as a feminist inversion of a film noir plot: an investigator suspects a beautiful woman of murdering her husband for money and sets out to catch her, then becomes emotionally involved with her and faces danger due to that involvement. The catch is that the investigator here is female, presenting spectators with the rarely seen case of a female investigator tracking a female villain.

This female investigator trapped in a masculine plot is given an androgynous name: Alex Barnes. The androgynous quality of Alex's name presumably allows male spectators to identify with her as an investigative protagonist more easily than if she were saddled with a distinctively feminine name. Carol Clover notes that the "final girl" in horror films — the investigative female protagonist with whom the male spectators will eventually come to identify — is commonly given an androgynous name.[21] As Tania Modleski has pointed out in a discussion of *Notorious*, the name "Alex" can also be broken down into A-lex, outside/without the Law.[22] While such a name might seem to be a misnomer for protagonist Alex Barnes, who is employed by the Justice Department and later works with the Hawaiian police, it is in fact appropriate: Alex quits her Justice Department job to pursue her own investigation, thus breaking with the Law as an organized policing system (and following in the footsteps of many male *noir* protagonists); Alex also breaks the "Law of the Father" by not submitting to compulsory heterosexuality.

Accordingly, the sanity of detective Alex Barnes (Debra Winger) is doubted when she exercises her investigative powers. Alex's male boss, angry when she quits her Justice Department job in order to track down suspected serial murderess "Catherine" (Theresa Russell) in Hawaii, grumbles to her, "All I know is that she's obsessed with killing and that you're obsessed with her. What worries me is that you might be as wacky as she is." It is interesting to note that this relatively mild challenge to a female investigator's sanity ("wacky" doesn't have the same force as "paranoid") occurs in response to a situation in which it is specifically a woman's guilt — not a man's — that is being investigated. The investigation of a woman's guilt is less psychically threatening to the male spectator than the investigation of a man's guilt. Thus, it is portrayed as less "crazy" for Alex to investigate a possibly murderous wife than for the women in the Gothic films of the forties to investigate their possibly murderous husbands. Also, unlike a murderous male character who is often constituted as somehow radically other (psychologically female-identified, non-human, etc.) in order to protect the male spectator from unpleasure, the murderous female character can appear as quite a "normal" example of femininity (Catherine is an attractive, pleasant blonde), since she is already coded as other to the male spectator by her sex.

Another way in which the enunciation of *Black Widow* molds the narrative to minimize unpleasure for the male spectator can be seen in the way it handles the problematic of desire. In the typical film noir formulation, the investigator should become romantically involved with the *femme fatale*, perhaps even having sex with her (especially in modern noirs like *Body Heat* that do not have to work within the confines of the Production Code). If that plot were to be followed in *Black Widow*, the female investigator Alex would sleep with Catherine, and the spectator would observe a "lesbian" love scene. Although this might be a source of pleasure for the male spectator in that observing two women making love is a common male fantasy, it might simultaneously be a source of unpleasure for the male spectator in that a lesbianism poses a definite challenge to the current patriarchal order, and to men's privileges under that order.[23] *Black Widow* manipulates this tension to guarantee maximum pleasure for the male spectator by simultaneously suggesting and disavowing a homoerotic relationship between Alex (now masquerading as Jessie, another butch name) and Catherine. On the one hand, the friendship that Jessie strikes up with Catherine involves titillating physical contact: At the scuba class where they meet, Jessie practices mouth-to-mouth resuscitation on Catherine; when they end the friendship as adversaries, Catherine grabs Jessie and kisses her full on the mouth as her parting gesture; when Catherine is caught for her murders, she gazes longingly at Jessie and tells her that their relationship has been more important that any of her relationships with men. Between this homoerotic frame to their relationship, however, the narrative introduces a male love interest for the two women to compete over, thus channeling their mutual attraction onto a suitable male object (in much the way that male homosocial desire is often channeled through competition over a female love object.)[24] This strategy allows the film to bring up the possibility of lesbian desire only to disavow it as abnormal and obsessive.[25] It is no accident that it is exactly at the point when finding Catherine becomes the preeminent project of Alex's life that her boss decides she's "wacky."

But while the film may constitute Alex as "wacky" in her trajectory of desire, it does eventually validate her investigative abilities, although in a rather ambiguous manner. Surprisingly enough, the ending of *Black Widow* initiates a play of knowledge between investigator and spectator similar to that described in the *Maltese Falcon* example above. In a trick ending, the spectator sees events from Catherine's point of view as she is told about her last husband's mysterious death while she was out of town and that the police suspect an obsessed Alex of killing him to throw suspicion on Catherine. Since Catherine has, in fact, framed Alex by planting poison in her apartment, she readily believes this tale, and when Alex is eventually arrested for murder, she goes to visit in her in prison to gloat. There, although she does not say anything to Alex that actually incriminates her, Catherine is suddenly confronted with her supposedly dead husband, still alive, and by a witness to one of her earlier identities. She is now led off to face charges, and we see that Alex has really been working in collaboration with the local police. Although this ending may strike the viewer as unsatisfactory[26] in that Alex's ruse does not directly lead to a confession from Catherine, the stratagem is successful in keeping Catherine from skipping town immediately (her usual modus operandi after a murder) so that she can be arrested. Although the ending doesn't work particularly well as drama, it does serve as an important marker of Alex's investigative power that the film's spectators are not privy to her plan and that they are presumably as surprised as Catherine is when they find out that Alex is most in control of her investigation precisely when she appears to be most unsuccessful at it. Somehow, though, Alex does not gain the same symbolic capital as Sam Spade does by similar ruses that show off his superior knowledge. Perhaps this is because Alex's strategy also works to mitigate male spectatorial discomfort with female investigation by withholding information about her sanity rather than about her emotions. The effect of letting spectators think she has gone mad is quite different than if she had let spectators think she had trouble controlling her temper, as Spade pretends to do. The fact that Alex allows representatives of the law to label her investigations publicly as "obsessive" (reminding the audience of Alex's boss's speculation that she's "wacky") works to reinforce the idea that female investigators are intrinsically at risk for developing unhealthy obsessions, and that it is only a lucky accident that Alex herself both happened to be right in her suspicions and did not degenerate into madness in her attempts to prove them.

Another film that has a female investigator investigating another woman is *Goodbye Lover* (Roland Joffé, 1999). *Goodbye Lover* is a complex tale of murderous double crossing among a group of spouses, lovers, and relatives all after corporate insurance money. At the center of the murders is sexpot Sandra Dunmore (Patricia Arquette), who manages to escape a murder plot aimed at herself and to murder her own way to eight million dollars. Wisecracking detective Rita Pompano (Ellen DeGeneres, in one of her first films after coming out as a lesbian) solves the mystery handily and bravely saves Sandra from a hit man.

At first glance, Rita seems like the perfect, cynical, world-weary, phallic investigator. Yet her madness is implied in her actions: Rita is a "bad cop"—having solved the mystery, instead of acting like a rational, sane police officer and hauling Sandra off to jail, Rita shakes her down for half of the insurance money. Both Rita and Sandra, the film implies, live happily ever after. The fact that instead of staying true to her police officer role, Rita turns criminal herself implies madness.

The film also explicitly calls Rita mad. In a scene that has no diegetic significance (Rita and her superior officer poke around the scene of an unrelated homicide), they start discussing her superior's upcoming tropical vacation. "I don't think men should wear spandex, do you?" Rita opines to her boss. "You are so nuts!" he replies. It is interesting to note that the context of Rita's madness is a discussion of male sexuality, especially as Ellen DeGeneres's own sexuality would have been much in the minds of the contemporary viewing audience.

Charlie's Angels *and* Charlie's Angels: Full Throttle: *The Trope of Madness Is Independent of the Gender of the Producers*

Even when a woman is intimately involved with the making of a film, as Drew Barrymore was as a producer and driving force behind the film *Charlie's Angels* (McG [Joseph McGinty Nichol],[27] 2000), intimations of madness still appear. The film has little to do with the 1970s television series it updates, but is enjoyable taken on its own terms—a coup considering that shooting on the film started without a script in place.[28] Initially, the three Angels are overdetermined as competent. Natalie, a.k.a.

"Nat" (Cameron Diaz), is goofy, but smart, apparently a big winner on the game show *Jeopardy*. Alex (Lucy Liu), is a former astronaut and equestrienne champion. Dylan (Drew Barrymore) is a tough police academy dropout who is shown knocking out her drill instructor.[29] The Angels all prove themselves capable of jumping out of aircraft — sometimes with parachutes, sometimes without. Nat pilots a speedboat. All three are deft fighters, knocking out their opponents — though in one early fight scene, it takes three of them to fight one male opponent (Crispin Glover), and he escapes them in the end. Yet in making the Angels super-competent, the film paradoxically undercuts that same competence. Rather than having realistic fight scenes, several of the Angels' fighting scenes and gymnastic scenes in which they fly through the air (á la *Crouching Tiger, Hidden Dragon*) are so spectacular that it is clear that wires are being used — you can't see the wires, but you know they're there.[30] This puts the Angels' competence into the realm of fantasy, as something unreal, impossible. This is in stark contrast to the *Charlie's Angels* television series, which never had the Angels do any gravity-defying stunts. This lack of realism helps underscore the point that the Angels aren't really that competent.

The Angels are also poor investigators. Hired by Vivian Wood (Kelly Lynch) to solve the kidnapping of her boss Eric Knox (Sam Rockwell), purportedly by business competitor Roger Corwin (Tim Curry), the Angels find him easily. When they find him, with ridiculous ease, it does not occur to them that they are being set up. At Knox's insistence, they steal a tracking technology from Corwin that Knox claims is his — but in fact, they've just stolen Corwin's formula for Knox's own use. Moreover, they mistakenly think that Knox is in danger, and set Dylan to guard him. Knox sleeps with her, then reveals his trickery and attempts to kill her. The plot of Angel-falls-in-love-with-the-villain is used occasionally on the television series, but the television Angels are never as roundly fooled as the Angels are here.

The intimation of madness comes at the end of the opening sequence of the film, when Dylan, disguised as an African American man (LL Cool J) in kente-cloth dress, jumps out of a plane dragging a would-be hijacker with her. After they land safely in the the Angels' speedboat and he stops screaming, he stares at her and says, "You crazy bastard!" Dylan calmly removes her mask and corrects him: "I think you mean: 'You crazy bitch!'" Here, the intimation of madness is directly linked to gender and race. Dylan[31] is a crazy white woman, not a crazy black man. But the invocation of black maleness is telling in itself, as American culture also uses the trope of madness in relation to African American men.

An African American man turns the tables on that stereotype in the film's sequel, *Charlie's Angels: Full Throttle* (McG [Joseph McGinty Nichol], 2003), as the new Bosley (Bernie Mac as the foster brother of the "old Bosley" [Bill Murray]) tells the Angels "You all fine, but you crazy." Even before Bosley meets them, however, the film has overdetermined the Angels as mad. After a dramatic rescue in the film's pre-credit opening sequence, one villain explains to a colleague who their adversaries are: "Three crazy beautiful girls!" Moreover, in the film's opening credits, Dylan (still played by Drew Barrymore) wears a t-shirt that says "Lady Insane" in a flashback to Dylan's career as a professional wrestler. As Barrymore also was a producer of this film,[32] and thus presumably had extensive creative control, it is clear that the gender of the producer does not insulate a film from intimations of madness of the female investigator.

Cleopatra Jones, Foxy Brown, *and* Friday Foster: *The Trope of Madness Is Independent of Race*

Race is another factor that doesn't appear to affect accusations of madness much. In the black action film *Cleopatra Jones* (Jack Starrett, 1973), African American Cleopatra "Cleo" Jones (Tamara Dobson) is a glamorous government secret agent who spends her spare time protecting her boyfriend's L.A. drug rehab center from crooked cops and violence from the drug-smuggling gang headed by "Mommy" (a leather-clad Shelley Winters). The film presents Cleo as almost superhumanly competent. Aside from being a martial arts master, Cleo handles cars, dirt bikes, knives, and big guns with ease. Moreover, whenever men dare to question her competence, she is supremely unaffected by self-doubt. When her boyfriend Reuben pleads with her, "Don't make anything worse. This isn't exactly your jurisdiction," Cleo snaps back: "My jurisdiction extends from Ankara, Turkey to Watts Tower, Baby." After Cleo leaves a scene, the camera routinely lingers on the men who stare after her, awestruck at her power. The chief of police sums up their attitude when he gazes at her receding form and asks a subordinate rhetorically, "Do you ever feel inadequate?"

Yet even the superhuman Cleo is relentlessly cut down to size, partly by the obligatory reference to insanity, and partly by the film's plot. The reference to insanity comes when Cleo is at her most phallically competent, driving a black corvette up along the walls of the dry L.A. River basin in a chase scene that looks like it could have come straight out of the Bond films of the early seventies. One of the bad guys chasing Cleo looks at his partner, shakes his head and mutters, "That crazy broad!" Note how the charge of madness is specifically linked to Cleo's femininity by the use of the word "broad."

Furthermore, at the film's climactic moment, Cleo must be rescued from a junked car headed for the shredder — rescued by her two *male* friends, the karate-chopping Johnson brothers. To add insult to injury, the Johnson brothers are only present to rescue Cleo in the first place because they disobeyed her direct order not to follow her to her meeting with "Mommy."

In the black action revenge drama *Foxy Brown* (Jack Hill, 1974), the titular heroine (Pam Grier) infiltrates the prostitution arm of the crime ring responsible for her lover's death. Like *Cleopatra Jones*, this film constructs its heroine as extremely competent in the traditionally-masculine fields of weaponry and transportation — Foxy even pilots a plane. Yet at the moment of Foxy's greatest triumph, the accusation of insanity surfaces. When Foxy presents the female crime ring leader Katherine (Kathryn Loder) with her boyfriend's severed penis, Katherine shrieks, "You're crazy!"

It is intriguing that both films pit their African American female superheroines not against male villains (though some of these are also portrayed in the films), but against female villains. Perhaps a superheroine can only be "super" as compared to a female foil. To allow these female heroines to triumph over male-headed crime rings might suggest that a complete triumph over patriarchy is not far behind. It is also intriguing that the female villains are both white. This might be simply a response to the ubiquitous male black action film trope of showing blacks triumphing over whites, a scenario that was replayed countless times perhaps because it would have been so unthinkable onscreen just a few years before. Or perhaps the trope of the white female villain suggests a new threat to black women: the burgeoning women's liberation movement, blamed then and now for being exclusionary to women of color.

Friday Foster (Arthur Marks, 1975) stars Pam Grier as the eponymous African American heroine, a former fashion model turned investigative journalist[33] who winds up foiling an assassination plot. While Friday is in some ways portrayed as brave and capable (she runs after a man who had previously attacked her, even stealing a hearse to chase him), her mastery is undercut in other ways (she gets arrested for stealing the hearse; even though she lives in L.A., she doesn't own a car, leaving her stuck taking taxis and catching rides with friends in order to get around town). The hearse-stealing incident also leads to an intimation of madness, perhaps predictably ensconced in an exchange between two men. A police detective notes: "Man, the gal's got more balls than brains. She nuts, or what?" The reply from Colt Hawkins (Yaphet Kotto) is "She's just all woman, Lieutenant." In a nutshell, this exchange summarizes the problem of suturing the female investigator into a traditionally male position as a filmic detective protagonist. A woman who takes direct action, daring to chase after a man who has attacked her is, this exchange implies, somehow unwomanly. The police detective implies that courage can only be measured in masculine terms, in terms of "balls." This is an inversion of the the typical castration anxiety crisis leading to fetishization: instead of saying, this woman has been castrated, oh wait, no, she is perfectly whole after all, in this case, one man says, this woman has something she shouldn't have, and another man says, oh no, she doesn't, she's "all woman." The tension between "masculine" action being performed by a "feminine" form is resolved by the accusation of madness — if she's not fitting into her proper gender role, she must be "nuts." The accusation of madness allows suture to take place, and resolves the cognitive dissonance and spectatorial unpleasure Friday's brave actions may cause for male spectators.

Virgins and Matrons: The Trope of Madness in Nancy Drew, Reporter, Smart Blonde, Compromising Positions, *and* Manhattan Murder Mystery

The trope of madness appears whether the female investigator is unmarried or married. In *Nancy Drew, Reporter* (William Clemens, 1939)[34] teen detective Nancy Drew (Bonita Granville) is initially presented as spunky, capable, and competent. The opening and closing titles are superimposed on an image of Nancy typing, emphasizing her mastery of language. Nancy also shows mastery over driving: Nancy hunts down a man who has hit her car in an exciting high-speed car chase and successfully catches him, then demands payment for repairing her damaged fender. When she is searching for crucial evidence, she quickly finds the tin she seeks and escapes from a villain who chases her.

Nancy is not above a few mischievous tricks. Nancy steals another reporter's assignment so she can go cover an inquest. Nancy cleverly sneaks a prohibited camera into a jail by hiding the camera under her hair and putting a block of wood in Ted's camera case as a decoy. She has Ted distract a policeman so that she can search for evidence in a murder victim's home, and tricks Ted into going undercover as a boxer to investigate. Nancy even tricks her father, lawyer Carson Drew (John Litel), into agreeing to represent a falsely accused murder suspect. In her most audacious move, she even plants a fake story in the newspaper in order to catch the crooks. All of these tricks subvert various patriarchal forces: the press, the prison system, the police, the boxing game, and the law.

Yet Nancy's mastery is undercut in several ways: Because she chases the hit-and-run driver, she doesn't get her story on the inquest in on time and gets scooped. She bases her assertion that a murder suspect is innocent solely on her "woman's intuition," saying " ... she just doesn't look like the type who'd poison anybody." Nancy is also shown as scaring easily. When two pre-teens, Ted's little sister Mary (Mary Lee) and Mary's friend "Killer" Parkins (Dickie Jones), put a harmless whistle-bomb (a noisemaking device) under the hood of Nancy's car, Nancy leaps out of her car, hides in her garage, and yells for Ted to help her. Moreover, once Nancy has found the missing evidence but has been left by Ted to deliver it herself, the crook's moll snatches the tin out of her hands. Although Nancy chases her on foot, she loses her and winds up knocking over a policeman. The implication is that Nancy needs Ted by her side to be successful.

Nancy's mastery over language is undercut when she loses verbal exchanges with her father and Ted. When Nancy criticizes herself, saying, "Everything's gone wrong. I've failed all around," and "Maybe I'm just not intelligent," her Dad teasingly responds, "That's right." Moreover, when Nancy says, "You can always get information from women. They just love to talk," Ted wryly counters, "Yeah, I've noticed." Although these scenes are played as jokes, their valence is clear.

The film makes a few important changes from the novels. As on TV, Nancy has no female sidekicks of her own age. Moreover, Ted is not Nancy's boyfriend in the film, although in the books Ned [sic] Nickerson is her boyfriend. This works in some ways to desexualize Nancy, who is presented simply as having a crush on Ted, who in turn is oblivious to her feelings and appears to regard her as a nuisance.

Another change is that Nancy's overwhelming intelligence is underplayed in the films. Rick Altman quotes Warner Brothers' advertising for the series:

> She may get the wrong answers in school ... but she gets the right men in jail!... Her homework may not be so hot ... but her policework is 100%... [S]he's got ... feminine intuition![35]

Altman charitably reads this campaign as a rejection of "traditional (male) modes of success."[36] I would say rather that this advertising campaign undercuts Nancy's investigative authority by portraying her as weak at book learning and reliant on intuition as opposed to logic.

Nancy gets called crazy whether she's pursuing her dream of winning a student journalism award, investigating, or mooning over neighbor Ted Nickerson (Frank Thomas, Jr.). She is first called crazy as part of a group of mostly female aspiring journalists. The crusty editor of *The River Heights Tribune* remarks "Why anyone is simpleminded enough to want to work on a newspaper, I've never been able to find out," and mutters "imbecile schoolchildren" as the student journalists leave. Nancy is also called crazy when she investigates with Ted. Ted's little sister Mary speculates, "Maybe they're both insane." Ted himself calls Nancy crazy when she is unaccountably (to him) overjoyed to find out that the "older woman" he's been meeting for tennis dates is really just a tennis pro. Ted, oblivious to Nancy's jealousy, suggests to her, "Maybe you ought to get psychoanalyzed," implying that her healthy interest in the opposite sex is somehow abnormal.

A female detective of marriageable age is also typed as insane in *Smart Blonde* (Frank McDonald, 1936), a film starring the series character Torchy Blane (Glenda Farrell).[37] Torchy is an intrepid reporter who gives back as good as she gets — often better. The opening shots of the film illustrate her mastery. The first shot after the opening credits is of a newspaper story written by reporter Torchy Blane. Torchy's words then fade and are penetrated by a new phallic image, an oncoming train heading almost straight towards the camera and the viewer. This image of penetration initially seems to have destroyed the mastery of language represented by Torchy's ruined story. Then we see, however, that Torchy is in a taxicab going alongside the train. She pays the cabbie (demonstrating economic mastery), leaps for the back of the train (demonstrating physical mastery), and hops on without paying (demonstrating mastery over Law). She bluffs her way past the conductor (demonstrating mastery over the representative of Law) and uses him to find the man she wants to interview for her story. So in some sense, she co-opts the phallus here, making it work for her by using the train and its authority figure to re-assert her own linguistic mastery as a reporter.

Torchy follows the same path throughout the film, co-opting or bettering all who challenge her. For example, when her friend Lt. Steve McBride gets called into a private conversation at a nightclub and won't let Torchy accompany him, she simply discovers what she wants to know from the hatcheck girl. When Steve drives a car that has obviously been sabotaged,

Torchy criticizes his driving and then insists on driving his car herself to discover what's wrong with it. When Steve keeps her waiting outside while he enters a sketchy rooming house, Torchy sneaks in anyway and makes important deductions about the missing man Steve sought to question. Torchy also sneaks into a murder scene from which she has been barred and steals a key piece of evidence. Of course, it turns out in the end that Torchy has been way ahead of Steve the whole time and that she eventually comes up with the information that leads to the solution of the mystery.

After Torchy explains to him how she has solved the case, Steve responds by intimating that she's crazy: "Don't make any difference what I was," he says, "I'd never figure out what goes on in that dizzy brain of yours." Steve then attempts to domesticate the independent Torchy via a smart-alecky marriage proposal, which she accepts.

The detecting housewife heroine of *Compromising Positions* (Frank Perry, 1985) is also a journalist — though not such an emphatically capable one — and is also typed as insane. When Judith Singer (Susan Sarandon), a journalist-turned-homemaker who is intrigued by the murder of her philandering dentist (Joe Mantegna), comes home late after investigating, her husband Bob (Edward Herrmann) gives her the third degree about where she's been and then impugns her sanity:

JUDITH: I don't have to give you an accounting of my every move. I mean what, do you think I was out with another man?
BOB: Don't be melodramatic.
JUDITH: And don't tell me I'm being melodramatic. You know, for ten years I have trusted you and now —
BOB: You're acting crazy. Maybe you should see a psychiatrist.

Judith continues her investigations and then comes home to find that her house has been vandalized by someone warning her off the case. Bob's reaction is to cut Judith off when she tries to explain and again to impugn her sanity:

JUDITH: I've been doing a little investigative reporting and I —
BOB: *What?*
JUDITH: I just, I asked a few people some questions and maybe what hap —
BOB: Are you *crazy?*

....

BOB: I've had it, Judith. I've had it with your evasions and your obsession with this thing.

Bob, who comes off as a big jerk, then belittles his wife's profession, trying to put her "in her place": "You are a wife and a mother and *former* journalist, so don't get grandiose with me." He then orders Judith to stop investigating.

The film has an ambivalent relationship with Judith's supposedly-conflicting roles as wife, mother, and detective. On the one hand, she breezily defies Bob and continues her investigations anyway, enjoying a flirtation with hunky police detective Lt. David Suarez (Raul Julia) along the way. She also manages to turn the murder into a story for her local paper and ends the film planning to resume her reporting career. On the other hand, she decides to stay with her horrid husband — "Bob can be a big pain, but he's a good father and he's trying to be a good husband" — and she's not portrayed as the world's best investigator, either. Despite her best efforts, her theory about who the killer is proves to be wrong, and she is almost killed herself by the real killer.

In Woody Allen's *Manhattan Murder Mystery* (1993),[38] detection is seen as the antidote to approaching old age for middle-aged couple Larry (Woody Allen) and Carol Lipton (Diane Keaton). Because this is a Woody Allen film, we should not be surprised that intimations of madness appear even for the men in the film: Larry is claustrophobic and a self-described neurotic, and Larry and Carol's friend Ted (Alan Alda) has a shrink. Still, the vast majority of intimations of madness in the film are aimed at Carol, the investigating housewife.

The intimations that Carol is mad are not only far more numerous than the intimations that any other character is mad, but are also all directly connected to Carol's investigation of her neighbor Paul House (Jerry Adler), whom Carol suspects has murdered his wife. (This association of her madness with investigation contrasts with Larry's claustrophobia, triggered by a stuck elevator, and Ted's visits to a psychiatrist, which are unexplained.) When Carol and Ted (who has a crush on her) start eagerly discussing the case, a jealous Larry interjects: "You guys are slipping into a mad obsession." Undaunted, Carol spies on her neighbor as he lurks around the building at night. Again, Larry thinks she's mad: "Can you go back to bed? This is crazy.... Leave the poor guy alone. You're crazy.... This is insane." When Carol tells Larry about her further investigations, he responds: "You snuck into his apartment? Are you nuts? ... Save a little craziness for menopause." When Carol decides to break into House's apartment a second time, Larry responds: "You gotta go back to your shrink." When Carol drags him in with her, he protests, "This is insane." When Carol spots the supposedly murdered woman on a bus, Larry accuses her of a "total psychotic breakdown." Even after Larry decides to humor Carol, he still asks "Are you nuts?" when she wants to investigate a suspicious hotel room.

Interestingly, Carol and Ted also suspect that what Carol is doing is crazy, but in a positive way. While snooping around House's apartment, Carol ecstatically calls Ted to report:

> CAROL: I'm telling you... I'm just dizzy with freedom. This is ... the crazi-
> est thing I've ever done.
> TED: Yes, it's crazy, but soon we'll be too old to do anything crazy.

Even more interestingly, Carol eventually decides to see a psychiatrist again for introspective reasons. Larry's response is a backhanded disavowal of her need for mental health assistance that implies that she is indeed crazy: "You don't have to see a shrink. There's nothing wrong with you that can't be cured with a little prozac and a polo mallet."

Carol is a reasonably competent detective, divining that there has been a crime in the first place, finding out that House has a mistress, following him successfully, etc. Neither she nor Larry (nor Ted) really understands the details of House's complex crime. The role of interpreter of events is left to their *femme fatale* friend Marcia Fox (Anjelica Huston), but even she has to interpret the story twice to get it right. One is left with the impression that the solution of the mystery is secondary to the act of detecting and how the detecting transforms its characters.

The film also gradually undercuts Carol's initial competence. As the film progresses, Larry takes on an increasingly active role, detecting with — and later replacing — Carol. Carol, whose competence has been previously challenged in little things — House finds the reading glasses she accidentally leaves in his apartment — finds her competence completely undercut when House kidnaps her and she must wait for Larry to rescue her. The act of detecting together and of Larry taking on the traditionally masculine role of rescuer rejuvenates the couple's love life and stems the twin threats of Larry's attraction to Marcia and Carol's attraction to Ted.

Dotty Old Ladies: The Trope of Madness Is Independent of the Investigator's Age

Even little-old-lady detectives, powerful in print and on television because of their traditional position outside of heterosexual desire, fall victim to imputations of madness when they appear in film.[39] In the old 1930s[40] Hildegarde Withers series, the frumpy middle-aged female detective (Edna May Oliver),[41] has her sanity challenged when investigating the deaths of people with whom she is not directly connected. In *Murder on a Honeymoon* (Lloyd Corrigan, 1935), when she is eavesdropping on some suspects in an attempt to solve the murder of one of her fellow hydroplane passengers, her comic foil, Inspector Oscar Piper (James Gleason) of the New York Police Department, sneaks up behind her and says "Hildegarde, you get screwier every day." Again, when she makes a suggestion about the solution of the mystery, Piper says, "That's the dizziest theory I ever heard in my life." Note how Piper's accusations of madness directly criticize the efficacy of Withers' detective work, as if it were intrinsically insane for her to detect at all. Piper's comments are all the more striking because a central premise of the series is that he blunders around making false accusations at the drop of a hat while Withers not only keeps uncovering evidence that proves his suspicions wrong, but also investigates more thoughtfully than he does and eventually solves the various parts of the mystery. The insistence of the trope of madness, however mildly worded here, underscores the tendency for female investigative competence to be undercut by intimations of instability.[42]

The popular series of 1960s films based on Agatha Christie's little old lady detective Miss Jane Marple (Margaret Rutherford) plays out similar mild — yet damning — accusations of madness, with two twists: Miss Marple is made to express others' accusations of madness and is also set up as a potential object of desire despite her age. In the first film in the series, *Murder, She Said* (George Pollock, 1961),[43] Miss Marple witnesses a murder on a passing train but is not believed by the police. She complains to her close friend, mystery-reading librarian Jim Stringer (Stringer Davis):[44]

> MISS MARPLE: Mr. Stringer, would you say I was an unstable woman?
> MR. STRINGER: Certainly not.
> MISS MARPLE: In full possession of my faculties?
> MR. STRINGER: Absolutely.
> MISS MARPLE: Not given to hallucinations?
> MR. STRINGER: Why, no.
> MISS MARPLE: Thank you, Mr. Stringer. The police think I'm dotty.

Here, the film's enunciation forces Miss Marple to articulate several possible descriptions of her own madness. Moreover, she depends upon a man's judgement that she is not mad — she needs Mr. Stringer's stamp of approval to confirm her sanity.

The film allows Miss Marple great strength as an investigator. First, she takes the accusation of madness as a personal challenge to prove the police wrong. "If you imagine that I am going to sit back and let everybody regard me as a dotty old maid, you are very much mistaken," she tells a skeptical Inspector Craddock. Yet the phrase "dotty old maid" itself reduces Marple's power, recalling the nineteenth-century "medical" relationships between virginity, menopause, and madness. The implied relationship between lack of desire and madness puts the female investigator in a Catch-22 situation: Female investigators can be called crazy either because they're in love or because they're *not* in love — either way, they lose.

To guard against the spectator's seeing Miss Marple as just a "dotty old maid," the film constructs her as sexually desirable by giving her a faithful male assistant, Mr. Stringer, a character who does *not* appear in Christie's Miss Marple stories,[45] and by having the decidedly unpleasant head of the household that she infiltrates in her investigation propose marriage to her at the end of the film. Yet when Miss Marple rejects his proposal, we get more madness imagery: "The woman must be completely unbalanced!" he exclaims at her refusal. His words imply that the only woman more mad than an old maid is an old maid who won't marry when she has the chance to do so.

Miss Marple is, however, allotted a strong degree of competence in these films: she is correct about the killer's identity; she is allowed a great sense of humor about herself and others; and she is decidedly athletic in an English girls'-school sort of way. The films have a running gag about her athletic accomplishments: in one, we learn she was a golfing champion; in another, a riding champion. In the two other films, she captures the murderer by the deft application of her championship fencing and shooting skills. Yet even this seemly unambiguous testament to Marple's abilities may connote madness: her hearty athleticism might seem to carry overtones of English girls'-school lesbianism — the other "madness" that may afflict old maids.

Crazy Continental Ops: The Trope of Madness in European and Japanese Films

The association of female investigation with madness is not restricted to Hollywood film, and it can even appear as a central trope in Continental feminist cinema. In Morleen Gorris's provocative film, *A Question of Silence* (*De Stilte Rond Christine M.*, Netherlands, 1983), investigating psychiatrist Janine Van den Bos (Cox Habbema) gradually comes to realize that the three women who have apparently murdered a male boutique owner on impulse were really acting out of years of accumulated anger at sexism in Dutch society. While the perspective of the film is indubitably feminist, it frames Janine's investigation very much in terms of a battle over the definition of women's sanity.[46] When she initially rejects the easy assumption that the murderous women are insane, Janine herself gets typed as slightly unbalanced, both by the enunciation of the film — we see Janine take up smoking again, which marks her as having an addictive personality — and by characters within the film — Janine's husband complains bitterly, "these women occupy all your thoughts," coding Janine as obsessive. When Janine repeats her contention that the women are sane in court, the chilly, unperceptive reception she and her theories get from the male-dominated court provokes the laughter of the defendants and the silent female witnesses of their crime, who have come to court to cheer them on. Janine perceives the true oppressive nature of a male-dominated legal system, joins in with their laughter, then stalks out of court. At the end of the film, then, while Janine is typed as eminently sane to the implied spectators of the film, she appears to all of the male characters within the diegesis to be just as insane as the women she's been investigating.

On a lighter note, in Philippe de Broca's French comedy-thriller *Dear Detective* (*Tendre Poulet*, 1977)[47] the heroine, Lise (Annie Girardot), is typed as a very competent police inspector who battles sexism on the job daily. Here, the accusation that Lise is crazy comes after she has temporarily resigned from the force. As she's rushing around the house tidying up, her aunt Simone makes the international "she's nuts" handsign to Lise's mother. Even though this reference seems to type Lise's NOT working as a detective and becoming superhousewife instead as the mad facet of her character, I would argue that the implication of insanity spills over onto other areas of her life. The damage is done — in the spectator's eyes, the female investigator has become implicated in madness.

It is also important to note that the phenomenon of the mad female investigator is not limited to America, England, and Continental Europe. Another light film is Juzo Itami's Japanese police procedural film *A Taxing Woman* (1987), in which Japanese IRS agent Ryoko Itakura (Nobuko Miyamoto) attempts to discover the ill-gotten gains of mobster Hideki Gondo (Tsutomu Yamazaki). No one in the film explicitly calls Ryoko crazy, but her relentless hunt for Gondo's money — which stretches over years and includes pawing through his garbage — marks Ryoko as obsessive. Moreover, Ryoko is presented as a divorced single mother with a child, but we never see her child. The film positions Ryoko as if the true joy of her life is work, a characteristic that — at least in Japan, where gender norms of the 1980s still mirrored American gender norms of the 1950s — marks her as transgressive.

The Trope of Madness Appears in Avant-Garde Film

Sally Potter's avant-garde film *Thriller* (1979) investigates how traditional narratives use women as objects, not as subjects, and how this leads to women's deaths.[48] Potter has Mimi, the dead "heroine" of the opera *La Boheme*, narrate her search for meaning, her attempt to solve the mystery of her own death. After a brief introduction that shows her maniacally laughing and contains music from the score of *Psycho* (Alfred Hitchcock, 1960) [Our first intimation of madness! What's crazier than the word "psycho"?], Mimi is shown in a still photograph looking in the mirror, while in voiceover, she muses: "I'm trying to remember, to understand. There were some bodies on the floor. One of them is mine. Did I die? Was I murdered? If so, who killed me and why?" Then, after a brief summary of the plot of *La Boheme*, Mimi starts her challenge to the narrative: "Can these be the facts? Is that what really happened? Is this the story of my life? Was that the story of my death?" She wonders: "What if I had been the subject of this scenario instead of its object?"

Potter's point is that the narrative conventions of *La Boheme* (and by extension, many of our cultural narratives) murdered Mimi by requiring her death in order to prop up the subjectivity of the male heroes. After realizing that allowing Mimi to live would give her a subjectivity unwelcome to male fantasy (Mimi the hardworking mother of small children, Mimi the laborer, Mimi the old woman) Mimi concludes: "I had to be young, single, and vulnerable, with a death that serves their desire to become heroes with the display of their grief."

Even a progressive film such as this one, however, which investigates and seeks to subvert narrative conventions, uses the trope of the madness of the female investigator. Aside from the use of music from *Psycho* and the initial maniacal laughter, Potter introduces more of Mimi's maniacal laughter at a critical point. Mimi has been reading a long excerpt of literary theory in French. The last words she reads are names: "Mallarmé, Marx, Freud." When she gets to "Freud," she starts laughing maniacally again. As in *The Silence of the Lambs*, the evocation of the psychiatrist evokes its concomitants, the patient (here particularly appropriate in its literal sense of "the one who suffers") and the patient's presumed madness. Thus, even self-aware feminist avant-garde filmmakers like Sally Potter engage with the problematic of the female investigator on film by evocations of madness. Even as she is busy investigating male guilt of patriarchal narratives in a self-aware fashion, Mimi is pushed into a semblance of madness by the narrative here.[49]

The Trope of Madness May Be Metaphorized or Displaced

As the above description of foreign films suggests, the accusation of madness need not be an accusation of literal madness, nor need it be applied to the act of investigating. Nevertheless, the accusation has its effect: it undercuts the competence of the female investigator. In *Stranger on the Third Floor* (Boris Ingster, 1940)—sometimes held to be the first example of film noir[50]—the heroine, Jane (Margaret Tallichet), searches for the murderer whom her boyfriend has seen and for whose crime he has been arrested. When she finally finds him and tries to capture him by luring him to the front of a boarding house and ringing for help, the land-lady promptly calls her drunk, yells at her for disturbing the house late at night, and slams the door on her. In this instance, the accusation of drunk-enness has the same valence as an accusation of madness.

Occasionally, the madness may be displaced onto another character or characters closely associated with the female detective. In *Phantom Lady* (Robert Siodmak, 1944), the heroine, Carol "Kansas" Richman (Ella Raines), is a particularly aggressive investigator on behalf of her jailed boss, who has been unjustly accused of murdering his wife. Kansas sets out to track down the "phantom lady" who can give her boss an alibi, a woman he knows only by the distinctive hat she was wearing on the eve-ning of the murder. In her initial investigation, Kansas is powerful indeed. Hounding a reluctant witness who appears to have been paid off, she sits staring at him at his bar, then boldly stalks him through the streets of the city, staring all the while. He is so unnerved by her look that he gets hit by a car and killed. Such a direct visual assault by a woman on a man is almost unseen in Hollywood film.[51]

Accordingly, this investigative acuity is counterbalanced by an equally large suggestion of madness. While Kansas herself is not accused of being mad, the trope of madness is decidedly overdetermined in the film. Kansas does find the "phantom lady," (Fay Helm), but she has had a complete nervous breakdown[52] and will be useless as a witness. As she waits for the police with her boss's best friend Marlow (Franchot Tone), who has been helping her investigate, it becomes clear that *he* is in fact a crazed stran-gler, and that she is his next victim.[53] Kansas is saved only by the timely arrival of the police.

In their own ways, the phantom lady and Marlow are both doubles for Kansas:[54] the phantom lady went on a date with Kansas's boss, a posi-tion Kansas herself would have liked to occupy; and Marlow has been both a friend to Kansas's boss, as she is, and her co-investigator in the hunt for the phantom lady. It makes sense that the trope of madness is displaced onto the two characters who most closely double Kansas's position, and that the level of madness is in both cases extreme, to make up for the fact that it is displaced.

Christopher Nolan's *Insomnia* (2002) similarly displaces the madness of the female investigator onto the male subject of her investigation. The film chronicles a duel of wits between troubled LAPD detective Will Dormer (Al Pacino), on temporary reassignment in Alaska, and Walter Finch (Robin Williams), a killer who has seen Dormer accidentally-on-purpose shoot the partner who was about to report him to Internal Affairs for planting evidence. Finch blackmails Dormer into sharing information with him, into not pursuing Finch for a murder he committed, and into framing someone else for the crime. Although the film focuses on the relationship between the two men, the third side of their triangle is rookie Alaska policewoman Ellie Burr (Hilary Swank).

Ellie is a neophyte investigator assigned to investigate the shooting of Dormer's partner. Although she is tempted to do a softball job, Dormer himself tells her to be sure of all her facts before she files her report. She follows his advice and looks over the crime scene more carefully. She realizes from photographs that part of Dormer's story about what happened in the fog cannot be correct and questions him about the inconsistency. She reinvestigates the scene (bravely going to a creepy location by herself) and finds the bullet from Dormer's gun, suggesting that he shot his partner. She consults a case study she had made of one of Dormer's cases to show that Dormer's backup weapon is a 9mm automatic, the same caliber as the bullet that killed Dormer's partner. In the process of her investigation, Ellie goes from hero worship of Dormer to a more critical view of him.

Ellie is portrayed as thorough, increasingly competent, and brave. She drives Detective Dormer and his partner around when they arrive in Alaska (although she later hands over her car keys to Dormer). She also goes alone to pick up some letters from killer Walter Finch at his lake house, knowing that he's a murder suspect, but not thinking that he's the murderer. In a scene reminiscent of *The Silence of the Lambs*, she sees the dress of the murder victim and realizes Finch is the killer. Although she tries to act casually, Finch immediately sees what she has seen, hits her over the head, and imprisons her. When Dormer arrives to rescue her, she accuses him of shooting his partner on purpose, but then joins forces with him to fight Finch. After Dormer has been mortally wounded, she offers to hide evidence that incriminates him. Only after Dormer specifically instructs her not to hide the evidence that he shot his partner — "Don't lose your way"— does she decide to tell her superior officers the truth.

Ellie is never explicitly called crazy, but she is presented as radically over-indentified with Detective Dormer — his number-one fan. She knows about all of his most famous cases, and has used one of them as her case study at the police academy. She quotes Dormer to himself, when even he has forgotten what he once said. Ellie is highly identified with Dormer, and the film *does* explicitly call Dormer crazy. Finch says to Dormer at one point, "I'm trying to help you and you're running around like a fucking maniac." Dormer is also described as "under a lot of pressure." Dormer is also typed as crazy by his guilt-racked inability to sleep in the never-ending Alaska summer sunlight.

The trope of madness is also displaced onto Ellie's male colleagues in general. "We're not a bunch of hotheads who are going to jump to a lot of crazy conclusions," says one of the male detectives to a witness. In fact, that's *exactly* what Ellie's colleagues do, leaping to incriminate an innocent man. Ellie, overidentified with the masculine power-structure of the police force, picks up a taint of madness in the process.

In some cases, however, the accusation of madness is evoked by much more direct methods. *The Mad Miss Manton* (Leigh Jason, 1938), for example, mainly uses the film's title to impugn the sanity of its socialite-detective protagonist Melsa Manton (Barbara Stanwyck). The only other suggestion of madness occurs when Melsa confronts police officers after having reported finding a dead body that has since disappeared. The officers crowd around Melsa and tap her knee to test her reflexes. When she kicks one of them, they decide "Hey, she's not nuts!" and proceed to berate her for playing games with them. This is an implication of madness by its denial. "Hey, she's not nuts!" means "The natural assumption would be that she *is* nuts."

The Implication of Madness Occurs Even When the Film Is Based on "Real" Events: Fargo

The opening titles of the Coen brothers' modern film noir *Fargo* (Joel Coen, 1995) claim that all details are true except for the names of the survivors. That cannot objectively be true, as all films "based on a true story" differ in which facts they highlight, and which they downplay or omit. Perhaps because it is supposedly fact-based, however, *Fargo* provides one of the stronger images of the female detective on film.[55] Small-town Minnesota police chief Marge Gunderson (Frances McDormand) is physically brave — she captures a dangerous man single handedly — and is exceptionally competent and logical.

Because she is such a powerful figure, it is significant that the Coen brothers highlight the fact that Marge is pregnant — *very* pregnant — during her investigation. Her pregnancy is overdetermined by the visuals of the film. Although we later learn that she is only 7 months pregnant, Marge looks so large that she might be expected to give birth any minute. She also suffers from morning sickness, which doesn't make sense: She is in late pregnancy, while morning sickness occurs mainly in the first trimester of pregnancy. The excessiveness of Marge's pregnancy is also emphasized — and played for laughs — by her taking an unrealistically huge amount of food at a buffet lunch.[56]

The choice to emphasize Marge's pregnancy has several effects: First, it despecularizes Marge, allowing the viewer to perceive her more as protagonist and less as visual material for consumption. Second, it allows the Coen bothers a telling visual contrast. The film ends with Marge and her milquetoast husband anticipating the birth of their first child — an affirmation of life[57] arriving via the birth canal. One of the images shortly before this conversation is of a kidnapper feeding his co-conspirator head first into a woodchipper — an affirmation of death arriving via a "death canal." This mechanical *vagina dentata* is disavowed by the final shot of the film, but the image still lurks below the surface.

The third, and most important, use of Marge's pregnancy is as metaphor for madness. Pregnancy (and all conditions relating to the female reproductive cycle, such as menstruation, menopause, etc.) have been historically blamed for causing women to be mad, unstable creatures.[58] To underscore this point, the Coen brothers include a seemingly-meaningless subplot: When Marge goes to the Twin Cities to investigate her case, her old high school friend Mike (Steve Park) contacts her, and she agrees to meet him for a drink. He makes a clumsy pass at her, then tells her he's a grieving widower. She swallows his story whole, but she later learns that he is in fact a stalker with psychiatric problems. By associating Marge with a madman, the film again undercuts her investigative prowess. Competent in every other way, like Ryoko in *A Taxing Woman*, Marge cannot detect effectively when she is the object of someone else's desire.

Hilary Radner similarly reads this scene as implying that Marge is mad, in effect saying that Marge's failure to perceive/acknowledge her place as an object of desire amounts to madness. "The 'insanity' of Marge's sensibility also reveals itself in this scene. She fails again and again to recognize the signs of Mike's instability," opines Radner.[59]

Moreover, although Radner's essay initially concentrates on the madness of the men in *Fargo* ("Murder like a hysterical symptom is passed from one lunatic to another — all men"),[60] Radner eventually focuses on the madness of the female investigator herself. Indeed, Radner reads Marge as mad in several respects: for her strict moral code ("an ethical imperative so overwhelming that it verges on lunacy"), for her persistence on the job (her "irrational pursuit of the rational"), for her relentlessly optimistic rejection of the capitalist greed that drives men to murder ("Here again we must question Marge's sanity"), and for her contentment with the comforts of a dull domesticity that are sometimes not enough for her husband ("Marge's 'pretty good' seems no more rational than Norm's 'more.'")[61]

Madness by Implication

The hegemony of the codes by which the specular and desire are imbricated in the very fabric of the female investigative film is so overarching that even recent films that might be expected to have a greater degree of distance from these codes ultimately prove to follow them as well. The 1995 Jon Amiel film *Copycat* is a case in point. The tale of two female investigators on the trail of a serial killer makes one of these investigators, Dr. Helen Hudson (Sigourney Weaver) (the one who investigates serial killers professionally), not only called mad (she's called a crank) but also quite literally the bearer of madness. Her role as an investigator into the crimes of men (specifically white men between the ages of 20 and 35 — a profile that fits many serial killers)[62] leads directly to her madness: an escaped serial killer whom she has studied and helped to imprison attacks her, causing her severe agoraphobia. Helen is radically overdetermined as insane: Besides being agoraphobic, she also becomes an alcoholic, pill-popping insomniac prone to anxiety attacks.[63]

While a film like *Copycat* shows how closely bound up ideas of female investigation and madness can still be in Hollywood film, the slightly earlier, immensely popular *The Silence of the Lambs* (Jonathan Demme, 1990) provides, perhaps, a best-case scenario. In this film, eminently capable[64] FBI-trainee Clarice Starling (Jodie Foster) is never explicitly called mad or considered mad by other characters in the film as she investigates to hunt down a serial killer. The film proceeds from a relatively feminist perspective,[65] portraying Clarice as deftly deflecting a constant barrage of sexist remarks and attitudes from the men with whom she works. Yet the narrative of even this film hints, if only obliquely, at the mental disturbance of its female investigator. Significantly, a large part of Clarice's investigation involves speaking with imprisoned cannibalistic serial killer Dr. Hannibal Lecter (Anthony Hopkins) — a psychiatrist by trade. He probes her mind, forcing her to relate painful memories in exchange for information, and reveals that her current desire to save lives through her career in law enforcement is really an attempt to end her nightmares about animal slaughter she witnessed as a child. This is portrayed as a mild obsession, to be sure, and Dr. Lecter does not frame his analysis of Clarice in terms of madness and sanity, yet the very fact that Clarice spends much of the film talking about her life to a psychiatrist positions her as slightly unbalanced. Clarice's mental health is also marked as a central concern of the film by the revelations that as an undergraduate, she double majored in psychology and criminology, and that she aspires to work permanently in the FBI's behavioral sciences unit upon completing her training. The trope of the female psychiatrist who is herself unstable is a familiar one,[66] and its implications need little elaboration here.

It is also important to note that *The Silence of the Lambs* switches genres slightly at the end of the film, when Dr. Lecter has already escaped from prison and is therefore no longer around to imply that Clarice is at all mad. At Clarice's moment of greatest competence, when her hard work and quick thinking have led her unwittingly to the killer's doorstep and she has recognized him as such, the film takes on several aspects of the horror genre.[67] Clarice winds up chasing the killer through the horror film's "terrible place" — in this case, an impossibly labyrinthine basement — and then gets chased herself by the killer, who is wearing night vision glasses. In a scene reminiscent of the opening scene of John Carpenter's 1978 film *Halloween* (and important scenes in many other horror films) the spectator and camera are aligned with the killer's perspective through the use of the frame of the night vision glasses. While Clarice does eventually track the killer by sound, killing him a fraction of a second before he would have killed her, the spectator is left to focus on scenes of a terrified Clarice fumbling in the dark, showing just as much panic as any other horror film victim.[68] I would read this genre switch as a compensatory mechanism á la *Blue Steel* — the enunciation switches genres in order to undercut Clarice's competence while she investigates male guilt, since the structure that has implied her mental imbalance is no longer in place.

The sequel to *Silence of the Lambs*, *Hannibal* (Ridley Scott, 2001) replays the themes of the earlier film. Clarice Starling (played by Julianne

Moore in the sequel)[69] is still typed as a highly competent investigator who faces gender discrimination, and blatant sexual harassment, on the job. Dr. Hannibal Lecter is still psychoanalyzing Clarice — when she suffers a public humiliation at work, he writes Clarice a letter inquiring into her emotional state and hinting at the psychological motivations behind her feelings.

Clarice is more explicitly typed as mad in this film than she is in *The Silence of the Lambs*. After a failed attempt to avert the kidnapping of Dr. Lecter, she tells the police that she is not hysterical, but that of course hysterical people always say they are not hysterical.[70] By her own words, then, Clarice implies a hint of madness.

In a bravura performance, Clarice rescues Dr. Lecter from maneating swine, only to be shot herself and then carried off to safety in Dr. Lecter's arms. After Dr. Lecter has nursed her back to a modicum of health at his hideout, she unsuccessfully tries to capture him with a steak knife. In the ensuing scuffle, he slams her pony tail in a refrigerator door, holding her captive. As the smitten Dr. Lecter leans in to steal a kiss, Clarice handcuffs him to herself. "Now that," opines Dr. Lecter, "is very interesting." Indeed it is. Throughout, the film has typed Clarice as a woman unable to have a relationship with a man. Having her think solely of police work when being kissed by a serial killer, albeit a charming one, signifies Clarice as a woman unable to work in the field of heterosexual desire.[71]

The film climaxes with a symbolic castration/disavowal of castration. To escape the handcuffs, Dr. Lecter hacks off a hand with a cleaver. At first the audience thinks it is Clarice's hand that has been cut off, but cannot be sure. In this film with an otherwise graphic, gory *mise en scène*, director Ridley Scott hides the actual dismemberment from the audience. The next scene, however, is a classic fetishization of a woman that is extensively marked as a disavowal of castration.[72] Clarice appears outside Lecter's hideout, wearing her revealing black dinner dress, and holding up her hands — both hands — as authorities arrive on the scene.[73]

Similar to the troubled Clarice Starling is the protagonist of *Murder By Numbers* (Barbet Schroeder, 2002), Cassie Mayweather (Sandra Bullock, who also executive produced). Cassie is a highly competent police investigator who is battling demons of her own while she solves a modern-day Leopold and Loeb type of murder. Many years before, Cassie's abusive husband had stabbed her and left her for dead. While her husband was imprisoned, Cassie changed her name and became a police officer, but her personal relations with her co-workers and men in general have been affected by her victimization. The film clearly establishes that Cassie's pattern is to sleep with her new partners, then push them away before they can hurt her. No one in her homicide unit wants to work with her anymore, and they all call her "the hyena," a reference she explains by saying, "Female hyenas have kind of a mock penis." Her ex-boyfriend, the district attorney, calls her "the scorpion." It later develops that he abused her also, and that she broke his nose in self-defense.

Cassie's relations with her new partner Sam Kennedy (Ben Chaplin) follow a similar pattern. Cassie dominates him from the start, making him serve the other cops donuts, telling him not to ruin her crime scene, and cutting him off in mid-sentence. She is also sexually domineering, standing him up for a date, then kissing him aggressively and almost forcing him into bed when he catches up with her, then kicking him out of her bed after sex.

Cassie lives on a houseboat, like other freedom-seeking detectives, e.g., Quincy from the television series *Quincy, M.E.*, or Travis McGee, hero of the series of detective novels by John D. MacDonald, or the male hero of *Foul Play* (Colin Higgins, 1978). In Cassie's case, however, this freedom-seeking rootlessness is presented as pathological, as if a woman seeking freedom is intrinsically mad.

The film doesn't just settle for implications of madness, however. The dialogue consistently overdetermines Cassie as mad. When Cassie refers to the murder victim by her first name, her boss chides her: "You're supposed to identify with the killer, not the victim"—an odd description of police work! Later, when she persists in suspecting the real killers, her boss chides her again—"You're getting way too involved in this, Cassie"—and threatens to send her to the department psychiatrist. When she tells her boss she's fine, he responds, "You're never *really* fine, are you, Cass?" Her partner Sam also thinks her interest in the case is mentally unhealthy: "Are you so obsessed with [one of the killers] that you can't see straight?" he asks. "...They think you're losing it." When one of the killers attacks her, she opens a car door in his face, which again makes the department threaten to send her "to the department shrink." Even the killer who assaults her thinks that Cassie is crazy, psychoanalyzing her to her face in much the same way that Cassie's co-workers do.

Like Clarice Starling of the *Silence of the Lambs* pictures and Alex Barnes of *Black Widow*, Cassie triumphs through her intelligence (investigating beyond the false clues planted by the killers in order to solve the mystery), her physical courage (tracking and successfully winning a deadly struggle with one of the killers), and her psychological acuity (tricking the other killer into a confession.) Like the *Silence of the Lambs* films and *Black*

Widow, Murder By Numbers similarly focuses less on Cassie as an investigator and more on Cassie as a psychological case study. Somehow transformed by her success in the murder case, Cassie, who has before unaccountably resisted testifying at her ex-husband's parole hearing,[74] becomes brave and finds the courage to testify. The film ends with her acknowledging her former name as a witness to the brutality perpetrated on her. Ironically, though she has been previously chided for "identifying with the victim," the film posits that only by identifying herself *as* a victim can Cassie achieve true psychological health.

While the psychiatric assessments of the female investigators above at least make a certain amount of diegetic sense, in that they are clearly related to the plot of the films, sometimes the madness of the female investigator is so roughly sutured into films that it makes little or no sense. The film version of the 1960s television series *The Avengers* (Jeremiah Chechik, 1998) (un)balances one of the most competent female investigators of all time with radically overdetermined intimations of madness. The film is true to the television series' portrayal of Emma Peel as a competent, intelligent investigator. In the film, Emma (Uma Thurman) has a doctorate (though she unaccountably asks John Steed [Ralph Fiennes] to call her "*Mrs.* Peel" rather than Dr. Peel),[75] bests Steed in a chess match that she plays without looking at the board, drives a powerful sportscar competently under fire, is an accomplished high diver, and bests Steed twice at fencing.

Yet Emma's competence is undercut in a number of ways: She's not allowed the background of professional spy,[76] but is rather a scientist trying to clear her name after being falsely accused of sabotaging her own top secret project. The physical prowess that Emma displays in the television series is given to Steed instead — he fights off a gang of thugs in the kind of fight that Emma routinely handled in the television series, and the climactic fencing duel takes between Steed and the archvillain (Sean Connery, camping it up as the weather-obsessed August de Wynter), although it would be diegetically more appropriate for Emma, the better fencer, to fight this duel. Instead, she is relegated to fighting a minor villain in a particularly wimpy style (knocking him around with acrobatic kicks highly reminiscent of Batgirl's fighting style on the television series *Batman*) while Steed impales the villain with his phallically-cathected umbrella-sword.[77] Emma is never allowed to really fight men in the film the way she does in the television series — her only other fight scenes show her grappling briefly with her cloned (female, of course) doppelganger. The scenes of the women wrestling — thankfully, no mud is involved — are more a male fantasy than serious fight scenes.

Moreover, the physical and mental talents Emma displays are attributed to patriarchal influences. "You're a lady of hidden talents, Mrs. Peel...: Scientist, swordsman. To what do you attribute your overachievements?" asks Steed, as they fence. "My father always wanted a boy," replies Emma. Leaving aside the question of why competence in science and sport are necessarily overachievements for a woman, Emma's answer clearly aligns her with the gothic heroine tradition of the woman who inherits her competence from her father as a substitute son. The film also notes that Emma's missing husband was a government agent, suggesting that she has also acquired some of her "masculine" powers from him, in much the same way that widows acquire their dead husbands' congressional seats. In the television series, on the other hand, Emma's missing husband is simply an aviator.

Emma's sanity is severely challenged at several points during the film, none of which make diegetic sense.[78] The government agents speculate that she may have sabotaged her own government projects because she might suffer from mental illness: "amnesia," "split personality," or "trauma." This doesn't add much to the story, because the audience (and Steed) promptly see Emma meet and fight with her *doppelganger* and realize that Emma is clearly not a Jekyll-and-Hyde case, but merely the victim of a villainous double. Yet even after he has seen the *doppelganger* and knows that Emma must be telling the truth when she says a lookalike wrecked her project, Steed delivers the following amazing statement:

> According to your file, you're a psychopathic personality with schizophrenic delusions suffering from recurring amnesia based on traumatic repression leading to outbursts of anti-social and violent behavior.

Clearly, Steed knows this isn't true (as does the audience) since he has seen the *doppelganger* and Emma at the same time (as the audience has). So why is this indictment of Emma's sanity in the film at all? A similarly non-diegetic implication of madness comes when Emma is arrested by another villain, placed in a padded cell in a straightjacket, and then confronted with her *doppelganger* by the villain. The villains then immediately knock her unconscious, remove her straightjacket, and take her out of the padded cell with them — so why weren't the straightjacket and the padded cell skipped? They're certainly superfluous to the story.

I would suggest that these non-diegetically motivated intimations of madness are a direct response to an exceptionally competent female investigator — the old 1960s *Avengers* series still beats almost any latter-day film or television series as a portrayal of female investigative competence. The woman who can do everything "has it all"—except her sanity.

Male Spectatorship/Male Guilt— On a Collision Course in the Gothic Film

I have noted above many instances where the enunciation of a film types the female investigator as mad. To test my theory about how enunciatory intimations of madness affect male spectators, I will now consider male spectators' own descriptions of their responses to these films. The clearest responses to enunciatory implications of female madness appear in the writings of those most self-conscious of male spectators: film critics. Specifically, I will consider male critical responses to the subgenre of film that portrays the most explicit enunciatory implications of the female investigator's madness, the 1940s female gothic.

Many of Hitchcock's Gothic films, which feature female protagonists investigating potential male guilt,[79] imply paranoia on the part of their female investigators. The play of paranoia in these films is decidedly affected by the mechanisms of sexual difference. Diane Waldman notes:

> ... [T]he central feature of the Gothics is ambiguity, the hesitation between two possible interpretations of events by the protagonist and often ... by the spectator as well.... This hesitation is experienced by a character (and presumably a spectator) who is female. Within a patriarchal culture, then, the resolution of the hesitation carries with it the ideological function of validation or invalidation of feminine experience.[80]

It is interesting that Waldman postulates a specifically female spectator here. For the investment that a female spectator might be presumed to make in the Gothic heroine may be quite different than the investment of a male spectator: For female spectators, finding out that the male character under suspicion is actually guilty would be a *validation* of female knowledge and investigative potency — and perhaps a welcome respite from the relentless images of guilty women flooding the silver screen. For male spectators, however, the gothic heroine's success at investigation comes at the expense of the exposure and censure of a guilty male character, a potentially problematic locus of identification for male spectators.

In non–Gothic films, this uncomfortable identification may be mitigated by aspects of a film's enunciation that code the guilty party as not-male no matter how male he may at first appear to be. Sometimes, the not-maleness is biological: In her classic essay on the horror film, "When the Woman Looks," Linda Williams notes that (male) spectators perceive "monsters" as threatening precisely because these monsters are constructed as sexually different from (and perhaps more powerful than) men:

> ... [T]he monster's power is one of sexual difference from the normal male. In this difference he is remarkably like the woman in the eyes of the traumatized male: a biological freak with impossible and threatening appetites that suggest a frightening potency precisely where the normal male would perceive a lack.... What is feared in the monster ... is similar to what [Susan] Lurie says is feared in the mother: not her own mutilation, but the power to mutilate and transform the vulnerable male.[81]

Little wonder, then, that the monster is eventually vanquished, and that women who align themselves with the monster through looking are "violently punished."[82]

Sometimes, when the killer appears to be a human male, the monster's not-maleness is played out metaphorically and constructed as a psychological rather than a biological problem: For example, the killers in *Psycho*, *Dressed to Kill*, and *The Silence of the Lambs* are all biological males who are in some way absolved of guilt because it is their evil "female" side that is portrayed as responsible for their violence against women. Thus women are simultaneously the cause and perpetrators of violence against themselves. Thus we see that filmic enunciation can compensate for potential male spectatorial discomfort with an unpleasant identification by a neat trick of disavowal: a man didn't murder a woman — it wasn't a man at all; it was really a woman all along; and it was the victim's own fault anyway.[83]

In the Gothic film, however, these avenues for the denial of male guilt are unavailable. In this genre, the guilty male character is indubitably a human male, the gothic heroine's object of investigation/desire. Thus, other compensatory mechanisms swing into play. If this character can't be shown to be "not-male," the film's enunciation can compensate by showing him to be "not-guilty," as in *Spellbound* (Alfred Hitchcock, 1945). At other times, the enunciation may compensate by showing the character to be "not-the-hero," so that the male spectator will transfer his identification to a more comfortable locus, as in *Stage Fright* (Alfred Hitchcock, 1950).

But what if the male character *is* guilty and has *not* been replaced with another potential locus of male identification? If the enunciation gives the male spectator no out, then we would reasonably expect to see some compensatory mechanism at work in the male spectator's interpretation of what he sees. If the character is male and the hero and guilty, the safest interpretation to compensate for that uncomfortable set of facts is: "Of course he's not guilty. The woman's insane!" Examples of this compensatory strategy can be seen by an examination of male critics' interpretations of two Gothic films, both of which center on a woman's suspicions that her husband plans to kill her. Although the first, Alfred Hitchcock's *Suspicion* (1941), invalidates the female investigator's interpretations of events, while the second, Fritz Lang's *The Secret Beyond the Door* (1948), confirms them, respected critics of these films (Donald Spoto and Reynold Humphries, respectively) have responded to the female investigators in both films in remarkably similar ways.

Suspicion consists of a series of episodes in which petty crook Johnny Aysgarth (Cary Grant) performs "suspicious" actions that are (as the spectator finally learns) sadly misinterpreted by his wealthy wife Lina (Joan Fontaine). The camera first purports to trick us by showing Grant and Fontaine (while they are still merely acquaintances) struggling on a windy hillside, then having Grant explain that she has misunderstood his "friendly" gesture to fix her hair as an attempted (sexual) assault. Some male critics may agree with Grant's explanation of the gesture. Donald Spoto describes the scene thus:

> Cut to a medium shot, and it certainly seems as if he's attacking her — he has her by the wrists, and she's in a panic. "Nothing less than murder could justify such violent self-defense!" he tells her with a smile. But he says he was only trying to fix her hair. This could be regarded as a deliberate red herring unworthy of Hitchcock — until we see that the scene is exactly reduplicated at the film's finale — and the false emotionalism of the scene might also be easily dismissed because of the exaggerated musical accompaniment (in the fashion of the early 1940s). But once again, a Hitchcock film is more sophisticated than the sophisticates. The hysterical score is apt as an expression of the mind of this woman — and the film is, after all, presented entirely from her highly neurotic viewpoint, that of a woman who extrapolates (from her husband's childish irresponsibility) to the wrongheaded conviction that he's a killer.[84]

But female spectators may have a completely different response to the red herring scene — uninvited overtures from men may well be perceived not as romantic, but as threatening, especially in a deserted location. In a rape culture, why *is* it paranoid for a woman to fear a man who is larger and stronger than she is when he makes a sudden move towards her?[85]

Spoto's belief in Fontaine's madness is further demonstrated by his unorthodox assertion that Hitchcock lied when he claimed that he had originally planned to have Grant be guilty — that is, that he had planned to have Fontaine be absolutely correct in her suspicions of him. Spoto says:

> Hitchcock always claimed that he wanted to end *Suspicion* quite differently, with Johnny indeed killing his wife; before she willingly drinks the

poisoned milk he offers — rather than face life without her beloved — she writes a letter implicating him in the crime, then asks him to post it. But this ending was foiled, Hitchcock maintained, when RKO refused to cast Cary Grant as a killer.... But Hitchcock is the master of red herrings.... Had he presented us with a woman who *rightly* suspects her husband is her would-be killer, we'd be left with a story of her rather demented passion unto death — not very convincing psychologically (without much possibility of audience identification), and with no twist at the end, no payoff.[86]

Spoto's insistence on Grant's innocence is concomitantly an insistence on Fontaine's paranoia. The illogic of this argument is clear: Spoto's claim that the audience cannot identify with a female protagonist whose suspicions are confirmed suggests then that the audience must identify with a female protagonist whom (he claims) the film has constructed as "neurotic"[87] — hardly a more attractive locus for audience identification.

I do not mean to criticize an individual critic for his interpretation of a film with a female detective protagonist. Rather, I am fascinated by the dynamics of film that channel critics (and countless other spectators) into the interpretation that the female investigator is mad. Indeed, Spoto is by no means alone in this sort of interpretation. In his analysis of Fritz Lang's thriller *Secret Beyond the Door*, Reynold Humphries asserts that the unconscious project of this film is to demonstrate that the female detective-protagonist Celia (who correctly suspects that her husband is a murderous psychotic) is herself mad — "that she is as neurotic as he is."[88] Furthermore, Humphries worries that "it is the very institution of the cinema that is at stake," when the [male] spectators of the film "are now identifying with someone who is unbalanced," inasmuch as they "are constituted by Celia's discourse and are therefore spoken by her."[89] The way in which Humphries intertwines several concerns about gender, investigation, sanity, and enunciation here is thought-provoking.

Part of this anxiety stems from the implicit assumption of a male spectator forced to identify with an "unbalanced" female protagonist who investigates, exposes, and neutralizes murderous male desires. The concerns Humphries voices about "spectatorial identification" with a female protagonist are specifically concerns about *male* spectatorial identification.

As I suggest above, if the male spectator gains pleasure from identifying with the enunciation along familiar paths of desire, any aspects of the enunciation that frustrate (without eventually fulfilling) the male spectator's expected trajectory of desire might be sources of unpleasure to him.[90] While male spectators can be expected to tolerate *some* unsettling aspects of a film's enunciation, if the enunciation frustrates their trajectory of desire too completely, they will experience a radical inconcinity between their own cultural screen[91] and the place which the enunciation of the film expects its spectators to occupy. If the real spectator does not match the implied spectator,[92] he will likely respond in one of two ways: He will either perform a work of masquerade in order to suture himself into the film's project by trying to view the film as the implied spectator ought, or he will experience profound unpleasure and perhaps, as has happened here, a fundamental rejection of the film's project.

This lack of suture — this inability to become the implied spectator (an implied *female* spectator) — is what leads Humphries to assert that "it is the very institution of the cinema that is at stake" when he fundamentally misreads the project of *The Secret Beyond the Door* as the demonstration that the female protagonist is mad. Celia is not a threat to the institution of the cinema because she is "unbalanced"; on the contrary, Celia is coded as "unbalanced" because — as a female investigator who uncovers male guilt — she is a threat to the institution of cinema in its traditional role of maximizing the pleasure of the male spectator.

* * *

This chapter has explored different possible explanations for the problematic of the female investigator's madness in film. This insistent trope of madness appears independently of gendered agency in film production, feminist or non-feminist perspectives, and the female investigator's position within or outside desire. Instead, it might be explained better as the product of the male spectator's relationship with the cinematic apparatus and with the figure of the investigator.

·5·

A Case Study of *Rebecca*

Daphne du Maurier's 1938 novel *Rebecca* and the adaptations that followed it provide an ideal case study for theorizing the female detective, as the narrative has been adapted to all the areas of inquiry covered by this project: The narrative is available in its original gothic novel format, as the inspiration for a lesbian detective novel, as three made-for-television movies, and as a film.[1] By tracing the evolution of the narrative as it is transformed into these different formats, we can see how the theory of the flawed female investigator is played out in different genres and media.

Rebecca *as Gothic Novel*

The modern gothic novel *Rebecca*—published nearly 150 years after *Mysteries of Udolpho*—retains many of the qualities of earlier gothic novels. The nameless narrator is, like her gothic foremothers, an "almost-detective," whose investigations do not lead directly to her solving the mystery of her husband's first wife's death. The narrator's initial mastery of language and vision is steadily eroded as the narrative progresses, and the narrator's body is constructed as a problematic site.

A Nameless Narrator

Much ink has been spilled over the fact that the narrator of *Rebecca* herself is given no name. On this topic, Daphne du Maurier later noted:

> ... I continue to receive letters from all over the world asking me ... why did I never give the heroine a Christian name? The answer to the ... question is simple, I could not think of one, and it became a challenge in technique[,] the easier because I was writing in the first person.[2]

Yet du Maurier teases the reader throughout the novel with tantalizing glimpses of the narrator's name. The narrator notes: "...[M]y name was on the envelope, and spelt correctly, an unusual thing" (20). When she lunches with Maxim de Winter, he compliments her: "You have a very lovely and unusual name" (24). The narrator notes of Maxim "...[F]rom the very first he had called me by my [given name]" (43).

Interestingly, the narrator's given name is apparently her *father's* name (25). She bears this Name-of-the-Father not, as most do, solely in her last name, but in both of her names. Being named for her father suggests that the narrator stands in relation to him as a substitute son, and that any strengths she has inherited from him are those that a son would inherit from the patriarchy. This recalls Emily St. Aubert's relationship to her father in *Mysteries of Udolpho*. Like Emily St. Aubert and the other gothic heroines described in Chapter One, the narrator is conveniently orphaned — placed outside the family structure (24). The narrative details her flawed attempts to become reincorporated into a family.

The narrator's glory in attempting to join a family is reflected in her reaction to Maxim's marriage proposal. Her reaction to his proposal is characterized by her joy in being given a name, Maxim's name: "Mrs. de Winter. I would be Mrs. de Winter," (55) she repeats thrice in close succession. Shortly thereafter, she repeats almost the same words (57, 61).

The fetishistic repetition of the family name glorifies the patriarchal structure defining women as their husband's wives. The narrator also glorifies her dead father, a man so patriarchally dominant that upon his death, the narrator's mother "lingered behind him for five short weeks and stayed no more" (24). This inability to survive her husband suggests that a woman's identity is inextricably bound with that of her husband — when he exists no more, she exists no more. The narrator's mother's attitude foreshadows what the narrator's attitude will be when she finds that Maxim has killed his first wife: Her only thoughts are of protecting him, not of protecting herself.

Critics have dealt with the narrator's namelessness in different ways.[3] I shall simply call her the narrator, in recognition of the function she serves. This choice is no less problematic than other solutions, for as we shall see below, the fact that the narrator narrates does not ensure her mastery over language.

The *Rebecca* Narrator, Narrative, and Language

The narrator recalls her gothic foremothers by her powerful connection to books and reading. She constantly measures her life against the lives of characters in books and finds her life wanting. Her first kiss from Maxim is described as "[n]ot as dramatic as in books" (43). His proposal to her is similarly disappointing: "In books men knelt to women, and it would be moonlight. Not at breakfast, not like this" (53). Her bridal wardrobe is also disappointing: "Brides one read about had trousseaux, dozens of sets at a time, and I had never bothered" (138).

In terms of language, the narrator initially appears powerful. She narrates the novel from beginning to end, as opposed to being discussed in the third person (like Emily St. Aubert and Catherine Morland), or having her narrative stopped mid-novel (like Marian Halcombe), or having her narrative interrupted by a trial account (like Valeria Woodville). Moreover, the narrator's initial words, "Last night I dreamt I went to Manderley again," resonate powerfully because of the great popularity of the novel and its adaptations (1). This opening phrase ranks with "It was the best of times; it was the worst of times," "All happy families are alike..." and "Reader, I married him" as a phrase from a novel so famous that even people who have not read the novel know to which novel the words belong. Thus, curiously, the success of the novel boosts the authority of its narrator.

Yet the narrator's initial linguistic mastery is swiftly undercut. She ends her first narrative, her dream of the lost estate Manderley, with a vow of self-silence, resolving not to share her dream with her husband Maxim. "We would not talk of Manderley[.] I would not tell my dream," she vows(4). Similarly, the narrator initially indicates that she has found her voice through reading: "I have [found] a genius for reading aloud," she notes, describing her life in exile with Maxim (6). A few paragraphs later, however, it becomes clear that she has no mastery over what she reads, but rather is mastered by the text. An article that recalls Manderley to her and to Maxim makes her "falter as [she] read[s] aloud" (7). Maxim's response silences her permanently. "...I had learnt my lesson.... [I]n future keep the things that hurt to myself alone" (7). Though the narrator couches her silence in terms of protecting her husband, the fact remains that a man has made her limit her speech.

Even when the narrator speaks freely, that too, is controlled by men. The narrator dominates the conversation during her first lunch alone with Maxim, which might seem to indicate linguistic mastery (24). The topic of her conversation is limited to a man, however (the narrator's dead father), and it turns out that her conversation has been elicited from her almost against her will by her future husband Maxim. "I felt impelled to speak," she says, "because his eyes followed me..." (24).

The narrator duels over language with the dead Rebecca, jealous that Rebecca could call her husband Max, while she is relegated to calling him Maxim (44). This jealousy over language takes a visceral turn when the narrator physically destroys the title page of a book inscribed from Rebecca to "Max":

> I cut the page right out of the book. I left no jagged edges, and the book looked white and clean when the page was gone. A new book, that had not been touched. I tore the page up in many little fragments and threw them into the wastepaper basket.... But I kept thinking of the torn scraps in the basket, and after a moment I had to get up and look in the basket once more. Even now the ink stood up on the fragments thick and black, the writing was not destroyed. I took a box of matches and set fire to the fragments. The flame had a lovely light, staining the paper, curling the edges, making the slanting writing impossible to distinguish. The fragments fluttered to grey ashes. The letter R was the last to go, it twisted in the flame, it curled outwards for a moment, becoming larger than ever. Then it crumpled too; the flame destroyed it. It was not ashes even, it was feathery dust.... I went and washed my hands in the basin. I felt better, much better [58–59].

This is a curious way of turning over a new leaf, of starting the marriage with a blank slate. It is ineffective. Despite her burning of Rebecca's writing, the narrator is still forced to confront Rebecca's linguistic mastery at Manderley, where she sits at Rebecca's old writing desk using Rebecca's writing instruments and Rebecca's stationery. The comparison in their writing points out her own inadequacies related to caste: "...[A]s I wrote, in halting, laboured fashion ... I noticed for the first time how cramped and unformed was my own hand-writing, without individuality, without style, uneducated even, the writing of an indifferent pupil taught in a second-rate school," she says (89).

The narrator's mastery over language is compromised here by her class. The narrator occupies a liminal position in the British class structure. On the one hand, she has had an education, and is the daughter of respectable parents. On the other hand, when she meets her future husband, she is working as a servant ("companion") to a boorish American woman on holiday. The higher class position that is her birthright is highlighted by her relationship with language when she, Maxim de Winter, and her employer meet. The narrator understands Maxim's sarcasms, while her *nouveau riche* employer does not (16–18).

The narrator is also linguistically dominant over those who cannot or do not challenge her class status. She linguistically dominates Maxim's agent Frank Crawley, who immediately accepts her in her new role as mistress of

Manderley. This domination is underlined by the narrator's choice to call Frank Crawley by his given name: "I called him Frank because Maxim did, but he would always call me Mrs. de Winter"[4] (129). The narrator presses Frank in a way that she dares to question few others: "I had to go on with my questions [about Rebecca's death]," she says. "He did not want to talk about it, I knew that, but although I was sorry for him and shocked at my own self I had to continue, I could not be silent" (132). The narrator continues to extract information from Frank about Rebecca, and freely confesses her own sense of inadequacy, making Frank even more uncomfortable: "I saw that I had upset him far more than I had upset myself, and the realisation of this calmed me and gave me a feeling of superiority" (135).

The narrator's linguistic dominance over Frank is also shown by the fact that she can joke at his expense: "I turned away to hide my smile," she says, having jokingly told Frank that she will dance with no one with him and Maxim, and Frank has remonstrated that this would not be proper. "It was a joy to me the way he never knew when his leg had been pulled" (198). It is telling that the narrator's joke is a joke about class. She proposes to do something rude, and Frank believes that she is serious. The narrator, confident that she is well bred, shows here that she is secure in at least this aspect of her manners.

The narrator similarly dominates the mentally-disabled tenant of the estate, Ben, whom she characterizes as "even more frightened than I" (156). Ben is timid when she questions him about hanging around the abandoned boat house, and the narrator winds up lecturing Ben about stealing a fishing line and ordering him firmly to go home (156–157).

Yet, there is also an intimation that her work as a servant has problematized the narrator's class position. This is emphasized by her relationship with her servant, the forbidding Mrs. Danvers, after her marriage to Maxim. In a reverie about the luxurious teas at Manderley, the narrator recalls: "...[T]he waste used to worry me sometimes. But I never dared ask Mrs. Danvers what she did about it" (8). Here we see the reverse of Emily St. Aubert's position of linguistic mastery with regard to her servant Annette, as noted in Chapter One above. Emily, secure in her class position, dominates Annette linguistically. Here, the narrator, tainted by the suggestion of having married above her station, is dominated by Mrs. Danvers.

The *Rebecca* Narrator and Vision

Like Emily St. Aubert and Jane Eyre, the narrator finds her initial mastery over vision swiftly undercut. Like Emily and Jane, the narrator is an artist. She sketches a fanciful image of Maxim costumed as a medieval gentleman, asserting her mastery over the man she desires by representing the male figure according to her own desire and imagination (19–20). Yet after she receives an unsigned note from him, she chastises herself for her inability to draw realistically: "[I] turned once more to my pencil drawing, but for no known reason it did not please me any more[.] [T]he face was stiff and lifeless, and the lace collar and the beard were like props in a charade" (20). It is telling that the interruption from Maxim's note, an intrusion whose source is the very object of her painting, makes her doubt her visual mastery. She goes from a desiring viewing subject mastering the viewed desired object to being mastered by it.

The narrator's sketching is brought up several more times throughout the narrative, but is similarly undercut each time. "Maxim says you paint," says her sister-in-law Beatrice. "That's very nice, of course, but there's no exercise in it, is there? All very well on a wet day when there's nothing better to do" (96–97). Here, the narrator's painting is seen as a pale substitute for the more vigorous and upper-class sports that Beatrice pursues, such as riding to the hunt. Similarly, a bishop's wife damns the narrator's hobby with faint praise, saying, "It's a nice little talent to have" (127).

The last time the narrator sketches in the novel, her sketches lead to her downfall: In planning her costume for a ball, the narrator sketches a few ideas from a book, then rejects them and tosses them in the wastepaper basket (201). Mrs. Danvers looks through the wastepaper baskets — a curiously personal invasion of privacy — sees the narrator's rejected sketches, and persuades the narrator to copy a costume from one of the family portraits hanging at Manderley (201–202). The narrator sketches the portrait and sends off for her costume (206). Initially, her sketches seem to lead to success: the delivered costume made from her sketches is "perfect" (208). This "perfect" costume, made when the narrator has let Mrs. Danvers substitute her choice of artistic subject for the narrator's own taste, is also a spectacular failure, however. Mrs. Danvers has led the narrator to base her costume on a portrait that was also used by the late Rebecca as the model for an identical costume (220). Rather than mastering the subject of the portrait and asserting her own artistic vision of self-presentation, the narrator has been again mastered by the matter she sought to sketch. The narrator's appearance in the copied gown leads to shocked stares of horror (216–217). She finds herself not admired as the creating subject of a brilliant artistic creation but reviled as a grotesque object who is spoken by her costume in a way she cannot comprehend.

The narrator's problematized relationship with vision is intimately tied to her liminal class position. As the new mistress of Manderley, the narrator is the object of many inquisitive stares, a fit object of vision for the curious of all classes. Her upper-class sister-in-law Beatrice looks her "up and down" upon meeting her, and the narrator catches Beatrice glancing at her often (95, 103). Rebecca's disreputable lower-class cousin Favell likewise looks the narrator "up and down" on meeting her (161).

As a bride, the narrator finds that even her sexual status is an object for visual speculation. She is also given the once over by a bishop's wife: "I saw her eye ... dubious ... taking in my clothes from top to toe, wondering, with that swift downward glance given to all brides, if I was going to have a baby" (128). This assessment of her as a newlywed bride is fairly impersonal, however — any new bride of the rural gentry might face similar curiosity.

Much more personal and clearly class-based, however, is the narrator's duel on the field of vision with the formidable housekeeper Mrs. Danvers. The narrator is radically over-determined as the object of Mrs. Danvers' vision. The narrative is peppered with references to Mrs. Danvers' visual mastery over the narrator: "[Mrs. Danvers] began to speak..., her hollow eyes never leaving my eyes, so that my own wavered and would not meet hers..." (68) "I knew her eye to be upon me" (68). "[Mrs. Danvers] stood waiting for me ... the hollow eyes watching me intently from the white skull's face" (71). "I wondered why she must go on standing there, watching me..." (73). "I found myself held by [Mrs. Danvers'] eyes, that had no light, no flicker of sympathy towards me" (73). "[Mrs. Danvers] was like a shadow ... watching me, appraising me..." (75). "Mrs. Danvers ... went on looking at me" (162). "...[W]hy did Mrs. Danvers have to stand there looking at me..." (163)?

This inspection of the narrator by Mrs. Danvers — theoretically, the narrator's social inferior — clearly carries a class valence. The narrator is held up to a servant's scrutiny and found lacking, unworthy of her class position.

The *Rebecca* Narrator and Clothing

The narrator's clothed body is also a problematic site. She recalls what she looked like when first meeting Maxim, describing herself as "...dressed in an ill-fitting coat and skirt and a jumper of [her] own creation ... like a shy, uneasy colt" (9). When she approaches Manderley for the first time, she is "unsuitably dressed as usual" (62). Her sister-in-law comments, "I can tell by the way you dress that you don't care a hoot what you wear" (101).

The narrator's relationship to clothes is, like her relationship to vision, a marker of class anxiety. She is so ashamed of her worn underclothes that she mends them herself rather than have the housemaid see them, and she is quite relieved to get a lady's maid of such humble origins that she does not disdain the narrator's clothes (138).

The narrator's dowdy wardrobe is compared to the dead Rebecca's expensive, tasteful trousseau. Rebecca's gowns and underthings are maintained in perfect condition, as if Rebecca were still alive, by the devoted Mrs. Danvers, who fetishizes the physical objects chosen and worn by Rebecca (172).

As noted above, the narrator's lone attempt to control her own self-presentation through clothing, her attempt to play dress-up at a costume ball, ends in a resounding failure.

The *Rebecca* Narrator's Distrust of Her Own Perceptions

The narrator is clearly able to perceive danger, but quickly doubts her own perceptions. After Maxim has almost driven her off a cliff and is staring at her oddly, lost in another world, as they stand by the cliff's edge, the narrator is understandably alarmed. She reasonably suspects that he might be slipping into madness and might really push her off the cliff in a trance. As soon as she manages to recall Maxim to himself, however, she minimizes her prior perceptions of danger: "I had misjudged him of course," she says, "[and] there was nothing wrong after all" (29). In fact, something *is* very wrong. As Maxim will later confide, he stood on this very cliff with the late Rebecca and almost pushed her off it, and he later did indeed kill Rebecca (276, 284).

The narrator tends to ascribe all of her reasonable curiosity about Maxim and Rebecca to her own supposed psychological inadequacies. The narrator is disturbed by things that remind her of Rebecca's death: "I wanted to forget them but at the same time I wanted to know why they disturbed me, why they made me uneasy and unhappy. Somewhere, at the back of my mind, there was a frightened furtive seed of curiosity that grew slowly and stealthily, for all my denial of it..." (123). This curiosity and anxiety is quite natural, given the mysterious circumstances of Rebecca's death and Maxim's odd behavior whenever Rebecca is mentioned, yet the narrator swiftly disavows it. Instead of trusting her instincts, she focuses on protecting Maxim from any reminders of Rebecca's death. When Frank brings up something about sailing that she fears will remind

Maxim of Rebecca's death, she indulges in a frenzy of self-blame: "I was wrong of course, morbid, stupid; this was the hyper-sensitive behaviour of a neurotic, not the normal happy self I knew myself to be" (123). After she has questioned Frank about Rebecca, but he has begged her to forget the past, the narrator feels guilty over her investigative impulses: "I had been selfish and hyper-sensitive, a martyr to my own inferiority complex" (136).

This inaccurate psychologizing hides the narrator's real psychological problem, discussed further below, of identifying so profoundly with Maxim and the patriarchal privilege he represents that her greatest aim in life becomes to prevent Maxim from suffering the consequences of having killed Rebecca. The narrator only gains confidence in her own perceptions after Maxim has told her that he killed Rebecca. Only then is she able confidently to perceive things that Maxim cannot perceive: "...I saw Frank looking at Maxim. He looked away again immediately but not before I had seen and understood the expression in his eyes. Frank knew. And Maxim did not know that he knew" (302). This change is so important that du Maurier repeats it a few pages later (308).

The *Rebecca* Narrator and Same-Sex Desire

Rebecca has been a text fascinating to theorists of gay and lesbian literature.[5] The narrator's relation to heterosexual desire is mediated by several same-sex metaphors. For example, in describing her initial crush on Maxim, the narrator likens herself to a schoolboy smitten with an older male schoolmate: "...I was young enough to win happiness in the wearing of his clothes, playing the schoolboy again who carries his hero's sweater and ties it about his throat choking with pride..." (36) she says. The image of the sweater tied about a throat and the image of choking may suggest to the modern reader auto-erotic asphyxiation. That association aside, the image certainly links desire to death, to an extinguishing of identity.

In several other places, the narrator associates herself with being a young boy. She likens her role *vis à vis* her employer to that of a "whipping boy" (42). More significantly, when she fears that she will be unable to be a wife to Maxim, she offers him instead a life of masculine companionship with her, offering to be "a sort of boy" for him (269).

The *Rebecca* Narrator's Body

The narrator's body betrays her as she is unable to control her tears: "I could not check them, for they came unbidden.... I thought of all those heroines of fiction who looked pretty when they cried, and what a contrast I must make with blotched and swollen face, and red rims to my eyes" (41). This lack of control of body is replayed throughout the narrative. The narrator faints at the inquest into Rebecca's death (316–318). Her legs likewise betray her as Maxim drives back to the house after the inquest: "I tried to get up but my legs were things of straw, they would not bear me" (323), she says.

The *Rebecca* Narrator as Almost-Investigator

Despite her attempts to investigate, the narrator is prone to misinterpret the information that others give her.[6] Like other gothic heroines, she leaps to inaccurate conclusions and winds up having others explain the truth to her, not divining it herself. The narrator is blind to the mentally-disabled Ben's hints as to what happened to Rebecca. Ben cogently notes that a tall, dark woman used to come to the cottage by night and that she threatened to send him to the asylum if he looked in at the cottage windows again (157). Not only does the narrator have no idea to whom Ben refers, but she dismisses his coherent narrative solely because he is mentally disabled (158). When Ben later says that the "fishes have eaten her"—"the other one"—the narrator still mistakes to which "her" Ben refers (263). Both of the narrator's informational encounters with Ben are followed immediately afterwards by long scenes with Mrs. Danvers in Rebecca's old rooms, in which Mrs. Danvers provides contextual clues that should allow the narrator (and the reader) to decipher Ben's tale. Mrs. Danvers lets the narrator know that Rebecca was tall and had dark hair (171) and used to frequent the cottage (173), often for liaisons (249)—just like the tall dark woman in Ben's tales. Yet the narrator still makes no sense of what Ben has said. Only when the blackmailing Favell explicitly threatens to produce a witness to Maxim's crime does the narrator realize what Ben has been telling her all along (339).

Similarly, despite the narrator's continuing fascination with Rebecca's death and sunken boat, she completely misinterprets a number of clues to the past. When the narrator innocently mentions that Maxim must have married her because the narrator is unlikely to cause any gossip, Maxim becomes furious. The narrator is baffled by his rage, evincing no suspicion that Rebecca may have indeed given rise to local gossip. Likewise, when Frank Crawley says, "kindliness, and sincerity, and if I may say so — modesty — are worth far more to a man, to a husband, than all the wit and beauty in the world" (135), the narrator fails to understand Frank's implication that Rebecca was neither kind, nor sincere, nor modest.

The narrator also completely misinterprets the meaning of the body found when Rebecca's sunken vessel is discovered, believing the body in the boat to be that of another person. Only after Maxim explicitly narrates his killing of Rebecca does the narrator understand the truth about what he has done.

The *Rebecca* Narrator and Patriarchy

Patriarchy never had such a friend as the narrator of *Rebecca*. Far from being horrified and/or terrified by Maxim's revelation that he killed Rebecca, the narrator is simply pleased that *she*, not Rebecca, is the prize desired by Maxim. Rather than seeking to escape him, she unreflectingly throws all of her energies towards helping him escape punishment for his crime. Indeed, she seems briefly to consider murdering the blackmailing Favell, who correctly accuses Maxim of Rebecca's murder: "In a book or in a play I would have found a revolver and we should have shot Favell, hidden his body in a cupboard. There was no revolver. There was no cupboard. We were ordinary people. These things did not happen" (334). This wistfully expressed desire to kill Favell is astounding not only for its murderous wish, but also for the depth of the narrator's denial about what has already happened. There certainly *is* a revolver in the house — the one that Maxim used to shoot Rebecca. Moreover, these things *do* happen — "ordinary people" like Maxim do kill.[7]

Divine Victim: *A Lesbian Re-imagining of* Rebecca

Divine Victim,[8] a modern gothic novel by lesbian mystery novelist Mary Wings, is a creative re-imagining of du Maurier's *Rebecca*.[9] With its lesbian and gay undertones, du Maurier's *Rebecca* easily lends itself to a lesbian re-writing. The initial parallels between Wings' *Divine Victim* and du Maurier's *Rebecca* are many: Both narratives have nameless first-person narrators. Both narratives open with the narrator's approach to a house owned by her partner, the female occupant of which has recently died. Both dead women are named Rebecca, and the narrator of each narrative is compelled to piece together the dead Rebecca's life while living in the dead woman's home. Both narrators have a strong relationship with art and the visual: the narrator of *Rebecca* is an artist herself; the narrator of *Divine Victim* is an art historian. Both narrators are fish out of water: the narrator of *Rebecca* is a commoner living among the gentry; the narrator of *Divine Victim* is a cosmopolitan lesbian living in a small homophobic town in Montana. All of these similarities initially lead the reader to expect that *Divine Victim* will be a straightforward adaptation of *Rebecca* where the characters and events of the earlier narrative will map directly onto the later narrative.

Wings emphasizes the *Rebecca* allusion via explicit references. Upon first seeing the house of the dead Rebecca, the *Divine Victim* narrator soliloquizes: "Last night I dreamt I went to Manderley again..." (8). Moreover, the narrator's lover Marya explicitly refers to the film version of *Rebecca*: "I'm being Judith Anderson playing Mrs. Danvers!" (54) she exults, laughing. The narrative also offers its own menacing Mrs. Danvers figure in the avenging homophobic Helen Danroy, who can't come to terms with the fact that her grandmother was the lover of Marya's late Aunt Rebecca.

The reader eventually finds, however, that the seemingly simple one-to-one correspondence of characters and events is more complicated than it initially appears. Initially, the *Divine Victim* narrator's current lover Marya seems to be a potentially homicidal double for *Rebecca's* Maxim de Winter. Like Maxim de Winter, Marya is not "forthcoming about her background" (5). The *Divine Victim* narrator looks up to see Marya coming at her with an ice axe over her head (53–54), and the narrator is the victim of several mysterious attacks by an unknown assailant, who might be Marya. It turns out, however, that Marya's ice axe is for mountain climbing, that Marya really is just acting out a part from the film version of *Rebecca*, and that the mysterious attacks are not Marya's doing.

Initially, Marya's dead Great Aunt Rebecca seems like a double for the dead Rebecca in *Rebecca*. The *Divine Victim* Rebecca turns out to be merely a red herring, an interesting side-line to the real narrative, however. She turns out to be the heroine of the piece: a transgressive lesbian ex-nun who used her wits to fashion a beautiful sanctuary of religious sculpture where she could pursue her own brand of matriarchal worship in peace.

The real Rebecca-figure of *Divine Victim* is the narrator's unfaithful (42) former girlfriend Ilona, who (as the reader later learns) has been murdered by the narrator in a fit of rage. Moreover, the reader slowly grows to realize that the narrator of *Divine Victim* is *not* a double for the mousy narrator of *Rebecca*. Rather, the *Divine Victim* narrator is a double for the murderous Maxim: she has murdered her former lover Ilona and is waiting for the authorities to catch up with her.

Who doubles the mousy narrator of *Rebecca*? Not the *Divine Victim* narrator's current lover Marya, who is rather hearty, over-inquisitive, and not particularly timid or weak. I suggest that *Divine Victim* thrusts the *reader* into the role occupied by the mousy *Rebecca* narrator: The reader is led to wonder about Ilona's fate, but is only given access to what happened through bits of the tale sparingly doled out by the *Divine Victim* narrator. In contrast to the implied reader of *Rebecca*, who should understand more than the narrator does, the implied reader of *Divine Victim* knows *less* than the narrator does, and has access to the story only through the narrator's gradual revelations. The narrator is initially misleading about how her relationship with Ilona ended, mentioning initially only a "horrendous break-up" (5), quite an understated way of saying that she pushed Ilona off a cliff.[10] When the *Divine Victim* narrator finally reveals the truth, the reader is already highly identified with the narrator. *Divine Victim* places its implied reader in the position in which the reader is most likely to understand, and in some measure be tempted to forgive/excuse, the narrator's objectively unforgivable murderous act. The reader has followed the narrator-protagonist through so many vicissitudes that the text almost forces the implied reader into a position of wondering if— or even hoping that — the narrator will get away with her heinous crime.

I would suggest that one effect of Wings' strategy here is to force the implied lesbian/feminist reader of *Divine Victim* to grapple with the understudied phenomenon of domestic violence within the lesbian community.[11] Here, the "masculine" guilt that underlies the gothic is placed instead upon the narrator herself and, by implication, upon the implied reader who has been identifying with the narrator up to this point. Moreover, by putting the reader in the position of the *Rebecca* narrator, in *Divine Victim* Mary Wings answers the "How could she!?" response that many a feminist reader has had to the *Rebecca* narrator's acceptance of Maxim's crime — if we identify with the murderous *Divine Victim* narrator and hope for her somehow to escape her just deserts, we are guilty of the same folly as the *Rebecca* narrator. Wings shows us the seductive compulsion of identification with the storyteller, even if the story told is of the storyteller's own guilt. This lesbian gothic novel tells the reader unpleasant truths not about the Other, but about *herself*.

Domestic Violence in *Divine Victim*

Is it an accident that the initial letters of "Divine Victim" are DV, the same abbreviation used by family law attorneys and courts nationwide to indicate domestic violence? I suspect not. The narrative of *Divine Victim* is rife with violence committed by women against women, and domestic violence seems to be one of the main motifs of the novel.[12] The violence spans quite a range. At one end is violence against property by the narrator's lover Marya, although she is one of the characters in the book portrayed more positively. Marya keeps destroying religious art that the narrator values: Marya kicks a Madonna statue, topples a statue of St. Bridget, purposely shatters a collection of saints that the narrator has carefully arranged, accidentally knocks over a statue of St. Frances, and unintentionally discards a priceless Madonna painting for which the narrator has been searching (122, 90–91, 44, 122, 241–243). Marya justifies her violence against this religious art as a political statement. Her description of the priceless Madonna: "...Elizabeth Taylor violet eyes and an aquiline nose. Totally Aryan. Catholic imagery has no racial integrity..." (242). She follows her toppling of St. Bridget by interpreting fasting nuns as early anorexics, describing them as "sick" and "pathological" (91). Marya is also not immune from the threat of violence based upon sexual jealousy: Her expression is "near-violent" when she incorrectly suspects the narrator of infidelity (131).

The nuns at the convent where the late Rebecca fell in love with a fellow postulant are also parties to violence committed against other women, though their excuse is religion. In the name of religious purity, the mother superior forces Rebecca to kneel on broken shards of pottery and hold her hands over her head every night for a week (160). To keep Rebecca from pride in her accomplishments as a sculptor, the mother superior grabs Rebecca by the ear, forces her to crush one of her statues, and then eat the raw clay (156). When Rebecca and her love kiss openly, the mother superior hits Rebecca in the arm and slashes Rebecca in the face, causing a scar that will never heal (173). Other nuns are complicit in the violence, not warning the lovers that the mother superior holds scissors behind her back and physically restraining Rebecca's lover and stopping her from screaming when Rebecca is attacked (173).

The narrator's former girlfriend Ilona is more directly violent toward the narrator, constantly putting her down, blaming her for their fights, and playing mind games with her. "The truth was," admits the narrator, "Ilona had tried to convince me I was crazy" (95). Ilona is also physically violent towards the narrator, grabbing her wrist and attempting to strangle her with a brasierre (63).

The narrator herself, initially passive with Ilona, eventually becomes violent towards her also. In their final confrontation, the narrator hits Ilona after Ilona dares her to do so (232). Their argument intensifies after Ilona threatens to leave the narrator stranded by the roadside and throws a dead cat at the narrator (232–233). Ilona then makes her infidelity clear, though her jab is not at the narrator's sexuality, but at the narrator's intellectual prowess:

> "Do you know what?" she jeered. "The only way your dissertation was accepted was because I was fucking your advisor. Five months we fucked and you didn't even guess! We couldn't believe it" [234].

The narrator responds by waiting until Ilona puts her car in neutral and then pushing Ilona and the car off the edge of a cliff (234–235).

Although the narrator tries to rehabilitate herself with the reader and seems to suffer genuine pangs of guilt, she clearly is capable of repeating her violent behavior against other women: When the narrator is trying to discover what Marya did with the priceless Madonna, she shakes her by the shoulders (242).

Divine Victim as Lesbian Detective Novel

Despite its highly original twist on the *Rebecca* narrative, *Divine Victim* also exhibits aspects of the lesbian detective novel: car trouble, concerns over the protagonist's physical integrity, and a fear of a sexual loss of control. This is not surprising, as author Mary Wings is also the author of a popular series of more traditional lesbian detective novels.[13]

Car Trouble in *Divine Victim*

The narrator of *Divine Victim*, like many lesbian detectives, has car trouble. The narrative opens with anxiety about driving: "It was the final freezing night of driving and I was nervous.... A sudden slip would mean a trip to the ditch and an entrance to the sleepy world just beyond freezing" (3). The car slips, skids, sways, and swerves as the narrator and Marya draw up to their destination (3, 8). The women's car is also vandalized in a way directly connected to their lesbianism: "QUEERS DIE" is scratched on it (125–126). In a flashback to Italy, the narrator drives drunk, without headlights, and the narrator's terrible secret also involves "car trouble": The narrator kills Ilona by pushing her over the edge of a cliff in her car (230, 235).

The *Divine Victim* Narrator's Physical Integrity

The narrative also shares the same concerns over the narrator's physical integrity as other lesbian detective narratives do. The narrator suffers frequent physical attacks from the evil Helen Danroy, who cannot get over the fact that her very Catholic grandmother had a long-ago lesbian relationship with the dead Rebecca. The narrator is scalded by a water heater that has been tampered with, almost electrocuted, gassed with carbon monoxide and with an industrial solvent, hit on the back of the head, bound, and gagged by Helen Danroy (28–29, 115–116, 207, 196, 197–198). Yet the narrator never sees the attacks coming. Although the narrator eventually triumphs over Helen Danroy by working free from her bonds and hitting Helen over the head with a plaster statue of St. Jude, her physical integrity remains threatened (209): She slips and falls while trying to rescue the valuable Madonna picture from the bowels of a garbage truck (242).

The *Divine Victim* Narrator and Sexual Domination

The narrator, like many other lesbian detectives, struggles with the fear of becoming femme-inized. The narrator describes her first time making love with Ilona as an experience that makes her unaccountably passive: "I let Ilona touch me where she wanted, without knowing how I'd suddenly become so passive, except that my breathing was making me faint" (38). The narrator is bound and gagged by Helen Danroy in a position that she would relish with another partner: "I wouldn't mind Sister Redmpta putting me in this position, I thought, as I tugged at the leather thongs," says the narrator (199). Moreover, there is a hint of bondage play in the relationship between the narrator and Marya, as Marya's copy of *Bad Attitude* contains a bondage pictorial (213).

The *Divine Victim* Narrator as Almost-Detective

The *Divine Victim* narrator shows her gothic roots by being an almost-detective. She scores some successes, like figuring out that Helen Danroy is not a nurse, as she initially pretends to be (101–102). The narrator does not notice, however, when Helen Danroy steals her wallet to investigate *her* (209). The narrator visits the nunnery where the late Rebecca was a postulant, but finds out what happened only because, in a scene reminiscent of *The Mysteries of Udolpho*, an old nun tells her the whole story (148–185). Although the narrator seeks a valuable Madonna painting stolen by the late Rebecca, she does not actually find it, even though it is in a fairly obvious hiding place. Instead, her lover Marya finds it and tosses it out with the trash, while the narrator is powerless to save it from being crushed by a garbage truck (242–243).

The *Divine Victim* Narrator in the Field of Vision

As an art historian, the narrator initially seems to occupy a privileged position in the field of looking relations. Her profession is to look, to interpret, to pronounce judgment upon works of art. Yet her visual mastery is swiftly undercut. The text makes much of her failing eyesight — she is constantly squinting or getting her glasses whenever she has to read a business card or any other writing. Moreover, the narrator finds herself in an unwelcome position as viewed object when she runs into Mrs. Danroy, who recalls Mrs. Danvers as an all-powerful viewing subject. "I found it hard to escape from her gaze," the narrator notes (74). The narrator also is "hypnotized" by the gaze of a nun, whose look makes the narrator physically uncomfortable: "Two points of light, like hot coals, burned into my face," she says. "My skin flushed as I stood transfixed" (148).

The narrator's most damning transformation into viewed object rather than viewing subject comes when Ilona urges a lecherous man to take the narrator's picture over the narrator's protests (226). This picture is the link that will ultimately allow the narrator to be traced as Ilona's murderer (237).

Rebecca *as Made-for-Television Movie*

The narrative of *Rebecca* has been made over into made-for-television movies at least three times: in 1962, 1978, and 1997. I consider here all three made-for-television movies. The two earlier versions were somewhat difficult to obtain, and for that reason, I believe that heretofore they have not been much studied. The 1962 version is available at the Museum of Television and Radio in New York City.[14] The 1980 version was never released commercially on video, and after an exhaustive search, the only place I was able to view it was at Britain's National Film and Television Archive in London.[15]

The 1962 *Theatre '62* presentation of *Rebecca* aired on NBC on April 8th, 1962 as a live television adaptation of the novel. The end titles of this version say "Based on the David O. Selznick film." They certainly *should* give credit to the film version, as several sequences are stolen nearly shot-for-shot from the Selznick/Hitchcock film, especially from Hitchcock's ending where the viewer sees Manderley burn down. Mrs. Danvers is silhouetted against the flames, just as in the Hitchcock film, and the last shot of the production is the burning "R" on Rebecca's hand-embroidered nightie-case.

Sponsored by "your local gas company," the 1962 *Theatre '62* adaptation is interrupted by commercials for a dizzying array of gas-guzzling products — gas kitchen appliances, gas clothes dryers, outdoor gaslights,[16] gas ranges, gas heaters, and gas cooling systems. Due to time constraints and the constraints of live television, this version skips a fair amount of du Maurier's narrative,[17] but keeps the opening voiceover from the novel,[18] and generally remains true to the feel of the du Maurier novel.

The narrator is not as de-glamourized as she is in the novel.[19] Her hair is styled in a fashionable 1960s flip, suggesting obliquely that the events portrayed are contemporaneous with the time of the production. She wears nice tailored clothes that fit her well: a skirted suit, a rather mannish vest, a jacket and skirt, a sweater and skirt, a twin-set and skirt. There is no hint, as there is constantly in the novel, that she is wearing clothes (and metaphorically a familial role) that are too big for her. Because she seems to have no problems with her image, she likewise doesn't need to over-compensate for it. The ball at which she unwittingly wears Rebecca's old costume is not her idea in this version of the narrative. It is the choice of Maxim (James Mason)—a means to present the narrator to the county and to his relatives. This narrative shift emphasizes the narrator's indifferent relationship to self-specularization.

The 1962 television production interestingly presents the most assertive narrator (Joan Hackett). Instead of merely dominating Frank Crawley (Murray Matheson), as she does in the novel, the narrator is assertive with all of her servants. For example, rather than pretending she knows where the morning room is and being corrected by the butler Frith, as she is in all the other versions of the narrative, in this version, she boldly asks him outright where it is. Moreover, the narrator is assertive with her husband. When she has heard Maxim's terrible tale, she is impressively level-headed and cheerful as she tries to buck him up. The rather unsettling effect is as if a perky 1960s heroine like Annette Funicello, Sally Field, or Mary Tyler Moore suddenly found herself in the narrator's unenviable position.

More remarkably, the narrator is far less dominated by Mrs. Danvers (Nina Foch) than in other versions. She isn't too shy to admit in front of Mrs. Danvers that she broke a cupid figurine, as she is in all of the other versions of the narrative. Instead, she boldly announces, "I'm afraid I broke it" in front of Mrs. Danvers as soon as Mrs. Danvers mentions the figurine, and she generally speaks to Mrs. Danvers with an air of self-assurance. Incredibly, she even forgets Mrs. Danvers' name at one point. Also, the narrator is not subjected to Mrs. Danvers' investigation: Mrs. Danvers doesn't root through the narrator's garbage to find her discarded sketches for the ball; instead, a minor servant, Robert, finds them left in the family portrait gallery. Finally, even when Mrs. Danvers throws her most potent dart, asking "Do you believe the dead come back and watch the living?", the narrator has the presence of mind to answer back clearly: "No, no, no — I don't believe that." This blithe self-confidence with servants and employees may be due to American notions of upward mobility and a classless society, for this is the most American of all the film and television versions of *Rebecca*, produced specifically for an American television audience. Hence, the narrator here does not seem to feel that she has married above her station as much as the narrator does in the British versions of *Rebecca*, and accordingly feels less like she has to impress the servants with signs that she deserves the class status derived from her marriage.

The narrator is also presented as physically hardy in the 1962 version. She skips the inquest into Rebecca's death in favor of a brief description of the proceedings. This feature of the production may perhaps have been a time-saving strategy, but it means that the audience never sees the narrator faint, as she does in all of the other versions.

Rebecca's death is presented here much as in the Hitchcock film, as an unpremeditated/accidental crime of passion. Maxim narrates: "She said: 'All right, Maxim, what're you going to do about it? Kill me?' She wouldn't stop laughing.... I went mad for a minute, and I must've struck her, perhaps more than once.... She stumbled and suddenly she fell. She didn't get up. She hit her head against a heavy piece of ship's tackle." Here the ship's tackle is made the villain, absolving Maxim of some responsibility for Rebecca's death.

The four-hour 1978 BBC/Time Life production of *Rebecca* is particularly memorable. Although it was never commercially released after airing in Britain in 1979 and although it aired in the United States in 1980, librarians on both sides of the Atlantic recalled it as a wonderful production. It is also noteworthy as an ambivalent work, simultaneously progressive and regressive, reflecting both the gains of the women's movement and the coming backlash against them.

The longer 1978 version has a distinct advantage over the shorter 1962 version, as it is able to include large chunks of dialogue from the du Maurier novel. The narrator[20] (Joanna David) does begin the film with "Last night I dreamt I went to Manderley again..." and continues with a goodly chunk of du Maurier's opening monologue. The film differs from the novel, however, in that the narrator is shown not to be addressing the audience with her opening monologue, but to be speaking to an older man, whom we only see from the back, but who is presumably Maxim (Jeremy Irons). This is interesting in that, in the novel, the narrator deliberately does not bring up anything about Manderley that could upset Maxim, whereas here, she seems to think nothing of stirring up possibly painful memories for him. It suggests that her role is not necessarily to restrict her own speech to protect her man, and that her own right to self-expression is as important as his preferences. This fits in with some of the ideas of the women's consciousness-raising movements of the early 1970s.

The narrator is shown to be more of an investigator in the 1978 version than in other versions of the narrative. She specifically asks Mrs. Van Hopper what happened to the first Mrs. de Winter, and Mrs. Van Hopper gives her the important information that Rebecca drowned in a bay near Manderley. She also insists on answers to the questions she poses to Maxim. "Do you know this place? Have you been here before?" the narrator asks as Maxim broods looking out over a cliff. He doesn't answer her, and she has to remind him twice that it's getting late and that they should be going home before Maxim snaps out of his trance. As they get back into the car, the narrator persists, "*Have* you been here before?" Maxim finally answers, "Yes, some years ago. I wanted to see if it had changed." The narrator presses on, asking, "And has it?", eliciting from Maxim the admission, "No ... No, it has not changed." Later she asks Maxim whether he bought the cupid that she broke and why he has to go to London. Both times, she apparently elicits honest answers from Maxim. The narrator also openly grills Frank Crawley about Rebecca's death, asking him questions such as "What happened when she was drowned?", "How long afterwards did they find her?", "How did they know it was her?", and "...Was Rebecca very beautiful?" Frank, like Maxim and Mrs. Van Hopper, answers her honestly. In no other version of the narrative is the narrator such an insistent and successful investigator. This investigative competence may also be a reflection of the times.

The longer time frame of the 1978 version also allows the breakfast scene where Maxim asks the narrator to marry him to be emphasized and more unhurried and to include more dialogue from the novel. This version has the narrator slated to leave Monte Carlo the next day,[21] not in a few hours. Maxim is not in dishabille and not shaving (as he is in the Hitchcock film) when they begin their discussion:

MAXIM: I'm asking you to marry me, you little fool! ... You think I'm asking you to marry me ... to be kind, don't you?
NARRATOR: Yes.
MAXIM: Yes, well one of these days you'll realize that being kind *isn't* my strongest quality.

Maxim's last comment here touches on another subject that the 1978 version deals with more directly than any other version: domestic violence.

In this version, Maxim begins with verbal abuse of his new bride's sartorial choices as they approach his home: "Why don't you take off that mackintosh. It hasn't rained at all down here. And put that little fur thing straight." Although this is adapted from dialogue in the novel, it has a more critical valence on-screen: in the novel, Maxim seems concerned about not having gotten the narrator a trousseau; in the television movie, he appears controlling. Another exchange between the couple makes explicit the threat of domestic violence:

> NARRATOR: ... I do so wish you wouldn't treat me like a silly little girl.
> MAXIM: How do you want to be treated?
> NARRATOR: Like other men treat their wives.
> MAXIM: Heh, heh, heh ... Knock you about, you mean?
> NARRATOR: Oh, don't be absurd. Why must you make a joke of everything I say?
> MAXIM: I'm not joking. I'm very serious.

Maxim's last lines here have a chilling valence when one realizes he did indeed kill his first wife — often in real life the culmination of domestic violence. Jeremy Brett's Maxim is by far the angriest Maxim in any of the adaptations — e.g., Maxim yells loudly at the narrator when she wears the offending dress to the costume ball. He also yells loudly at the narrator several other times. This angry portrayal of Maxim makes it plausible that he committed a crime of violence.

In some ways, the emphasis on Maxim's potential for violence is a reflection of increasing awareness of domestic violence in the late 1970s and early 1980s.[22] On the other hand, the actual killing of Rebecca is portrayed in a way that absolves Maxim of responsibility for it. "I fired at her heart," Maxim explains. His language makes it sound as if Rebecca were killed by a firing squad, as if she were being justly punished by the forces of (a masculine) law for daring to threaten the legitimacy of patriarchal succession. The only visual portrayal of the scene is a shot of the barrel of the gun, firing in the fog (although diegetically, the killing took place indoors, where there would be no fog). This disembodied gun, with no shot of Maxim's hand pulling the trigger and no reaction shot of Rebecca as victim, makes the murder seem curiously detached from Maxim, and in some ways absolves him of responsibility.

This ambiguous treatment of domestic violence — acknowledging it more openly, but implying that in Rebecca's case it was justified — reflects ambivalent public attitudes of the late 1970s and early 1980s, when growing awareness of the problem was countered by a tendency to blame abused women themselves for domestic violence. Susan Faludi has detailed how films like *Fatal Attraction* expressed this ambiguity.[23] The 1978 version of *Rebecca* simply did so earlier.

The 1978 production, like the 1962 production, offers feminist viewers an assertive narrator who seems more comfortable with her role as mistress of Manderley than her predecessors in the novel and the Hitchcock film. As with the 1962 version, I attribute this change to changing societal attitudes about the fluidity of class boundaries.

The 1997 Mobil Masterpiece Theatre production of *Rebecca* shares some important characteristics with television series that feature female investigators. A made-for-television movie necessarily differs from a television series in that the television series has a great deal of time for characters to change and grow, while a made-for-television movie must condense character development, much like a traditional film. Nevertheless, the 1997 television movie production of *Rebecca* is similar to television series in several ways: the female investigator is portrayed as competent, self-confident, and sexually knowledgeable; the female investigator is not necessarily specularized; and the portrayal of the female investigator is very much influenced by the socio-cultural milieu of the time of production.

More so than the film version of *Rebecca* (discussed below), the 1997 television movie changes Daphne du Maurier's words — skipping and altering large portions of du Maurier's dialogue. Notably, the opening voiceover narration — "Last night I went to Manderley again..." — is entirely gone from the opening of the television movie, though this monologue opens both the novel and the film. Instead, rather than opening the television movie, the voiceover drawn from the monologue in first and second chapters of the novel becomes an epilogue, following du Maurier's original scheme.[24] I call the second Mrs. de Winter "the narrator" here for consistency's sake, though she narrates nothing until the conclusion of the television movie.

The 1997 television movie portrays the narrator as far more competent and self-confident than the novel and film versions of *Rebecca* do. In the novel and the film, the narrator is too cowed by the imperious Mrs. Van Hopper to dare to tell her of her impending nuptials herself. Instead, Maxim has to speak for her. In the television movie, however, the narrator boldly tells Mrs. Van Hopper (Faye Dunaway, in a scene-chewing performance) the news herself and keeps her chin well up when Mrs. Van Hopper makes catty comments to her. In the novel, the narrator is so overwhelmed by the crying Mrs. Danvers (Diana Rigg, in a disappointingly camp-less portrayal) that she cannot look at her (347); in the television movie, she calmly helps Mrs. Danvers sit down. In the novel, the narrator is initially afraid to go to the inquest; in the television movie, she shows no such fear (though she does faint, just as she does in the novel [p. 310] and the film).

The narrator is also portrayed as more knowledgeable about sex in this television movie. In the novel, the 1978 BBC production, and the film, Mrs. Van Hopper asks the narrator "Have you been doing anything you shouldn't?"—clearly implying that the narrator has had sex with Maxim and must marry to hide an unanticipated pregnancy. The narrator is so sexually innocent that she simply answers: "I don't know what you mean." In the 1997 television movie, however, the narrator stares at Mrs. Van Hopper coolly. She understands exactly what Mrs. Van Hopper means, and does not deign to answer, though there is no suggestion that she has been having pre-marital sex. This may be explainable by the fact that the novel, published in 1938, and the film, produced in 1940 under the Hays code, were more restricted by censorship in what they could imply about the narrator's sexual knowledge. In 1978, it was at least still possible for audiences to imagine a young woman of the 1920s as sexually innocent.[25] I would suggest that television audiences of the 1990s, in contrast, may be unable conceive of, let alone identify with, a protagonist who is a sexual ignoramus.

Moreover, the 1997 television movie makes clear that Maxim and the narrator have an active, enjoyable sex life. When Mrs. Danvers asks the narrator whether she thinks the dead ever come back to watch the living and whether she thinks Rebecca watches her and Maxim together, the narrator immediately has a flashback to an image of herself and Maxim rolling around nude having sex. A later scene also suggests that they have just made love. I would again suggest that the television spectators of the 1990s are not only comfortable with, but have also almost grown to expect such scenes. (One thinks of the consummation scenes of 1980s and 1990s television dramas — e.g., *Hotel*, *Moonlighting*, *The Practice*— that typically showed a lot of skin.)[26]

The 1997 television movie de-specularizes the narrator. Although she does not appear as poorly dressed as her own description in the gothic novel would suggest, she is dressed generally in drab colors — gray and white — in baggy clothes that de-emphasize her curves to an extent extreme even for the late nineteen-twenties, when the story is set. Even at the end of the film, where she has made a foray into wearing brighter colors, her costume is still noticeably shapeless. The actress who plays the narrator — Emilia Fox[27] — is an almost boyish, slightly more robust Calista Flockhart lookalike, her hair cut in a plain bob. This extreme de-specularization focuses attention on the narrator as protagonist rather than as spectacle.

The 1997 television movie also emphasizes the narrator's position as viewing subject. The television movie opens with the narrator sketching, rather than with the monologue about dreaming of Manderley, and the narrator's sketching competence is supported. In the novel and film, the narrator sketches Maxim, but is interrupted by a note or by Maxim in person, and is embarrassed by her sketch. In this television movie, however, she sketches without interruption. The television movie also aligns the narrator with powerful vision by showing her photographing Maxim in his bathing costume. The narrator herself takes the picture while wearing a bathing costume that shows so little skin that it looks like the bathing costumes of the 1910s rather than the late 1920s. This too despecularizes her and emphasizes her as viewing subject, rather than viewed object.

In this context, the television movie's treatment of Rebecca (Lucy Cohu) herself is noteworthy. Rather than making her invisible, the television movie does show Rebecca in visual flashbacks. The way she is shown is a classic fetishization of the female body, however — the viewer never sees her as an organic whole. Instead, the viewer sees parts of her body — her eyes, her mouth, the back of her head — or only sees her in such a long-shot that her features are blurred and indistinct.

The 1997 television movie underscores the physical nature of Maxim's domestic violence towards Rebecca. Instead of hitting Rebecca so that she falls and accidentally hits her head (as in the film version and the 1962 television version), or shooting Rebecca (as in the novel and in the 1978 television version), the 1997 television movie shows Maxim strangling Rebecca.[28] This puts rather more guilt on Maxim's shoulders. He is not subject to an instantaneous impulse, like hitting someone or pulling a trigger, but has made a decision over a longer period of time to kill someone in a few minutes by strangling. This more damning portrayal of Maxim's violence may reflect more knowledgeable, progressive attitudes towards domestic violence in 1997 than in earlier times.

The confines of the narrative, however, require that Maxim become a sympathetic character. As a reaction to the heavy guilt the murder scene imposes on Maxim, the television movie goes to great lengths to rehabilitate him. In a brilliant stroke, the television movie has Maxim tell the narrator of Rebecca's murder neither in the neutral setting of the library (as in the novel) nor in the menacing setting of the boathouse (as in the film and in the 1962 television production), but in the sexually charged settings of lush gardens at Manderley and in their marital bed right after they have apparently made love.[29] Making Rebecca's murder the subject of pillow talk emphasizes — to the narrator and to the implied viewer — that Maxim has supposedly changed his stripes, that he only kills wives who "deserve it," not "good wives" like the narrator.

The narrative goes even further to rehabilitate Maxim. Borrowing a leaf from *Jane Eyre*, Maxim later rushes into the burning Manderley in an attempt to save Mrs. Danvers, crippling himself and burning a hand in the process. The epilogue specifically notes that, presumably because of injuries suffered in trying to save Mrs. Danvers, he cannot have children, focusing on the punishment fitting the crime. Since Rebecca's murder was sparked by his inability to tolerate the idea of someone else's son being raised as his own and occupying his place of privilege, he is deprived of children — a major departure from the gothic tradition that ends many novels with the birth of a firstborn son.

Maxim is also portrayed as more savvy than in the novel or the film. He knows that both Frank Crawley and Col. Julyan (Anthony Bate) know of his crime. This is in contrast to the novel, where the narrator knows that Frank knows — while Maxim does not — and serves to reduce the narrator's superior knowledge.

I suggest that all of the 1997 television movie's changes from the novel, the film, and the prior television movies are designed to make the narrator a more attractive locus of identification for the female spectator of the 1990s.

Rebecca *as Film*

Alfred Hitchcock's 1940 film *Rebecca* opens with the title: "THE SELZNICK STUDIO presents its production of DAPHNE DU MAURIER'S celebrated novel," and indeed, Hitchcock's *Rebecca* is very much du Maurier's *Rebecca*. As someone who saw the film before reading the novel, I had always assumed that much of the film was Hitchcock's invention. On the contrary, what struck me when reading the novel and then watching the film with the novel in hand is how much of the dialogue and action of the film is lifted directly from the novel.[30] Screenwriters Robert E. Sherwood and Joan Harrison and adaptors Philip MacDonald and Michael Hogan lift generously from du Maurier's text. The voiceover by the narrator (Joan Fontaine) that starts the film consists of large chunks lifted whole from the first chapter of *Rebecca*, starting with "Last night I went to Manderley again." Most of the dialogue is taken word for word from the novel, although the screenplay skips some dialogue and modifies some other parts.

Hitchcock and the screenwriters make a few changes to the images and plot of the novel. Some minor changes make some big filmic differences. For example, the potent image of the narrator tearing and burning Rebecca's handwriting, with the "R" in Rebecca the last thing to burn, is transposed to an even more potent last shot of the film where the "R" that has been embroidered by Mrs. Danvers (Judith Anderson) on Rebecca's nightgown case is the last thing to burn when Manderley burns. Hitchcock here uses the image to focus more on Mrs. Danvers' sexuality and less on the narrator's relationship to language and writing and her thoughts about occupying Rebecca's place.

The film also changes the mechanics of Rebecca's death. Instead of shooting Rebecca, Maxim hits her ("I suppose I went mad for a moment. I must've struck her"), and she falls and hits her head on a table. This change may have been added to make Maxim's character somewhat more palatable to an audience.[31] Hitting Rebecca doesn't carry the same taint of premeditated murder that bringing a gun to her cottage and shooting her does.

The movie also transposes the scene where Maxim goes into a trance and looks like he's going to push the narrator off a cliff into a scene where he looks like he's contemplating suicide himself off the same cliff. (The narrator, who doesn't know him at this point, breaks his trance by yelling at him, and stops the suicide attempt.) This change similarly rehabilitates Maxim for the filmgoing audience. A potential suicide, guilty over having killed his wife, is a more sympathetic character than a madman who's about to push his new girlfriend off a cliff.

The film glamourizes the narrator compared to the way she is represented in the novel, and seems to give her a higher class status than the novel accords her. The narrator's clothes always fit her (as opposed to being too big, as in the novel), and they are tasteful, if simple. The narrator's breeding is metonymized by the string of pearls that she wears throughout most of the film. Despite the fact that viewers of the film may find Joan Fontaine dreadfully mousy and subservient in her interactions with the household staff, she possesses a greater sense of command and grace in the film than in the novel, where her interactions with the staff are extraordinarily timid and servile.

The film also reduces the narrator's role in the solution of the mystery about Rebecca's last visit to a doctor, shutting the narrator out of the investigatory process. Unlike in the novel, the narrator does not go to

London with Maxim, Colonel Julyan, Frank Crawley, and Favell in order to question Dr. Baker. Instead, the narrator is left behind at Manderley. This tactic *does* improve the film's suspense. As Maxim approaches the burning Manderley, the audience wonders whether the narrator is trapped inside and whether she will survive. Yet the audience *knows* that the narrator has survived from her opening voiceover. (If she dreamt last night that she went to Manderley again, then surely, she survived the fire.)[32]

Moreover, the trip to London also differs in that Frank basically tells Maxim that he knows Maxim killed Rebecca. This shifts a very important locus of knowledge away from the narrator. In the novel, she knows that Frank knows about the murder, but Maxim does not realize that Frank knows. The film, however, does not allow the narrator to have any knowledge superior to her husband's.

Another change is in the treatment of the narrator's father. In the novel, both he and the narrator's mother have died long before the narrator meets Maxim. In the film, the narrator's mother has died years before, but her father has only died "last summer." Interestingly, the film enlarges upon the novel's description of the pair's lunchtime conversation about the narrator's father, adding the odd detail that he was a painter who painted the same tree over and over again — i.e., a bit of a kook, who may perhaps have passed some of his madness on to the narrator, whose hobby of sketching is mentioned shortly thereafter. She sketches Maxim shortly after that — a mild intimation of madness.

Hitchcock, Detection, and Madness

The other intimations of madness in the film are especially interesting in that they are bracketed by a wholly filmic addition to the novel — an addition that brilliantly elucidates the intimate connection between the medium of film itself and the madness of the female investigator. We should take Hitchcock's departure from the novel seriously, since, as noted above, he had to fight for the changes he wished to make to du Maurier's narrative. Moreover, Hitchcock is Hitchcock — the self-aware director whose work comments constantly on issues of knowing, seeing, madness, and the institution of the cinema itself. Thus, although the changes to du Maurier's narrative that I describe below may at first glance appear minor, they merit our consideration as the crystallization of the nexus between madness and the female detective on film.

The novel makes no mention of the narrator and Maxim having taken home movies on their honeymoon, nor of their ever viewing such movies. Hitchcock's filmed version, however, adds a scene of Maxim and the narrator viewing home movies to highlight intimations that the narrator is mad.[33] The scene starts with Maxim and the narrator looking at the movies from their honeymoon, but the film runs off the reel, and they have to stop. Immediately afterwards, the servant Frith comes in to announce a household problem: Mrs. Danvers has accused a servant of stealing an ornament. The narrator, too timid to confess in front of Frith, tells Maxim after Frith leaves that she herself has broken the ornament and hidden the pieces. When Maxim chides her for not speaking up sooner, the narrator responds: "I was afraid he'd think me a fool." Maxim is unsympathetic: "Well he'll think you much more of a fool now.... Don't be such a little idiot darling. Anybody would think you were afraid of them." This exchange is taken from the text of the novel, but its inclusion should not be minimized, as the screenplay elsewhere skips over large chunks of dialogue and alters others. The fact that the words "fool" and "idiot" appear here as intimations of madness should not be underplayed. The connection between film, female detection and madness is emphasized as Maxim again puts on the home movies, hoping that the clip he has rigged will hold — can film be contained in the face of female investigation? They argue while watching the film and we see the narrator as viewer, her face lit by the light of the projector, consuming filmic representations of her own happiness while having a fight with her husband. He turns off the projector in anger, and the narrator again faces an intimation of madness as she seems to be a bit deluded about the success of her marriage. "Our marriage is a success, isn't it? A great success. We're happy, aren't we? Terribly happy," she asks Maxim nervously. Maxim initially does not respond, but finally concedes, "If you say we're happy, let's leave it at that" — not exactly a ringing endorsement of marital bliss. Maxim starts the home movies again on a shot of him and the narrator cuddling together on their honeymoon, and the screen fades out. The narrator's delusion about the state of her marriage is also taken from the novel.[34] It is worthy of note, however, that this instance of implied madness is similarly bracketed by an image of film, just as the words "fool" and "idiot" are.

* * *

As I noted in the introduction to this work, the results of this study may be discouraging to feminist cultural critics: The concepts of "female" and "investigator" produce such an inconcinity in Anglo-American culture that representations of female investigators seem almost inevitably to portray them as fundamentally flawed bearers of Lack. The nature of this

Lack varies by genre and medium, but it is nearly omnipresent. Yet the burgeoning number of female investigative narratives in all genres and media suggests that, despite these flaws, our culture bears a deep fascination with, and affection for, the female investigator, however lacking.

> The basic characteristics of any good investigator are a plodding nature and infinite patience. Society has inadvertently been grooming women to this end for years.[35]

Chapter Notes

Introduction

1. Dorothy L. Sayers, "Introduction" to *Great Short Stories of Detection, Mystery and Horror*, Dorothy L. Sayers, ed., London, Victor Gollancz, 1928, p. 15, reprinted as "Introduction" to *The Omnibus of Crime*, Dorothy L. Sayers, ed., New York, Payson and Clarke, 1929, p. 15, and further reprinted in Howard Haycraft, ed., *The Art of the Mystery Story*, New York, Carroll & Graf, 1992, p. 79.

2. Julian Symons, for example, postulates a fundamental distinction between the "Great Detective" and the "hardboiled dick." Julian Symons, *Bloody Murder: From the Detective Story to the Crime Novel: A History*, New York, Viking, 1985, pp. 123–124.

3. Jacqueline Rose, "Woman as Symptom," in *Sexuality in the Field of Vision*, London, Verso, 1986, p. 221.

4. Mary Ann Doane, "Paranoia and the Specular," in *The Desire to Desire: The Woman's Film of the 1940s*, Bloomington, Indiana University Press, 1987, pp. 123, 129, 134–135.

5. Kathleen Gregory Klein, *The Woman Detective: Gender & Genre*, Urbana, U. of Illinois, 2nd edition, 1995, p. 1.

6. David Martindale, *Television Detective Shows of the 1970s: Credits, Storylines and Episode Guides for 109 Series*, Jefferson, NC, McFarland, 1991.

7. Dave Rogers, *The Complete Avengers: Everything you ever wanted to know about The Avengers and The New Avengers*, New York, St. Martin's, 1989.

8. Jack Condon & David Hofstede, *Charlie's Angels Casebook*, Beverly Hills, Pomegranate Press, 2000.

9. William K. Everson, *The Detective in Film: A Pictorial Treasury of the Screen Sleuth from 1903 to the Present*, Secaucus, NJ, The Citadel Press, 1972.

10. Howard Haycraft's introduction to Chesterton's "A Defence of Detective Stories," in Haycraft, ed., *The Art of the Mystery Story*, New York, Carroll & Graf, 1992, p. 3. Chesterton's essay was originally published in his *The Defendant*, London, R.B. Johnson, 1902.

11. Dorothy L. Sayers, "Introduction" to *Great Short Stories of Detection, Mystery and Horror*, Dorothy L. Sayers, ed., London, Victor Gollancz, 1928, pp. 9–47, reprinted as "Introduction" to *The Omnibus of Crime*, Dorothy L. Sayers, ed., New York, Payson and Clarke, 1929, also pp. 9–47, and further reprinted as "The Omnibus of Crime," in Howard Haycraft, ed., *The Art of the Mystery Story*, New York, Carroll & Graf, 1992, pp. 71–109; Dorothy L. Sayers, "Introduction" to *Great Short Stories of Detection, Mystery and Horror, Second Series*, Dorothy L. Sayers, ed., London, Victor Gollancz, 1931, pp. 11–26, reprinted as "Introduction" to *The Second Omnibus of Crime: The World's Great Crime Stories*, Dorothy L. Sayers, ed., New York, Blue Ribbon Books, 1939 [first published in the U.S. in 1932, with a different publisher], pp. 1–16. See James Sandoe, "Reader's Guide to Crime," in *The Art of the Mystery Story*, Howard Haycraft, ed., New York, Carroll & Graf, 1992, p. 497.

12. Robin W. Winks, "Introduction," to Howard Haycraft, ed., *The Art of the Mystery Story*, New York, Carroll & Graf, 1992, p. i. *Murder for Pleasure* has been reprinted by Carroll & Graf, 1984.

13. The pseudonym used by art critic Willard Huntington Wright when writing his Philo Vance detective novels. Howard Haycraft, ed.,

The Art of the Mystery Story, New York, Carroll & Graf, 1992, p. 33.

14. Pseudonym for William A. P. White. James Sandoe, "Readers' Guide to Crime," in *The Art of the Mystery Story*, Howard Haycraft, ed., New York, Carroll & Graf, 1992, p. 497.

15. Howard Haycraft, *The Art of the Mystery Story*, pp. vii–ix. Nash's claim to fame in the field of detective story criticism comes from coining the term "Had-I-But-Known" to describe this literary device. See Rosamund Bryce, "The Most Likely Victim," in Dilys Winn, ed., *Murder Ink: The Mystery Reader's Companion*, New York, Workman Publishing, 1977, p. 184 and Kathleen L. Maio, "Had-I-But-Known: The Marriage of Gothic Terror and Detection," in *The Female Gothic*, Juliann E. Fleenor, ed., Montréal, Eden Press, 1983, p. 82.

16. Leroy Lad Panek, *Watteau's Shepherds: The Detective Novel in Britain: 1914–1940*, Bowling Green, OH, Bowling Green Popular Press, 1979, p. 1.

17. A 1977 poll of customers at New York's Murder Ink mystery bookstore found that the third most popular occupation of mystery readers polled was "schoolteacher." I assume this covers post-secondary educators as well as those teaching earlier grades. Dilys Winn, ed., *Murder Ink: The Mystery Reader's Companion*, New York, Workman, 1977, p. 440. See also Marjorie Nicolson, "The Professor and the Detective," *The Atlantic Monthly*, April 1929, reprinted in *The Art of the Mystery Story*, Howard Haycraft, ed., New York, Carroll & Graf, 1992 [originally published 1946], pp. 110–127.

18. Note, for example, academic Carolyn Heilbrun's use of the pen name Amanda Cross while awaiting tenure at Columbia. See Carol Kountz, "You Call it a Pseudonym, We Call it an Alias," in Dilys Winn, ed., *Murder Ink: The Mystery Reader's Companion*, New York, Workman, 1977, p. 45.

19. Ray B. Browne, "Introduction," *Heroes and Humanities: Detective Fiction and Popular Culture*, Bowling Green, OH, Bowling Green State University Popular Press, 1986, p. 7.

20. Gary Hoppenstand, *In Search of the Paper Tiger: A Sociological Perspective of Myth, Formula and the Mystery Genre in the Entertainment Print Mass Medium*, Bowling Green, OH, Bowling Green Popular Press, 1987.

21. George N. Dove, *The Police Procedural*, Bowling Green, OH, Bowling Green Popular Press, 1982, pp. 112–143. For a recent example of a mythic approach to the analysis of detective fiction, see Christine A. Jackson, *Myth and Ritual in Women's Detective Fiction*, Jefferson, NC, McFarland, 2002.

22. Nadya Aisenberg, *A Common Spring: Crime Novel and Classic*, Bowling Green, OH, Bowling Green Popular Press, 1980.

23. Leroy Lad Panek, *Watteau's Shepherds: The Detective Novel in Britain: 1914–1940*, p. 1.

24. Leroy Lad Panek, *An Introduction to the Detective Story*, Bowling Green, OH, Bowling Green State University Popular Press, 1987, pp. 6–11.

25. Larry Landrum, "Criticism and Theory," in *American Mystery and Detective Novels: A Reference Guide*, Westport, CT, Greenwood Press, 1999, pp. 39–115.

26. As this manuscript began making the rounds at various presses, a new study of the female investigator by Linda Mizejewski came out from Routledge. While Mizejewski and I are fascinated by many of the same texts, our approaches to them are fundamentally different. See Linda Mizejewski, *Hardboiled & High Heeled: The Woman Detective in Popular Culture*, New York, Routledge, 2004.

27. Horace Newcomb, ed., *Television: The Critical View*, New York, Oxford, 1979, pp. 118–150 and pp. 151–159, respectively.

28. Sally R. Munt, "The Inverstigators," [sic] in *Murder by the Book?: Feminism and the Crime Novel*, London, Routledge, 1994, pp. 120–146.

29. Sally R. Munt, "The Inverstigators," [sic] in *Murder by the Book?: Feminism and the Crime Novel*, London, Routledge, 1994, p. 125.

30. Others that I have found are Paulina Palmer, *Lesbian Gothic: Transgressive Fictions*, London, Cassell, 1999, Paulina Palmer, "The Lesbian Feminist Thriller and Detective Novel," in *What Lesbians Do in Books*, Elaine Hobby and Chris White, eds., London, The Women's Press, 1991, pp. 9–27, Paulina Palmer, "The Lesbian Thriller: Transgressive Investigations," in *Criminal Proceedings: The Contemporary American Crime Novel*, Peter Messent, ed., London, Pluto Press, 1997, pp. 87–110, Gillian Whitlock, "'Cop it Sweet': Lesbian Crime Fiction," in *The Good, The Bad, and the Gorgeous: Popular Culture's Romance with Lesbianism*, Diane Hamer and Belinda Budge, eds., London, Pandora, 1994, pp. 96–118, Barbara Wilson, "The Outside Edge: Lesbian Mysteries," in *Daring to Dissent: Lesbian Culture from Margin to Mainstream*, Liz Gibbs, ed., London, Cassell, 1994, pp. 217–228, Mary Wings, "Rebecca Redux: Tears on a Lesbian Pillow," in *Daring to Dissent: Lesbian Culture from Margin to Mainstream*, Liz Gibbs, ed., London, Cassell, 1994, pp. 11–33.

31. Frances A. DellaCava and Madeline H. Engel list 41 lesbian detective series characters. Frances A. DellaCava & Madeline H. Engel, *Sleuths in Skirts: Analysis and Bibliography of Serialized Female Sleuths*, New York, Routledge, 2002, p. 8.

32. Sally R. Munt, "The Inverstigators," [sic] in *Murder by the Book? Feminism and the Crime Novel*, London, Routledge, 1994, p. 122.

33. Joseph Hansen, "Homosexuals: Universal Scapegoats," in *Murder Ink: Revived, revised, still unrepentant*, Dilys Winn, ed., New York, Workman Publishing, 1984, pp. 131–133.

34. See Gillian Whitlock, "'Cop it Sweet': Lesbian Crime Fiction," in *The Good, The Bad, and the Gorgeous: Popular Culture's Romance with Lesbianism*, Diane Hamer and Belinda Budge, eds., London, Pandora, 1994, pp. 98–101. For example, in an early survey of lesbian literary criticism, Bonnie Zimmerman mentions lesbian detective novels only as a counter-example to the "rhetoric of non-violence" extant in other lesbian literature of the times. Bonnie Zimmerman, "What Has Never Been: An Overview of Lesbian Feminist Criticism," in Gayle Greene and Coppélia Kahn, eds., *Making A Difference: Feminist Literary Criticism*, London, Routledge, 1990 [originally printed in 1985], p. 197.

35. For example, female detective theorist Kathleen Gregory Klein focuses on Barbara Wilson's early detective novels to postulate that lesbian detective fiction offers an alternative to the "dualistic universe" that leads to the formula reflected so often in detective fiction with female protagonists: "If female, then not detective; if detective, then not really female." Kathleen Gregory Klein, "*Habeas Corpus*: Feminism and Detective Fiction," in *Feminism in Women's Detective Fiction*, Glenwood Irons, ed., Toronto, University of Toronto Press, 1995, pp. 175–185. Similarly, in another important early survey of lesbian detective novels, Maureen T. Reddy concentrates on novels that commingle crime solving with exploration of lesbian identity and "coming out." Maureen T. Reddy, "Lesbian Detectives," in *Sisters in Crime: Feminism and the Crime Novel*, New York, Continuum, 1988, p. 123. I agree with Klein and Reddy that these particular novels grapple with intriguing feminist and lesbian issues and that they deviate from conventions of the detective genre in significant and fascinating ways; however, I think of these novels as examples that do not necessarily reflect the entire spectrum of lesbian detective fiction.

36. See, for example, Liahna Babener, "Uncloseting Ideology in the Novels of Barbara Wilson" in *Women Times Three: Writers, Detectives, Readers*, Kathleen Gregory Klein, ed., Bowling Green, OH, Bowling Green State University Popular Press, 1995, pp. 143–161. Babener notes that her interest lies in examining the resistance to formula in novels that leads to "the deconstruction of the genre" (p. 147) and hence focuses on Barbara Wilson's early works. See also Susan Elizabeth Sweeney, "Gender-Blending, Genre-Bending and the Rendering of Identity in Barbara Wilson's *Gaudí Afternoon*," in *Multicultural Detective Fiction: Murder from the "Other" Side*, Adrienne Johnson Gosselin, ed., New York, Garland, 1999, pp. 123–141.

37. For example, Erin A. Smith's discussion of gay and lesbian re-writings of the hardboiled genre focuses on Wilson's *Murder in the Collective* and *Gaudí Afternoon* and on Wings's Emma Victor novel *She Came Too Late*. Erin A. Smith, *Hard-Boiled: Working Class Readers and Pulp Magazines*, Philadelphia, Temple University Press, 2000, pp. 170–172.

38. For example, see Lois A. Marchino, "Katherine V. Forrest: Writing Kate Delafield for Us," in *Women Times Three: Writers, Detectives, Readers*, Kathleen Gregory Klein, ed., Bowling Green, OH, Bowling Green State University Popular Press, 1995, pp. 65–79, which focuses on the early Kate Delafield novels.

39. Barbara Wilson, "The Outside Edge: Lesbian Mysteries," in *Daring to Dissent: Lesbian Culture from Margin to Mainstream*, Liz Gibbs, ed., London, Cassell, 1994, pp. 217–228 and Mary Wings, "Rebecca Redux: Tears on a Lesbian Pillow," in *Daring to Dissent: Lesbian Culture from Margin to Mainstream*, Liz Gibbs, ed., London, Cassell, 1994, pp. 11–33.

40. Cf. Barbara Wilson, "[T]hrillers and mysteries could just as well be called novels of investigation.... For the focus of the thriller is not the crime but the solving of the crime, not the mystery, but the demystifying process." Barbara Wilson, "The Outside Edge: Lesbian Mysteries," in *Daring to Dissent: Lesbian Culture from Margin to Mainstream*, Liz Gibbs, ed., London, Cassell, 1994, pp. 220–221.

41. The problem of scope is, of course, not limited to scholars studying female detective novels. The field of mystery fiction is now so large that any survey must be of a somewhat cursory nature, and as a result, scholars of mystery and detective fiction in general also focus on narrower subparts of the field. See, e.g., Patricia Merivale and Susan Elizabeth Sweeney, eds., *Detecting Texts: The Metaphysical Detective Story from Poe to Postmodernism*, Philadelphia, University of Pennsylvania Press, 1999 (a collection of essays focusing on certain metaphysical detective stories).

42. Patricia D. Maida and Nicholas B. Spornick, *Murder She Wrote: A Study of Agatha Christie's Detective Fiction*, Bowling Green, OH, Bowling Green State University Popular Press, 1982. See also Michele Slung, "Let's Hear It for Agatha Christie: A Feminist Appreciation," in *The Sleuth and the Scholar: Origins, Evolution, and Current Trends in Detective Fiction*, [a collection of papers from a 1986 symposium], Barbara A. Rader and Howard G. Zettler, eds., Contributions to the Study of Popular Culture No. 19, Westport, CT, Greenwood Press, 1988, pp. 63–68.

43. Earl F. Bargainnier, ed., *10 Women of Mystery*, Bowling Green, OH, Bowling Green State

University Popular Press, 1981. See also Moira Davison Reynolds's biographies of selected women mystery writers combined with brief descriptions of some of their works. Moira Davison Reynolds, *Women Authors of Detective Series: Twenty-One American and British Writers, 1900–2000*, Jefferson, NC, McFarland, 2001. See also Cora Kaplan's wonderfully insightful, though maddeningly brief, piece entitled "An Unsuitable Genre for a Feminist." Cora Kaplan, "An Unsuitable Genre for a Feminist, in *The Study of Popular Fiction: A Source Book*, Bob Ashley, ed., Philadelphia, University of Pennsylvania Press, 1989, pp. 199–203. Kaplan discusses female authors of detective fiction from the early 20th century onward and finds that the majority of them replicate patriarchal and class biases in their detective stories. *Id.*

44. Carolyn Stewart Dyer and Nancy Tillman Romalov, eds., *Rediscovering Nancy Drew*, Iowa City, IA, University of Iowa Press, 1995.

45. Sabine Vanacker, "V.I. Warshawski, Kinsey Millhone and Kay Scarpetta: Creating a Feminist Detective Hero," in *Criminal Proceedings: The Contemporary American Crime Novel*, Peter Messent, ed., London, Pluto Press, 1997, pp. 62–86.

46. Frances A. DellaCava and Madeline H. Engel, *Sleuths in Skirts: Analysis and Bibliography of Serialized Female Sleuths*, New York, Routledge, 2002. This useful reference work has lists categorizing female detectives by sociological characteristics, indexes of pen names, book titles, and detectives' occupations, and an opening essay detailing how the characteristics of female detectives have changed over time. As the title suggests, it focuses only on series characters, and it focuses only on series fiction from the United States.

47. Bobbie Ann Mason, *The Girl Sleuth: A Feminist Guide*, Old Westbury, NY, The Feminist Press, 1975.

48. Sally R. Munt, *Murder by the Book? Feminism and the Crime Novel*, London, Routledge, 1994. See also Kimberly J. Dilley, *Busybodies, Meddlers, and Snoops: The Female Hero in Contemporary Women's Mysteries*, Westport, CT, Greenwood Press, 1998. For a collection of essays focusing on feminist readings of female investigative narratives over a wide range of eras, see *Feminism in Women's Detective Fiction*, Glenwood Irons, ed., Toronto, University of Toronto Press, 1995.

Chapter 1

1. For an excellent discussion of gothic conventions and their psychological underpinnings, see Linda Bayer-Berenbaum, "Literary Gothicism," in *The Gothic Imagination: Expansion in Gothic Literature and Art*, Rutherford, NJ, Fairleigh Dickinson University Press, 1982. See also Tania Modleski, "The Female Uncanny: Gothic Novels for Women," in *Loving With A Vengeance: Mass-Produced Fantasies for Women*, New York, Methuen, 1982, p. 59. For a deliciously detailed longer description of the components of the modern gothic novel, see Joanna Russ, "Somebody is Trying to Kill Me and I Think It's My Husband: The Modern Gothic," *Journal of Popular Culture*, Vol. 6, No. 4 (Spring 1973), pp. 667–670. For a discussion of the psychological attributes of the female gothic novel, see Juliann E. Fleenor, "Introduction: The Female Gothic," in *The Female Gothic*, Juliann E. Fleenor, ed., Montréal, Eden Press, 1983, pp. 15–16.

2. Interestingly, the modern gothic novel has even more hapless detectives than does the traditional gothic novel. Joanna Russ details these women's ineffective efforts thus: "...[E]ither because of other people's detective work or by chance — [a] *Secret is Revealed.*... [Modern gothic novels] are not stories of detection.... [A]ny necessary detective work is done by other persons...." Joanna Russ, "Somebody is Trying to Kill Me and I Think It's My Husband: The Modern Gothic," *Journal of Popular Culture*, Vol. 6, No. 4 (Spring 1973), pp. 669, 671. According to Russ, while the protagonists of modern gothic novels do sometimes dig up clues to various mysteries, they tend to misinterpret those clues or to find them only after others have already found them. *Id.* at p. 679. Indeed, in her closing analysis, Russ aptly puts first the fact that the heroine of the modern gothic novel "cannot ... [s]olve an intellectual puzzle (whodunit or science fiction.)" *Id.* at p. 686.

3. Discussing the Gothic film, Diane Waldman notes that in cases where "the heroine's suspicions about the Gothic male are confirmed," she requires the assistance of a man to "corroborate [her] experience." Diane Waldman, "'At last I can tell it to someone!': Feminine Point of View and Subjectivity in the Gothic Romance Film of the 1940s," *Cinema Journal* 23, no. 2, Winter 1983, p. 31. In her reading of the Gothic film *Rebecca*, Waldman further notes: "...[T]he heroine's happiness is purchased at the price of her independent judgement." *Id.*

4. See Bonamy Dobrée, "Introduction" to Ann Radcliffe, *The Mysteries of Udolpho*, New York, Oxford University Press, 1970, p. v. Indeed, although *Udolpho* went through periods of relative obscurity, in 1938, Montague Summers opined: "All men of taste, all cognoscenti, all who can have the slightest claim to literary knowledge or are fond of books have read at least *The Mysteries of Udolpho....*" Montague Summers, *The Gothic Quest: A History of the Gothic Novel*, New York, Russell & Russell, Inc., 1964 [originally published in 1938], p. 397.

5. See Elizabeth Gaskell, *The Life of Charlotte Brontë*, ed. and intro. by Alan Shelston, New York, Penguin, 1985 [originally published in 1857], pp. 320–321.

6. R.F. Stewart, ... *And Always a Detective: Chapters on the History of Detective Fiction*, North Pomfret, VT, David & Charles, 1980, p. 47.

7. This included "Woman in White perfume, bonnets, and quadrilles." See Tamar Heller, "*The Woman in White*: Portrait of the Artist as a Professional Man," in *Dead Secrets: Wilkie Collins and the Female Gothic*, New Haven, Yale University Press, 1992, p. 110.

8. Julian Symons, "Introduction," to Wilkie Collins, *The Woman in White*, New York, Penguin, 1974, p. 15.

9. Jenny Bourne Taylor, "Introduction," to Wilkie Collins, *The Law and the Lady*, New York, Penguin, 1992, p. ix. I am extremely grateful to Lesley Mandros Bell for bringing this work to my attention.

10. Earlier critics have noted the similarity between the suspense in Radcliffe's works and that in later detective fiction. See, for example, Devendra P. Varma, *The Gothic Flame*, New York, Russell & Russell, 1966, pp. 110, 237–241.

11. For an interesting reading of *The Mysteries of Udolpho* as in some ways analogous to the modern detective story through its locked-room imagery, see Mark S. Madoff, "Inside, Outside, and the Gothic Locked Room Mystery," in *Gothic Fictions: Prohibition/Transgression*, Kenneth W. Graham, ed., AMS Press, New York, 1989, pp. 49–62.

12. Ann Radcliffe, *The Mysteries of Udolpho*, Bonamy Dobrée, ed. and intro., Frederick Garber, notes, New York, Oxford University Press, 1970, p. 5. Italics mine. All further page references are to this edition.

13. On real-life successful women who were "substitute sons," see Maureen T. Reddy, *Sisters in Crime: Feminism and the Crime Novel*, New York, Continuum, 1988, p. 52.

14. Linda Bayer-Berenbaum postulates that garrulous maids in the gothic generally function as foils as for the well-spoken gothic heroines they serve. Linda Bayer-Berenbaum, *The Gothic Imagination: Expansion in Gothic Literature and Art*, Rutherford, NJ, Fairleigh Dickinson University Press, 1982, p. 23. Varma notes that the "garrulous maid" is a typical Radcliffe character. Devendra P. Varma, *The Gothic Flame*, p. 114.

15. Patricia Parker also notes the connection between class and excessive female language in *Udolpho*, and emphasizes how Emily's speech is carefully separated from the "hysteria and pointlessness" shown by lower-class women in the text. Patricia Parker, *Literary Fat Ladies: Rhetoric, Gender, Property*, New York, Methuen, 1987, p. 34.

16. Ellen Moers notes how the themes of "physical heroics" and "risk-taking" were common in the works of nineteenth-century female writers. This theme is continued in the girls' detective fiction of the early twentieth century. Ellen Moers, *Literary Women: The Great Writers*, New York, Oxford, 1977, p. 131.

17. Interestingly, there is apparently *less* fainting in *The Mysteries of Udolpho* than in Radcliffe's earlier works. David S. Miall has noted that "the frequency of fainting fits steadily diminishes across Radcliffe's novels." David S. Miall, "The Preceptor as Fiend: Radcliffe's Psychology of the Gothic," in *Jane Austen and Mary Shelley and Their Sisters*, Laura Dabundo, ed., Lanham, MD, 2000, p. 35. Miall has even calculated the fainting frequency in Radcliffe's works: "Someone faints on average after every 11 pages in *Athlin* ... , 18 pages in *Sicilian*, 40 pages in *Forest*, 48 pages in *Udolpho*, and 52 pages in *The Italian*." *Id.* at p. 43, note 2.

18. Austen does mention, however, several contemporaneous popular thrillers of the same kind: "*Castle of Wolfenbach, Clermont, Mysterious Warnings, Necromancer of the Black Forest, Midnight Bell, Orphan of the Rhine*, and *Horrid Mysteries*." Jane Austen, *Northanger Abbey*, London, Penguin, p. 27. All further page references are to this edition. For some description of these works, see Devendra P. Varma, *The Gothic Flame*, New York, Russell & Russell, 1966, pp. 4–5. See also Bette B. Roberts, "The Horrid Novels: *The Mysteries of Udolpho* and *Northanger Abbey*," in *Gothic Fictions: Prohibition/Transgression*, Kenneth W. Graham, ed., AMS Press, New York, 1989, pp. 89–111 and Montague Summers' digression in "A Great Mistress of Romance: Ann Radcliffe, 1764–1823," in *Essays in Petto*, Freeport, NY, Books For Libraries Press, 1928 [reprinted 1967], pp. 21–22.

19. I focus here on women and writing in this work; others have focused on the relationship between women and reading in *Northanger Abbey*. See, e.g., Barbara M. Benedict, "Jane Austen and the Culture of Circulating Libraries: The Construction of Female Literacy," in *Revising Women: Eighteenth-Century "Women's Fiction" and Social Engagement*, Paula R. Backscheider, ed., Baltimore, MD, The Johns Hopkins University Press, 2000, pp. 178–181 and Kate Ferguson Ellis, *The Contested Castle: Gothic Novels and the Subversion of Domestic Ideology*, Urbana, IL, University of Illinois Press, 1989, p. 7.

20. Jane Austen, *Northanger Abbey*, New York, Penguin, reprinted 1994. All further page references are to this edition. Allan D. McKillop postulates that these comments of Tilney's are meant to be jibes at Samuel Richardson and his dutifully journalizing heroines. See McKillop, "Critical Realism in *Northanger Abbey*," in *From Jane Austen to Joseph Conrad: Essays Collected in the*

Memory of James T. Hillhouse, Robert C. Rathburn and Martin Steinmann, Jr., eds., Minneapolis, University of Minnesota Press, 1958, p. 40.

21. Sandra M. Gilbert and Susan Gubar interpret the laundry list as perhaps "the real threat to women's happiness," presumably because of the connotations of an oppressive domesticity surrounding it. Sandra M. Gilbert and Susan Gubar, *The Madwoman in the Attic: The Woman Writer and the Nineteenth-Century Literary Imagination*, New Haven, Yale University Press, 1979, p. 135. As I've implied above, though, the world in which Catherine travels when she finds the list would not categorize her as the type of woman expected to do laundry. While the list might suggest a threat to the happiness of the marginalized washerwomen who might perform their work under unjust or unpleasant conditions, it hardly seems like much of a threat to someone of Catherine's class.

22. The fact that Catherine's attempts to interpret the world around her are structured like the investigations of a (terrible) detective is underscored by the language critics have used to describe her interpretive struggles. Gilbert and Gubar note Catherine's inability to follow up on the linguistic "clues" that Isabella is always giving her and deem her "mystified" by the behavior of the Thorpes and the Tilneys. Gilbert and Gubar, *The Madwoman in the Attic*, pp. 130, 142.

23. For a discussion of Jane Austen and violence against women, see Kate Ferguson Ellis, "The Language of Domestic Violence," in *The Contested Castle: Gothic Novels and The Subversion of Domestic Ideology*, Urbana, IL, University of Illinois Press, 1989, pp. 3–19.

24.Charlotte Brontë, *Jane Eyre*, ed. and intro. by Q.D. Leavis, New York, Penguin, reprinted 1988. All further page references are to this edition.

25. For a class-based interpretation of Jane's spying on the rich, see Susan Fraiman, "Jane Eyre's Fall from Grace," in *Unbecoming Women: British Women Writers and the Novel of Development*, New York, Columbia University Press, 1993, pp. 107–108.

26. Jean Wyatt explicitly links Jane's failures of vision and understanding to the mysteries of sexual desire. See Jean Wyatt, "A Patriarch of One's Own: Oedipal Fantasy and Romantic Love in *Jane Eyre*," in *Reconstructing Desire: The Role of the Unconscious in Women's Reading and Writing*, Chapel Hill, NC, University of North Carolina Press, 1990, p. 29.

27. In this respect, Jane is quite different from Emily St. Aubert, who has no qualms about explicitly pushing her servants into serving her investigative aims. I attribute this disjunction to the fact that, being herself a servant and having experienced ill treatment at the hands of her

social superiors, Jane might be particularly sensitive about pulling rank on anyone. This is not to say that Jane displays no linguistic mastery whatsoever. Nancy Armstrong, for one, interprets many of Jane's little rebellions as particularly linguistic ones. Nancy Armstrong, *Desire and Domestic Fiction: A Political History of the Novel*, New York, Oxford, 1987, pp. 42–43, 46, 200, 205.

28. Like the names of many of Collins's characters, Marian's name possesses a special significance, in this case pointing to her investigative role in the novel. Miss Halcombe does indeed comb the Hall where she and Laura are staying for clues as to the intentions of Sir Percival Glyde and Count Fosco towards Laura's fortune.

29. On similarities between *The Woman in White* and *The Mysteries of Udolpho*, see Nicholas Rance, *Wilkie Collins and Other Sensation Novelists: Walking the Moral Hospital*, Rutherford, NJ, Fairleigh Dickinson University Press, 1991, p. 96.

30. Wilkie Collins, *The Woman in White*, reprinted London, Penguin, 1985, p. 63. All future page references are to this edition.

31. Critics have not always seen Marian as a detective, giving that role in the novel rather to Walter Hartright. See, e.g., Winifred Hughes, *The Maniac in the Cellar: Sensation Novels of the 1860s*, Princeton, NJ, Princeton University Press, 1980, p. 139.

32. Tamar Heller points out that Marian's diary is subject to the editing of Walter Hartright, however. Tamar Heller, "*The Woman in White*: Portrait of the Artist as a Professional Man," in *Dead Secrets: Wilkie Collins and the Female Gothic*, New Haven, Yale University Press, 1992, pp. 115, 136. U.C. Knoepflmacher similarly calls Walter "the novel's prime orderer," as Walter claims to have selected, excerpted, and expurgated the various narratives that together make up the novel. U.C. Knoepflmacher, "The Counterworld of Victorian Fiction and *The Woman in White*," in *The Worlds of Victorian Fiction*, Jerome H. Buckley, ed., Harvard English Studies No. 6, Cambridge, MA, Harvard University Press, 1975, p. 362.

33. Marian's "modesty" is, of course, a gender-inflected trait coded as specifically feminine. Thus it is important that, in examining Marian's and Jane's descriptions of their actions, we differentiate between what modesty may require these heroine-narrators to *say*, and what they actually *do*.

34. Kimberley Reynolds and Nicola Humble read this seemingly liberating description of Marian casting off the confining clothes of nineteenth-century upper-class womanhood as nevertheless emphasizing the physical and sexual restriction of women. They point out that the image of the petticoat has earlier been associated

by Marian with the oppression of women. See Kimberley Reynolds and Nicola Humble, *Victorian Heroines: Representations of Femininity in Nineteenth-Century Literature and Art*, New York, Harvester/Wheatsheaf, 1993, pp. 54–55.

35. See Luce Irigaray, "The Mechanics of Fluids," *This Sex Which Is Not One*, trans. Catherine Porter and Carolyn Burke, Ithaca, Cornell University Press, 1985, pp. 106–118.

36. Tamar Heller aptly notes this point and compares it to Emily's fainting in *Udolpho*:

"Marian's detection represents the moment when she obtains knowledge of male oppression, paralleling the moment in *The Mysteries of Udolpho* when Emily lifts the veil that evokes the mystery of the mother's oppression. Like Emily, however, who is denied a chance to attain this knowledge, Marian is deprived of the chance to use it."

Tamar Heller, "*The Woman in White*: Portrait of the Artist as a Professional Man," in *Dead Secrets: Wilkie Collins and the Female Gothic*, New Haven, Yale University Press, 1992, p. 136.

37. Natalka Freeland notes: "...[A]lmost all of the novel's critics have agreed [that the novel's] most viscerally unsettling effects result from the violation, amounting to a virtual rape, of Marian's diary...." Natalka Freeland, "From 'Foreign Peculiarities' to 'Fatal Resemblance': Detecting Villainy in *The Woman in White*," in *The Devil Himself: Villainy in Detective Fiction and Film*, Stacy Gillis and Philippa Gates, eds., Westport, CT, Greenwood Press, 2002, p. 49.

38. Peter Brooks, *Reading for the Plot: Design and Intention in Narrative*, Cambridge, MA, Harvard University Press, 1984, p. 169.

39. D.A. Miller argues for two simultaneously existing readings of the effects of Fosco's intrusion: one, which he terms "homosexual," as a violation of the (impliedly male) reader, and the other, which he terms "heterosexual," as implicating the reader in Marian's violation: "Having just finished reading Marian's diary ourselves, we are thus implicated in the sadism of his act...." D.A. Miller, "*Cage aux Folles*: Sensation and Gender in Wilkie Collins' *The Woman in White*," in *The Novel and the Police*, Berkeley, University of California Press, 1988, p. 164.

40. Wilkie Collins, *The Law and the Lady*, Jenny Bourne Taylor, ed. and intro., New York, Oxford U. Press, 1992. All future page references are to this edition.

41. Speaking of earlier gothics, David Punter writes: "Eighteenth-century fiction, the 'site' of the Gothic, is obsessed with the law, with its operations, justifications, limits." David Punter, *Gothic Pathologies: The Text, the Body and the Law*, New York, St. Martin's Press, 1998, p. 19.

42. Interestingly, the last character who has used the capitalized "Me" is the crippled Miserrimus Dexter — another character whose masculinity is at issue.

43. Philip O'Neill also makes the point that Valeria "is only forceful ... when she is operating in her husband's interests." Philip O'Neill, *Wilkie Collins: Women, Property, and Propriety*, London, Macmillan Press, 1988, p. 202.

44. Kathleen O'Fallon reads this shift of investigative prowess from Valeria to her male associates in the rosiest light possible:

"In the course of her investigation, Valeria enlists the aid of several men, but none of them determines what she will or will not do. She is plainly the one who drives the investigation, so forcefully that it eventually takes on a life of its own, continuing even after she has withdrawn from it to sit by Eustace's sickbed."

Kathleen O'Fallon, "Breaking the Laws about Ladies: Wilkie Collins' Questioning of Gender Roles," in *Wilkie Collins to the Forefront: Some Reassessments*, Nelson Smith and R.C. Terry, eds., New York, AMS Press, 1995, p. 236.

45. Jenny Bourne Taylor similarly notes Valeria's lack of control over writing here. Wilkie Collins, *The Law and the Lady*, Jenny Bourne Taylor, ed. and intro., New York, Oxford U. Press, 1992, p. xvi.

46. Philip O'Neill notes that this passage also undercuts the importance of Valeria's investigatory efforts. Philip O'Neill, *Wilkie Collins: Women, Property, and Propriety*, London, Macmillan Press, 1988, p. 201.

Chapter 2

1. Frances A. DellaCava & Madeline H. Engel, *Sleuths in Skirts: Analysis and Bibliography of Serialized Female Sleuths*, New York, Routledge, 2002, p. 8.

2. Sally R. Munt, "The Inverstigators," [sic] in *Murder by the Book?: Feminism and the Crime Novel*, London, Routledge, 1994, p. 122.

3. Joseph Hansen, "Homosexuals: Universal Scapegoats," in *Murder Ink: Revived, revised, still unrepentant*, Dilys Winn, ed., New York, Workman Publishing, 1984, pp. 131–133.

4. See Gillian Whitlock, "'Cop it Sweet': Lesbian Crime Fiction," in *The Good, The Bad, and the Gorgeous: Popular Culture's Romance with Lesbianism*, Diane Hamer and Belinda Budge, eds., London, Pandora, 1994, pp. 98–101. For example, in an early survey of lesbian literary criticism, Bonnie Zimmerman mentions lesbian detective novels only as a counter-example to the "rhetoric of non-violence" extant in other lesbian literature of the times. Bonnie Zimmerman, "What Has Never Been: An Overview of Lesbian Feminist Criticism," in Gayle Greene and Coppélia Kahn, eds., *Making A Difference: Feminist*

Literary Criticism, London, Routledge, 1990 [originally printed in 1985], p. 197.

5. Carol Clover notes similar failures of technology for the "final girl" in horror films. Carol J. Clover, *Men, Women, and Chain Saws*, Princeton, Princeton U. Press, 1992, p. 31.

6. On the importance of the mastery of transportation, particularly the automobile, as a symbol of self-assertion in early juvenile series girls' fiction, see Bobbie Ann Mason, *The Girl Sleuth: A Feminist Guide*, Old Westbury, NY, The Feminist Press, 1975, pp. 11, 16, 141.

7. Heterosexual female detectives generally *don't* have car trouble. They are usually portrayed as having a certain mastery over transportation. There are exceptions, however, the most notable being the Stephanie Plum novels by Janet Evanovich, in which there is a running gag about Stephanie's cars exploding, getting stolen, getting crushed, and getting vandalized. I am indebted to Mike Greenfield for pointing out the series' fascination with lesbian topics — at one point, Stephanie's mother accuses her of being a lesbian because she dons Doc Martens, and Stephanie's sister flirts briefly with the idea of "becoming" a lesbian.

8. A counterexample is detective Archie Goodwin's car crash in the opening scene of the delightful 1938 Nero Wolfe novel *Some Buried Caesar*. Even then, however, Archie almost completely disavows responsibility for the crash, blithely blaming it on garagemen and an inconveniently-placed tree. See Rex Stout, *Some Buried Caesar*, New York, Bantam, 1994, p. 2.

9. Of course, there are heterosexual female detectives who need a lot of rescuing as well. See Maureen T. Reddy, *Sisters in Crime: Feminism and the Crime Novel*, New York, Continuum, 1988, p. 66.

10. Paulina Palmer, "The Lesbian Thriller: Transgressive Investigations," in *Criminal Proceedings: The Contemporary American Crime Novel*, Peter Messent, ed., London, Pluto Press, 1997, pp. 89–90.

11. Paulina Palmer notes: "A focus on sex is, in fact, a distinctive feature of lesbian crime fiction, differentiating it from lesbian fiction of a more general kind." Paulina Palmer, "The Lesbian Feminist Thriller and Detective Novel," in *What Lesbians Do in Books*, Elaine Hobby and Chris White, eds., London, The Women's Press, 1991, p. 21.

12. Elizabeth Pincus, *The Two-Bit Tango*, Spinsters Book Company, San Francisco, 1992.

13. Elizabeth Pincus, *The Solitary Twist*, Spinsters Ink, Minneapolis, 1993.

14. Elizabeth Pincus, *The Hangdog Hustle*, Spinsters Ink, Duluth, MN, 1995.

15. Author biography, Elizabeth Pincus, *The Two-Bit Tango*, Spinsters Book Company, San Francisco, 1992, end pages.

16. See Mabel Maney, *The Case of the Not-So-Nice Nurse*, Pittsburgh, Cleis Press, 1993, back cover. For more on the relationship between these novels and traditional girls' adventure fiction, see Julia D. Gardner, "'No Place for a Girl Dick': Mabel Maney and the Queering of Girls' Detective Fiction," in *Delinquents & Debutantes: Twentieth-Century American Girls' Cultures*, Sherrie A. Inness, ed., New York, New York University Press, 1998, pp. 247–265.

17. Mabel Maney, *The Case of the Good-for-Nothing Girlfriend*, Pittsburgh, Cleis Press, 1994.

18. Mabel Maney, *A Ghost in the Closet*, Pittsburgh, Cleis Press, 1995.

19. Seymour Chatman, *Coming to Terms: The Rhetoric of Narrative in Fiction and Film*, Ithaca, Cornell University Press, 1990, pp. 149–154.

20. The Nancy Drew series is also peppered with car trouble: "...[I]ndignant male chauvinists are always puncturing [Nancy's] tires or shoving her into a ditch." Bobbie Ann Mason, *The Girl Sleuth: A Feminist Guide*, Old Westbury, NY, The Feminist Press, 1975, p. 65.

21. Nancy also has some other transgressive, masculine-identified abilities: identifying precious minerals, identifying strange insects, and picking locks (95, 154, 169).

22. Maney may have intended to highlight the gendered marketing of tie-ins to juvenile series fiction. In real life, while "the Hardy Boys [had] a detective handbook," Nancy Drew had her own cookbook, and "Cherry Ames [had] her own nursing handbook." Bobbie Ann Mason, *The Girl Sleuth: A Feminist Guide*, Old Westbury, NY, The Feminist Press, 1975. p. 128.

23. According to Nicole Décuré, Virginia Kelly is the first black woman detective heroine to be written by a black woman (although there were a few earlier novels featuring black women detectives that were written by white women). Nicole Décuré, "In Search of Our Sisters' Mean Streets: The Politics of Sex, Race, and Class in Black Women's Crime Fiction," in *Diversity and Detective Fiction*, Kathleen Gregory Klein, ed., Bowling Green, OH, Bowling Green State University Popular Press, 1999, p. 158. Stephen Soitos, however, cites a serialized novel *Hagar's Daughter*, published in 1901 and 1902, as the first novel to feature a black female investigator written by a black woman. Stephen F. Soitos, "Queering the 'I': Black Lesbian Detective Fiction," in *Multicultural Detective Fiction: Murder from the "Other" Side*, Adrienne Johnson Gosselin, ed., New York, Garland, 1999. p. 107. For general discussions of Nikki Baker's detective fiction, see Décuré, "In Search of Our Sisters' Mean Streets," pp. 169–171, and Soitos, "Queering the 'I'," pp. 107–119.

24. Nikki Baker, *The Lavender House Murder*, Tallahassee, Naiad Press, 1992.

25. Nikki Baker, *Long Goodbyes*, Tallahassee, Naiad Press, 1993.

26. Stephen F. Soitos, "Queering the 'I': Black Lesbian Detective Fiction, in *Multicultural Detective Fiction: Murder from the "Other" Side*, Adrienne Johnson Gosselin, ed., New York, Garland, 1999, p. 112.

27. Carol Clover notes the "virtual indestructibility" of the typical horror-movie killer. Carol J. Clover, *Men, Women, and Chainsaws: Gender in the Modern Horror Film*, Princeton, NJ, Princeton University Press, 1992, p. 30.

28. Jackie Manthorne, *Deadly Reunion*, Charlottetown, Prince Edward Island, Canada, Gynergy Books, 1995.

29. Katherine V. Forrest, *Murder at the Nightwood Bar*, Tallahassee, FL, Naiad Press, 1987.

30. Katherine V. Forrest, *The Beverly Malibu*, Tallahassee, FL, Naiad Press 1989.

31. Anthony Slide, *Gay and Lesbian Characters and Themes in Mystery Novels: A Critical Guide to Over 500 Works in English*, Jefferson, NC, McFarland & Co., 1993, pp. 55–56.

32. For another sex scene in which Kate seems to be losing control, though not worrying too much about it, see *Murder at the Nightwood Bar*, pp. 123–124.

33. Lillian Faderman notes: "'[S]tone butches' ... observed taboos similar to those that were current among working-class heterosexual males. For example, letting another woman be sexually aggressive with you if you were a stone butch was called being flipped, and it was shameful in many working-class lesbian communities because it meant that a butch had permitted another woman to take power away from her by sexually 'femalizing' her, making a 'pussy' out of her...." Lillian Faderman, *Odd Girls and Twilight Lovers: A History of Lesbian Life in Twentieth-Century America*, New York, Penguin, 1991, pp. 169–170. While Faderman is discussing the 1950s and 1960s, these codes still appear to apply somewhat to the character of Kate Delafield, in that her sexual coming-of-age occurred in the late 1960s. While she may have rejected the bar scene of that era (*Nightwood Bar* 32–34), some of the more rigid butch-femme codes have apparently influenced her in these early novels. Kate's eventual accomodation to switching roles reflects the more fluid conception of roles made possible in the 1980s. See Faderman, *Odd Girls and Twilight Lovers: A History of Lesbian Life in Twentieth-Century America*, pp. 264–267.

34. Sally Munt says, "Not only does Kate revision herself as a femme, she also has to change her construction of that role as passive, and allow for a new conception of these roles as fluid, not fixed. Indeed, oral and narrative histories of butches and femmes often relate the complexity of these identities, with women having switched from one to the other within and between different relationships." Sally R. Munt, "The Inverstigators," [sic] in *Murder by the Book?: Feminism and the Crime Novel*, London, Routledge, 1994, p. 138. Munt notes a similar "slip[] from butch to femme" for lesbian detective Emma Victor in Mary Wings's *She Came Too Late* [London, The Women's Press, 1986]. Munt notes that "[T]his passivity is indulged because the reader knows Emma Victor is really a strong woman permitting her submission fantasies a limited expression." Munt, *op. cit.*, p. 142. Interestingly, Lois A. Marchino quotes a brief excerpt from a sex scene between Kate and Aimee in a later Kate Delafield novel, *Murder By Tradition*, that suggests that Kate is now taking a more dominant role in their lovemaking. Lois A. Marchino, "Katherine V. Forrest: Writing Kate Delafield for Us," in *Women Times Three: Writers, Detectives, Readers*, Kathleen Gregory Klein, ed., Bowling Green, OH, Bowling Green State University Popular Press, 1995, p. 74. If Kate is now reasserting a more "dominant" role, however, doesn't that suggest even more strongly the underlying fear of "turning femme"?

Chapter 3

1. This chapter is based in large part on research conducted over several weeks at the Museum of Television and Radio in New York during December 1993, June 1994, and May 2002.

2. Susan J. Douglas, *Where the Girls Are: Growing Up Female With the Mass Media*, New York, Random House, 1994, p. 168.

3. Anne Francis, the star of *Honey West*, studied karate for two hours a day for the show. Ronald L. Smith, *Sweethearts of '60s TV*, New York, S.P.I. Books, 1993, p. 192.

4. Yvonne Craig, the actress who played Batgirl recalls: "The producer didn't want Batgirl to do anything considered unfeminine, like punch villains. He wanted her to spin madly — and since I had a ballet background, I could do that — or kick people with balletic high kicks or skinny out from under them. It was somewhat limiting, because there are things that are far more interesting to do than kicking people." Panel discussion reported in "Feminine Wiles: Empowered Women, Heroic and Evil," in *Television Quarterly*, Vol. XXVII, No. 2, p. 22.

5. See Dave Rogers, *The Complete Avengers*, New York, St. Martin's Press, 1989, p. 90. The rule was established only part-way through the series, during the Emma Peel years. *Id.*

6. *Cagney and Lacey: The Return* aired November 6, 1994 on CBS.

7. Jack Condon & David Hofstede, *Charlie's Angels Casebook*, Beverly Hills, Pomegranate Press, 2000, p. 231.

8. Condon & Hofstede, *Charlie's Angels Casebook*, p. 174.

9. Condon & Hofstede, *Charlie's Angels Casebook*, p. 259.

10. Indeed, many actresses left shows in the 1970s and early 1980s because of contract, creative, and workplace disputes. Lynn Redgrave left *House Calls* in a contract dispute with producers; Suzanne Somers left *Three's Company* in a salary dispute; Esther Rolle temporarily left *Good Times* in a creative dispute with the producers [she felt that the character of J.J. Evans (Jimmie Walker) was degenerating into a stereotyped portrayal of African American young men]; Cybill Shepherd almost left *Moonlighting* in a dispute with producers about working conditions — she also had problems with the treatment of herself and her character, facing "a behind-the-scenes campaign, conducted by both executive producer Glenn Caron and actor Bruce Willis ... to curb [her] 'aggressive' personality"; Valerie Harper left *Valerie* "in a well-publicized dispute with the producers"— her absence was explained by her character's death; Shelley Long left *Cheers* because of creative differences with the producers. Tim Brooks and Earle Marsh, *The Complete Directory to Prime Time Network and Cable TV Shows: 1946–Present*, 6th ed., New York, Ballantine Books, 1995, pp. 483, 1039, 411, 696, 466 and Susan Faludi, *Backlash: The Undeclared War Against American Women*, New York, Anchor, 1991, pp. 143, 157.

11. Jack Condon & David Hofstede, *Charlie's Angels Casebook*, Beverly Hills, Pomegranate Press, 2000, pp. 9, 81–82.

12. The only actors in recent memory whose disputes with producers were as well publicized were David Caruso of *NYPD Blue* and Pierce Brosnan of *Remington Steele*. Both had no creative or financial disagreements with producers but simply wanted a more flexible shooting schedule in order to pursue film offers. Brosnan stayed with *Remington Steele* and was later rewarded with the James Bond role he had missed out on during *Remington Steele*; Caruso quit *NYPD Blue* and *was* characterized as "difficult."

13. Her lackluster performance might be partly explained by the fact that "Kirk ... had never seen the original movies." Tom Soter, *Investigating Couples: A Critical Analysis of The Thin Man, The Avengers, and The X-Files*, Jefferson, NC, McFarland, 2002, p. 155.

14. The Dumont network series is apparently lost. See Graham Russell Gao Hodges, *Anna May Wong: From Laundryman's Daughter to Hollywood Legend*, New York, Palgrave Macmillan, 2004, pp. 216–217, 264 note 9.

15. Tim Brooks and Earle Marsh, "The Gallery of Mme. Lui-Tsong [sic]," in *The Complete Directory to Prime Time Network and Cable*

TV Shows: 1946–Present, 6th ed., Ballantine, NY, 1995, p. 384. Max Allan Collins and John Javna note: "...Anna May Wong played Madame Liu Tsong (Anna's real name), an art gallery owner who doubled as a sleuth. Probably the first woman detective with her own TV show." Max Allan Collins & John Javna, *The Best of Crime & Detective TV: Perry Mason to Hill Street Blues, The Rockford Files to Murder, She Wrote*, New York, Harmony Books, 1988, p. 94.

16. Tim Brooks and Earle Marsh, *The Complete Directory to Prime Time Network and Cable TV Shows: 1946–Present*, 6th ed., Ballantine, NY, 1995, p. 384.

17. Interestingly, Anna May Wong had earlier played a Chinese American female investigator on *film*, in 1937's *Daughter of Shanghai*. William K. Everson, *The Detective in Film: A Pictorial Treasury of The Screen Sleuth from 1903 to the Present*, Secaucus, NJ, Citadel Press, 1972, p. 122. Anna May Wong also played a character who did some detecting in *When Were You Born?* (1938). Everson, *The Detective in Film*, p. 227.

18. Kathi Maio, *Popcorn and Sexual Politics*, Freedom, CA, the Crossing Press, 1991, pp. 99–100. Maureen T. Reddy also calls Modesty Blaise "not altogether praiseworthy." Maureen T. Reddy, *Sisters in Crime: Feminism and the Crime Novel*, New York, Continuum, 1988, p. 2. I respectfully disagree. I think that the character of Modesty Blaise is a lot like the women of *Charlie's Angels*— she can be perceived from radically different perspectives by different audiences. Personally, I adored the Modesty Blaise books.

19. On the timing of his literary creation, O'Donnell writes: "There is a theory which asserts that when it's steam-engine time, somebody will invent the steam-engine. So with Modesty Blaise. The beginning of the Sixties was the time for someone like her to appear...." O'Donnell's own conception of Modesty Blaise does lend some credence to Maio's claims about the intended audience for the character: "...[I]t delighted me to contemplate writing about a marvellous [sic] female creature who would be as good as any male hero in the crunch, yet would remain entirely feminine withal. Yes, feminine. No bra-burning Women's Libber, she." Peter O'Donnell, "Becoming Modesty," in *Murder Ink: The Mystery Reader's Companion*, Dilys Winn, ed., New York, Workman Publishing, 1977, p. 158.

20. Gary Warren Niebuhr, *A Reader's Guide to The Private Eye Novel*, New York, G.K. Hall & Co., 1993, p. 87.

21. For a thorough analysis of the series that includes both pre- and post-Diana Rigg seasons of *The Avengers*, see "Is There Honey Still for Tea?: *The Avengers*," in James Chapman, *Saints & Avengers: British Adventure Series of the 1960s*, London, I.B. Tauris, 2002, pp. 52–99. This study

investigates literary and filmic influences on *The Avengers* and examines its changing artistic, generic, and ideological underpinnings. *Id.* For a discussion of *The Avengers* in the context of class, contemporary attitudes towards technology, and the pop movement in Britain, see David Buxton, *From The Avengers to Miami Vice: form and ideology in television series*, New York, Manchester University Press/St. Martins, 1990, pp. 96–107.

22. Dave Rogers, *The Complete Avengers*, New York, St. Martin's Press, p. 87.

23. Dave Rogers, *The Complete Avengers*, New York, St. Martin's Press, p. 89.

24. See George Lipsitz, "The Meaning of Memory: Family, Class, and Ethnicity in Early Network Television Programs," in *Private Screenings: Television and the Female Consumer*, Lynn Spigel and Denise Mann, eds., Minneapolis, University of Minnesota Press, pp. 77–83.

25. On the pen=penis equation in detective fiction, see Maureen T. Reddy, *Sisters in Crime: Feminism and the Crime Novel*, New York, Continuum, 1988, pp. 96–98.

26. In a 1992 interview by Bill Warren made available on the Showbiz RoundTable on the computer network GEnie, Patrick Macnee (Steed) says, in answer to the question of whether Diana Rigg was mistreated in the production of the *Avengers* in any other way besides being underpaid, "Oh yes. She personified, as I said earlier, women's lib, but she was employed by the male chauvinist pigs. There were four or five of them, and they were as piggy and as chauvinistic as you can possibly imagine. And she said, after 18 months of this, 'I'm off.'" Concerning the show's sexual politics, Macnee remarks that the actress originally slated to play Emma Peel didn't work out because "She was too much of a woman. [Emma] needs to be a hermaphrodite, in a way." *Id.*

27. One thinks of another British series, *Dr. Who*, that has kept the main character constant for over 20 years (through a science-fiction feint in which he —*always* a he — is allowed to change appearances and personalities every few years), but has gone through a dizzying number of (mostly female) sidekicks.

28. This incident may seem to be an exception to the cultural taboo against hitting women discussed above. It is explained by two circumstances: first, the suspect doesn't hit her directly as he would a male opponent in a fair fight — instead, he slaps her face and throws her on a couch. Second, physical violence against prostitutes *is* often represented in mass media, and Julie, as the daughter of a prostitute, is marked as a potential prostitute. The violence against prostitutes is often portrayed as violence against a completely passive victim who has given up her rights to control over and safety of her body by her choice of profession. Moreover, by agreeing to date a suspect for information, Julie re-enacts her mother's role as a prostitute.

29. The original version of *Scooby-Doo, Where Are You?* ran in 1969–72, 1974–76, Fall 1978, and Fall 1984. Various other versions of the show ran until 1993. Hal Erickson, *Television Cartoon Shows: An Illustrated Encyclopedia, 1949 through 1993*, Jefferson, NC, McFarland, 1995, pp. 433–435.

30. The human characters on the show were based on the characters from one of television executive Fred Silverman's favorite sitcoms, *The Many Loves of Dobie Gillis*. All-American Dobie Gillis was represented by Freddy; plain but brainy Zelda Gilroy, by Velma; pretty but vacuous Thalia Menninger, by Daphne; and beatnik Maynard G. Krebs, by Shaggy. Hal Erickson, *Television Cartoon Shows: An Illustrated Encyclopedia, 1949 through 1993*, Jefferson, NC, McFarland, 1995, p. 437.

31. Velma, though generally correct in her suspicions, was not infallible. 1970 was a particularly bad television season for Velma. The show seemed to delight in highlighting the unsuccessful parts of her investigations. In an episode entitled "Scooby's Night With a Frozen Fright" (1970), Velma says "I'll bet he's up to something," about a suspect who turns out *not* to be guilty. In "Mystery Mask Mix-Up" (1970), Velma says "I can read Chinese, but I can't make heads or tails of this." The mystery writing turns out to be simply mirror writing. It it telling that the form of Velma's incapacity turns on her ability to interpret writing. In "Jeepers, It's the Creeper" (1970), Velma loses her glasses twice (undercutting her authoritative vision) and states: "That hermit disguise doesn't fool me. I think he's the Creeper." Velma is entirely wrong again. The bank president, not the hermit, turns out to be the Creeper. To be fair, though, Fred, the only other person who ever solves mysteries on the series, agrees with Velma's mistaken suspicions. Velma and Freddy are also wrong in "Nowhere to Hyde" (1970), when they suspect the criminal is Helga the housekeeper instead of her employer, Dr. Jekyll. Velma also occasionally undercuts her own prowess. In "Spooky Space Kook" (1969), when Freddy is trapped by a meathook, he pleads "Velma, surely you can figure this out." She responds "Mechanics aren't my cup of tea, Freddy." Velma does not solve the mystery in this episode — Freddy does. On the other hand, Velma's deductions, when she makes them, are pretty spectacular. In "A Night of Fright is No Delight" (1969) Velma takes the lead in investigating and correctly interprets several clues, the most memorable of which is understanding that the words "FEED the organ" mean playing the notes F-E-E-D on the organ.

32. Timothy and Kevin Burke note: "...Velma represented a distillation of virtually every noxious stereotype about intelligent women that one could find. Timothy Burke and Kevin Burke, *Saturday Morning Fever*, New York, St. Martin's Press, 1999, p. 218. They also note that "[viewers] have joked about Velma being a lesbian...." *Id.*

33. Hal Erickson, *Television Cartoon Shows: An Illustrated Encyclopedia, 1949 through 1993*, Jefferson, NC, McFarland, 1995, p. 437.

34. Fred generally drives the gang's van, the Mystery Machine.

35. Jeffery Davis, *Children's Television: 1947–1990*, Jefferson, NC, McFarland, 1995, p. 83.

36. The sexual politics of referring to the female member of the couple simply as "wife," as if she is defined by her husband, are clear.

37. David Martindale, *Television Detective Shows of the 1970s: Credits, Storylines and Episode Guides for 109 Series*, Jefferson, North Carolina, McFarland, 1991, p. 318.

38. The reason that Sally, unlike most female investigators who go undercover as prostitutes, is not punished for her action (other than by having raised Mac's ire) is that, as an upperclass woman, she's shown not to be "naturally" good at playing a prostitute — she requires coaching from her earthy housekeeper Mildred (Nancy Walker) to play the part.

39. Robert Daley noted in 1974 that the portrayal of Sally did not ring true with real police officers. Robert Daley, "Police Report on the TV Cop Shows," in *Detective Fiction: Crime and Compromise*, Dick Allen and David Chacko, eds., New York, Harcourt Brace Jovanovich, 1974, p. 437. To be fair, Daley, a former deputy police commissioner [Daley, op. cit., p. 439], criticizes *every* detective show that he reviews on the grounds that they are all inaccurate and unrealistic. Robert Daley, "Police Report on the TV Cop Shows," in *Detective Fiction: Crime and Compromise*, Dick Allen and David Chacko, eds., New York, Harcourt Brace Jovanovich, 1974, pp. 430–444.

40. "McMillan and Wife," in Tim Brooks and Earle Marsh, *The Complete Directory to Prime Time Network and Cable TV Shows: 1946–Present*, 6th ed., Ballantine, NY, 1995, pp. 663–664.

41. One wonders if some wag naming the character was making a "Sgt. Pepper" joke. Pepper's character had originally appeared as a character on the series *Police Story*, then named Lisa Beaumont. David Martindale, *Television Detective Shows of the 1970s: Credits, Storylines and Episode Guides for 109 Series*, Jefferson, NC, McFarland, 1991, p. 389. Susan J. Douglas notes that star Angie Dickinson herself came up with the name "Pepper," claiming, "Somehow I can't

imagine a woman police officer named 'Lisa.'" Susan J. Douglas, *Where the Girls Are: Growing Up Female With the Mass Media*, New York, Random House, 1994, p. 209, citing Sue Cameron, "Police Drama: Women Are on the Case," *Ms.*, October 1974, p. 104.

42. Susan J. Douglas, *Where the Girls Are: Growing Up Female With the Mass Media*, New York, Random House, 1994, p. 210. [Italics hers.] Douglas also makes a convincing argument linking of the rise of the representation of rape on television in the seventies (and on *Police Woman* in particular) to male backlash against the sexual liberation of women. Douglas, *Where the Girls Are*, pp. 209–211. Douglas also makes other persuasive arguments to locate the beginnings of the backlash against women's liberation in the media of the early 1970s. Douglas, *Where the Girls Are*, pp. 193–199. On backlash trends, see also Tania Modleski's analyses of a wide variety of antifeminist 1980s film and television texts in *Feminism Without Women: Culture and Criticism in a "Postfeminist" Age*, London, Routledge, 1991; Julie D'Acci's account of how the successful "'80s feminist police "buddy show" *Cagney and Lacey* suffered continual attacks by network executives trying to undercut its feminist perspective in "Defining Women: The Case of *Cagney and Lacey*," in *Private Screenings: Television and the Female Consumer*, Lynn Spigel and Denise Mann, eds., Minneapolis, U. of Minnesota, 1992, pp. 169–201; and Susan Faludi's fascinating (and disturbing) description of how behind-the-scenes machinations of television producers in the early 1980s quite deliberately pitched shows to antifeminist audiences in *Backlash: The Undeclared War Against American Women*, New York, Doubleday, 1991, pp. 142–168.

43. Co-workers call her "Pep," implying the energy she radiates.

44. The advertisements shown during a later episode, "Pattern for Evil" (airing 10/3/75), suggest that advertisers assumed the show had a large male audience. That episode featured a beer ad, a car ad featuring a male consumer, an ad for men's razors, an ad for automobile shocks, another car ad with a male spokesperson, an ad for dog food, an ad for a male hardboiled detective show, a cola ad featuring a country boy, and another car ad portraying a group of mostly male office workers. Almost everyone in the ads is white. The only advertisements aimed at women are an ad for hair conditioner featuring soon-to-be Angel Farrah Fawcett and an ad for Dristan nasal mist that shows a female sufferer of sinus trouble. To judge by these ads, at least the marketing department thought that the viewers of *Police Woman* were almost exclusively white and male. I think that this is unlikely, but it may partially explain why the show seemed to undercut

Pepper over time and to give more screen time to her co-workers. The ad lineup for a later episode, "Sweet Kathleen," is a little less macho. That episode featured the following ads: an ad for asthma medicine, an ad for an antiseptic oral anesthetic, an ad for a Dustin Hoffman movie, a car ad with a male spokesperson, an ad for camera film, an ad for *House Calls*, an aspirin ad featuring a male headache sufferer, an ad for a different male detective series, an ad for a Dean Martin roast, another car ad with a male spokesperson, a hamburger ad, another car ad, an ad for telephone equipment, an ad for a John Wayne movie, an ad for a science-fiction series, and an ad for anti-perspirant, featuring Tina Louise (*Gilligan's Island*'s Ginger).

45. Jack Condon and David Hofstede, *Charlie's Angels Casebook*, Beverly Hills, Pomegranate Press, 2000, p. 147. This seems to be the episode of *Charlie's Angels* that is the most remembered by the series' fans and detractors alike. Paradoxically, this sex-ploitation episode reportedly led to greater power for the actresses who portrayed the Angels, as they demanded and received more script control. Patricia Burstein, *Farrah: An Unauthorized Biography of Farrah Fawcett-Majors*, New York, Signet, 1977, p. 89.

46. I suspect that the inclusion of a scene showing tough men who cook pasta sauce in *The Godfather* (Francis Ford Coppola, 1972) made this kind of cooking more acceptable to men in the early seventies — a type of cooking analogous in its gender-typing to grilling on the barbecue.

47. Diana M. Meehan, *Ladies of the Evening: Women Characters of Prime-Time Television*, Metuchen, N.J., The Scarecrow Press, Inc., 1983, pp. 73–84. Meehan also typed as decoys Cinnamon Carter of *Mission Impossible*, Eve Whitfield of *Ironside*, Julie Barnes of *Mod Squad*, all the women of *Charlie's Angels* (but especially Jill, Kelly, and Kris), and Jennifer Hart of *Hart to Hart*.

48. Meehan, *Ladies of the Evening: Women Characters of Prime-Time Television*, p. 78.

49. Martindale includes both theories in his review. David Martindale, *Television Detective Shows of the 1970s: Credits, Storylines, and Episode Guides for 109 Series*, Jefferson, NC, McFarland, 1991, p. 175.

50. In the series that followed, Reardon's first name became Matt, and he was played by Charles Cioffi. David Martindale, *Television Detective Shows of the 1970s: Credits, Storylines and Episode Guides for 109 Series*, Jefferson, NC, McFarland, p. 175.

51. Susan J. Douglas, *Where the Girls Are: Growing Up Female With the Mass Media*, p. 209. For a parody of the Christie Love arrest style, see Beyoncé Knowles' portrayal of Foxxy Cleopatra in *Austin Powers in Goldmember* (Jay Roach, 2002).

52. J. Fred MacDonald, *Blacks and White TV*, p. 204. Others echo this suggestion that *Get Christie Love!* required more than the usual suspension of disbelief from its viewers: "Unfortunately, poorly written scripts and unbelievable characters caused the ABC drama to be cancelled after one season." George Hill, Lorraine Raglin, and Chas Floyd Johnson, *Black Women in Television: An Illustrated History and Bibliography*, New York, Garland Publishing, 1990, p. 9.

53. David Martindale, *Television Detective Shows of the 1970s: Credits, Storylines, and Episode Guides for 109 Series*, Jefferson, NC, McFarland, 1991, p. 175. Martindale conflates here two *different* real-life policewomen who influenced the series: author Dorothy Uhnak, upon whose novels the series was based, and the series' technical advisor Olga Ford. Ford was "a black New York City second-grade detective with 15 years on the force." Sue Cameron, "Police Drama: Women are on the Case," *Ms.*, October 1974, p. 108. Cameron does confirm that Ford's experiences as a police officer formed the basis of at least one episode's plot on the show. *Id.*

54. Paul Leon Bail, "Dorothy Uhnak," in *Great Women Mystery Writers: Classic to Contemporary*, Kathleen Gregory Klein, ed., Westport, CT, Greenwood Press, 1994, p. 343. For another real-life account of the discrimination suffered by a capable female police officer in the 1950s and later, see Maureen T. Reddy's description of Marie Cirile's autobiography. Maureen T. Reddy, *Sisters in Crime: Feminism and the Crime Novel*, New York, Continuum, 1988, pp. 70–73. Reddy aptly comments on "the conflicts inherent in the term "woman police officer" in a patriarchal society." *Id.* at 71.

55. *Julia* (1968–71), a popular program about an African American nurse, is one counterexample. Tim Brooks and Earle Marsh, *The Complete Directory to Prime Time Network and Cable TV Shows: 1946–Present*, 6th ed., New York, Ballantine Books, 1995, p. 542.

56. Interestingly, Charles Cioffi, who plays Reardon in the regular series, was also in the film version of *Shaft*, which underscores the series' ties to the blaxploitation genre. See Martin Connors & Julia Furtaw, eds., *VideoHound's Golden Movie Retriever 1995*, Detroit, Visible Ink, 1995, p. 826.

57. David Martindale, *Television Detective Shows of the 1970s: Credits, Storylines, and Episode Guides for 109 Series*, Jefferson, NC, McFarland, 1991, pp. 442–443. Martindale attributes the failure of *Shaft* as a television series not to white America's discomfort with a powerful black detective but rather to the series' failure to remain true to the style, sex appeal, and violence that made the movies such hits in the first place. Martindale quotes *Los Angeles Times* critic Cecil Smith's immortal line: "*Shaft* on TV makes Barn-

aby Jones look like Eldridge Cleaver." Martindale, *Television Detective Shows of the 1970s*, p. 443.

58. Thus 1970s Saturday morning television, for example, combined *Isis*, about a young female superhero, with *Shazaam!*, about a young male superhero. Likewise, the female "Batman-and-Robin" of Saturday morning television, "Electrawoman and Dynagirl," had episodes of their serial carefully circumscribed by other serials ("Dr. Shrinker" and "Wonderbug") aimed more at a mixed-gender audience as part of *The Krofft Supershow*. *Captain Caveman and the Teen Angels* (a *Charlie's Angels* ripoff) was similarly circumscribed by other less female-centered programming. To be fair, however, some programming for young girls in the seventies stood on its own, e.g., *Josie and the Pussycats*.

59. ABC News: World News Tonight, May 29, 2002. Ms. Benson died in May, 2002. *Id.*

60. David Martindale, *Television Detective Shows of the 1970s: Credits, Storylines and Episode Guides for 109 Series*, Jefferson, NC, McFarland, 1991, pp. 179–80. Tim Brooks and Earle Marsh, *The Complete Directory to Prime Time Network and Cable TV Shows: 1946-Present*, New York, Ballantine Books, 1995, p. 437. Perhaps network executives thought that both male and female audiences would watch the *Hardy Boys*, but that only female audiences would watch *Nancy Drew*. Maureen T. Reddy notes the male/female anomaly in detective fiction, using the book versions of *The Hardy Boys* and *Nancy Drew* as examples. See Maureen T. Reddy, *Sisters in Crime: Feminism and the Crime Novel*, New York, Continuum, 1988, p. 6.

61. An example of this phenomenon is the role of Peggy Maxwell (Susan Saint James) on *The Name of the Game* (1968–1971). Peggy played girl-friday/sidekick to three different investigative journalists working for the same magazine syndicate who rotated episodes weekly. Peggy acted as the main narrative link between the three men, who seldom investigated together, but never got her own segment. David Martindale, *Television Detective Shows of the 1970s: Credits, Storylines and Episode Guides for 109 Series*, Jefferson, NC, McFarland, 1991, pp. 351–352.

62. The also-rans include the following series: *Amy Prentiss*, about a woman chief of detectives (3 episodes aired); *The American Girls*, about female investigative reporters (6 episodes aired); *The Snoop Sisters*, about elderly sibling mystery writers (4 episodes aired, preceded by one TV-movie); *Kate McShane*, about an investigating lawyer (8 episodes aired, preceded by one TV-movie); *McNaughton's Daughter*, about a deputy DA (3 episodes aired, preceded by one TV-movie); *Mrs. Columbo* (renamed *Kate Loves a Mystery*, and sometimes known as *Kate the Detec-*

tive or *Kate Columbo*), about the famed male detective's never-seen wife (11 episodes aired, preceded by one TV-movie). See David Martindale, *Television Detective Shows of the 1970s: Credits, Storylines and Episode Guides for 109 Series*, Jefferson, NC, McFarland, 1991, pp. 16, 18–19, 252–254, 323, 346–349, 445–446. Of course, shows that featured male investigators as well as female investigators sometimes failed as well. Martindale also notes the 4-episode run of *Khan!*, featuring a Chinese American detective and his daughter and son, the 6-episode run of *Dog and Cat*, about a male-female police investigating team, the 12-episode run of *The Most Deadly Game*, featuring two men and a woman as an investigating team, and the 14-episode run of *The Silent Force*, also featuring two men and a woman as an investigating team. See Martindale, *Television Detection Shows of the 1970s*, pp. 131–32, 257, 340–343, 443–445. There was a trend in the early 70s towards shows featuring female lawyer protagonists, who usually had associates or family members who did much of their detective work for them, *à la* Perry Mason. Another "woman lawyer" show was *The Feather and Father Gang*. See Martindale, *Television Detection Shows of the 1970s*, pp. 173–175.

63. See Susan J. Douglas, *Where the Girls Are: Growing Up Female with the Mass Media*, New York, Random House, 1994, pp. 214, 216. See also below on the power of the disembodied voiceover. In his telephone calls to the Angels, the unseen Charlie keeps up a steady stream of double entendres about his sex life that are marked by shots tantalizing the viewer with a glimpse of Charlie's arm (or some other appendage) and a view of his sybaritic surroundings. Significantly, the Angels, although well aware of Charlie's double entendres, are cut off from the slightly more privileged viewing position of the audience.

64. Typical is the assessment of Max Allan Collins and John Javna: "The three perpetrators, Farrah Fawcett, Jackie [sic] Smith, and Kate Jackson, did more damage to the cause of feminism than the Susan B. Anthony dollar.... [The program is] [n]ot just a crime show, but a crime. The braless Angels jiggled their way into American culture, paving the way for even worse atrocities." Max Allan Collins & John Javna, *The Best of Crime & Detective TV: Perry Mason to Hill Street Blues, The Rockford Files to Murder, She Wrote*, New York, Harmony Books, 1988, p. 47.

65. David Bianculli, *Teleliteracy: Taking Television Seriously*, New York, Continuum, 1992, p. 4.

66. David Martindale, *Television Detective Shows of the 1970s: Credits, Storylines and Episode Guides for 109 Series*, Jefferson, NC, McFarland, 1991, p. 81. This is true even of very recent male critical assessments of the show. "Sex, pure and

simple, seemed to be the principal ingredient in the considerable success of this detective show," say Brooks and Marsh. Tim Brooks and Earle Marsh, *The Complete Directory to Prime Time Network and Cable TV Shows: 1946-Present*, New York, Ballantine Books, 1995, p. 178. Their commentary includes a discussion of the Farrah Fawcett-Majors swimsuit poster "which showed the fine points of her anatomy [i.e., her nipples] in marvelous detail." Brooks and Marsh, *Directory*, pp. 178–179.

67. John Fiske, *Television Culture*, London, Routledge, 1987, p. 39.

68. See Fiske, *Television Culture*, pp. 39–40. A similar, though more female-positive reading of *Charlie's Angels* is that of Caren J. Deming: "Even such phallocentric series as *Policewoman* [sic] and *Charlie's Angels* contained moments when female actors were able to use their performances (if not often the script) to enter what Edwin Ardener called 'the zone of difference,' that tiny space created by the mismatch of dominant visions with muted ones." Caren J. Deming, "For Television-Centred Television Criticism: Lessons from Feminism" in *Television and Women's Culture: The Politics of the Popular*, Mary Ellen Brown, ed., London, SAGE, 1990, p. 58.

69. Susan J. Douglas, *Where the Girls Are: Growing Up Female with the Mass Media*, New York, Random House, 1994, pp. 213–216.

70. For those who like charts, Condon and Hofstede have compiled "The Charlie's Angels Swimsuit Guide," in which they chart the episodes where any Angel wears a bikini, a one-piece swimsuit, or a towel. Interestingly, fewer than one third of the episodes featured swimwear or towels. Jack Condon and David Hofstede, *Charlie's Angels Casebook*, Beverly Hills, Pomegranate Press, 2000, Appendix B, pp. 289–291.

71. Douglas interprets the occupation-switching as a way for the Angels to build solidarity with other women across class barriers. See Susan J. Douglas, *Where the Girls Are: Growing Up Female with the Mass Media*, New York, Random House, 1994, p. 214.

72. Andrea L. Press, *Women Watching Television: Gender, Class, and Generation in the American Television Experience*, Philadelphia, University of Pennsylvania Press, 1991, pp. 148–150. The impressive diversity of viewership of *Charlie's Angels* can be seen by the fact that Queen Elizabeth II, Prince Phillip, and Prince Charles were all fans of the show when it originally aired. In an age when VCR use was not common, the Queen made sure that dinner didn't interfere with watching *Charlie's Angels*. Condon & Hofstede, *Charlie's Angels Casebook*, p. 64.

73. Ella Taylor, *Prime-Time Families: Television Culture in Postwar America*, Berkeley, University of California Press, 1989, p. 54.

74. Laura Henderson and Bradley S. Greenburg, *Life on Television: Content Analyses of U.S. TV Drama*, Norwood, N.J., Ablex Publishing Corp., 1980, pp. 90–94.

75. *Entertainment Tonight: Charlie's Angels Uncovered* (syndicated television program, viewed 11/6/99). The same program noted that the *Charlie's Angels* movie, then in pre-production, was not going to have the Angels using guns. *Id.*

76. Peter Travers, *Discovering Paperbacks Brings You Peter Travers' Favorite TV Angels*, Middletown, CT, Xerox Education Publications, 1978, p. 66.

77. The centrality of the concept of female friendship to *Charlie's Angels* is reaffirmed by a more recent re-telling of the narrative. In the film *Charlie's Angels: Full Throttle* (McG, 2003), rebellious former Angel Madison Lee (Demi Moore) has broken away from Charlie and the later Angels and has become their enemy. In what is obviously meant to be a crushing remark, one of the current "good" Angels tells Madison, "I have something you'll never have ... friends."

78. The segment in question is a part of the infamous 1976 "Angels in Chains" episode mentioned above, which finds the Angels stripped and doused with disinfectant by a sadistic matron as they go undercover in a women's prison.

79. This perspective is a *topos* in criticism of *film noir* in general and of certain films (e.g., *Mildred Pierce*) in particular. See, for example, Frank Krutnik, *In a Lonely Street: Film noir, Genre, Masculinity*, London, Routledge, 1991, pp. 61–65; Linda Williams, "Feminist Film Theory: *Mildred Pierce* and the Second World War," in *Female Spectators: Looking at Film and Television*, Deidre Prisnam, ed., London, Verso, 1988, pp. 12–30; Joyce Nelson, "'Mildred Pierce' Reconsidered," *Film Reader* no. 2 (1977), p. 70, reprinted in Bill Nichols, *Movies and Methods: An Anthology*, Vol. 2, Berkeley, University of California Press, 1985, pp. 450–458; Pam Cook, "Duplicity in *Mildred Pierce*," in *Women in Film Noir*, E. Ann Kaplan, ed., London, British Film Institute, 1980, pp. 68–82 (though Cook takes a broader view than the specific historical period after World War Two, p. 69); and Sylvia Harvey, "Woman's Place: The Absent Family of Film Noir," in *Women in Film Noir*, E. Ann Kaplan, ed., London, British Film Institute, 1980, p. 25.

80. There is one role-reversal episode in which Laura Holt, the female member of the detective couple, demonstrates her extensive knowledge of television series in a parody of Steele's obsession with cinema. Her prowess is undercut, however, by the fact that television still suffers from being a less-respected medium than film, and by the fact that her prowess is demonstrated only in a single episode and only in order to parody Steele's.

81. On the dangers of cinematic overidentification, see Mary Ann Doane, "Misrecognition and Identity," *Ciné-Tracts* [outside cover says 11 or II], Vol. 3, No. 3 (Fall 1980), p. 25, reprinted in *Explorations in Film Theory: Selected Essays From Ciné-Tracts*, Ron Burnett, ed., Bloomington, Indiana University Press, 1991, pp. 15–25.

82. E. Ann Kaplan, "Introduction" to *Women in Film Noir*, London, BFI Publishing, 1980, pp. 2–3, [italics in original].

83. Compare the voiceover on *Charlie's Angels*: "Once upon a time, there were three little girls who went to the police academy.... But I took them away from all that. *Now they work for me. My name is Charlie.*" Apparently, the Angels' names are irrelevant; only the fact that these "little girls" belong to Charlie matters.

84. Indeed, Suzanna Danuta Walters suggests that a central project of shows like *Moonlighting* is to "create narratives in which educated, accomplished women get their comeuppance and are 'put in their place' by their working-class [male] counterparts." Suzanna Danuta Walters, *Material Girls: Making Sense of Feminist Cultural Theory*, Berkeley, University of California Press, 1995, p. 134.

85. The female : male::amateur : professional distinction — typical on shows like *McMillan and Wife*— can be found even on such a seemingly feminist romantic investigative show as *The Avengers*. The American version of *The Avengers'* opening credits specifically identifies John Steed as a "top professional" and his female partner Emma Peel as a "talented amateur."

86. Interestingly, this voiceover is the voice of the female detective herself, as opposed to the voice of an observer (like Max on *Hart to Hart*) or a boss (like Charlie on *Charlie's Angels*). Significantly, later seasons drop Laura's voiceover.

87. Julie D'Acci, *Defining Women: Television and the Case of Cagney and Lacey*, Chapel Hill, NC, University of North Carolina Press, 1994, p. 144.

88. The schoolgirl detective genre that flourished in the 1920s and '30s featured almost exclusively young female detectives who had inherited their detecting abilities from their fathers. Patricia Craig and Mary Cadogan note: "Both [Sylvia Silence and Nancy Drew] started their careers by helping their investigator fathers, who were quickly relegated to off-stage roles. Almost all the young female investigators were followers in their fathers' footsteps.... Mothers were either nonexistent or merely psychological wallpaper." Patricia Craig and Mary Cadogan, *The Lady Investigates: Women Detectives and Spies in Fiction*, London, Victor Gollancz, 1981, p. 115.

89. Peter O'Donnell, "Becoming Modesty," in *Murder Ink: The Mystery Reader's Companion*, Dilys Winn, ed., New York, Workman Publishing, 1977, pp. 158–159.

90. Kaja Silverman, *The Acoustic Mirror: The Female Voice in Psychoanalysis and Cinema*, Bloomington, Indiana U. Press, 1988, p. 48.

91. *Id.*

92. The nature of the alibis on his passports undercuts any claim to creative self-authorship, however, since they are not original inventions but rather the names of film characters played by Humphrey Bogart. Even when choosing a name for himself, the jewel thief steps into prepared roles.

93. The jewel thief's overidentification with the cinematic (mentioned above) is now likewise shown to be traceable to his desire to consolidate his own identity. In a paraphrase of the work of Christian Metz, Mary Ann Doane succinctly explains Metz's take on the relationship between the spectator's concept of self and the misrecognition inherent in primary identification:

"...[T]he pleasure of misrecognition ultimately lies in its confirmation of the subject's mastery over the signifier, its guarantee of a unified and coherent ego capable of controlling the effects of the unconscious. This is, essentially, a guarantee of the subject's identity.... Primary cinematic identification entails not only the spectator's identification *with* the camera but his identification *of* himself as the condition of the possibility of what is perceived on the screen. The film viewer, according to Metz, is positioned by the entire cinematic apparatus as the site of an organization — the viewer lends coherence to the image and is simultaneously posited as a coherent entity."

Mary Ann Doane, "Misrecognition and Identity," reprinted in *Explorations in Film Theory: Selected Essays from Ciné-Tracts*, Ron Burnett, ed., Bloomington, Indiana University Press, 1991, p. 19. [Originally published as Mary Ann Doane, "Misrecognition and Identity," *Ciné-Tracts* (outside cover says 11 or II), Vol. 3, No. 3 (Fall 1980), pp. 25–32]. (Italics Doane's.) Doane suggests that, while Metz's theory may apply to male spectators, women's identification with the cinematic does not follow such a straightforward trajectory, pp. 28, 31–32 in original.

94. After its demise, the regular series (1982–1986) was followed by two one-hour episodes and two two-hour television movies in early 1987 that wrapped up the narrative. Tim Brooks and Earle Marsh, *The Complete Directory to Prime Time Network and Cable TV Shows: 1946–Present*, 6th ed., New York, Ballantine Books, 1995, p. 862.

95. It is telling that "real" families apparently subscribe to the traditionally masculine value of struggle for dominance through open conflict, whereas "inauthentic" families subscribe to the traditionally feminine value of compromise for the sake of preserving the peace.

96. Luce Irigaray, "Women on the Market," *This Sex Which Is Not One*, Catherine Porter and Carolyn Burke, trans., Ithaca, Cornell University Press, 1985, p. 172. See also Gayle Rubin, "The Traffic in Women: Notes Toward a Political Economy of Sex," in *Toward an Anthropology of Women*, Rayna R. Reiter, ed., New York, Monthly Review Press, 1975, pp. 157–210 and Eve Kosofsky Sedgwick, "Gender Asymmetry and Erotic Triangles," in *Between Men: English Literature and Male Homosocial Desire*, New York, Columbia University Press, 1985, pp. 21–27.

97. Irigaray notes: "As among signs, value [among commodities] appears only when a relationship has been established. It remains the case that the establishment of relationships cannot be accomplished by the commodities themselves, but depends upon the operation of two exchangers. The exchange value of two signs, two commodities, two women, is a representation of the needs/desires of consumer-exchanger subjects.... [T]here is no such thing as a commodity, either, so long as there are not *at least two men* to make an exchange. In order for a product — a woman? — to have value, two men, at least, have to invest (in) her."

Luce Irigaray, "Women on the Market," in *This Sex Which is Not One*, Catherine Porter and Carolyn Burke, trans., Ithaca, Cornell University Press, 1985, pp. 180–181. [Italics hers.]

98. See Irigaray, "Women on the Market," p. 175.

99. Compare the doomed Italian wedding ceremony between Frasier Crane and Diane Chambers on *Cheers*.

100. For an exploration of some of the cultural politics behind this type of rhetorical strategy, see Judith Williamson, "Woman is an Island: Femininity and Colonization," in *Studies in Entertainment: Critical Approaches to Mass Culture*, Tania Modleski, ed., Bloomington, Indiana University Press, 1986, pp. 99–118. See also Mary Ann Doane, "Dark Continents: Epistemologies of Racial and Sexual Difference in Psychoanalysis and the Cinema," in *Femmes Fatales: Feminism, Film Theory, and Psychoanalysis*, New York, Routledge, 1991, pp. 209–248.

101. Just as romance writer Joan Wilder is recognized in a small Central American town in *Romancing the Stone*, so Remington Steele is recognized in an obscure Mexican town: "You're the big dick from Los Angeles," a hotel clerk quips.

102. The intertextuality between the film and the television series is interesting: The film, produced after the beginning of the television series, may well have been partly inspired by it. The television series then uses the film reference as a signifier of the problematic of female authorship. This self-referentiality is a hallmark of the series. The opening titles of later seasons of the series

show Laura and the jewel thief in a darkened movie theater exchanging sly glances as they watch images of themselves from earlier episodes.

103. The same dynamic appears in another '80s series: *Cheers*. Diane Chambers sleeps with Sam Malone almost immediately after rejecting Sam's brother Derek. The fact that the identity of the romantic rival is irrelevant, that he is simply a place-marker to promote the structure of exchange, is underscored here by the fact that the audience never even gets to see or hear the actor who plays Derek — he is always hidden by a crowd of admirers. Similarly, Sam's surprise proposal to Diane (at the start of Shelley Long's last season on the show) is prompted by his rejection of his current girlfriend, councilwoman Janet Eldridge. I would argue that this does not necessarily indicate that women are the consumers on the market of men here, but rather that both of these situations reflect different aspects of the patriarchal exchange of women described above: For women to have value as commodities, as Irigaray notes, they must have their value determined by a comparison against other women (Diane vs. Janet); for an exchange to take place, there must be at least two possible "consumer-exchanger subjects" (Sam and Derek). Similar dynamics of competition occur on others of the plethora of "Will they or won't they?" shows of the 1980s, including *Who's the Boss?* and *Night Court*.

104. This sort of metonymy for the sex act is comparatively rare in '80s television. Programs like *Hotel* and *Moonlighting* preferred to show a lot of flesh when a relationship was finally consummated.

105. In 1984, Marjorie Hansen Shaevitz writes: "I am concerned about those of us who are trying to be perfect workers, perfect wives, perfect mothers, and perfect housekeepers all at the same time." Marjorie Hansen Shaevitz, *The Superwoman Syndrome*, New York, Warner Books, 1984, p. 2.

106. *TV Guide*, vol. 37, no. 18, (5/6/89), p. 51.

107. Patricia Mellencamp argues that *Murder, She Wrote* in fact offers a "TV critique of the heterosexual couple and the family," and that Jessica herself, as an asexual, independent woman, is meant to offer a positive alternative to those roles. See Patricia Mellencamp, *High Anxiety: Catastrophe, Scandal, Age, & Comedy*, Bloomington, Indiana University Press, 1992, p. 305

108. The sexual dynamics of the show, namely Jessica getting help from nice old men who are fond of *her* and showing up a police chief who is both charmed by and exasperated with her, may owe much to the Margaret Rutherford Miss Marple movies of the early sixties. That series introduced a mild-mannered, would-be beau

who acted as Miss Marple's assistant on her cases — an assistant who had never appeared in the corresponding novels. Since Angela Lansbury played Miss Marple in a later Miss Marple film (in *The Mirror Crack'd* [1980]), she may well have studied the earlier Miss Marple films when preparing her own version of Miss Marple, and her portrayal of Jessica Fletcher may accordingly have been influenced by the earlier films. Parrish and Pitts note the similarities in the character portrayals. Parrish and Pitts, *The Great Detective Pictures*, p. 379.

109. For example, Maude (Bea Arthur) on *Maude*, Momma Carlson (Carol Bruce) on *WKRP in Cincinnati*, Mona (Katherine Helmond) on *Who's the Boss?*, and Endora (Agnes Moorehead) on *Bewitched*.

110. *Larry King Live*, 9/30/94.

111. Apparently, Jessica also does not wield that weapon of phallic privilege — the gun. Collins and Javna quote Lansbury as saying "We ... have no car chases[,] and I don't carry a gun." Max Allan Collins & John Javna, *The Best of Crime & Detective TV: Perry Mason to Hill Street Blues, The Rockford Files to Murder, She Wrote*, New York, Harmony Books, 1988, p. 107. The authors also make the interesting observation that "Lansbury played the role of Agatha Christie's Miss Marple in the 1980 film *The Mirror Crack'd*, and Jessica Fletcher is a clever hybrid of Christie and her famous character." Collins & Javna, *The Best of Crime & Detective TV*, p. 106.

112. *Murder She Wrote: The Celtic Riddle* (2003).

113. Julie D'Acci, *Defining Women: Television and the Case of Cagney and Lacey*, Chapel Hill, University of North Carolina Press, 1994, p. 16. See also Molly Haskell, *From Reverence to Rape: The Treatment of Women in the Movies*, Chicago, University of Chicago Press, 2nd edition, 1987, pp. 362–363.

114. Julie D'Acci, *Defining Women: Television and the Case of Cagney and Lacey*, Chapel Hill, University of North Carolina Press, 1994, pp. 17–18, 25.

115. Susan Faludi, *Backlash: The Undeclared War Against American Women*, New York, Doubleday, 1991, p. 152.

116. D'Acci, "Negotiating Feminism," *Defining Women: Television and the Case of Cagney and Lacey*, Chapel Hill, University of North Carolina Press, 1994, pp. 142–167.

117. For a great critique of the *anti*-feminist subtext of the birth episode on Murphy Brown, see Suzanna Danuta Walters, *Material Girls: Making Sense of Feminist Cultural Theory*, Berkeley, University of California Press, 1995, pp. 15–18.

118. Interestingly, the character of Jackie was originally planned as a lesbian, reflecting the sexual orientation of Roseanne's real-life sister. Tania

Modleski, "The White Negress and the Heavy-Duty Dyke," in *Old Wives' Tales and Other Women's Stories*, New York, New York University Press, 1998, p. 97, citing Geraldine Barr (with Ted Schwarz), *My Sister Roseanne: The True Story of Roseanne Barr Arnold*, New York, Birch Lane Press, 1994, pp. 197–198, 280. Other gay and gay-friendly characters *were* featured on the show, though perhaps the most stunning revelation is that Roseanne and Jackie's conservative mother eventually comes out as gay.

119. Susan Faludi, *Backlash: The Undeclared War Against American Women*, New York, Doubleday, 1991, pp. 150, 152.

120. The show apparently *did* have some lesbian fans. In *Murder at the Nightwood Bar*, the lesbian detective novel discussed above, the lesbians at the bar choose to watch *Cagney and Lacey*. Katherine V. Forrest, *Murder at the Nightwood Bar*, Tallahassee, Naiad Press, 1994, p. 75.

121. As with *Charlie's Angels*, women's response to *Cagney and Lacey* was, of course, not monolithic. Andrea L. Press notes a similar generational split wherein older women viewers value Cagney and Lacey's working relationship and professional competence, while even those younger women viewers who enjoy the show focus on how they cannot visualize themselves doing what Cagney and Lacey do for a living. Andrea L. Press, *Women Watching Television: Gender, Class, and Generation in the American Television Experience*, Philadelphia, University of Pennsylvania Press, 1991, pp. 146–148.

122. Robert J. Thompson notes, however, that Cagney and Lacey's "first assignment after being promoted to the rank of detective was 'hooker detail,'" and that "the two women ... spent several scenes dressed as prostitutes." Robert J. Thompson, *Television's Second Golden Age: From Hill Street Blues to ER*, New York, Continuum, 1996, p. 109. Danae Clark also notes an episode where the pair dress up as hookers, but their parody of the markers of femininity is so extreme that it subverts any voyeuristic possibility for the viewer. Danae Clark, "*Cagney & Lacey*: Feminist Strategies of Detection," in *Television and Women's Culture: The Politics of the Popular*, Mary Ellen Brown, ed., London, SAGE Publications, 1990, pp. 131–133.

123. For a study of the feminist implications of how Cagney and Lacey's detective work is presented and of their progressive place in the world of looking relations, see Danae Clark, "*Cagney & Lacey*: Feminist Strategies of Detection," in *Television and Women's Culture: The Politics of the Popular*, Mary Ellen Brown, ed., London, SAGE Publications, 1990, pp. 117–133.

124. Mary Murphy, "Cagney and Lacey: The Beat Goes On," *TV Guide*, Vol. 42, No. 45, Issue # 2171, Nov. 5–11, 1994, p. 24.

125. Sandra Tomc, "Questing Women: The Feminist Mystery after Feminism," in *Feminism in Women's Detective Fiction*, Glenwood Irons, ed., Toronto, University of Toronto Press, 1995, p. 58.

126. In a thorough reading of the first *Prime Suspect* series, Sandra Tomc observes that this seemingly progressive text has several regressive elements, including a rejection of the series' initial critique of male culture and an agenda that locates Jane Tennison's chances for self-actualization firmly within the patriarchal structure of the police department. Sandra Tomc, "Questing Women: The Feminist Mystery after Feminism," in *Feminism in Women's Detective Fiction*, Glenwood Irons, ed., Toronto, University of Toronto Press, 1995, pp. 46–63. For another close reading of the first and later *Prime Suspect* series, see Priscilla L. Walton and Manina Jones, *Detective Agency: Women Re-Writing the Hardboiled Tradition*, Berkeley, University of California Press, 1999, pp. 249–261.

127. That is, *The X-Files* tends not to offer neat solutions to the mysteries it poses — things are often left unexplained. This is anathema to classic notions of detection that seek knowledge, order, and finality.

128. See, e.g., David Lavery, Angela Hague, and Marla Cartwright, eds., *"Deny All Knowledge": Reading the X-Files*, Syracuse, NY, Syracuse University Press, 1996 and Jan Delasara, *PopLit, PopCult and The X-Files: A Critical Exploration*, Jefferson, NC, McFarland & Co., 2000. On the scientific aspects of *The X-Files*, see Anne Simon, *The Real Science Behind the X-Files: Microbes, Meteorites, and Mutants*, New York, Simon & Schuster, 1999 and Jeanne Cavelos, *The Science of the X-Files*, New York, Berkley Boulevard Books, 1998.

129. Rhonda Wilcox and J.P. Williams similarly observe: "Ironically, [Scully and Mulder's] frequent sex role reversals result in Scully's investigative gaze being disempowered. Time and again, Mulder sees evidence of the supernatural that Scully, by the structure of the episode, is disallowed from seeing." Rhonda Wilcox and J.P. Williams, "'What Do You Think?': The X-Files, Liminality, and Gender Pleasure," in *"Deny All Knowledge": Reading the X-Files*, David Lavery, Angela Hague, and Marla Cartwright, eds., Syracuse, NY, Syracuse University Press, 1996, p. 99.

130. For an in-depth discussion of the gendered implications of *X-Files* fan culture, see Susan J. Clerc, "DDEB, GATB, MPPB, and Ratboy: *The X-Files'* Media Fandom, Online and Off," in *"Deny All Knowledge": Reading the X-Files*, David Lavery, Angela Hague, and Marla Cartwright, eds., Syracuse, NY, Syracuse University Press, 1996, pp. 36–62.

131. The writers were not themselves blind to the gender implications of their choices. In one

X-Files episode, Scully wonders why Mulder always drives.

132. Lest we think their interest *entirely* intellectual, I should note that there was also a lengthy discussion thread about whether Dana Scully wears silk, cotton, or nylon underwear. To be fair, however, in the newsgroup there was also a cadre of female fans of David Duchovny, the DDEB (David Duchovny Estrogen Brigade) which in fact predates the GATB (Gillian Anderson Testosterone Brigade). There was a similarly long discussion thread in the newsgroup commenting on Duchovny's appearance in a Speedo swimsuit.

133. On Scully as "scientific object," see Lisa Parks, "Special Agent or Monstrosity?: Finding the Feminine in *The X-Files*," in *"Deny All Knowledge": Reading the X-Files*, David Lavery, Angela Hague, and Marla Cartwright, eds., Syracuse, NY, Syracuse University Press, 1996, pp. 121–134.

134. The episode is entitled "Emily," and it aired on 12/14/97.

135. Mark Nollinger, "The Exit Files" (sidebar entitled "Mything Links"), *TV Guide*, 5/18/02, pp. 16–17.

136. For example, their views on women's bodies appear to be more progressive than those held by American society as a whole. When one male participant wrote in to say that men don't find pregnant women's bodies attractive (a topic sparked by the fact that Gillian Anderson was pregnant during taping of the show), many men wrote in to criticize him for A. presuming to speak for all men and B. having unrealistic views about women's bodies. Married men wrote in to talk about how they were attracted to their pregnant wives, and pro-feminist men criticized our society in general for putting a premium on anorexic-looking female bodies. Several women wrote in to thank the men for being supportive. I would guess that the active participants on the newsgroup are mostly well-educated young adults in business or academia, judging from their e-mail addresses and signatures, and that there are slightly more men than women participating.

137. The strength of the female characters may be due to the fact that star Pamela Anderson executive produced the series.

138. Tania Modleski points out that "Columbo appear[s] *not* to possess the phallus, but in the end, of course, [he] always reveal[s] that he d[oes]." Tania Modleski, *Feminism Without Women: Culture and Criticism in a "Postfeminist" Age*, New York, Routledge, 1991, p. 106. Modleski further notes that Columbo is "infallible." *Id.*

Chapter 4

1. Christian Metz, *The Imaginary Signifier: Psychoanalysis and the Cinema*, Celia Britton,

Annwyl Williams, Ben Brewster, and Alfred Guzzetti, trans., Bloomington, Indiana UP, 1977, p. 56. Significantly, the spectator here and elsewhere in Metz is assumed to be male.

2. Christian Metz, *id.* at pp. 55–56.

3. To take an extreme example, in his article "Hitchcock, The Enunciator," Raymond Bellour notes a particular instance in the film *Marnie* when the purpose of Hitchcock's cameo appearance seems to be to act as a relay (via his own look reduplicating the looks of male characters in the film) between the enunciation and the male spectator. Raymond Bellour, "Hitchcock the Enunciator," Bertrand Augst and Hilary Radner, trans., in *Camera Obscura*, No. 2 (Fall 1977), p. 73.

4. On the alignment of male characters with spectacle, see Steve Neale, "Masculinity as Spectacle: Reflections on Men and Mainstream Cinema," in *Screening the Male: Exploring Masculinities in Hollywood Cinema*, Steven Cohan and Ina Rae Hark, eds., London, Routledge, 1993, pp. 9–20, originally published in *Screen*, Vol. 24, No. 6 (Nov.- Dec. 1983), pp. 2–16. Neale's main project is to complicate and extend Laura Mulvey's work in "Visual Pleasure in Narrative Cinema" by examining instances in which a male protagonist is offered up as spectacle to the viewing audience. He also makes some particularly telling comments about the position of women in all films, not just detective films:

> While mainstream cinema ... can constantly take women and the female image as its object of investigation, it has rarely investigated men and the male image in the same kind of way.... Where women are investigated, men are tested. Masculinity, as an ideal, at least, is implicitly known. Femininity is, by contrast, a mystery.

Steve Neale, "Masculinity as Spectacle: Reflections on Men and Mainstream Cinema," p. 19.

5. Elaborating, Mulvey asserts: "The determining male gaze projects its fantasy onto the female figure, which is styled accordingly. In their traditional exhibitionist role women are simultaneously looked at and displayed, with their appearance coded for strong visual and erotic impact so that they can be said to connote *to-be-looked-at-ness.*" Laura Mulvey, "Visual Pleasure and Narrative Cinema," in *Visual and Other Pleasures*, Bloomington, Indiana University Press, 1989, p. 19. Of course, much work has been done on cinematic spectatorship since Mulvey's original work, including much theorizing of the possibilities for female spectatorship. Within mainsteam cinema, however, the cinematic codes Mulvey details that assume a male spectatorship have remained all but unchanged in the 1990s and beyond.

6. Christian Metz's "primary cinematic identification" (=the spectator's identification with the enunciation) and "secondary cinematic identification" (=the spectator's identification with one or more characters in the diegesis) often seem to be interpreted exclusively in terms of the male spectator. See Christian Metz, "Identification, Mirror," in *The Imaginary Signifier: Psychoanalysis and the Cinema*, Celia Britton, Annwyl Williams, Ben Brewster, and Alfred Guzzetti, trans., Bloomington, Indiana University Press, 1977, p. 56. Even when theorists do not explicitly postulate a male spectator, their theories often assume one. For example, Metz's chapter entitled "Disavowal, Fetishism," is presented as a general case, although it is applicable only to male spectators (For women spectators, what's to disavow? What's to fetishize?). Metz, *The Imaginary Signifier*, pp. 69–78. Doane notes: "The cinema in general, outside of the genre of the woman's picture, constructs its spectator as the generic 'he' of language. The masculine norm is purportedly asexual while sexually defined seeing is relegated to the woman." Mary Ann Doane, *The Desire to Desire: The Woman's Film of the 1940s*, Bloomington, Indiana University Press, 1987, p. 3. This tendency holds true for theory on film spectatorship as well: the theoretical text often constructs the spectator as a generic "he," as the representative of a masculine norm; the question of sexual difference is left to theoretical texts dealing with the "special case" of the female spectator.

7. As Doane aptly notes in her discussion of a cycle of "paranoid woman's films," the "attribution of the investigating gaze to the female protagonist ... effects a major disturbance in the cinematic relay of the look." Mary Ann Doane, "Paranoia and the Specular," *The Desire to Desire*, p. 135.

8. I am not suggesting that male spectators *never* identify with female protagonists. Carol Clover has demonstrated in her study of horror films how adolescent boys can identify with the female protagonists of these films, deriving masochistic pleasure from identifying with the heroine as she is menaced. Yet the enunciation ensures that the male spectators' masochistic fantasy never hits too close to home. The fact that the protagonist is a girl allows them space to disavow their identification with her. Furthermore, although slasher films often portray male victims, Clover notes that the deaths of male victims are allotted substantially less screen time than the deaths of female victims. Male spectators only get the chance to experience masochistic desire fully when the victim is carefully coded as not-they. Here we have a case similar to the general principle that I am arguing: If one facet of the enunciation has the potential to lead to unpleasure for the male spectator through a problematic identification, then another facet of the enunciation carefully compensates for it. Carol J.

Clover, *Men, Women, and Chain Saws: Gender in the Modern Horror Film*, Princeton, Princeton University Press, 1992, pp. 23, 205–230, 18, 51, 35. On masochistic male identification, see also Frank Krutnik, *In a Lonely Street: Film Noir, Genre, Masculinity*, London, Routledge, 1991, pp. 90–91.

9. That a central project of traditional film noir detective films is the control of transgressive, powerful women is not much debated. For a discussion of this pattern, see Janey Place, "Women in Film Noir," in *Women in Film Noir*, E. Ann Kaplan, ed., London, BFI Publishing, 1980, pp. 35–67. (See especially pp. 42–50 on "The Spider Woman.") Moreover, E. Ann Kaplan notes woman's traditional status as an obstacle to and/or subject of investigation in *film noir*:

> In the typical film noir, the world is presented from the point of view of the male investigator, who ... seeks to unravel a mystery.... [W]e identify with him and rely on him ... to solve the enigma. By contrast, the female characters in film noir stand outside the male order and represent a challenge to it. They symboli[z]e all that is evil and mysterious ... [and use their sexuality] to entrap the investigator and prevent him from accomplishing his task.... [W]omen become the element that the male investigator must guard against if he is to succeed in his quest.

E. Ann Kaplan, "The Place of Women in Fritz Lang's *The Blue Gardenia*," in *Women in Film Noir*, E. Ann Kaplan, ed., BFI publishing, London, 1980, p. 83. See also Christine Gledhill, "*Klute* 1: A Contemporary Film Noir and Feminist Criticism," in *Women in Film Noir*, E. Ann Kaplan, ed., BFI publishing, London, 1980, p. 15.

10. Mary Ann Doane, "Film and the Masquerade: Theorizing the Female Spectator," in *Femmes Fatales: Feminism, Film Theory, Psychoanalysis*, London, Routledge, 1991, p. 27. [originally published as "Film and the Masquerade: Theorising the Female Spectator," *Screen* 23, nos. 3–4 (September-October 1982), pp. 74–87.]

11. Mary Ann Doane, "The 'Woman's Film': Possession and Address," in *Home is Where the Heart Is: Studies in Melodrama and the Woman's Film*, Christine Gledhill, ed., London, BFI Publishing, 1987, pp. 285–286, originally published in *Re-Vision: Essays in Feminist Film Criticism*, Mary Ann Doane, Patricia Mellencamp, and Linda Williams, eds., American Film Institute Monograph Series, Vol. III, Frederick, MD, University Publications of America, 1984, pp. 67–82.

12. I diverge from Doane on the exact cause of this phenomenon, however. Doane argues that paranoia is a consequence of these films' postulation "of a specifically female spectator" and of a "process of seeing" that is "object-less, free-floating." Mary Ann Doane, "The 'Woman's Film': Pos-

session and Address," in *Home is Where the Heart Is: Studies in Melodrama and the Woman's Film*, Christine Gledhill, ed., London, BFI Publishing, 1987, p. 286, originally published in *Re-Vision: Essays in Feminist Film Criticism*, Mary Ann Doane, Patricia Mellencamp, and Linda Williams, eds., Frederick, MD, University Publications of America, 1984, pp. 67–82. See also Mary Ann Doane, "Paranoia and the Specular," in *The Desire to Desire: The Woman's Film of the 1940s*, Bloomington, Indiana University Press, 1987, p. 129. I suggest instead that intimations of madness are a response to potential male spectatorial unpleasure at a female gaze that — far from being "object-less" — often has as its object the specter of male guilt.

13. My comments here on the psychic structure of *Coma* (and Jacqueline Rose's comments quoted below) are heavily indebted to Elizabeth Cowie's analysis of the film. Elizabeth Cowie, "A Discussion of 'Coma'," in *Films for Women*, Charlotte Brunsdon, ed., London, British Film Institute, 1986, pp. 155–165. This is an extract from a longer paper: "The Popular Film as a Progressive Text — a discussion of *Coma*," in *m/f* no. 3, 1979, pp. 59–81. The second part of Cowie's essay is purportedly in *m/f* no. 4, 1980, pp. 57–69. Elizabeth Cowie, "A Discussion of 'Coma'," in *Films for Women*, Charlotte Brunsdon, ed., London, British Film Institute, 1986, p. 164.

14. Jacqueline Rose, "Woman as Symptom," in *Sexuality in the Field of Vision*, London, Verso, 1986, p. 221. [Italics hers.] Rose's analysis here is part of a larger discussion of how filmic enunciation sometimes maps problems in the cinematic system onto the female body.

15. Not all feminist critics agree that the film unambiguously undercuts the female investigator's authority. Christine Geraghty, for example, sees the film as part of a 1970s revival of women's films. She focuses on how the film sets the protagonist up as a competent professional woman whose investigation is furthered when she does not give in to stereotypically feminine emotions and is thwarted when she does. Geraghty also asserts that the audience is made to doubt the competence of the male love interest (who *does* eventually rescue the protagonist) in much the same way as the competence of female love interests in traditional action films is often questioned. See Christine Geraghty, "Three Women's Films," in *Films for Women*, Charlotte Brunsdon, ed., London, BFI Publishing, 1986, pp. 142–145. [Originally published in *Movie* no. 27/29 Winter/Spring, 1980–81, pp. 85–90.]

16. On paranoia as a response to female investigation and "looking" in 1940s gothic films, see Mary Ann Doane, "The 'Woman's Film': Possession and Address," in *Home is Where the Heart Is: Studies in Melodrama and the Woman's Film*, Christine Gledhill, ed., London, British Film Institute Publishing, 1987, pp. 285–286.

17. Francis M. Nevins, "Translate and Transform: From Cornell Woolrich to Film Noir," in Film Noir Reader 2, Alain Silver and James Ursini, eds.; New York, Limelight, 1999, p. 140.

18. Bigelow co-wrote the script for Blue Steel as well as directed it. Pam Cook notes that the multitalented Bigelow is also a producer. Pam Cook, "No Fixed Address: The Women's Picture from Outrage to Blue Steel, in Contemporary Hollywood Cinema, Steve Neale and Murray Smith, eds., London, Routledge, 1998, p. 244. Blue Steel came out at the same time as another, less-successful policewoman drama directed by a woman — Sondra Locke's Impulse (1990), a film about a female vice cop who has to see a psychiatrist and who eventually leaves her job to become "redomesticated." See William Covey, "Girl Power: Female-Centered Neo-Noir," in Film Noir Reader 2, Alain Silver and James Ursini, eds., New York, Limelight, 1999, pp. 316–319. The representation of the crazed female cop apparently maintains its appeal today: the recent reviews of Twisted (Philip Kaufman, 2004), written by Sarah Thorp, position it as a similar crazed-female-cop film.

19. The famous exception is Robert Montgomery's The Lady in the Lake (1947) in which the trajectories of the camera and the look of detective Philip Marlowe are coincidental. See Peter Humm, "Camera Eye/Private Eye," in American Crime Fiction: Studies in the Genre, Brian Docherty, ed., New York, St. Martins, 1988, p. 34. Humm's essay generally discusses the use of the "camera-eye technique" in hardboiled detective fiction and other works of the 1930s and 1940s.

20. Frank Krutnik, In a Lonely Street: Film Noir, Genre, Masculinity, London, Routledge, 1991, p. 94.

21. Carol J. Clover, Men, Women, and Chain Saws: Gender in the Modern Horror Film, Princeton, Princeton University Press, 1992, p. 40. Kathi Maio remarks on the name's masculine associations too. See Kathi Maio, Feminist in the Dark: Reviewing the Movies, Freedom, CA, the Crossing Press, 1988, p. 199. On the importance of names and naming in women's detective fiction, see Maureen T. Reddy, Sisters in Crime: Feminism and the Crime Novel, New York, Continuum, 1988, pp. 92–94.

22. Tania Modleski, The Women Who Knew Too Much: Hitchcock and Feminist Theory, New York, Routledge, 1989, p. 64. Such a name might seem to be a misnomer for Alex Barnes, who is employed with the Justice Department and later works with the Hawaiian police, but it is appropriate for two reasons: A. She quits her Justice Department job to pursue her own investigation, thus breaking with the Law as an organized policing system. B. She breaks the "Law of the Father"

by not submitting to compulsory heterosexuality: When the film begins, she is single and decidedly uninterested in dating men; as the film progresses, she feels desire for a woman; and, although she eventually has a brief love affair with the murderess's latest conquest, she does not pair up with him at the film's end.

23. Linda Williams notes that the popular "lesbian" scenes in pornographic films aimed at male audiences are carefully circumscribed by images of heterosexual sex, posing little psychic threat to the male spectator. Linda Williams, Hard Core: Power, Pleasure, and the "Frenzy of the Visible," Berkeley, University of California Press, 1989, pp. 127, 140. On how the exchange system of women under patriarchy leads to a repression of female homosexuality, see Gayle Rubin, "The Traffic in Women: Notes on the 'Political Economy' of Sex," in Toward an Anthropology of Women, Rayna R. Reiter, ed., Monthly Review Press, New York, 1975, p. 183.

24. See Eve Kosofsky Sedgwick, "Gender Asymmetry and Erotic Triangles," in Between Men: English Literature and Male Homosocial Desire, New York, Columbia University Press, 1985, pp. 21–27.

25. On how Black Widow defines "normality" and "abnormality" by a change to more traditional cinematic signifiers of desire when Alex and Catherine are in close contact, see Judith Mayne, The Woman at the Keyhole: Feminism and Women's Cinema, Bloomington, Indiana University Press, 1990, p. 47.

26. Mayne, for one, calls it "a somewhat silly conclusion." Judith Mayne, The Woman at the Keyhole: Feminism and Women's Cinema, Bloomington, Indiana University Press, 1990, p. 48.

27. Krista Smith, "The Nine Lives of Drew Barrymore," Vanity Fair, No. 514, June 2003, p. 219.

28. The sequel to the film also made it at least to the casting stage without a complete script. Jennifer Kasle Furmaniak, "Why Drew Kicks Butt," Cosmopolitan, July 2003, p. 184.

29. Note the masculine names — Alex, Dylan, and "Nat" — as discussed above.

30. Another aspect of the film that undercuts the Angels' physical competence is the fact that none of them use guns. Apparently, this was a deliberate choice. Entertainment Tonight: Charlie's Angels Uncovered (syndicated television program, viewed 11/6/99) noted that the (first) Charlie's Angels film, then in pre-production, was not going to have the Angels using guns.

31. As the Angels work as a unit — both in the opening sequence and in the film as a whole — this implication of madness really applies to all three women.

32. A July 2003 article in Cosmopolitan magazine shows a picture of Barrymore staring

intently into a camera. The caption reads: "On the other side of the camera, producing *Charlie's Angels: Full Throttle*." Jennifer Kasle Furmaniak, "Why Drew Kicks Butt," *Cosmopolitan*, July 2003, p. 185.

33. The character is apparently "[b]ased on [a] *Chicago Tribune* comic strip." (italics mine) Martin Connors and Julia Furtaw, eds., *VideoHound's Golden Movie Retriever 1995*, Detroit, Visible Ink Press, 1995, p. 411.

34. This film is the second of a series of four films. The others are *Nancy Drew, Detective* (William Clemens, 1938), *Nancy Drew, Trouble Shooter* (William Clemens, 1939), and *Nancy Drew and the Hidden Staircase* (also William Clemens, 1939). Michael R. Pitts, *Famous Movie Detectives*, Metuchen, NJ, Scarecrow Press, 1979, pp. 306–308. See also Jon Tuska, *The Detective in Hollywood*, Garden City, NY, Doubleday, 1978, pp. 81–82.

35. Rick Altman, *Film/Genre*, London, BFI Publishing, 1999, p. 160.

36. Rick Altman, *id.* at pp. 159–160.

37. There were a total of nine Torchy Blane films, seven of which starred Glenda Farrell. Michael R. Pitts, *Famous Movie Detectives*, Metuchen, NJ, Scarecrow Press, 1979, p. 280. The films starring Glenda Farrell are *Smart Blonde* (Frank McDonald, 193[6]), *Fly-Away Baby* (also Frank McDonald, 1937), *The Adventurous Blonde* (also Frank McDonald, 1937), *Blondes at Work* (Frank McDonald, 1938), *Torchy Gets Her Man* (William Beaudine, 1938), *Torchy Blane in Chinatown* (William Beaudine, 1939), and *Torchy Runs for Mayor* (Raymond McCarey, 1939). Michael R. Pitts, *Famous Movie Detectives*, Metuchen, NJ, Scarecrow Press, 1979, pp. 281–284. Pitts gives the date of *Smart Blonde* as 1937. Perhaps that was the release date, but the print of the film I saw distinctly gives the copyright date as 1936. The other two Torchy Blane films are *Torchy Blane in Panama* (William Clemens, 1938), starring Lola Lane, and *Torchy Plays With Dynamite* (Noel Smith, 1939), starring Jane Wyman. *Id.* Torchy's capable can-do attitude, so similar to that of Nancy Drew in the Bonita Granville Nancy Drew films, may be due to the fact that *Smart Blonde* had the same scriptwriter as the Nancy Drew series, Kenneth Gamet. William K. Everson, *The Detective in Film*, Secaucus, NJ, Citadel Press, 1972, p. 136. It is also interesting that William Clemens, who directed all four of the Bonita Granville Nancy Drew films (see note above), tried his hand at a Torchy Blane film.

38. In 1994, Peggy Li, one of the students in an undergraduate class I taught at Berkeley entitled "The Rise of the Female Investigator," wrote an excellent paper on *Manhattan Murder Mystery*. While I do not recall the specifics of her

work, I imagine that my later analysis of the film is at least partly indebted to her.

39. Of course, menopause itself is associated with cultural expectations of madness. See Elaine Showalter, *The Female Malady*, New York, Pantheon Books, 1985, pp. 55, 59.

40. 1930s and 1940s film featured many female detectives, both in individual films and in several series. William K. Everson discusses several female detective films of the 1930s and 1940s that I have as yet been unable to view: The late 1930s Joel and Garda Sloane series *Fast Company* (Edward Buzzell, 1938), *Fast and Loose* (Edward L. Marin, 1939), and *Fast and Furious* (Busby Berkeley, 1939); *Daughter of Shanghai* (Robert Florey, 1937, starring Anna May Wong as an Asian American amateur detective and "Phillip Ahn as a Chinese FBI man"); *Miss Pinkerton* (Lloyd Bacon, 1932 [based on Mary Roberts Rinehart's novels about nurse-detective "Miss Adams."); *The Girl from Scotland Yard* (Robert Vignola, 1937); *So's Your Aunt Emma* (Jean Yarbrough, 1942); *Mary Ryan, Detective* (Abby Berlin, 1949); *Mrs. Pym of Scotland Yard* (Fred Elles, 1939, a British film); *Lady on a Train* (Charles David, 1945); *Remember Last Night?* (James Whale, 1935); *When Were You Born?* (William McGann, 1938, also starring Anna May Wong as an astrologer-detective); *Midnight Mystery* (George B. Seitz, 1930); and *Mr. and Mrs. North* (Robert B. Sinclair, 1941). See William K. Everson, *The Detective in Film*, Secaucus, NJ, Citadel Press, 1972, pp. 106, 122, 129, 132, 135–136, 137, 140, 179, 193, 212–213, 224–225, 227, 229. See also the following sources: James Robert Parish and Michael R. Pitts, *The Great Detective Pictures*, Metuchen, NJ, Scarecrow Press, 1990, p. 337 [Parish and Pitts also mention *Private Detective* (Noel Smith, 1939 [featuring Jane Wyman as "the owner of a private detective agency"]) and *A Night to Remember* (Richard Wallace, 1943 [featuring a detecting couple]). Parish and Pitts, *The Great Detective Pictures*, pp. 424–426, 397–398]; Michael R. Pitts, *Famous Movie Detectives*, Metuchen, NJ, Scarecrow Press, 1979, p. 310; Larry Langman and Daniel Finn, *A Guide to American Crime Films of the Forties and Fifties*, Bibliographies and Indexes in the Performing Arts No. 19, 1995, pp. 161, 179, 184; Larry Langman and Daniel Finn, *A Guide to American Crime Films of the Thirties*, Bibliographies and Indexes in the Performing Arts No. 18, Westport, CT, Greenwood Press, 1995, pp. 82–83, 97, 160–161, 163, 291; Denis Gifford, *The British Film Catalogue, 1895–1985: A Reference Guide*, New York, Facts on File Publications, 1986, film #10651 [there are no page numbers in this work]; and *American Film Institute Catalog of Motion Pictures Produced in the United States: Feature Films, 1941–1950*, Vol. M-

Z, Patricia King Hanson and Amy Dunkleberger, eds., Berkeley, CA, University of California Press, 1999, pp. 2279–2280. Another female detective series of the thirties was the one featuring Nurse Sarah Keate (variously, Keating), a series based on a character created by Mignon G. Eberhart. The films were *While the Patient Slept* (Ray Enright, 1935), *The Murder of Dr. Harrigan* (Frank McDonald, 1936), *Murder By an Aristocrat*, (also Frank McDonald, 1936), *The Great Hospital Mystery* (James Tinling, 1937), *The Patient in Room 18* (Crane Wilbur, 1938), and *Mystery House* (Noel Smith, 1938). Larry Langman and Daniel Finn, *A Guide to American Crime Films of the Thirties*, Bibliographies and Indexes in the Performing Arts No. 18, Westport, CT, Greenwood Press, 1995, pp. 103, 169–170, 172, 177, 201, 291. Female detective films of the 1940s also included *The Lady Confesses* (Sam Newfield, 1945) and the Kitty O'Day series: *Detective Kitty O'Day* (William Beaudine, 1944), *Adventures of Kitty O'Day* (William Beaudine, 1945), and *Fashion Model* (also William Beaudine, 1945). Langman and Finn, *A Guide to American Crime Films of the Forties and Fifties*, pp. 3, 76, 95–96, 159. Langman and Finn also list series featuring female detectives from the silent era: The "Bess the Detectress"series included *Bess the Detectress in Tick Tick Tick* (1914), *Bess the Detectress or the Dog Watch* (1914), and *Bess the Detectress or the Old Mill at Midnight* (1914). Larry Langman and Daniel Finn, *A Guide to American Silent Crime Films*, Bibliographies and Indexes in the Performing Arts No. 15, Westport, CT, Greenwood Press, 1994, p. 18 and appendix B. Langman and Finn also note a trio of "Ethel the Detective" films: *Ethel Gets the Evidence* (1915), *Ethel's Burglar* (1915), and *Ethel's First Case* (1915). Larry Langman and Daniel Finn, *A Guide to American Silent Crime Films*, p. 80 and Appendix B. There's no index that allows convenient identification of female detective films, but some other female detective films that I noted while browsing were *Lady Raffles* (William Neill, 1928), *The Girl Detective's Ruse* (1913), and *The Bedroom Window* (Willaim De Mille, 1924). Larry Langman and Daniel Finn, *A Guide to American Silent Crime Films*, pp. 153, 104, and ? Langman and Finn also note a series entitled "Lady Baffles and Detective Duck." *Id.* p. 152 and appendix B. They also note a "Girl Detective" series, but it seems to have a different date than that of *The Girl Detective's Ruse* above. *Id.* appendix B.

41. The first three entries in the series, *The Penguin Pool Murder* (George Archainbaud, 1932), *Murder on the Blackboard* (George Archainbaud, 1934), and *Murder on a Honeymoon* (Lloyd Corrigan, 1935) all starred Edna May Oliver as the heroine; Helen Broderick took over the role in *Murder on a Bridle Path* (Edward Killy,

1935 [or 1936]); and Zasu Pitts took over the role in *The Plot Thickens* (Ben Holmes, 1936) and *Forty Naughty Girls* (Eddie Cline, 1937). See William K. Everson, *The Detective in Film*, pp. 132–135. See also Jon Tuska, *The Detective in Hollywood*, Garden City, NY, Doubleday, 1978, pp. 78, 80 and Larry Langman and Daniel Finn, *A Guide to American Crime Films of the Thirties*, Westport, CT, Greenwood Press, 1995, pp. 90, 173. Langman and Finn give the date of *Murder on a Bridle Path* as 1936. *Id.* at 173. Interestingly, a later film, *Mrs. O'Malley and Mr. Malone* (Norman Taurog, 1950), was originally supposed to be a Hildegarde Withers film, but her character was "replaced by a housewife." Michael R. Pitts, *Famous Movie Detectives*, Metuchen, NJ, Scarecrow Press, 1979, p. 152. See also Larry Langman and Daniel Finn, *A Guide to American Crime Films of the Forties and Fifties*, Bibliographies and Indexes in the Performing Arts No. 19, 1995, p. 187.

42. Significantly, the 1931 Stuart Palmer novel, *The Penguin Pool Murder*, on which the first film in the series is based, ends with Withers and Piper heading for the marriage license bureau. Stuart Palmer, *The Penguin Pool Murder*, Bantam, 1986, p. 182. A marriage proposal also ends the filmed version of *The Penguin Pool Murder*, but apparently, no marriage takes place. See Jon Tuska, *The Detective in Hollywood*, Garden City, NY, Doubleday, 1978, p. 78. Indeed, this plot element is disavowed in the later films. A marriage between the two protagonists would ruin the trope of the asexual — and therefore mad — elderly female detective.

43. The series continues in *Murder at the Gallop* (George Pollock, 1963), *Murder Ahoy* (George Pollock, 1964), and *Murder Most Foul* (George Pollock, 1965). *VideoHound's Golden Movie Retriever 2002*, Jim Craddock, Ed., Detroit, Gale Group, 2002, pp. 495–497.

44. *VideoHound's Golden Movie Retriever 1995* notes: "[Miss] Marple's assistant, Mr. Stringer, is the real life Mr. Dame Margaret [Rutherford]." It is also interesting to note that this video guide explicitly refers to Miss Marple as "the dottie [sic] detective." "Murder at the Gallop" and "Murder Ahoy," in *VideoHound's Golden Movie Retriever 1995*, Martin Connors and Julia Furtaw, eds., Detroit, Visible Ink Press, 1995, p. 659. For more about the relationship between Stringer Davis and Margaret Rutherford, see Jon Tuska, *The Detective in Hollywood*, Garden City, NY, Doubleday, 1978, pp. 85 & ff.

45. Interestingly, these Miss Marple films are mostly based on mysteries written about Agatha Christie's other famous sleuth: Belgian *male* detective Hercule Poirot. Miss Marple's basic strength of character in these films may be related to the fact that the plots originally featured a male

detective. *VideoHound's Golden Movie Retriever 1995*, Martin Connors and Julia Furtaw, eds., Detroit, Visible Ink Press, 1995, pp. 659–660. See also James Robert Parish and Michael R. Pitts, *The Great Detective Pictures*, Metuchen, NJ, Scarecrow Press, 1990, pp. 376–379.

46. See Jeanette Murphy, "A Question of Silence," in *Films for Women*, Charlotte Brunsdon, ed., London, British Film Institute Publishing, 1986, p. 102.

47. Apparently, a 1978 American made-for-television movie based on this film exists. It starred Brenda Vaccaro. See *VideoHound's Golden Movie Retriever 1995*, Detroit, Visible Ink, 1995, p. 313.

48. For an excellent analysis of this film, see E. Ann Kaplan, "Investigating the Heroine: Sally Potter's 'Thriller,'" in *Women and Film: Both Sides of the Camera*, New York, Routledge, 1983, reprinted 1990, pp. 154–161. Potter astutely dubs Mimi's "status ... as investigating subject" as "a psychoanalytic problem." Kaplan, "Investigating the Heroine," p. 155.

49. Kaplan interprets Mimi's laughter here positively, as "not so much laughing at male theory *per se* ... but signal[ing] a realization that the answers [the investigating Mimi seeks] cannot be found in *texts*...." E. Ann Kaplan, "Investigating the Heroine: Sally Potter's 'Thriller,'" in *Women and Film: Both Sides of the Camera*, New York, Routledge, 1983, reprinted 1990, p. 160. Potter sees the laughter as ushering in "the next stage in Mimi[]'s psychological growth." *Id.*

50. "*Stranger on the Third Floor* is the first true film noir...." Bob Porfirio, "Stranger on the Third Floor," in Alain Silver and Elizabeth Ward, eds., *Film Noir: An Encyclopedic Reference to the American Style*, Woodstock, NY, Overlook Press, 1992, p. 269. Other candidates for the first film noir include *Rebecca* (Alfred Hitchcock, 1940) and *The Maltese Falcon* (John Huston, 1941). See Ronald Schwartz, *Noir, Now and Then: Film Noir Originals and Remakes (1944–1999)*, Contributions to the Study of Popular Culture No. 72, Westport, Greenwood Press, 2001, p. xiii.

51. Tony Williams also notes Kansas' startling appropriation of "the sadistic power of the [traditionally masculine] gaze." Tony Williams, "*Phantom Lady*, Cornell Woolrich, and the Masochistic Aesthetic," in *Film Noir Reader*, Alain Silver and James Ursini, eds., New York, Limelight, 1996, p. 134. Jennifer M. Bean has noted another instance of a powerful investigating woman's gaze: The moment in *Shadow of a Doubt* (Alfred Hitchcock, 1943) when niece Charlie stares at her uncle Charlie going up the stairs hard enough to stop him in his tracks. Jennifer M. Bean, "Male Paranoia and Feminist Film Theory: The Gothic Woman's Film of the 1940's," paper delivered at Society for Cinema

Studies National Conference, March 5, 1995. In a sub-chapter entitled "Men Seldom Make Passes at Girls Who Wear Glasses," Mary Ann Doane details other filmic instances of transgressive female "appropriation of the gaze" in non-detective films — transgressions typically punished by death for the woman who dares to look. Mary Ann Doane, "Film and the Masquerade: Theorizing the Female Spectator," in *Femmes Fatales: Feminism, Film Theory, Psychoanalysis*, London, Routledge, 1991, pp. 26–28.

52. The "Phantom Lady" is overdetermined as mad. Even when she first appears in the film, Tom Flinn describes her as "neurotic." Tom Flinn, "Three Faces of Film Noir," reprinted in *Film Noir Reader 2*, Alain Silver and James Ursini, eds., New York, Limelight, 1992, p. 38 [orig. published 1972].

53. Interestingly, Williams reads Kansas as mad when she is menaced by Marlow, describing her as "collapsing into hysteria." Tony Williams, "*Phantom Lady*, Cornell Woolrich, and the Masochistic Aesthetic in Film," in *Film Noir Reader*, Alain Silver and James Ursini, eds., New York, Limelight, 1996, p. 138.

54. The introduction to *The BFI Companion to Crime* notes that Marlow is also a "double" of her boss, "acting out his repressed desires." *The BFI Companion to Crime*, Phil Hardy, ed., Richard Attenborough, fwd., Berkeley, University of California Press, 1997, p. 18.

55. The "truth" of *Fargo* may be illusory, however. According to Thomas Leitch, "the published screenplay of *Fargo* ... describes the film as one that '...pretends to be true.'" Thomas Leitch, *Crime Films*, Cambridge, Cambridge University Press, 2002, pp. 287, 328 (note 9).

56. Nicole Rafter also notes the excessiveness of Marge's pregnancy, calling her "hugely pregnant" and "obsessed by food." Nicole Rafter, *Shots in the Mirror: Crime Films and Society*, New York, Oxford University Press, 2000, p. 88.

57. Hilary Radner notes that this life-affirming cop "does not kill" in the performance of her duties — an interesting deviation from conventions of the detective genre. Hilary Radner, "New Hollywood's New Women: Murder in Mind — Sarah and Margie," in *Contemporary Hollywood Cinema*, Steve Neale and Murray Smith, eds., London, Routledge, 1998, p. 254.

58. "...Victorian ... theories of female insanity were specifically and confidently linked to the biological crises of the female life-cycle — puberty, pregnancy, childbirth, menopause — during which the mind would be weakened and the symptoms of insanity might occur." Elaine Showalter, *The Female Malady*, New York, Pantheon Books, 1985, p. 55.

59. Hilary Radner, "New Hollywood's New Women: Murder in Mind — Sarah and Margie,"

in *Contemporary Hollywood Cinema*, Steve Neale and Murray Smith, eds., London, Routledge, 1998, p. 257.

60. Hilary Radner, *id.* at p. 255.

61. Hilary Radner, *id.* at pp. 249, 257, 259.

62. This profile also fits a large part of Hollywood's target audience, and accordingly a large part of the implied spectators of the film.

63. Priscilla L. Walton and Manina Jones also note that "she is dismissed as hysterical" by the police. Priscilla L. Walton and Manina Jones, "'She's Watching the Detectives': The Woman PI in Film and Television," in *Detective Agency: Women Rewriting the Hard-Boiled Tradition*, Berkeley, University of California Press, 1999, p. 270.

64. Nicole Rafter notes Clarice's initially privileged position in the field of vision: "Like male officers, Clarice does not drop her eyes when others stare, but returns looks with a steady gaze." As I note below, this privileged vision eventually is taken away from Clarice as she stumbles blindly around the serial killer's basement while he stalks her wearing night-vision glasses. Nicole Rafter, *Shots in the Mirror: Crime Films and Society*, New York, Oxford University Press, 2000, p. 87. Interestingly, Clarice's competence in the film may have had an effect on the career choices of female spectators. Rafter reports that "droves of young women decided to join the FBI" after the release of the film. Rafter, *op. cit.*, p. 66. For a discussion and analysis of the reception of *The Silence of the Lambs* among other groups, see Janet Staiger, "Taboos and Totems: Cultural Meanings of *The Silence of the Lambs*," in *Film Theory Goes to the Movies*, Jim Collins, Hilary Radner, and Ava Preacher Collins, eds., New York, Routledge, 1993, pp. 142–154.

65. Amy Taubin calls it "a profoundly feminist movie." Amy Taubin, "Grabbing the Knife: 'The Silence of the Lambs' and the History of the Serial Killer Movie," in Pam Cook and Philip Dodd, eds., *Women and Film: A Sight and Sound Reader*, Philadelphia, Temple University Press, 1993, p. 129.

66. Cf. the female psychiatrists in *Copycat* and *A Question of Silence* above, and those in Hitchcock's *Spellbound* (1945) and David Mamet's *House of Games* (1987).

67. Carol Clover notes these horror aspects of *The Silence of the Lambs* in *Men, Women, and Chain Saws: Gender in the Modern Horror Film*, Princeton, NJ, Princeton University Press, 1992, p. 232.

68. B. Ruby Rich offers a positive reading of this scene, suggesting it as a vision of female empowerment and a reversal of Foster's portrayal of the rape victim in *The Accused*: "Here, she can win, saving not only herself ... but also ... [another menaced woman].... Who[m] does she

represent? Every actress done for by a killer in a horror movie? Every woman assaulted? You? Me?" B. Ruby Rich, "Never a Victim: Jodie Foster: A New Kind of Female Hero," in Pam Cook and Philip Dodd, eds., *Women and Film: A Sight and Sound Reader*, Philadelphia, Temple University Press, 1993, p. 57.

69. Richard B. Schwartz notes that "...Jonathan Demme passed on directing [*Hannibal*] and Jodie Foster passed on reprising the role of Clarice...." *Nice and Noir*, Columbia, MO, U. of Missouri Press, 2002, p. 122.

70. The words Clarice uses are taken from the Thomas Harris novel *Hannibal*, upon which the film is based, but as director Ridley Scott chose to depart radically from other parts of the novel (see note below), the words should be considered for their cinematic effect. See Thomas Harris, *Hannibal*, Dell, Movie Tie-In Edition, 2001, p. 443.

71. The 1999 novel *Hannibal*, upon which the film is based, makes Clarice's psychosexual problems even more explicit. In the novel, Clarice is shown having crushes on a series of father-figures, but being unable to proceed to sexual relationships with them because of her unresolved emotions about her own father's violent death. The novel and the film take radically different plot paths after Dr. Lecter rescues Clarice. In the novel, which requires from the reader more than a typical suspension of disbelief, instead of attempting to capture Dr. Lecter, the drugged Clarice is subjected to intensive psychotherapy by him. Through the power of therapy and psychoactive drugs, Dr. Lecter cures Clarice's psychosexual problems, fosters her resentment against the FBI, convinces her to join him in eating the brains of the man who sexually harassed her, and becomes her long-term lover as they travel the world as fugitives from justice. Interestingly, their affair starts when Clarice takes a stab at psychoanalyzing *him*. See Thomas Harris, *Hannibal*, New York, Dell, Movie Tie-In Edition, 2001, pp. 494–544. Brian Jarvis rightly notes Clarice's Electra Complex. Brian Jarvis, "Watching the Detectives: Body Images, Sexual Politics, and Ideology in Contemporary Crime Film," in *Criminal Proceedings: The Contemporary American Crime Novel*, Peter Messent, ed., London, Pluto Press, pp. 223–224.

72. See Laura Mulvey, "Visual Pleasure and Narrative Cinema," in *Visual and Other Pleasures*, Bloomington, Indiana University Press, 1989, pp. 21, 26.

73. Interestingly, the final scene of the film also disavows the castration of Dr. Lecter. While the shot of Dr. Lecter on an airplane with a bandaged arm confirms that he has lost his hand, the scene ends with Lecter introducing a precocious boy to the pleasures of cannibalism. Although

Dr. Lecter has not succeeded in siring children and although he wears the badge of castration on his mutilated arm, the scene emphasizes that his generative powers are unimpaired — passing his knowledge along to a child symbolizes his ability to father, to pass on his legacy.

74. One might think that Cassie resists testifying because she fears her ex-husband discovering her new identity, but the film demonstrates that he has already tracked her down.

75. This emphasizes her place in the world of gendered relations rather than the world of professional relations.

76. To be fair, the television series also identifies Emma as a "talented amateur," as noted above.

77. Perhaps the producers worried that if Emma were shown impaling/penetrating de Wynter, they would be open to a charge of male-bashing, particularly since Emma has earlier survived being drugged and almost raped by de Wynter. Such a scene would have added a rape-revenge drama twist to the film, however, and would have been more diegetically appropriate. On the rape-revenge genre, see Carol J. Clover, "Getting Even," in *Men, Women, and Chain Saws: Gender in the Modern Horror Film*, Princeton, NJ, Princeton University Press, 1992, pp. 114–165.

78. James Chapman notes that "...the film of *The Avengers* has several glaring plot loopholes — the result, it seems, of last-minute cuts by the studio following adverse reaction from test screenings." James Chapman, "Is There Honey Still for Tea?: *The Avengers*" in *Saints & Avengers: British Adventure Series of the 1960s*, London, I.B. Tauris, 2002, p. 97. The fact that the plot loopholes making Emma seem insane might have been caused by the "adverse reaction" of test audiences to the original full-strength portrayal of a phallic Emma only proves my point.

79. E.g., *Rebecca* (1940), *Suspicion* (1941), *Shadow of A Doubt*(1943), *Spellbound* (1945), *Stage Fright*(1950).

80. Diane Waldman, "'At last I can tell it to someone!': Feminine Point of View and Subjectivity in the Gothic Romance Film of the 1940s," *Cinema Journal* 23, no. 2, Winter 1983, p. 31.

81. Linda Williams, "When the Woman Looks," in *Re-Vision: Essays in Feminist Film Criticism*, Mary Ann Doane, Patricia Mellencamp, and Linda Williams, eds., Frederick, MD, American Film Institute, 1984, pp. 87, 90. Barbara Creed postulates that "the gaze of *both* male and female spectators is constructed as masochistic by the ... horror text" [italics in orig.], but acknowledges that the viewing male's position is "not necessarily identical to that offered to the female spectator." Barbara Creed, "Dark Desires: Male Masochism in the Horror Film," in *Screening the*

Male: Exploring Masculinities in Hollywood Cinema, Steven Cohan and Ina Rae Hark, eds., London, Routledge, 1993, p. 131.

82. Linda Williams, "When the Woman Looks," p. 90.

83. On *Psycho* and *Dressed to Kill*, see Linda Williams, "When the Woman Looks," in *Re-Vision: Essays in Feminist Film Criticism*, Mary Ann Doane, Patricia Mellencamp, and Linda Williams, eds., Frederick, MD, American Film Institute, 1984, p. 93. Williams credits unpublished work by Henry Herrings [sic] for the observation about *Psycho* and *Dressed to Kill*. On *Silence of the Lambs*, see Carol J. Clover, *Men, Women, and Chain Saws: Gender in the Modern Horror Film*, Princeton, Princeton University Press, 1992, pp. 28, 232–233. Clover similarly notes the tendency of male killers displaying "gender confusion" or being desexualized. Thus the male audience is never forced by the film to identify with someone who is simultaneously sexually masculine and evil. See Clover, *Men, Women, and Chain Saws*, pp. 25–28.

84. Donald Spoto, *The Art of Alfred Hitchcock: Fifty Years of His Motion Pictures*, 2nd edition, New York, Doubleday, 1992, pp. 103–104. Of course, this interpretation will not hold true for male critics who consider feminst film theory. See, for example, Stephen Heath, who explicitly reads the scene as violent. Stephen Heath, *Questions of Cinema*, Bloomington, Indiana University Press, 1981, p. 185.

85. Diane Waldman notes that one project of the film is to "correct" spectators' perceptions that "the erotic" is really "the violent." Diane Waldman, "'At last I can tell it to someone!' Feminine Point of View and Subjectivity: The Gothic Romance Film of the 1940s," *Cinema Journal*, Vol. 23, No. 2, Winter 1983, p. 33.

86. Donald Spoto, *The Art of Alfred Hitchcock: Fifty Years of His Motion Pictures*, 2nd edition, New York, Doubleday, 1992, p. 101.

87. Spoto's comments on the protagonist's sanity are not isolated to those I have quoted at length. He also calls her "disturbed," "exploitative," "vulnerab[le] to her own fantasies," "in a haze of romantic fixation," "[given to] romantic obsession," and he discusses her "perverse psychology" and "pathology." Donald Spoto, *The Art of Alfred Hitchcock: Fifty Years of His Motion Pictures*, 2nd ed., New York, Doubleday, 1992, pp. 104–106.

88. Reynold Humphries, *Fritz Lang: Genre and Representation in His American Films*, Baltimore, Johns Hopkins University Press, 1989, p. 136.

89. Reynold Humphries, *id.* at p. 145.

90. I am not speaking here of the pleasure inherent in the act of desiring itself. Obviously, the alternating pattern of showing/withholding

the female body, for example, in Hollywood films works as a source of pleasure to the male spectator by playing on his frustration when the female body is temporarily veiled or absent and on his vicarious sense of power in the look when the female body is revealed or returns — a grown man's *fort-da* game. Rather, I mean the frustration attendant upon the male spectator's being forced by the enunciation into identifications and trajectories of desire that are unfamiliar and pose a threat to his subjectivity as it is constituted under the current patriarchal order.

91. Kaja Silverman interprets the Lacanian "screen" as an ideologically inflected configuration, described as "that culturally generated image or repertoire of images through which subjects are not only constituted, but differentiated in relation to class, race, sexuality, age, and nationality." Kaja Silverman, "Fassbinder and Lacan: A Reconsideration of Gaze, Look, and Image," in *Male Subjectivity at the Margins*, London, Routledge, 1992, p. 150.

92. I am slightly recasting narratologist Seymour Chatman's terms "implied audience" and "implied viewer" (developed from Wayne Booth's "implied author") to fit the terminology of my argument. In a discussion of the "implied reader" that prefigures the application of his ideas to film, Chatman notes: "...the implied author informs the real reader how to perform as implied reader, which *Weltanschauung* to adopt ... Of course, the real reader may refuse his projected role at some ultimate level ... But such refusal does not contradict the imaginative or 'as if' acceptance of implied readership necessary to the elementary comprehension of the narrative." Seymour Chatman, *Story and Discourse: Narrative Structure in Fiction and Film*, Ithaca, Cornell University Press, 1978, p. 150.

Chapter 5

1. Indeed, the narrative has also inspired a stage play, a radio presentation, a musical, and other novels. The Museum of Television and Radio owns a 1938 radio adaptation of *Rebecca* produced and directed by Orson Welles, and starring Welles as Maxim de Winter and Margaret Sullavan as the narrator. According to the Museum of Television and Radio's catalogue, this radio production, which aired 12/9/38, was the first in a series called Campbell Playhouse (apparently sponsored by Campbell's Soup) that adapted fiction to the radio. "[The stage version of] *Rebecca* was first performed March 11, 1940, at the Opera House in Manchester, England." Daphne du Maurier, *Rebecca: Acting Edition*, New York, Dramatists Play Service, 1943, p. 3. The stage play contains significant variations from the other versions and would therefore be a fascinating locus of further study.

2. Daphne du Maurier, excerpt from *The Rebecca Notebook and Other Memories*, as published in Daphne du Maurier, *Rebecca*, New York, Harper Perennial Edition, 2001, p. 388. Originally published in Daphne du Maurier, *The Rebecca Notebook and Other Memories*, Garden City, NY, Doubleday, 1980, p. 3. All further page references to the du Maurier novel are to the Harper Perennial edition.

3. Tania Modleski calls her "the heroine." Tania Modleski, *The Women Who Knew Too Much: Hitchcock and Feminist Theory*, New York, Routledge, 1988, p. 45. Although she is certainly the focus of the narrative, I hesitate to call her "the heroine" — as we will see, her actions throughout the narrative are not necessarily heroic. In discussing the film version of the narrative, Mary Ann Doane calls her by the name of the actress who plays her: "the Fontaine character" or "the Joan Fontaine character." Mary Ann Doane, "Paranoia and the Specular," in *The Desire to Desire: The Woman's Film of the 1940s*, Bloomington, Indiana University Press, 1987, p. 143. Helene Meyers calls her both "the second Mrs. de Winter" (emphasizing her place within the patriarchal family unit) and "the narrator." Meyers notes: "Perhaps unwittingly, the text legitimizes the narrator's anxieties [about her own identity] by rendering her nameless in stark contrast to Rebecca, who managed to retain an independent identity not only after marriage but also after death." Helene Meyers, *Femicidal Fears: Narratives of the Female Gothic Experience*, Albany, NY, State University of New York Press, 2001, p. 35.

4. Interestingly, Frank refers to the narrator's husband as "Maxim" (301) rather than as "Mr. de Winter," showing that his deference to the narrator must be due both to her gender and her newly-acquired class status and not to her class status alone. If class were the only determinant, Frank would also address Maxim by his honorific and surname.

5. See, e.g., Mary Wings, "Rebecca Redux: Tears on a Lesbian Pillow," in *Daring to Dissent: Lesbian Culture from Margin to Mainstream*, Liz Gibbs, ed., London, Cassell, 1994, pp. 11–33. Wings highlights many lesbian images in the text and speculates that Rebecca is really punished not for being unfaithful to Maxim, but for being a lesbian. *Id.*, pp. 11–12, 14–24 (especially pp. 20–22).

6. Michelle A. Massé notes that the heroine's problems with investigation extend to the minutest details of life at Manderley: "All knowledge she seeks seems to be forbidden." Michelle A. Massé, "This Hurts Me More Than It Does You: The Beater and *Rebecca*," in *In the Name of Love: Women, Masochism, and the Gothic*, Ithaca, Cornell University Press, 1992, p. 170. This is also an

excellent study of masochism and domestic violence in *Rebecca*.

7. Michelle A. Massé explains the narrator's behavior here in terms of a masochist identifying with her oppressor and co-opting the mechanisms of dominance. Michelle A. Massé, "This Hurts Me More Than It Does You: The Beater and *Rebecca*," in *In the Name of Love: Women, Masochism, and the Gothic*, Ithaca, Cornell University Press, 1992, pp. 147–191.

8. Mary Wings, *Divine Victim*, New York, Plume, 1992. All further page references to the Wings novel are to this edition.

9. It recalls, but does not follow the pattern of, *Wide Sargasso Sea*, Jean Rhys's creative reimagining of *Jane Eyre* from the point of view of Rochester's first wife, the so-called Bertha Mason (Rhys problematizes the name). Jean Rhys, *Wide Sargasso Sea*, New York, Norton, 1966, p. 135.

10. Interestingly, pushing Rebecca off a cliff is a strategy considered by Maxim in the novel *Rebecca*. Daphne du Maurier, *Rebecca*, New York, Harper Perennial Edition, 2001, p. 276.

11. The fact that lesbian-on-lesbian (or lesbian-on-anyone) violence is seldom publicly acknowledged can be seen by Paulina Palmer's observation that "[some] characteristics of the investigator in the American crime novel, such as his ... ruthlessness and propensity to violence, are, as critics observe, distinctly unsuited to the portrayal of the lesbian." Paulina Palmer, "The Lesbian Thriller: Transgressive Investigations," in *Criminal Proceedings: The Contemporary American Crime Novel*, Peter Messent, ed., London, Pluto Press, 1997, p. 90. Moreover, when Palmer specifically considers *Divine Victim*, she focuses on its humorous, parodic aspects, to the exclusion of any serious consideration of the horror of the narrator's murder of Ilona. Paulina Palmer, *Lesbian Gothic: Transgressive Fictions*, London, Cassell, 1999, pp. 141–145.

12. Wings appears quite purposely to have raised the issue of domestic violence in the lesbian community. "I have updated the lesbian gothic to current standards of fear and terror ... The fear of being the victim. The terror of lost selfhood in being complicit in a victim abuser relationship...." Mary Wings, "Rebecca Redux: Tears on a Lesbian Pillow," in *Daring to Dissent: Lesbian Culture from Margin to Mainstream*, Liz Gibbs, ed., London, Cassell, 1994, p. 32.

13. Wings is the author of a series of detective novels featuring lesbian detective Emma Victor: *She Came Too Late* (1987), *She Came in a Flash* (1988), *She Came By the Book* (1996), *She Came to the Castro* (1997), and *She Came in Drag* (1999). See Frances A. DellaCava and Madeline H. Engel, *Sleuths in Skirts: Analysis and Bibliography of Serialized Female Sleuths*, New York, Routledge, 2002, pp. 258–259.

14. I am grateful to an anonymous reference librarian at the Museum of Television and Radio for finding this version for me while I was in search of the 1978 version, and I am grateful to the Museum of Television and Radio for allowing me research access to their collection.

15. The version that aired in the United States in 1980 as part of the *Mystery!* series on PBS was originally a BBC/Time Life Films production. It was produced in 1978 and aired in Britain in January 1979. I am most grateful to Olwen Terris at the BBC and Margaret Deriaz at the bookings office of Britain's National Film and Television Archive for their assistance in tracking down this hard-to-find version for me, and I am most grateful to the National Film and Television Archive for granting me permission to view it on the BFI premises in London in July 2002.

16. One wonders whether the gas-happy sponsors of *Theatre '62* considered mounting a production of *Gaslight*.

17. For example, the 1962 production skips all of the scenes in the South of France, beginning the narrative as the narrator and Maxim are returning to England by ship from their honeymoon, and referring to the events of their courtship in a few sentences of voiceover only. The dog Jasper is entirely missing from the narrative, probably a wise move in live television, as is the mentally-disabled Ben. Missing narrative scenes that need to be summarized account for several digressions from du Maurier's dialogue. A curious detail (from the Hitchcock film, not the novel) that is left in as part of the shipboard dialogue is the recounting of the narrator's father painting the same tree over and over again. The narrator also doesn't know on shipboard how Rebecca has died. "She had died in some sort of an accident," the narrator says, clearly unaware that Rebecca drowned. Jack Favell is played by Lloyd Bochner, of later *Dynasty* fame.

18. Probably as a time-saving measure, the narrator narrates an endless series of voiceovers designed to summarize scenes that were deleted from this version. The net effect is very chatty.

19. Interestingly, even Mrs. Danvers is glamourized compared to the novel, film, and 1997 made-for-television movie.

20. End titles for the first hour-long episode call her "The Girl"; end titles for later episodes call her "Mrs. de Winter." Neither choice seems to fit the feminist mores of the 1970s — one defines her in terms of her gender and infantilizes her, while the other defines her as her husband's spouse.

21. Interestingly, the 1978 version uses someone's appendicitis attack as the reason for Mrs. Van Hopper to suddenly go to New York rather than the pregnancy of Mrs. Van Hopper's daughter as is used in other versions. The switch may

be due to a late-1970s audience having trouble believing that a daughter's pregnancy is an emergency medical condition requiring her mother's presence. The publication of books like *Our Bodies, Ourselves* in the early 1970s had done much to naturalize and demystify childbirth, and the portrayal of pregnancy as analogous to an illness would not have rung true with an audience of that day. For example, while the 1976 edition of *Our Bodies, Ourselves* acknowledges that pregnant women need "their family and friends," it also quotes Lester Hazell as saying that "[p]regnancy, labor[,] and delivery are states unto themselves[,] but they are by no means illnesses." The Boston Women's Health Collective, *Our Bodies, Ourselves: A Book By and For Women*, 2nd edition, New York, Simon & Schuster, 1976, p. 249 and note, citing Lester Dessez Hazell, *Commonsense Childbirth*, New York, Putnam, 1969, p. xxxiv.

22. I believe that the term "domestic violence" was itself coined slightly earlier than this production. [My unsuccessful efforts to track its first appearance through the *Oxford English Dictionary* and other dictionaries left me horrified at how few dictionaries include the term at all and how late the term seems to make it into those dictionaries. I did, however, find Maria Roy's 1977 edited collection of essays on domestic violence that includes the phrase "domestic violence" in the title. Roy comments on the difficulty she had in the mid-1970s finding scholarly material about domestic violence. Maria Roy, ed., *Battered Women: A Psychosocial Study of Domestic Violence*, New York, Van Nostrand Reinhold Co., 1977, p. 3. A cursory search of Cambridge Scientific Abstracts in the field of sociology revealed few articles published before the mid-1970s that discussed domestic violence under *any* of its earlier names (like "wife beating" or "wife battering" or "family violence.")] *The Burning Bed*, the made-for-television movie (starring Farrah Fawcett as an abused wife) that introduced much of America to the horrors of domestic violence, appeared a few years later than the 1978 *Rebecca* in 1985. *VideoHound's Golden Movie Retriever 1995*, Detroit, Visible Ink, 1995, p. 231.

23. Susan Faludi, *Backlash: The Undeclared War Against American Women*, New York, Anchor Books, 1991, pp. xiv, 117.

24. See excerpts from *The Rebecca Notebook and Other Memories*, as published in Daphne du Maurier, *Rebecca*, New York, Harper Perennial Edition, 2001, pp. 390, 401–410. Originally published in Daphne du Maurier, *The Rebecca Notebook and Other Memories*, Garden City, NY, Doubleday, 1980, pp. 4, 7, 23–32.

25. One might be tempted to think that BBC censors of the 1970s restricted what could be implied in the 1978 version, but I think that unlikely given the highly risqué content of, e.g.,

I, Claudius, which aired shortly afterwards in 1980.

26. In contrast, the 1978 version offers tamer hints of sex. Although there is a shot of Maxim and the narrator in bed on their honeymoon, Maxim wears light blue pajamas and the narrator is so completely hidden by bedcovers that it is impossible to know what she's wearing. While this honeymoon shot shows them sharing a bed and implies that they are about to make love, the 1978 version also makes clear that they have separate beds at Manderley. This too contrasts with the 1997 version, which has the couple emphatically sharing a bed.

27. Interestingly, Emilia Fox is the daughter of Joanna David, who played the narrator in the earlier BBC made-for-television movie. *VideoHound's Golden Movie Retriever 2001*, Jim Craddock, ed., Detroit, Visible Ink Press, 2001, p. 782.

28. This fits nicely with an *Othello* reference taken from the novel (p. 332). On Maxim as a murderer in the novel, see Mary Wings, "Rebecca Redux: Tears on a Lesbian Pillow," in *Daring to Dissent: Lesbian Culture from Margin to Mainstream*, Liz Gibbs, ed., London, Cassell, 1994, pp. 19–22.

29. The suggestion that they have been making love comes from the fact that they are both (tastefully) nude. Elsewhere in the production, they are shown wearing nightclothes to bed.

30. The film is also very much Selznick's *Rebecca*. The film's close adherence to the novel was apparently due to a command by David O. Selznick, who overruled many changes Hitchcock wanted to make. See "Woman and the Labyrinth: *Rebecca*," in Tania Modleski, *The Women Who Knew Too Much: Hitchcock and Feminist Theory*, New York, Routledge, 1989, p. 43.

31. Mary Wings declares that the transformation of murder to "accident" was a direct response to the Hays Code. Mary Wings, "Rebecca Redux: Tears on a Lesbian Pillow," in *Daring to Dissent: Lesbian Culture from Mainstream to Margin*, Liz Gibbs, ed., London, Cassell, 1994, p. 19.

32. *Rebecca* was of course made a decade before *Sunset Boulevard* (Billy Wilder, 1950) introduced filmgoers to the concept of a voiceover by a narrator who was already dead. One thinks also of the modern *American Beauty*.

33. Mary Ann Doane has examined this scene in detail as it relates to female spectatorship, calling it "a crucial scene in which the film effects a decomposition of the elements which collaborate in making the position of female spectatorship an impossible one." Mary Ann Doane, "Female Spectatorship and Machines of Projection: *Caught* and *Rebecca*," in *The Desire to Desire: The Woman's Film of the 1940s*, Bloomington, Indiana University Press, 1987, p. 163. I agree that it is a crucial scene, though for different reasons.

34. For an alternative adaptation of the scene from the novel, we need look no farther than the 1978 television movie, which makes the narrator look considerably less deluded simply by putting her affirmations in the future tense:

MAXIM: "Do you think you'll be happy here?"
NARRATOR: "Of course I'll be happy. You know I'll be happy. I love Manderley."
MAXIM: "Well, I hope so."
NARRATOR: "We'll both be happy. You know that."
MAXIM: "Do I?"

NARRATOR: "Don't you?"
MAXIM: "Yes. If you say so. I'll take your word for it. We'll both be happy. It's agreed. That's settled."

35. Female investigator Kinsey Millhone, in Sue Grafton's *'A' Is for Alibi*, New York, Bantam Books, 1982, p. 27.

Bibliography

1. Krista Smith, "The Nine Lives of Drew Barrymore," *Vanity Fair*, No. 514, June 2003, p. 219.

Bibliography

Primary Sources

1. Female Gothic Thrillers

Austen, Jane. *Northanger Abbey.* New York: Penguin, reprinted 1994.
Brontë, Charlotte. *Jane Eyre.* New York: Penguin, reprinted 1988.
Collins, Wilkie. *The Woman in White,* New York, Penguin, reprinted 1985.
_____. *The Law and the Lady.* New York: Oxford, reprinted 1992.
Radcliffe, Ann. *The Mysteries of Udolpho.* New York: Oxford, reprinted 1991.

2. The Lesbian Female Investigator

Baker, Nikki. *The Lavender House Murder.* Tallahassee: Naiad, 1992.
_____. *Long Goodbyes.* Tallahassee: Naiad, 1993.
Forrest, Katherine V. *Murder at the Nightwood Bar.* Tallahassee: Naiad, 1987.
_____. *The Beverly Malibu.* Tallahassee: Naiad, 1989.
Maney, Mabel. *The Case of the Not-So-Nice Nurse.* Pittsburgh: Cleis, 1993.
_____. *The Case of the Good-for-Nothing Girlfriend.* Pittsburgh: Cleis, 1994.
_____. *A Ghost in the Closet.* Pittsburgh: Cleis, 1995.
Manthorne, Jackie. *Deadly Reunion.* Charlottetown, Canada: Gynergy, 1995.
Pincus, Elizabeth. *The Two-Bit Tango,* San Francisco: Spinsters Ink, 1992.
_____. *The Solitary Twist.* Minneapolis: Spinsters Ink, 1993.
_____. *The Hangdog Hustle.* Duluth: Spinsters Ink, 1995.

3. The Socio-Cultural Determinants of the Role of the Female Investigator on Television

1950s

The Thin Man— September 1957–June 1959 (NBC)
Mr. and Mrs. North— October 1952–September 1953 (CBS), January 1954–July 1954 (NBC)
The Gallery of Mme. Liu-Tsong— September 1951–November 1951 (DuMont)

1960s

Honey West—September 1965–September 1966 (ABC)
The Avengers— March 1966–September 1969 (ABC) (episodes airing on American television)

The Girl from U.N.C.L.E.— September 1966–April 1967 (NBC)
The Mod Squad— September 1968–August 1973 (ABC)

1970s

Scooby-Doo, Where Are You?—1969–72, 1974–76, Fall 1978, Fall 1984 (ABC)
McMillan and Wife— September 1971–August 1977 (NBC)
Police Woman— September 1974–August 1978 (NBC)
Get Christie Love!— September 1974–July 1975 (ABC), preceded by TV-Movie (aired 1/22/74)
Nancy Drew Mysteries— February 1977–January 1978 (ABC) then w/Hardy Boys till Fall 1978
Charlie's Angels— September 1976–August 1981 (ABC)
Hart to Hart—August 1979–July 1984 (ABC)

1980s

Remington Steele— October 1982–March 1987 (NBC)
Moonlighting— March 1985–May 1989 (ABC)
Murder, She Wrote— September 1984–May 1996 (CBS); *Cagney and Lacey*— March 1982–
  August 1988 (CBS)
Hunter— September 1984–August 1991 (NBC)
21 Jump Street— April 1987–September 1990 (FOX)

1990s

Prime Suspect—1990–1996 (BBC — airing later on PBS in the United States)
Under Suspicion— September 1994–March 1995 (CBS)
The X-Files— September 1993–May 2002 (FOX)
VIP— September 1998 — 2002 (FOX)

2000s

TV-Movie: *Hunter: Return to Justice* aired 11/16/02 (NBC)
TV-Movie: *Murder She Wrote: The Celtic Riddle* (2003)
TV-Movie: *Hunter: Back in Force* aired 4/12/03 (NBC)

4. Why Female Investigators in Film Are Intrinsically Mad

Coma (Michael Crichton, 1978)
Blue Steel (Kathryn Bigelow, 1990)
Black Widow (Bob Rafelson, 1987)
Goodbye Lover (Roland Joffé, 1999)
Charlie's Angels (McG [Joseph McGinty Nichol],[1] 2000)
Charlie's Angels: Full Throttle (McG [Joseph McGinty Nichol], 2003)
Nancy Drew, Reporter (William Clemens, 1939)
Smart Blonde (Frank McDonald, 1936)
Compromising Positions (Frank Perry, 1985)
Manhattan Murder Mystery (Woody Allen, 1993)
Murder on a Honeymoon (Lloyd Corrigan, 1935)
Murder, She Said (George Pollock, 1961)
Murder at the Gallop (George Pollock, 1963)
Murder Ahoy (George Pollock, 1964)
Murder Most Foul (George Pollock, 1965)
Cleopatra Jones (Jack Starrett, 1973)
Foxy Brown (Jack Hill, 1974)
Friday Foster (Arthur Marks, 1975)
A Question of Silence (Morleen Gorris, 1983)

Dear Detective (Phillipe de Broca, 1977)
A Taxing Woman (Juzo Itami, 1987)
Thriller (Sally Potter, 1979)
Stranger on the Third Floor (Boris Ingster, 1940)
Phantom Lady (Robert Siodmak, 1944)
Insomnia (Christopher Nolan, 2002)
The Mad Miss Manton (Leigh Jason, 1938)
Fargo (Joel Coen, 1995)
Copycat (Jon Amiel, 1995)
The Silence of the Lambs (Jonathan Demme, 1990)
Hannibal (Ridley Scott, 2001)
Murder By Numbers (Barbet Schroeder, 2002)
The Avengers (Jeremiah Chechik, 1998)
Suspicion (Alfred Hitchcock, 1941)
Secret Beyond the Door (Fritz Lang, 1948)

5. A Case Study of *Rebecca*

du Maurier, Daphne. *Rebecca*. New York: HarperPerennial, 2001.
Wings, Mary. *Divine Victim*. New York: Plume, 1992.
Rebecca—1962 (NBC)
Rebecca—1978 (BBC/Time Life)
Rebecca—1997 (PBS)
Rebecca (Alfred Hitchcock, 1940)

Secondary Sources

CRITICISM OF THE GOTHIC NOVEL

Armstrong, Nancy. *Desire and Domestic Fiction: A Political History of the Novel.* New York: Oxford, 1987.
Bayer-Berenbaum, Linda. *The Gothic Imagination: Expansion in Gothic Literature and Art.* Rutherford, NJ: Fairleigh Dickinson University Press, 1982.
Benedict, Barbara M. "Jane Austen and the Culture of Circulating Libraries: The Construction of Female Literacy," in *Revising Women: Eighteenth-Century "Women's Fiction" and Social Engagement*, Paula R. Backscheider, ed. Baltimore: Johns Hopkins University Press, 2000, pp. 147–199.
Brooks, Peter. *Reading for the Plot: Design and Intention in Narrative.* Cambridge, MA: Harvard University Press, 1984.
Dobrée, Bonamy. "Introduction," to Ann Radcliffe, *The Mysteries of Udolpho.* New York: Oxford University Press, 1970.
Ellis, Kate Ferguson. "The Language of Domestic Violence," in *The Contested Castle: Gothic Novels and the Subversion of Domestic Ideology.* Urbana: University of Illinois Press, 1989, pp. 3–19.
Fleenor, Juliann E. "Introduction: The Female Gothic," in *The Female Gothic*, Juliann E. Fleenor, ed. Montréal: Eden Press, 1983, pp. 3–28.
Fraiman, Susan. "Jane Eyre's Fall from Grace," in *Unbecoming Women: British Women Writers and the Novel of Development.* New York: Columbia University Press, 1993, pp. 88–120.
Freeland, Natalka. "From 'Foreign Peculiarities' to 'Fatal Resemblance': Detecting Villainy in *The Woman in White*," in *The Devil Himself: Villainy in Detective Fiction and Film*, Stacy Gillis and Philippa Gates, eds. Westport, CT: Greenwood Press, 2002, pp. 39–55.

Gaskell, Elizabeth. *The Life of Charlotte Brontë*, Alan Shelston, ed. and intro. New York: Penguin, reprinted 1975 [originally published in 1857].

Gilbert, Sandra M., and Susan Gubar. *The Madwoman in the Attic: The Woman Writer and Nineteenth-Century Literary Imagination*. New Haven: Yale University Press, 1979.

Heller, Tamar. "*The Woman in White*: Portrait of the Artist as a Professional Man," in *Dead Secrets: Wilkie Collins and the Female Gothic*. New Haven: Yale University Press, 1992, pp. 110–141.

Hughes, Winifred. *The Maniac in the Cellar: Sensation Novels of the 1860s*. Princeton, NJ: Princeton University Press, 1980.

Knoepflmacher, U.C. "The Counterworld of Victorian Fiction and *The Woman in White*," in *The Worlds of Victorian Fiction*, Jerome H. Buckley, ed. Harvard English Studies No. 6. Cambridge, MA: Harvard University Press, 1975, pp. 351–369.

Madoff, Mark S. "Inside, Outside, and the Gothic Locked-Room Mystery," in *Gothic Fictions: Prohibition/Transgression*, Kenneth W. Graham, ed. New York: AMS Press, 1989, pp. 49–62.

Maio, Kathleen L. "Had-I-But-Known: The Marriage of Gothic Terror and Detection," in *The Female Gothic*, Juliann E. Fleenor, ed. Montréal: Eden Press, 1983, pp. 82–90.

Massé, Michelle A. "This Hurts Me More Than It Does You: The Beater and *Rebecca*," in *In the Name of Love: Women, Masochism, and the Gothic*. Ithaca: Cornell University Press, 1992, pp. 147–191.

McKillop, Allan D. "Critical Realism in *Northanger Abbey*," in *From Jane Austen to Joseph Conrad: Essays Collected in the Memory of James T. Hillhouse*, Robert C. Rathburn and Martin Steinmann, Jr., eds. Minneapolis: University of Minnesota Press, 1958, pp. 35–45.

Meyers, Helene. *Femicidal Fears: Narratives of the Female Gothic Experience*. Albany: State University of New York Press, 2001.

Miall, David S. "The Preceptor as Fiend: Radcliffe's Psychology of the Gothic," in *Jane Austen and Mary Shelley and Their Sisters*, Laura Dabundo, ed. Lanham, MD: University Press of America, 2000, pp. 31–43.

Miller, D.A. "*Cage aux Folles*: Sensation and Gender in Wilkie Collins' *The Woman in White*," in *The Novel and the Police*. Berkeley: University of California Press, 1988, pp. 146–191.

Modleski, Tania. "The Female Uncanny: Gothic Novels for Women," in *Loving with a Vengeance: Mass-Produced Fantasies for Women*. New York: Methuen, 1982, pp. 59–84.

Moers, Ellen. *Literary Women: The Great Writers*. New York: Oxford, 1977.

O'Fallon, Kathleen. "Breaking the Laws about Ladies: Wilkie Collins' Questioning of Gender Roles," in *Wilkie Collins to the Forefront: Some Reassessments*, Nelson Smith and R.C. Terry, eds. New York: AMS Press, 1995, pp. 227–239.

O'Neill, Philip. *Wilkie Collins: Women, Property, and Propriety*. London: Macmillan, 1988.

Parker, Patricia. *Literary Fat Ladies: Rhetoric, Gender, Property*. New York: Methuen, 1987.

Punter, David. *Gothic Pathologies: The Text, the Body, and the Law*. New York: St. Martin's Press, 1998.

Rance, Nicholas. *Wilkie Collins and Other Sensation Novelists: Walking the Moral Hospital*. Rutherford, NJ: Fairleigh Dickinson University Press, 1991.

Reynolds, Kimberley, and Nicola Humble. *Victorian Heroines: Representations of Femininity in Nineteenth-Century Literature and Art*. New York: Harvester/Wheatsheaf, 1993.

Roberts, Bette B. "The Horrid Novels: *The Mysteries of Udolpho* and *Northanger Abbey*," in *Gothic Fictions: Prohibition/Transgression*, Kenneth W. Graham, ed. New York: AMS Press, 1989, pp. 89–111.

Russ, Joanna. "Somebody Is Trying to Kill Me and I Think It's My Husband: The Modern Gothic," *Journal of Popular Culture*, Vol. 6, No. 4 (Spring 1973), pp. 666–691.

Summers, Montague. *The Gothic Quest: A History of the Gothic Novel*. New York: Russell & Russell, Inc., 1964 [originally published in 1938].

_____. "A Great Mistress of Romance: Ann Radcliffe, 1764–1823," in *Essays in Petto*. Freeport, NY: Books for Libraries Press, 1928 [reprinted 1967], pp. 1–29.

Symons, Julian. "Introduction," to Wilkie Collins, *The Woman in White*. New York: Penguin, 1974.

Taylor, Jenny Bourne. "Introduction," to Wilkie Collins, *The Law and the Lady*. New York: Penguin, 1992.

Uglow, Jennifer. "Introduction," to Mary E. Braddon, *Lady Audley's Secret*. New York: Penguin/Virago, 1985.

Varma, Devendra P. *The Gothic Flame*. New York: Russell & Russell, 1966.

Wyatt, Jean. "A Patriarch of One's Own: Oedipal Fantasy and Romantic Love in *Jane Eyre*," in *Reconstructing Desire: The Role of the Unconscious in Women's Reading and Writing*. Chapel Hill: University of North Carolina Press, 1990, pp. 23–40.

CRITICISM OF MYSTERY AND DETECTIVE FICTION

Aisenberg, Nadya. *A Common Spring: Crime Novel and Classic*. Bowling Green, OH: Bowling Green Popular Press, 1980.

Babener, Liahna. "Unclseting Ideology in the Novels of Barbara Wilson," in *Women Times Three: Writers, Detectives, Readers*, Kathleen Gregory Klein, ed. Bowling Green, OH: Bowling Green State University Popular Press, 1995, pp. 143–161.

Bailey, Frankie Y. *Out of the Woodpile: Black Characters in Crime and Detective Fiction*. Contributions to the Study of Popular Culture No. 27. New York: Greenwood Press, 1991.

Benvenuti, Stefano, and Gianni Rizzoni. *The Whodunit: An Informal History of Detective Fiction*, Anthony Eyre, trans. New York: Macmillan, 1981.

Brown, Patricia Leigh. "Nancy Drew fans pay homage to a heroine who is coming of age: Teen sleuth relied on smarts, not sex appeal." *San Jose Mercury News*, 4/19/93, p. 1.

Browne, Ray B. *Heroes and Humanities: Detective Fiction and Popular Culture*. Bowling Green, OH: Bowling Green State University Popular Press, 1986.

Bryce, Rosamund. "The Most Likely Victim," in Dilys Winn, ed., *Murder Ink: The Mystery Reader's Companion*. New York: Workman Publishing, 1977, pp. 183–185.

Charney, Hanna. *The Detective Novel of Manners: Hedonism, Morality, and the Life of Reason*. Rutherford, NJ: Fairleigh Dickinson University Press, 1981.

Coward, Rosalind, and Linda Semple. "Tracking Down the Past: Women and Detective Fiction," in *From My Guy to Sci-Fi: Genre and Women's Writing in the Postmodern World*, Helen Carr, ed. London: Pandora, 1989, pp. 39–57.

Craig, Patricia, and Mary Cadogan. *The Lady Investigates: Women Detectives and Spies in Fiction*. London: Victor Gollancz Ltd., 1981.

Décuré, Nicole. "In Search of Our Sisters' Mean Streets: The Politics of Sex, Race, and Class in Black Women's Crime Fiction," in *Diversity and Detective Fiction*, Kathleen Gregory Klein, ed. Bowling Green, OH: Bowling Green State University Press, 1999, pp. 158–185.

Dilley, Kimberly J. *Busybodies, Meddlers, and Snoops: The Female Hero in Contemporary Women's Mysteries*. Westport, CT: Greenwood Press, 1998.

Freeman, Lucy, ed. *The Murder Mystique: Crime Writers on Their Art*. New York: Frederick Ungar Publishing Co., 1982.

Gardner, Julia D. "'No Place for a Girl Dick': Mabel Maney and the Queering of Girls' Detective Fiction," in *Delinquents & Debutantes: Twentieth-Century American Girls' Cultures*, Sherrie A. Inness, ed. New York: New York University Press, 1998, pp. 247–265.

Hansen, Joseph. "Homosexuals: Universal Scapegoats," in *Murder Ink: Revived, Revised, Still Unrepentant*, Dilys Winn, ed. New York: Workman Publishing, 1984, pp. 131–133.

Haycraft, Howard, ed. *The Art of the Mystery Story*. New York: Carroll & Graf, 1992.

Hoppenstand, Gary C. *In Search of the Paper Tiger: A Sociological Perspective of Myth, Formula and the Mystery Genre in the Entertainment Print Mass Medium*. Bowling Green, OH: Bowling Green State University Press, 1987.

Humm, Peter. "Camera Eye/Private Eye," in *American Crime Fiction: Studies in the Genre*, Brian Docherty, ed. New York: St. Martin's, 1988, pp. 23–38.

Irons, Glenwood, ed. *Feminism in Women's Detective Fiction*. Toronto: University of Toronto Press, 1995.

Jackson, Christine A. *Myth and Ritual in Women's Detective Fiction*. Jefferson, NC: McFarland, 2002.

Kaplan, Cora. "An Unsuitable Genre for a Feminist?" in *The Study of Popular Fiction: A Source Book*, Bob Ashley, ed. Philadelphia: University of Pennsylvania Press, pp. 199–203. This piece was supposedly originally published in *Women's Review* 8 (1986), pp. 18–19, but I have been unable to track down the original version.

Klein, Kathleen Gregory. "*Habeas Corpus*: Feminism and Detective Fiction," in *Feminism in Women's Detective Fiction*. Toronto: University of Toronto Press, 1995, pp. 171–187.

_____. *The Woman Detective: Gender and Genre*, 2nd ed. Urbana: University of Illinois Press, 1995.

Kountz, Carol. "You Call It a Pseudonym, We Call It an Alias," in *Murder Ink: The Mystery Reader's Companion*, Dilys Winn, ed. New York: Workman, 1977.

Mandel, Ernest. *Delightful Murder: A Social History of the Crime Story*. Minneapolis: University of Minnesota Press, 1984.

Marchino, Lois A. "Katherine V. Forrest: Writing Kate Delafield for Us," in *Women Times Three: Writers, Detectives, Readers*, Kathleen Gregory Klein, ed. Bowling Green, OH: Bowling Green State University Popular Press, 1995, pp. 65–79.

Mason, Bobbie Ann. *The Girl Sleuth: A Feminist Guide*. Old Westbury, NY: Feminist Press, 1975.

Merivale, Patricia, and Susan Elizabeth Sweeney, eds. *Detecting Texts: The Metaphysical Detective Story from Poe to Postmodernism*. Philadelphia: University of Pennsylvania Press, 1999.

Munt, Sally R. *Murder by the Book? Feminism and the Crime Novel*. London: Routledge, 1994.

Nicolson, Marjorie. "The Professor and the Detective," *The Atlantic Monthly*, April 1929. Reprinted in *The Art of the Mystery Story*, Howard Haycraft, ed. New York: Carroll & Graf, 1992 [originally published 1946], pp. 110–127.

Niebuhr, Gary Warren. *A Reader's Guide to the Private Eye Novel*. New York: G.K. Hall & Co., 1993.

O'Donnell, Peter. "Becoming Modesty," in *Murder Ink: The Mystery Reader's Companion*, Dilys Winn, ed. New York: Workman, 1977, pp. 158–160.

Palmer, Jerry. *Thrillers: Genesis and Structure of a Popular Genre*. London: Edward Arnold, 1978.

Palmer, Paulina. "The Lesbian Feminist Thriller and Detective Novel," in *What Lesbians Do in Books*. Elaine Hobby and Chris White, eds. London: Women's Press, 1991, pp. 9–27.

_____. *Lesbian Gothic: Transgressive Fictions*. London: Cassell, 1999.

_____. "The Lesbian Thriller: Transgressive Investigations," in *Criminal Proceedings: The Contemporary American Crime Novel*, Peter Messent, ed. London: Pluto Press, 1997, pp. 87–110.

Panek, LeRoy Lad. *Watteau's Shepherds: The Detective Novel in Britain 1914–1940*. Bowling Green, OH: Bowling Green University Popular Press, 1979.

Paul, Robert S. *What Ever Happened to Sherlock Holmes? Detective Fiction, Popular Theology, and Society*. Carbondale: Southern Illinois University Press, 1991.

Priestman, Martin. *Detective Fiction and Literature: The Figure on the Carpet*. London: Macmillan, 1990.

Reddy, Maureen T. *Sisters in Crime: Feminism and the Crime Novel*. New York: Continuum, 1988.

Reynolds, Moira Davison. *Women Authors of Detective Series: Twenty-One American and British Writers, 1900–2000*. Jefferson, NC: McFarland, 2001.

Sayers, Dorothy L. "Introduction" to *Great Short Stories of Detection, Mystery and Horror*, Dorothy L. Sayers, ed. London: Victor Gollancz, 1928, pp. 9–47. Reprinted as "Introduction" to *The Omnibus of Crime*, Dorothy L. Sayers, ed. New York: Payson and Clarke, 1929, also pp. 9–47, and further reprinted as "The Omnibus of Crime," in Howard Haycraft, ed., *The Art of the Mystery Story*. New York: Carroll & Graf, 1992 [originally published in 1946], pp. 71–109.

_____. "Introduction" to *Great Short Stories of Detection, Mystery and Horror, Second Series*, Dorothy L. Sayers, ed. London: Victor Gollancz, 1931, pp. 11–26. Reprinted as "Introduction" to *The Second Omnibus of Crime: The World's Great Crime Stories*, Dorothy L. Sayers, ed. New York: Blue Ribbon Books, 1939 [first published in the U.S. in 1932, by a different publisher], pp. 1–16.

Schwartz, Richard B. *Nice and Noir: Contemporary American Crime Fiction*. Columbia: University of Missouri Press, 2002.

Shaw, Marion, and Sabine Vanacker. *Reflecting on Miss Marple*. London: Routledge, 1991.

Slung, Michele. "Let's Hear It for Agatha Christie: A Feminist Appreciation," in *The Sleuth and the Scholar: Origins, Evolution, and Current Trends in Detective Fiction* [a collection of papers from a 1986 symposium], Barbara A. Rader and Howard G. Zettler, eds. Contributions to the Study of Popular Culture No. 19. Westport, CT: Greenwood Press, 1988.

_____. *Crime on Her Mind: Fifteen Stories of Female Sleuths from the Victorian Era to the Forties*. New York: Michael Joseph, 1976.

Smith, Erin A. *Hard-Boiled: Working-Class Readers and Pulp Magazines*. Philadelphia: Temple University Press, 2000.

Soitos, Stephen F. "Queering the 'I': Black Lesbian Detective Fiction," in *Multicultural Detective Fiction: Murder from the "Other" Side*, Adrienne Johnson Gosselin, ed. New York: Garland, 1999, pp. 105–121.

Stewart, R.F. *...And Always a Detective: Chapters on the History of Detective Fiction*. North Pomfret, VT: David and Charles, 1980.

Sweeney, Susan Elizabeth. "Gender-Blending, Genre-Bending and the Rendering of Identity in Barbara Wilson's *Gaudí Afternoon*," in *Multicultural Detective Fiction: Murder from the "Other" Side*, Adrienne Johnson Gosselin, ed. New York: Garland, 1999, pp. 123–141.

Symons, Julian. *Bloody Murder: From the Detective Story to the Crime Novel: A History*. New York: Viking, 1985.

Vanacker, Sabine. "V.I. Warshawski, Kinsey Millhone and Kay Scarpetta: Creating a Feminist Detective Hero," in *Criminal Proceedings: The Contemporary American Crime Novel*, Peter Messent, ed. London: Pluto Press, 1997, pp. 62–86.

Whitlock, Gillian. "'Cop It Sweet': Lesbian Crime Fiction," in *The Good, The Bad, and The Gorgeous: Popular Culture's Romance with Lesbianism*. London: Pandora, 1994, pp. 96–118.

Wilson, Barbara. "The Outside Edge: Lesbian Mysteries," in *Daring to Dissent: Lesbian Culture from Margin to Mainstream*. Liz Gibbs, ed. London: Cassell, 1994, pp. 217–228.

Wings, Mary. "Rebecca Redux: Tears on a Lesbian Pillow," in *Daring to Dissent: Lesbian Culture from Margin to Mainstream*, Liz Gibbs, ed. London: Cassell, 1994, pp. 11–33.

Winks, Robin W. "Introduction" to *The Art of the Mystery Story*, Howard Haycraft, ed. New York: Carroll & Graf, 1992, pp. I–III.

_____. *Detective Fiction: A Collection of Critical Essays*. Englewood Cliffs, NJ: Prentice Hall, 1980.

Winn, Dilys, ed. *Murder Ink: The Mystery Reader's Companion*. New York: Workman, 1977.

_____, ed. *Murderess Ink: The Better Half of the Mystery*. New York: Workman, 1979.

CRITICISM OF MYSTERY AND DETECTIVE FILM AND TELEVISION

Bean, Jennifer M. "Male Paranoia and Feminist Film Theory: The Gothic Woman's Film of the 1940's," paper delivered at Society for Cinema Studies National Conference, March 5, 1995.

Buxton, David. *From The Avengers to Miami Vice: Form and Ideology in Television Series*, New York: Manchester University Press/St. Martin's, 1990.

Cameron, Sue. "Police Drama: Women Are on the Case," *Ms.* October 1974, pp. 104–108.

Chapman, James. "Is There Honey Still for Tea? *The Avengers*," in *Saints & Avengers: British Adventure Series of the 1960s.* London: I.B. Tauris, 2002, pp. 52–99.

Clark, Danae. "*Cagney & Lacey*: Feminist Strategies of Detection," in *Television and Women's Culture: The Politics of the Popular*, Mary Ellen Brown, ed. London: SAGE Publications, 1990, pp. 117–133.

Clerc, Susan J. "DDEB, GATB, MPPB, and Ratboy: *The X-Files*' Media Fandom, Online and Off," in *"Deny All Knowledge": Reading the X-Files*, David Lavery, Angela Hague, and Marla Cartwright, eds. Syracuse, NY: Syracuse University Press, 1996, pp. 36–51.

Clover, Carol J. *Men, Women, and Chain Saws: Gender in the Modern Horror Film.* Princeton: Princeton University Press, 1992.

Collins, Max Allan, and John Javna. *The Best of Crime & Detective TV: Perry Mason to Hill Street Blues, The Rockford Files to Murder, She Wrote.* New York: Harmony Books, 1988.

Cook, Pam. "Duplicity in *Mildred Pierce*," in *Women in Film Noir*, E. Ann Kaplan, ed. London: British Film Institute, 1980, pp. 68–82.

_____. "No Fixed Address: The Women's Picture from *Outrage* to *Blue Steel*," in *Contemporary Hollywood Cinema*, Steve Neale and Murray Smith, eds. London: Routledge, 1998, pp. 229–246.

Covey, William. "Girl Power: Female-Centered Neo-*Noir*," in *Film Noir Reader* 2, Alain Silver and James Ursini, eds. New York: Limelight, 1999, pp. 310–327.

Cowie, Elizabeth. "A Discussion of 'Coma'," in *Films for Women*, Charlotte Brunsdon, ed. London: British Film Institute, 1986, pp. 155–165.

Creed, Barbara. "Dark Desires: Male Masochism in the Horror Film," in *Screening the Male: Exploring Masculinities in Hollywood Cinema*, Steven Cohan and Ina Rae Hark, eds. London: Routledge, 1993, pp. 118–133.

D'Acci, Julie. *Defining Women: Television and the Case of* Cagney and Lacey. Chapel Hill: University of North Carolina Press, 1994.

_____. "Defining Women: The Case of *Cagney and Lacey*," in *Private Screenings: Television and the Female Consumer*, Lynn Spigel and Denise Mann, eds. Minneapolis: University of Minnesota Press, 1992.

Daley, Robert. "Police Report on the TV Cop Shows," in *Detective Fiction: Crime and Compromise*, Dick Allen and David Chacko, eds. New York: Harcourt Brace Jovanovich, 1974, pp. 430–444.

Delasara, Jan. *PopLit, PopCult and The X-Files: A Critical Exploration.* Jefferson, NC: McFarland, 2000.

Doane, Mary Ann. *The Desire to Desire: The Woman's Film of the 1940s.* Bloomington: Indiana University Press, 1987, pp. 123–175.

_____. "The 'Woman's Film': Possession and Address," in *Home Is Where the Heart Is: Studies in Melodrama and the Woman's Film*, Christine Gledhill, ed. London: British Film Institute Publishing, 1987, pp. 283–298. Originally published in *Re-Vision: Essays in Feminist Film Criticism*, Mary Ann Doane, Patricia Mellencamp, and Linda Williams, eds. Frederick, MD: University Publications of America, 1984, pp. 67–82.

Entertainment Tonight: Charlie's Angels Uncovered (syndicated television program, viewed 11/6/99).

Flinn, Tom. "Three Faces of Film Noir," reprinted in *Film Noir Reader 2*, Alain Silver and James Ursini, eds. New York: Limelight, 1999, pp. 35–43.

Geraghty, Christine. "Three Women's Films," in *Films for Women*, Charlotte Brunsdon, ed. London: British Film Institute, 1986, pp. 138–145.

Gledhill, Christine. "*Klute* 1: A Contemporary Film Noir and Feminist Criticism," in *Women in Film Noir*, E. Ann Kaplan, ed. London: BFI Publishing, 1980, pp. 6–21.

Harvey, Sylvia. "Woman's Place: The Absent Family of Film Noir," in *Women in Film Noir*, E. Ann Kaplan, ed. London: BFI Publishing, 1980, pp. 22–34.

Humphries, Reynold. *Fritz Lang: Genre and Representation in His American Films.* Baltimore, MD: Johns Hopkins University Press, 1989.

Jarvis, Brian. "Watching the Detectives: Body Images, Sexual Politics and Ideology in Contemporary Crime Film," in *Criminal Proceedings: The Contemporary American Crime Novel.* Peter Messent, ed. London: Pluto Press, 1997, pp. 214–240.

Kaplan, E. Ann. "The Place of Women in Fritz Lang's *The Blue Gardenia*," in *Women in Film Noir*, E. Ann Kaplan, ed. London: BFI Publishing, 1980, pp. 83–90.

Krutnik, Frank. *In a Lonely Street: Film Noir, Genre, Masculinity.* London: Routledge, 1991.

Lavery, David, Angela Hague, and Marla Cartwright, eds. *"Deny All Knowledge": Reading the X-Files.* Syracuse, NY: Syracuse University Press, 1996.

Leitch, Thomas. *Crime Films.* Cambridge: Cambridge University Press, 2002.

Mizejewski, Linda. *Hardboiled & High Heeled: The Woman Detective in Popular Culture.* New York: Routledge, 2002.

Modleski, Tania. "The Terror of Pleasure: The Contemporary Horror Film and Postmodern Theory," in *Studies in Entertainment: Critical Approaches to Mass Culture*, Tania Modleski, ed. Bloomington: Indiana University Press, 1986.

_____. *The Women Who Knew Too Much: Hitchcock and Feminist Theory.* London: Routledge, 1988.

Murphy, Jeanette. "A Question of Silence," in *Films for Women*, Charlotte Brunsdon, ed. London: British Film Institute, 1986, pp. 99–108.

Nelson, Joyce. "'Mildred Pierce' Reconsidered," *Film Reader*, no. 2 (1977), pp. 65–70, reprinted in Bill Nichols, *Movies and Methods: An Anthology*, Vol. 2. Berkeley: University of California Press, 1985, pp. 450–458.

Nevins, Francis M. "Translate and Transform: From Cornell Woolrich to *Film Noir*," in *Film Noir Reader 2*, Alain Silver and James Ursini, eds. New York: Limelight, 1999, pp. 137–157.

Parks, Lisa. "Special Agent or Monstrosity? Finding the Feminine in *The X-Files*," in *"Deny All Knowledge": Reading the X-Files*, David Lavery, Angela Hague, and Marla Cartwright, eds. Syracuse, NY: Syracuse University Press, 1996, pp. 121–134.

Place, Janey. "Women in Film Noir," in *Women in Film Noir*, E. Ann Kaplan, ed. London: BFI Publishing, 1980, pp. 35–67.

Radner, Hilary. "New Hollywood's New Women: Murder in Mind: Sarah and Margie," in *Contemporary Hollywood Cinema*, Steve Neale and Murray Smith, eds. London: Routledge, 1998, pp. 247–262.

Rafter, Nicole. *Shots in the Mirror: Crime Films and Society.* New York: Oxford University Press, 2000.

Rich, B. Ruby. "Never a Victim: Jodie Foster: A New Kind of Female Hero," in Pam Cook and Philip Dodd, eds., *Women and Film: A Sight and Sound Reader*, Philadelphia: Temple University Press, 1993, pp. 50–61. Originally published as "Nobody's Handmaid" in *Sight and Sound*, vol. 1, no. 8 (December 1991), pp. 7–10.

Schwartz, Ronald. *Noir, Now and Then: Film Noir Originals and Remakes (1944–1999)*, Contributions to the Study of Popular Culture No. 72. Westport, CT: Greenwood Press, 2001.

Soter, Tom. *Investigating Couples: A Critical Analysis of* The Thin Man, The Avengers, *and* The X-Files. Jefferson, NC: McFarland, 2002.

Spoto, Donald. *The Art of Alfred Hitchcock: Fifty Years of His Motion Pictures*, 2nd ed. New York: Doubleday, 1992.

Staiger, Janet. "Taboos and Totems: Cultural Meanings of *The Silence of the Lambs*," in *Film Theory Goes to the Movies*, Jim Collins, Hilary Radner, and Ava Preacher Collins, eds. New York: Routledge, 1993, pp. 142–154.

Taubin, Amy. "Grabbing the Knife: 'The Silence of the Lambs' and the History of the Serial Killer Movie," in Pam Cook and Philip Dodd, eds., *Women and Film: A Sight and Sound Reader*. Philadelphia: Temple University Press, 1993, pp. 123–131. Originally published as "Killing Men" in *Sight and Sound* vol. 1, no. 1 (May 1991), pp. 14–18.

Tomc, Sandra. "Questing Women: The Feminist Mystery after Feminism," in *Feminism in Women's Detective Fiction*, Glenwood Irons, ed. Toronto: University of Toronto Press, 1995, pp. 46–63.

Tuska, Jon. *The Detective in Hollywood.* Garden City, NY: Doubleday, 1978.

Waldman, Diane. "'At Last I Can Tell It to Someone!': Feminine Point of View and Subjectivity in the Gothic Romance Film of the 1940s," *Cinema Journal*, Vol. 23, No. 2, Winter 1983, pp. 29–40.

Walton, Priscilla L., and Manina Jones. "'She's Watching the Detectives': The Woman PI in Film and Television," in *Detective Agency: Women Rewriting the Hard-Boiled Tradition*. Berkeley: University of California Press, 1999, pp. 220–272.

Warren, Bill. "Interview with Patrick Macnee," Showbiz RoundTable, GEnie computer network, 1992.

Wilcox, Rhonda, and J.P. Williams, "'What Do You Think?': *The X-Files*, Liminality, and Gender Pleasure," in *"Deny All Knowledge": Reading* The X-Files, David Lavery, Angela Hague, and Marla Cartwright, eds. Syracuse, NY: Syracuse University Press, 1996, pp. 99–120.

Williams, Linda. "Feminist Film Theory: *Mildred Pierce* and the Second World War," in *Female Spectators: Looking at Film and Television*, Deidre Prisnam, ed. London: Verso, 1988, pp. 12–30.

_____. "When the Woman Looks," in *Re-vision: Essays in Feminist Film Criticism*, Mary Ann Doane, Patricia Mellencamp, and Linda Williams, eds., American Film Institute Monograph Series, Vol. III. Frederick, MD: University Publications of America, 1984, pp. 83–99.

Williams, Tony. "*Phantom Lady*, Cornell Woolrich, and the Masochistic Aesthetic," in *Film Noir Reader*, Alain Silver and James Ursini, eds. New York: Limelight, 1996, pp. 129–143.

FEMINIST FILM AND TELEVISION THEORY (AND CRITICISM)

Brown, Mary Ellen, ed. *Television and Women's Culture: The Politics of the Popular*. London: SAGE Publications, 1990.

De Lauretis, Teresa. *Alice Doesn't: Feminism, Semiotics, Cinema*. Bloomington: Indiana University Press, 1984.

Deming, Caren J. "For Television-Centred [sic] Television Criticism: Lessons from Feminism," in *Television and Women's Culture: The Politics of the Popular*, Mary Ellen Brown, ed. London: SAGE Publications, 1990, pp. 37–60.

Doane, Mary Ann. "Film and the Masquerade: Theorizing the Female Spectator," in *Femmes Fatales: Feminism, Film Theory, Psychoanalysis*. London: Routledge, 1991, pp. 17–32. [Originally published as "Film and the Masquerade: Theorising the Female Spectator," *Screen* 23, nos. 3–4 (September-October 1982), pp. 74–87.]

Douglas, Susan J. *Where the Girls Are: Growing Up Female with the Mass Media*. New York: Random House, 1994.

Erens, Patricia, ed. *Issues in Feminist Film Criticism*. Bloomington: Indiana University Press, 1990.

Faludi, Susan. *Backlash: The Undeclared War Against American Women*. New York: Doubleday, 1991.

Haskell, Molly. *From Reverence to Rape; The Treatment of Women in the Movies*. Chicago: University of Chicago Press, 2nd ed., 1987.

Kaplan, E. Ann. "Feminist Criticism and Television," in *Channels of Discourse: Television and Contemporary Criticism*, Robert C. Allen, ed. Chapel Hill: University of North Carolina Press, 1987.

_____. "Investigating the Heroine: Sally Potter's 'Thriller,'" in *Women and Film: Both Sides of the Camera*. New York: Routledge, reprinted 1990. [Originally copyright 1983], pp. 154–161.

Maio, Kathi. *Feminist in the Dark: Reviewing the Movies*. Freedom, CA: Crossing Press, 1988.

_____. *Popcorn and Sexual Politics*. Freedom, CA: Crossing Press, 1991.

Mayne, Judith. *The Woman at the Keyhole: Feminism and Women's Cinema*. Bloomington: Indiana University Press, 1990.

Meehan, Diana M. *Ladies of the Evening: Women Characters of Prime-Time Television*, Metuchen, NJ: Scarecrow, 1983.

Mellencamp, Patricia. *High Anxiety: Catastrophe, Scandal, Age, & Comedy*. Bloomington: Indiana University Press, 1992.

Mellencamp, Patricia. "Situation Comedy, Feminism, and Freud, in *Studies in Entertainment: Critical Approaches to Mass Culture,* Tania Modleski, ed. Bloomington: Indiana University Press, 1986.

Modleski, Tania. *Feminism Without Women: Culture and Criticism in a "Postfeminist" Age.* London: Routledge, 1991.

_____. "The White Negress and the Heavy-Duty Dyke," in *Old Wives' Tales and Other Women's Stories.* New York: New York University Press, 1998, pp. 80–100.

Mulvey, Laura. *Visual and Other Pleasures.* Bloomington: Indiana University Press, 1989.

Neale, Steve. "Masculinity as Spectacle: Reflections on Men and Mainstream Cinema," in *Screening the Male: Exploring Masculinities in Hollywood Cinema.* London: Routledge, 1993, pp. 9–20. Originally published in *Screen,* Vol. 24, No. 6 (Nov.-Dec. 1983), pp. 2–16.

Rose, Jacqueline. "Woman as Symptom," in *Sexuality in the Field of Vision.* London: Verso, 1986, pp. 225–233.

Silverman, Kaja. *The Acoustic Mirror: The Female Voice in Psychoanalysis and Cinema.* Bloomington: Indiana University Press, 1988.

_____. *Male Subjectivity at the Margins,* London: Routledge, 1992.

Walters, Suzanna Danuta. *Material Girls: Making Sense of Feminist Cultural Theory.* Berkeley: University of California Press, 1995.

Warren, Elaine. "Where Are the Real Women on TV?" *Los Angeles Herald Examiner,* Oct. 31, 1983, sec. E, pp. 1, 10.

Williams, Linda. *Hard Core: Power, Pleasure, and the "Frenzy of the Visible."* Berkeley: University of California Press, 1989.

Williamson, Judith. "Woman Is an Island: Femininity and Colonization," in Tania Modleski, ed., *Studies in Entertainment: Critical Approaches to Mass Culture.* Bloomington: Indiana University Press, 1986, pp. 99–118.

PSYCHOANALYTIC THEORY

Lacan, Jacques. *Ecrits: A Selection.* New York: Norton, 1977.

Silverman, Kaja. *The Subject of Semiotics.* Oxford: Oxford University Press, 1983.

GENERAL FILM AND TELEVISION THEORY AND CRITICISM

Allen, Robert C., ed. *Channels of Discourse: Television and Contemporary Criticism.* Chapel Hill: University of North Carolina Press, 1987.

Altman, Rick. *Film/Genre.* London: BFI Publishing, 1999.

Bellour, Raymond. "Hitchcock the Enunciator," Bertrand Augst and Hilary Radner, trans., in *Camera Obscura,* No. 2 (Fall 1977), pp. 66–91.

Bianculli, David. *Teleliteracy: Taking Television Seriously.* New York: Continuum, 1992.

Burke, Timothy, and Kevin Burke. *Saturday Morning Fever.* New York: St. Martin's Press, 1999.

Cashmore, Ellis.... *and there was television.* New York: Routledge, 1994.

Chatman, Seymour. *Story and Discourse: Narrative Structure in Fiction and Film.* Ithaca: Cornell University Press, 1978.

Doane, Mary Ann. "Misrecognition and Identity," *Ciné-Tracts* [outside cover says 11 or II], Vol. 3, No. 3 (Fall 1980), pp. 25–32. Reprinted in *Explorations in Film Theory: Selected Essays from Ciné-Tracts,* Ron Burnett, ed. Bloomington: Indiana University Press, 1991, pp. 15–25.

Fiske, John. *Television Culture.* London: Routledge, 1987.

Furmaniak, Jennifer Kasle. "Why Drew Kicks Butt," *Cosmopolitan,* July 2003, pp. 182–185.

Henderson, Laura, and Bradley S. Greenburg, *Life on Television: Content Analyses of U.S. TV Drama.* Norwood, NJ: Ablex Publishing Corp., 1980.

Hill, George, Lorraine Raglin, and Chas Floyd Johnson. *Black Women in Television: An Illustrated History and Bibliography.* New York: Garland, 1990.

Lipsitz, George. "The Meaning of Memory: Family, Class, and Ethnicity in Early Network Television Programs," in *Private Screenings: Television and the Female Consumer,* Lynn Spigel and Denise Mann, eds. Minneapolis: University of Minnesota Press, pp. 77–83.

MacDonald, J. Fred. *Blacks and White TV: Afro-Americans in Television Since 1948*. Chicago: Nelson-Hall, 1983.

Metz, Christian. *The Imaginary Signifier: Psychoanalysis and the Cinema*, Celia Britton, Annwyl Williams, Ben Brewster, and Alfred Guzzetti, trans. Bloomington: Indiana University Press, 1977.

Nollinger, Mark. "The Exit Files" (with sidebar entitled "Mything Links"), *TV Guide*, Vol. 50, No. 20, 5/18/02, pp. 14–23.

Rosen, Philip, ed. *Narrative, Apparatus, Ideology: A Film Theory Reader*. New York: Columbia University Press, 1986.

Smith, Krista. "The Nine Lives of Drew Barrymore," *Vanity Fair*, No. 514, June 2003, pp. 168–173, 218–221.

Taylor, Ella. *Prime-Time Families: Television Culture in Postwar America*. Berkeley: University of California Press, 1989.

Thompson, Robert J. *Television's Second Golden Age: From* Hill Street Blues *to* ER. New York: Continuum, 1996.

GENERAL FEMINIST/GENDER/SEXUALITY THEORY AND HISTORY

Faderman, Lillian. *Odd Girls and Twilight Lovers: A History of Lesbian Life in Twentieth-Century America*. New York: Penguin, 1991.

Irigaray, Luce. "Women on the Market," *This Sex Which Is Not One,* Catherine Porter and Carolyn Burke, trans. Ithaca: Cornell University Press, 1985, pp. 170–191.

Rubin, Gayle. "The Traffic in Women: Notes Toward a Political Economy of Sex," in *Toward an Anthropology of Women*, Rayna R. Reiter, ed. New York: Monthly Review Press, 1975, pp. 157–210.

Sedgwick, Eve Kosofsky. "Gender Asymmetry and Erotic Triangles," *Between Men: English Literature and Male Homosocial Desire*. New York: Columbia University Press, 1985, pp. 21–27.

Shaevitz, Marjorie Hansen. *The Superwoman Syndrome*. New York: Warner Books, 1984.

Showalter, Elaine. *The Female Malady*. New York: Pantheon Books, 1985.

Zimmerman, Bonnie. "What Has Never Been: An Overview of Lesbian Feminist Criticism," in Gayle Greene and Coppélia Kahn, eds., *Making a Difference: Feminist Literary Criticism*. London: Routledge, 1990 [originally printed in 1985], pp. 177–210.

REFERENCE WORKS, BIOGRAPHIES, AND MISCELLANEOUS OTHER WORKS

Bail, Paul Leon. "Dorothy Uhnak," in *Great Women Mystery Writers: Classic to Contemporary*, Kathleen Gregory Klein, ed. Westport, CT: Greenwood Press, 1994, pp. 343–345.

Barr, Geraldine, with Ted Schwarz. *My Sister Roseanne: The True Story of Roseanne Barr Arnold*. New York: Birch Lane Press, 1994.

Boston Women's Health Collective, *Our Bodies, Ourselves: A Book By and For Women*, 2nd edition. New York: Simon & Schuster, 1976.

Brooks, Tim, and Earle Marsh. *The Complete Directory to Prime Time Network and Cable TV Shows: 1946–Present*, 6th ed. New York: Ballantine, 1995.

Burstein, Patricia. *Farrah: An Unauthorized Biography of Farrah Fawcett-Majors*. New York: Signet, 1977.

Cavelos, Jeanne. *The Science of* The X-Files. New York: Berkley Boulevard Books, 1998.

Condon, Jack, and David Hofstede. *Charlie's Angels Casebook*. Beverly Hills: Pomegranate Press, 2000.

Connors, Martin, and Julia Furtaw, eds. *VideoHound's Golden Movie Retriever 1995*. Detroit: Visible Ink Press, 1995.

Craddock, Jim, ed. *VideoHound's Golden Movie Retriever 2001*. Detroit: Visible Ink Press, 2001.

Davis, Jeffery. *Children's Television: 1947–1990*. Jefferson, NC: McFarland, 1995.

DellaCava, Frances A., and Madeline H. Engel. *Sleuths in Skirts: Analysis and Bibliography of Serialized Female Sleuths*. New York: Routledge, 2002.

Du Maurier, Daphne. *Rebecca: Acting Edition.* New York: Dramatists Play Service, 1943.

———. *The Rebecca Notebook and Other Memories.* Garden City, NY: Doubleday, 1980.

Erickson, Hal. *Television Cartoon Shows: An Illustrated Encyclopedia: 1949–1993.* Jefferson, NC: McFarland, 1995.

Everson, William K. *The Detective in Film: A Pictorial Treasury of the Screen Sleuth from 1903 to the Present.* Secaucus, NJ: Citadel Press, 1972.

Gifford, Denis. *The British Film Catalogue, 1895–1985: A Reference Guide.* New York: Facts on File Publications, 1986.

Halliwell, Leslie. *The Filmgoer's Companion.* New York: Hill and Wang, 6th ed., 1977.

Hanson, Patricia King, and Amy Dunkleberger, eds. *American Film Institute Catalog of Motion Pictures Produced in the United States: Feature Films, 1941–1950,* Vol. M–Z. Berkeley: University of California Press, 1999.

Hardy, Phil, ed. *The BFI Companion to Crime.* Richard Attenborough, fwd. Berkeley: University of California Press, 1997.

Hazell, Lester Dessez. *Commonsense Childbirth.* New York: Putnam, 1969.

Hodges, Graham Russell Gao. *Anna May Wong: From Laundryman's Daughter to Hollywood Legend.* New York: Palgrave Macmillan, 2004.

Klein, Kathleen Gregory, ed. *Great Women Mystery Writers: Classic to Contemporary.* Westport, CT: Greenwood, 1994.

Landrum, Larry. *American Mystery and Detective Novels: A Reference Guide.* Westport, CT: Greenwood, 1999.

Langman, Larry, and Daniel Finn. *A Guide to American Crime Films of the Forties and Fifties.* Bibliographies and Indexes in the Performing Arts No. 19. Westport, CT: Greenwood, 1995.

———, and ———. *A Guide to American Crime Films of the Thirties.* Bibliographies and Indexes in the Performing Arts No. 18. Westport, CT: Greenwood, 1995.

———, and ———. *A Guide to American Silent Crime Films.* Bibliographies and Indexes in the Performing Arts No. 15. Westport, CT: Greenwood, 1994.

Martindale, David. *Television Detective Shows of the 1970s: Credits, Storylines and Episode Guides for 109 Series.* Jefferson, NC: McFarland, 1991.

Parish, James Robert, and George H. Hill. *Black Action Films: Plots, Critiques, Casts and Credits for 235 Theatrical and Made-for-Television Releases,* Richard Roundtree, foreword. Jefferson, NC: McFarland, 1989.

Parish, James Robert, and Michael R. Pitts. *The Great Detective Pictures.* Metuchen, NJ: Scarecrow, 1990.

Pitts, Michael R. *Famous Movie Detectives.* Metuchen, NJ: Scarecrow, 1979.

Rhys, Jean. *Wide Sargasso Sea.* New York: Norton, 1966.

Rogers, Dave. *The Complete Avengers: Everything You Ever Wanted to Know About* The Avengers *and* The New Avengers. New York: St. Martin's, 1989.

Roy, Maria, ed. *Battered Women: A Psychosocial Study of Domestic Violence.* New York: Van Nostrand Reinhold, 1977.

Sandoe, James. "Reader's Guide to Crime," in *The Art of the Mystery Story,* Howard Haycraft, ed. New York: Carroll & Graf, 1992 [originally published in 1946], pp. 492–507.

Silver, Alain, and Elizabeth Ward, eds. *Film Noir: An Encyclopedic Reference to the American Style.* Woodstock, NY: Overlook Press, 1992.

Simon, Anne. *The Real Science Behind* The X-Files: *Microbes, Meteorites, and Mutants.* New York: Simon & Schuster, 1999.

Slide, Anthony. *Gay and Lesbian Characters and Themes in Mystery Novels: A Critical Guide to Over 500 Works in English.* Jefferson, NC: McFarland, 1993.

Smith, Krista. "The Nine Lives of Drew Barrymore," *Vanity Fair,* No. 514, June 2003, p. 219.

Smith, Ronald L. *Sweethearts of '60s TV.* New York: S.P.I. Books, 1993.

Travers, Peter. *Discovering Paperbacks Brings You Peter Travers' Favorite TV Angels.* Middletown, CT: Xerox Education Publications, 1978.

Index

229